Advance Pr;

"Growing up, I loved hearing sto
touch with a part of our family st(
and spirit denomination; its time tu get back to our roots.

> — Dr. Fred A. Hartley, III
> Lead Pastor, Lilburn Alliance Church,
> Lilburn, Georgia

"It is time for The Christian and Missionary Alliance to return to the radical middle. Historically, we were a Deeper Life movement out of which missions was to flow. When we try to "get it done" without the emphasis on the Holy Spirit's empowerment, impotence and ineffectiveness are the result. Paul King is using our roots to call us forward based upon our historical calling. He has done an invaluable service to the future of the Alliance by showing us our true heritage."

> — Dr. Ron Walborn
> Dean of Bible and Christian Ministry,
> Department Head - Pastoral Ministry
> Nyack College
> Board of Directors, The Christian and
> Missionary Alliance

"Congratulations to Paul King on this solid piece of research uncovering the early interconnections between the Christian and Missionary Alliance and the emerging Pentecostal movement. The message of this book is that we share much and differ only slightly. Perhaps this message can inspire a new era of collaboration and shared mission."

> —Kenneth L. Draper, PhD
> Vice President, Academics
> Alliance University College
> Calgary, Alberta

"What a powerful document! *Genuine Gold* is an undeniable record of the impact of historical drift on the Christian & Missionary Alliance. It is a call to return to our roots and the ministry of the Holy Spirit in power in our churches. May this book receive a prayerful reading from Alliance leaders and members. Thank God for Paul King!"

> —John Harvey, Senior Pastor
> First Alliance Church, Toccoa, Georgia
> Former missionary and C&MA Director
> of Missions of Europe and Mideast

ISBN 0-9785352-0-0

Published by Word & Spirit Press, Tulsa, Oklahoma
www.WandSP.com

Cover and interior design by Bob Bubnis/BookSetters

Author website: www.higherlifeministries.com

Author queries: plking1@juno.com

GENUINE GOLD

THE CAUTIOUSLY CHARISMATIC STORY OF THE EARLY CHRISTIAN AND MISSIONARY ALLIANCE

PAUL L. KING

WORD & SPIRIT PRESS
TULSA, OKLAHOMA

Paul L. King, D.Min., Th.D.

Dr. Paul King is an ordained minister, historian, and theologian of The Christian and Missionary Alliance. He holds a D.Min. from Oral Roberts University and a Th.D. from the University of South Africa. As a professor of theology and administrator at Oral Roberts University, he oversees the ORU Bible Insititute program and teaches seminars on healing and ministry and leadership development internationally. Author of numerous articles, especially on 19th and 20th century faith, healing, and holiness movements, King bridges the charismatic and evangelical communities. He is co-author of *Binding and Loosing: Exercising Authority over the Dark Powers*, and author of *A Believer with Authority: The Life and Message of John A. MacMillan* and *Moving Mountains: Lessons in Bold Faith from Great Evangelical Leaders*. He was named the 2006 Oral Roberts University Scholar of the Year for his many publications.

Dedicated to

The Christian and Missionary Alliance pastors
of my formulative years:

Rev. Gene Bartmas,
under whom I received Christ as a six-year old

the late Rev. George Jones, Jr.,
under whom I received my call to ministry at 12 years old

Rev. Jerry MacCauley,
who gave me my first opportunities to preach as a 17-year old

the late Rev. Roland Gray, Sr.,
retired evangelist who mentored me like a grandfather

Rev. Ronald MacDonald,
under whom I served as Youth and Assistant Pastor

Dr. Keith Bailey,
who told me, "we need young men like you in the Alliance"

Contents

PART I:
PRE-AZUSA STREET CHARISMATIC BELIEFS AND PRACTICES

PART II:
THE 1906-1909 C&MA REVIVAL:
RESPONSE AND REACTION TO AZUSA STREET

PART III:
C&MA RESPONSE TO THE PENTECOSTAL MOVEMENT 1910-1919

PART IV:
CHARISMATIC TEACHING AND PRACTICE AFTER SIMPSON
(1920-PRESENT)

PART V:
ANALYSIS OF EARLY C&MA CHARISMATIC BELIEF AND PRACTICE

Abbreviations Used

AW	*The Alliance Weekly*
CMAW	*Christian Alliance and Missionary Weekly*
CMAW	*The Christian and Missionary Alliance Weekly*
CITB	*Christ in the Bible*
DPCM	*Dictionary of Pentecostal and Charismatic Movements*
LRE	*The Latter Rain Evangel*
NIDPCM	*The New International Dictionary of Pentecostal and Charismatic Movements*
WWW	*The Word, the Work, and the World*

Acknowledgements

Many people have been of great help to me in the research of this book: Dr. Joseph Wenninger, Patty McGarvey, and Brian Wiggins from The Christian and Missionary Alliance Archives; Wayne Warner, Brett Pavia, Glenn Gohr, and Dr. Gary McGee from the Flower Pentecostal Heritage Center, Assemblies of God Headquarters, Springfield, Missouri; Sandy Ayers, Director of Library, Alliance University College, Calgary, Alberta, Canada; library personnel from Simpson College and Nyack College; Dr. Mark Roberts, Holy Spirit Research Center, Oral Roberts University, Norweigian Pentecostal Archivist Geir Lie, many older Alliance and Pentecostal ministers and lay people, who have shared their memories and knowledge of earlier days and generations in the C&MA, and Dr. K. Neill Foster and Dr. Keith Bailey for imparting in me a love for Alliance history and theology.

Preface

As an ordained minister of The Christian and Missionary Alliance (C&MA), I love and believe in my denomination. Having believed in and experienced charismatic manifestations from the Holy Spirit for more than thirty-five years, I have been keenly curious and fascinated about such manifestations in our Alliance heritage.

Like many in the C&MA and some in the charismatic movement, I am also cautious and concerned about some elements of charismatic belief and practice. That often puts me in a place of walking a tightrope between the evangelical and charismatic movements. I am not charismatic enough for some charismatics and too charismatic for non-charismatics.

What I strive for, however, is to be a balance, a bridge, and a buffer between charismatics and non-charismatics. I encourage non-charismatics to be open to the supernatural working of God in their lives, and I exhort charismatics to exercise balance, discernment, and moderation. That is what this book is about—the attempts on the part of the early Christian and Missionary Alliance to be receptive to all the supernatural manifestations and gifts that God wants to give and, at the same time, to avoid extremes, exercise discernment, and try the spirits—as A. B. Simpson put it, to be watchful but not fearful, to shun both fear and fanaticism.

In the process of researching and writing this book, I have endeavored to document, as comprehensively and accurately as possible without being tedious, both positive and negative assessments and attitudes within the early C&MA toward charismatic/Pentecostal theology and practice. I have done so by extensively scouring primary sources—first-hand accounts, personal testimonies, conversations with older Alliance leaders, early Alliance documents, especially Alliance and proto-Alliance periodicals, books, and official records from 1881 to the 1930s, as well as Pentecostal and other sources, especially as they had connections to the early C&MA. At the same time, I have condensed nearly 500 pages of material for greater readability.

I have attempted, as well, to analyze and assess this historical and chronological survey as objectively as possible, recognizing my dual sympathetic biases toward both the C&MA and charismatic theology and practice. Some in the C&MA may be unhappy that I am too sympathetic to the Pentecostal and charismatic positions, while some charismatics and Pentecostals may be unhappy that I am too sympathetic to the C&MA. But this is precisely where I want to be—in the middle—finding the moderation and balance I believe is demonstrated in A. B. Simpson and the early C&MA. I desire, like Simpson envisioned, a church that is "cautiously charismatic" or "charismatic without chaos"—tongues and all gifts without controversy—the genuine gold.

Introduction

A minister was holding a healing meeting with about 1000 people present. The minister received prophetic insight (what some would call a word of knowledge) that someone in the congregation was resisting the Lord. A woman came forward and admitted that she was the one. She had been severely ill, but resisted coming for prayer. The minister anointed her with oil, laid hands on her, and prayed for her. She fell to the floor and seemed to be unconscious for about half an hour. When she recovered consciousness, she got up and discovered she was healed, without pain for the first time in more than twenty years.[1]

Sound like Benny Hinn or Kathryn Kuhlman or Richard Roberts? No, the date was 1885 and the minister was A. B. Simpson, the former Presbyterian minister who founded the Christian and Missionary Alliance (C&MA).

If I were to describe to you meetings that feature speaking and singing in tongues, prophecies, visions, holy laughter, shaking, and falling under the power of the Spirit, you might think I was describing the Toronto Blessing movement or the Pensacola/Brownsville revival, or the Azusa Street Pentecostal revival. In reality, I would be describing the revival in the C&MA from 1906 to 1909.

These are only two of hundreds of examples of charismatic-like incidents in the early C&MA. Although the C&MA is not considered a charismatic denomination today, manifestations and practices similar to those of the charismatic movement occurred in its early history. Years before the Azusa Street Pentecostal revival, A. B. Simpson declared that the C&MA "stands for an absolute faith in supernatural things and a supernatural God."[2] Even after losses sustained over Pentecostal controversies, Simpson continued to maintain, "This movement stands pre-eminently for the supernatural."[3] Another Alliance leader echoed Simpson's sentiment, avowing, "The Alliance is supernatural or it is nothing."[4]

This study thus seeks to document the history of belief and practice regarding supernatural gifts (*charismata*) and manifestations in the Christian and Missionary Alliance, especially in its earlier days. I have also included manifestations and practices often associated with the Pentecostal and charismatic movements such as trembling, shaking, shouting, holy laughter, falling under the power of the Spirit (often referred to in the early literature as prostration), lifting hands, dancing, visions, dreams, physical sensations or feelings of warmth, fire, or electricity, spontaneous vocal unison prayer, etc., and terminology such as "Pentecostal," "baptism in the Spirit," "Full Gospel," and "Latter Rain."

SCHOLARLY OPINION OF THE C&MA's CHARISMATIC CHARACTERISTICS

The Christian and Missionary Alliance, for the most part, does not like to identify itself with the Pentecostal and charismatic movements. However, several scholars view the C&MA as having Pentecostal or charismatic characteristics. Harold Lindsell, for example, has written that Simpson and the C&MA "stressed certain doctrines commonly manifested in the charismatic movement."[5] He mentions divine healing, the Spirit-filled life, and pneumatology (teaching on the Holy Spirit).

Donald Dayton, in his book *Theological Roots of Pentecostalism* notes that Simpson's fourfold pattern of "Christ as Savior, Sanctifier, Healer, and Coming King" provided roots for Pentecostal theology.[6] He observes, "By the middle of the last decade of the nineteenth century Simpson was moving, especially in his Bible studies, toward more explicitly Pentecostal language."[7] In his view, there was only "a hairsbreadth from Pentecostalism," that "hairsbreadth" of difference being tongues as the evidence of the baptism in the Holy Spirit.[8] While many C&MA people today might not be happy to be considered just a "hairsbreadth" from Pentecostalism, nonetheless, that is the perception of this non-Pentecostal scholar who has broadly researched Pentecostal and holiness movements.

Bruce Barron, author of *The Health and Wealth Gospel*, detects origins of the modern word of faith movement in Simpson: "The beginnings of positive confession with regard to healing can be spotted as far back as the work of A. B. Simpson, who wrote, 'We believe that God is healing before any evidence is given. It is to be believed as a present reality and then ventured on. We are to act as if it were already true.'"[9] Actually, Barron errs in saying the positive confession teaching *begins* with Simpson. In reality, as I demonstrate in my Doctor of Theology dissertation, *A Practical-Theological Investigation of Nineteenth and Twentieth Century "Faith Theologies"*, it begins much earlier through the teaching of Phoebe Palmer and many others, and has been present in some form throughout church history.[10] However, Simpson and early C&MA teaching on faith did influence various aspects of modern faith teaching, though modified, and in some cases distorted, in the modern faith movement.[11] The chapter on "The Early C&MA and Modern Faith Teaching" discusses the similarities and differences between the two movements.

Charles Nienkirchen demonstrates in his analysis *A. B. Simpson and the Pentecostal Movement* that Simpson was a forerunner of Pentecostalism, in that Simpson "raised questions and offered answers that anticipated some of the salient emphases of modern Pentecostalism."[12] Though Simpson was not uncritical of Pentecostalism, "an in-depth analysis of his theology reveals several themes that surface as points of ideological continuity between himself and early Pentecostals."[13] Among them, Nienkirchen includes "Simpson's restorationist and premillennial ideology, his doctrine of the baptism of the Holy Spirit, his understanding of spiritual gifts in the life of the church, and his hermeneutical approach to the book of Acts."[14]

The significance of these findings cannot be denied or ignored. Several professors at C&MA colleges and seminaries have shared with me that they believe that Simpson would be a Third Waver in today's theological climate regarding the supernatural. My assessment as a result of this research is that although he would not accept some Third Wave stances such as the belief that the baptism in the Spirit occurs at conversion, nonetheless, much of the Third Wave view regarding signs and wonders and the supernatural does coincide closely with Simpson' views.

MISCONCEPTIONS ABOUT C&MA CHARISMATIC BELIEFS AND PRACTICES

By piecing together a comprehensive, chronological reconstruction of views, practices, and the context of events in the early C&MA concerning charismatic phenomena, this study seeks to correct misconceptions about the C&MA's historic beliefs and practices regarding the supernatural. Some both within and outside of the C&MA mistakenly consider the C&MA as almost cessationists, believing that the supernatural gifts of the Spirit are not for today or that most manifestations of tongues are not from God.

We will see that some early Pentecostals such as Frank Bartleman erroneously claimed that Simpson and other C&MA leaders opposed the Pentecostal movement.[15] Further, Pentecostal historian Robert Mapes Anderson wrongly claimed that the C&MA changed their motto of Jesus Christ as "Savior, Baptizer in the Holy Ghost, Healer, and Coming King," substituting "Sanctifier" for "Baptizer."[16] Actually, the Alliance motto was coined in the 1880s, decades before Pentecostal movement. Rather, it was Pentecostals who modified Simpson's motto. For Simpson and the early Alliance, the sanctifying baptism in the Spirit was taught as part of the emphasis of Jesus Christ as Sanctifier (though not in the Wesleyan or Keswickean sense). Three stage Pentecostals later separated the crisis of sanctification from the baptism in the Spirit, sometimes advocating a "five-fold gospel." "Finished work" Pentecostals dropped the notion that sanctification is in any way involved with the baptism in the Spirit, and thus replaced "Sanctifier" with "Baptizer."

Grant Wacker mistakenly claimed, "Simpson became hostile to Pentecostalism about 1910."[17] Likewise Anderson erroneously asserted, "Articles in Alliance periodicals became exclusively representative of the anti-Pentecostal viewpoint."[18] Alliance articles were anti-evidential tongues, but they were not anti-tongues or other Pentecostal phenomena, nor were they exclusive. This study will also demonstrate that Menzies also came to an incorrect conclusion when he wrote, "The 'seek not, forbid not' Alliance position effectively closed the door to Pentecostal phenomena within their ranks."[19] Repeating Menzies' mistake, Blumhofer claimed that "tongue speech had been virtually eliminated from the Alliance."[20] On the contrary, tongues and other charismatic phenomena have continued throughout C&MA history, though to a much lesser degree than its earlier days.

Some C&MA people would deny, shun or ignore its charismatic history, seemingly embarrassed by its past. Others from a Pentecostal background claim the C&MA did not grow because it effectively quenched the Spirit or made a mistake in not totally accepting Pentecostalism with its evidential tongues doctrine.[21] Actually, the C&MA did grow, but not as rapidly or extensively as the Pentecostal movement.[22] On the other hand, due an over-eagerness to identify Simpson and the early Alliance closely with Pentecostalism, some from a C&MA background like Nienkirchen have misinterpreted Simpson's response as a seeker of tongues himself and mistakenly branded Tozer as a revisionist by originating the "seek not, forbid not" position of the Alliance. These errors have been further propagated in Pentecostal circles.[23] This will be specifically addressed in the chapter on "The Seek Not, Forbid Not Position."

From a historian's perspective this is a lost story that needs to be told both because it is fascinating and true, and also to correct misinformation and misinterpretation. From a theologian's point of view, the early Alliance charismatic theology and practice has a great heritage to contribute to scholars, Alliance pastors and members, and the broader evangelical community.

Among some of the fascinating charismatically-related historical facts in the C&MA related in these pages include the following:

- A black woman spoke in tongues in Simpson's church before 1897.

- A. B. Simpson experienced holy laughter for more than an hour.

- Prime leaders of the C&MA spoke in tongues—Vice President John Salmon, missionary statesman Robert Jaffray, Foreign Secretary Alfred Snead, District Superintendent and scholar Dr. Ira David, later C&MA Presidents H. M. Shuman and Dr. Harry Turner, the wives of Simpson associates and later Board of Manager members William T. MacArthur and William Christie.

- Simpson desired tongues but never received.

- Kathryn Kuhlman attended the C&MA's Simpson Bible Institute 1924-1926 and decades later donated $250,000 to Alliance missions.

- Alliance churches were formed out of the evangelistic and healing meetings of Pentecostal evangelist Charles Price.

- William Joseph Seymour, the catalyst of the Azusa Street revival, later embraced Alliance-like teaching on tongues and preached in a C&MA church.

- Jack Hayford as a teenager attended a C&MA church whose pastor spoke in tongues.

- C&MA leader John MacMillan endorsed the ministry of Oral Roberts in the 1950s.

- Chinese leader Watchman Nee's father-in-law was a native C&MA pastor.
- Healing with leg-lengthening took place in the 1890s and 1960s.
- The brother-in-law of Indonesian revival leader Mel Tari was a native C&MA pastor.

This is just a tiny fraction sampling the charismatic history of The Christian and Missionary Alliance in the following pages.

1. "Healing of Mrs. Williams," CAMW, May 9, 1890, 295-296.

2. A. B. Simpson, "Aggressive Christianity," CMAW, Sept. 23,1899, 260.

3. A. B. Simpson, "Our Trust," CMAW, May 28, 1910, 145.

4. W. T. MacArthur, "Watching the Father Work," *The Alliance Weekly* (AW), July 15, 1916, 244.

5. Harold Lindsell, *The Holy Spirit in the Latter Days* (Nashville, TN: Thomas Nelson, 1983), 23-24.

6. Donald W. Dayton, *Theological Roots of Pentecostalism* (Peabody, MA: Hendrickson, 1987), 22.

7. Ibid., 176.

8. Ibid.

9. Bruce Barron, *The Health and Wealth Gospel* (Downers Grove, IL: InterVarsity, 1987), 60, quoting A. B. Simpson, *The Four-fold Gospel* (Harrisburg, PA: Christian Publications, n.d.), 62.

10. Paul L. King, *A Practical-Theological Investigation of Nineteenth and Twentieth Century "Faith Theologies"*, Doctor of Theology thesis, University of South Africa, Pretoria, South Africa, November 2001, 223-238.

11. Ibid., 39-46, 53-54.

12. Charles W. Nienkirchen, *A. B. Simpson and the Pentecostal Movement* (Peabody, MA: Hendrickson, 1992), 52.

13. Ibid.

14. Ibid.

15. Frank Bartleman, *Azusa Street* (Plainfield, NJ: Logos, 1980), 109, 112.

16. Robert Mapes Anderson, *Vision of the Disinherited* (New York, Oxford: Oxford University Press, 1979), 147. Simpson coined the phrase "Jesus Christ as Savior, Sanctifier, Healer and Coming King" in the 1880s, decades before Pentecostals (and in particular Aimee Semple McPherson, with her Foursquare Gospel) adapted and modified Simpson's terminology from "Sanctifier" to "Baptizer." In Simpson's view, Christ as Baptizer was apart of His work as Sanctifier.

17. Grant Wacker, "The Assemblies of God: As Seen by the *Encyclopedia of Religion in the South*," *Assemblies of God Heritage*, Fall 1987, 10, as cited from Grant Wacker, "Assemblies of God," *Encyclopedia of Religion in the South*, edited by Samuel S. Hill (Macon, GA: Mercer University Press, 1984), 72-75.

18. Anderson, 147.

19. William W. Menzies, *Anointed to Serve* (Springfield, MO: Gospel Publishing House, 1971), 72.

20. Edith L. Blumhofer, *Restoring the Faith* (Urbana and Chicago: University of Illinois Press, 1993), 105.

21. Vinson Synan, *The Role of Tongues as Initial Evidence* (Tulsa, OK: Oral Roberts University Holy Spirit Research Center, n.d.), 11.

22. A study of the history of the C&MA demonstrates that a complex of factors contributed to the slower growth of the C&MA, of which its stance on tongues was but one.

23. Nienkirchen, 131-140; Blumhofer, *Restoring the Faith*, 102; Vinson Synan, *The Holiness-Pentecostal Tradition: Charismatic Movements in the Twentieth Century* (Grand Rapids, MI: Wm. B. Eerdmans, 1971, 1997), 127, 147.

PART ONE

PRE-AZUSA STREET C&MA CHARISMATIC BELIEFS AND PRACTICES

Development of
Simpson's Early
Charismatic Thought

We want to begin by examining the beliefs and practices of A. B. Simpson and The Christian and Missionary Alliance regarding the supernatural before the onset of the Pentecostal movement at Azusa Street in Los Angeles in April 1906. As noted above, Nienkirchen views Simpson as a forerunner to the Pentecostal movement and Dayton considers Simpson and the C&MA as significant sources for the theological roots of Pentecostalism.

SIMPSON'S EARLY ENCOUNTER WITH HOLY LAUGHTER
AND HEALING

Very early in Simpson's ministry he observed the healing power of God and what we would call today the phenomenon of "holy laughter." Before Simpson knew about divine healing he personally witnessed "the power of divine joy to heal disease." He recalled that in the "earliest years" of his ministry, which would have been in the 1870s, he visited a dying man not expected to live through the night. He led him to salvation and through what he called a "baptism of glory" and a "baptism of holy gladness" he was miraculously healed:

> But as I visited him, as I supposed for the last time, and tenderly led him to the Saviour, and as he accepted the gospel and became filled with the peace of God and the joy of salvation, there came upon him such a baptism of glory and such an inspiration of the very rapture of heaven, that he kept us for hours beside his bed as he shouted and sung, what we all believed to be the beginning of the songs of heaven, and we bad him farewell long after midnight, fully expecting that our next meeting would be above. But so mighty was the uplift in that soul that his body, unconsciously to himself, threw off the power of disease, and the next morning he was convalescent, to the

amazement of his physicians, and in a few days entirely well. I knew nothing, at that time, of divine healing, but simply witnessed with astonishment and delight, the power of divine joy to heal disease.[1]

Simpson writes that, "Many a time since have I seen the healing and the gladness of Jesus come together to the soul and body, and the night of weeping turned into a morning of joy. Many a time have I seen the darkly clouded and diseased brain lighted up with the joy of the Lord, and saved from insanity by a baptism of holy gladness." Such holy laughter occurred among other evangelical believers and churches in the nineteenth and early twentieth century, including the Keswick movement, Oswald Chambers, praying John Hyde, and Simpson himself.[2]

SIMPSON'S SANCTIFYING BAPTISM IN THE SPIRIT

After reading W. E. Boardman's *The Higher Christian Life*, A. B. Simpson received a sanctifying baptism in the Spirit in 1874.[3] He understood this experience to be a crisis of sanctification, though not eradication, as Wesleyans believed.[4] Rather, it was recognizing the Indwelling Christ transforming his life through the Holy Spirit, by "substitut[ing] His strength, His holiness, His joy, His love, His faith, His power, for all our worthlessness, helplessness and nothingness, and make it an actual living fact."[5] This would become a vital plank of his "Fourfold Gospel," proclaiming Jesus as Savior, Sanctifier, Healer and Coming King. George Müller later "told Dr. Simpson that his arrangement of truth was most evidently 'of the Lord' and suggested that he never change its mold."[6]

Simpson considered this his initial baptism in the Holy Spirit, and was a key to his understanding that speaking in tongues was not a necessary evidence of the baptism in the Spirit. He believed that there could be multiple baptisms in the Spirit, saying that there are "the Pentecosts and the second Pentecosts."[7] He compared this experience of sanctifying baptism of power to rising to greater heights, calling it "God's great Elevator, carrying us up to the higher chambers of His palace without our laborious efforts."[8] He would decades later pray for a "fuller" baptism of the Spirit "with all the gifts and graces,"[9] but would never doubt that he had received his initial baptism in 1874.

THE DREAMS THAT CHANGED SIMPSON'S LIFE

In 1877 Simpson experienced a vivid dream about Orientals wringing their hand in anguish going to hell, which stirred his missionary vision:

> I was awakened from sleep trembling with a strange and solemn sense of God's overshadowing power, and on my soul was burning the remembrance of a strange dream through which I had at that moment come. It seemed to me that I was sitting in a vast auditorium and millions of people were sitting around me. All the Christians in the world seemed to be there, and on the platform was a great multitude of faces

and forms. They seemed to be mostly Chinese. They were not speaking, but in mute anguish were wringing their hands, and their faces wore an expression I can never forget. As I woke with that vision on my mind, I trembled with the Holy Spirit, and I threw myself on my knees, and every fiber in my being answered, "Yes, Lord, I will go."[10]

This dream became the incentive that stirred Simpson's missionary vision and endeavors of faith. Simpson had another prophetic dream early on in his ministry that also had great impact on his trust in God, especially in the midst of the trials he would suffer periodically throughout his life:

> In the beginning of this life of faith God gave me a vision which to me was a symbol of the kind of life to which He had called me. In the dream a little sailboat was passing down a rapid stream, tossed by the winds and driven by the rapids. Every moment it seemed as if it must be dashed upon the rocks and crushed, yet it was preserved in some mysterious way and carried through all perils. Upon the sails of the little ship was plainly painted the name of the vessel in one Latin word, *Augustiae*, meaning "Hard Places." Through this simple dream the Lord seemed to fortify me for the trials and testings that were ahead, and to prepare me for a life's journey which would be far from a smooth one, but through which God's grace would always carry me in triumph.[11]

Although Simpson would not advise seeking meaning in all dreams, he became favorably inclined to recognize that God does often speak through dreams, visions, and impressions of various sorts. Throughout his life, in his periodicals he published dozens of testimonies of such dreams and visions, and their significance.

SIMPSON'S EXPERIENCE OF DIVINE HEALING

In the summer of 1881, Simpson was very ill with heart problems and not given much hope by his doctor. He received a miraculous healing at Dr. Charles Cullis' Old Orchard Camp Meeting at Old Orchard, Maine. Cullis was an Episcopalian medical doctor who began a faith healing ministry after visiting the faith works of George Müller. A. W. Tozer, in his biography of Simpson, recounts the incident of Simpson's healing:

> One Friday afternoon he walked out under the open sky, painfully, slowly, for he was always weak and out of breath in those days. A path into a pine wood invited him like an open door into a cathedral. There on a carpet of soft pine needles, with a fallen log for an altar, while the wind through the trees played an organ voluntary, he knelt and sought the face of his God.

Suddenly the power of God came upon him. It seemed as if God Himself was beside him, around him, filling all the fragrant sanctuary with the glory of His presence. "Every fiber in my soul," he said afterwards, "was tingling with the sense of God's presence." Stretching his hands toward the green vaulted ceiling he took upon himself the vow that saved him from an early grave.[12]

As a result, Simpson's experience, confirmed by Scripture, became another plank of his "fourfold Gospel," proclaiming Jesus as Healer. His new-found faith in healing was soon tested, however, for in the Fall of 1881, just a couple of months later, Simpson's daughter Margaret became deathly ill with raging fever from diphtheria. She was soon healed through faith without medicine.[13]

SIMPSON LAUNCHES HEALING MINISTRIES

In November 1881 Simpson launched an interdenominational ministry in New York City, with emphasis on evangelism, missions, and healing.[14] For Simpson, the three emphases went hand-in-hand. In 1882 Simpson began Friday afternoon healing meetings with 500-1000 in attendance.[15] These meetings, providing an atmosphere for teaching, faith, and hope, continued for more than thirty years. The following year, in May 1883, Simpson established Berachah Healing Home (first known as the "Home for Faith and Physical Healing).[16] In October 1883 Simpson established the first Bible Institute in North America—the Missionary Training Institute, later known as Nyack College.[17]

In 1884 and 1885 Simpson compiled his book *The Gospel of Healing*, containing both biblical support for healing and testimonies of healing. In 1887 Simpson organized The Christian and Missionary Alliance as two interdenominational para-church organizations (Christian Alliance and Evangelical Missionary Alliance) later joined as one in 1897, emphasizing missions and the fourfold "full gospel" of Jesus Christ as Savior, Sanctifier, Healer, and Coming King.

Carrie F. Judd, named to the Board of Managers as Recording Secretary of The Christian Alliance, would become one of the most significant "charismatic" leaders in the C&MA for more than twenty years. After a miraculous healing in 1880 through the ministry of black healing evangelist Mrs. Mix, she began a healing home called Faith Rest Cottage in Buffalo, New York. A year later she became editor of a monthly periodical about faith and healing entitled *Triumphs of Faith*. Her book on faith and testimony of healing had an impact on Simpson, and she became a frequent convention speaker for the C&MA. In 1889 she met holiness faith healing evangelist Maria Woodworth (Etter) and they became lifelong friends. Maria later became a popular Pentecostal evangelist. In 1890 she married George Montgomery and they founded another healing home in Oakland, California, called "Home of Peace."[18] George later became a Vice President of the C&MA and continued in that role through the 1920s, even years after he and Carrie became involved in the Pentecostal movement.

CHARISMATIC HEALING ANOINTING OF SIMPSON
AND EARLY ALLIANCE LEADERS

As mentioned in the Introduction, Simpson had a charismatic anointing in which sometimes he received prophetic insight, and dramatic healing touches with unusual manifestations at times occurred through his ministry. More than two decades before the Azusa Street Pentecostal Revival, a remarkable charismatic anointing for healing manifested as Simpson and others who became leaders of the fledging Christian and Missionary Alliance prayed for people for healing. Simpson's new Friday healing meetings, though low-key in comparison with many healing meetings today, along with Alliance conventions and healing homes, periodically nurtured charismatic-like manifestations such as visions, electric-like impulses, trembling, jerking, and falling under the power of the Spirit.[19]

In August 1887, at the Old Orchard Convention in Maine when C&MA was first formed (known as the Christian Alliance), people were seeking the presence of the Lord. All of a sudden the power of God came with a "flash of heat" and sensations like electrical shocks upon a schoolteacher on crutches, and she was instantly healed. People throughout the congregation were shouting, weeping and singing. As a demonstration of power evangelism, her two sisters were saved on the spot, and many more healings followed. These supernatural manifestations confirmed to Simpson the founding of the C&MA, and the message of Jesus Christ as Healer.[20]

Even the uneducated had an anointing of the Lord. Sophie Lichtenfels was a well-known scrubwoman who worked faithfully in Simpson's ministry. In 1893 she encountered a demonized woman, claimed God's Word that He would give her power over devils, and the woman became peaceful and no longer violent.[21]

In April 1894 in an article in the *Christian Alliance and Missionary Weekly*, the writer recounted his first impressions of Simpson's Friday healing meeting, saying that he was awed and overwhelmed by a sense of God's presence, like Jesus was physically in the midst. For a time, the man testified that he did not know whether he was in body or out of body.[22]

Simpson told of sensing the Spirit's anointing when he anointed the sick: "Dear friends, I never feel so near to the Lord . . . as when I stand with the Living Christ, to manifest His personal touch and resurrection power in the anointing of the sick." Yet Simpson never considered himself a faith healer, saying, "We do not claim to be healers and wonderworkers, but simply witnesses for the power of Jesus to do all He has promised."[23]

While supernatural manifestations periodically occurred in Simpson's ministry and the early Alliance, as early as 1885 he also cautioned not to depend on the anointing or feeling, nor look for a thrill or physical sensation.[24] Nearly two decades later, Simpson continued to caution not to look for a special vision, revelation or faith when helping the sick.[25] Even though Simpson was led by the Lord to launch out in this "special work of faith," as he called it,[26] he never wanted people to look to him for healing, avowing, "I have never allowed anyone to look to me as a healer, and have had no liberty to pray for others while they placed the least trust in either me or my prayers, or aught but the merits, promises and intercessions of Christ alone. My most important work has usually been to get myself and my shadow out of people's way, and set Jesus fully in their view."[27]

SIMPSON AFFIRMS SUPERNATURAL GIFTS FOR TODAY

Once Simpson was convinced of the reality of divine healing for today from his search of Scripture and seeking the Lord, confirmed by his own miraculous experience of healing, it was a logical conclusion to him that all supernatural gifts are to continue throughout the Christian age. He argued in the mid 1880s concerning Mark 16:

> A common objection is observed in this way,—Christ's last promise in Mark embraces much more than healing; but if you claim one, you must claim all. If you expect healing of the sick, you must include the gift of tongues and the power to overcome malignant poisons; and if the gift of tongues has ceased, so in the same way has the power over disease. We cheerfully accept the severe logic, we cannot afford to give up one of the promises. We admit our belief in the presence of the Healer in all the charismata of the Pentecostal church.[28]

He acknowledged that the gift of tongues had to a greater or less degree been continuous throughout church history, along with counterfeits, even in the present generation. With this acknowledgement, he became one of the prime advocates of restoration of the *charismata*, and hence a significant forerunner of the Pentecostal movement.

SIMPSON AND GORDON ON EDWARD IRVING'S MOVEMENT

Edward Irving was a Presbyterian minister who in the 1830s led his church into belief and practice of charismatic manifestations, including tongues and prophecy. There were accusations of a heretical Christology and reputed extravagances in manifestations, causing many to discount the authenticity of the entire movement.[29]

A. J. Gordon, a friend and associate of Simpson and founder of what today is known as Gordon College and Gordon-Conwell Seminary, had written in the early 1880s about Irving in his book *The Ministry of Healing* (which has been republished by the C&MA). Gordon acknowledged that Irving had shortcomings, yet also had extensive and quite positive things to say about Irving's ministry, calling him an "illustrious confessor bearing witness to the doctrine we are defending [healing]," and saying that his greatest gift was faith. Contrary to claims that his beliefs were heretical, Gordon averred, "He believed, with the whole strength and intensity of his nature, everything which he found written in the Scriptures." He commended Irving further:

But bating any extravagances into which he may have fallen, we confess that our heart has always gone out to him in reverence his heroic fidelity to the Word of God, and his willingness, in allegiance to that Word, to follow Christ "without the camp, bearing his reproach" (Hebrews 13:13). And we believe that when the Master shall come to recompense His servants, this one will attain a high reward and receive of the Lord double for the broken heart with which he went down to his grave.[30]

Simpson appears to have been influenced by Gordon, claiming that Irvingism was a genuine move of God but hurt by excesses:

The story of Edward Irving is well known. After a career of extraordinary brilliancy and power, in his last days he adopted the theory that the supernatural gifts of the Early Church should be claimed in our own day, and there were undoubted instances, not only of miraculous power, but especially in the exercise of the gift of tongues. But through exaggeration of this gift and the strong temptation to use it sensationally, it became a source of much confusion and even ridicule, and a work that had in it undoubted elements of truth and power was discredited and hindered.[31]

Simpson seems to be in essential agreement with Gordon's assessment. Other Alliance leaders such as well-known Baptist pastor F. L. Chapell and later C&MA pastor and Simpson Bible Institute interim president, T. J. McCrossan, likewise wrote approvingly of Irving.[32]

Ironically, some Alliance leaders in recent years have considered Irving's early charismatic movement a counterfeit of genuine spiritual gifts, even comparing it to the early heresies of Montanism. However, this was not the judgment of early Alliance leaders. They would have admitted that there were counterfeits among the authentic, but still acknowledged the genuineness of Irving's movement over all.

DEVELOPMENT OF SPIRITUAL WARFARE/DELIVERANCE MINISTRY

Recovery of the Concept of the Believer's Authority.
Among leaders in the Higher Life movement, Alliance-related pioneers were on the forefront of rediscovering the concept of the authority of the believer. In 1888, George B. Peck, a friend of Gordon and Simpson, wrote his book *Throne-Life, or The Highest Christian Life,* in which he wrote concerning "throne-power," or the "command of faith."[33] Also in the late 1800s George D. Watson, popular Methodist holiness leader affiliated with the C&MA, wrote *Steps to the Throne.*[34] Later Alliance missionary John A. MacMillan developed his concept of the authority of the believer most directly from Watson's book *Bridehood Saints,* paraphrasing and expanding upon Watson's writings.[35] Other Higher Life/

Keswick leaders such as A. T. Pierson, Jessie Penn-Lewis, and Andrew Murray taught embryonic concepts of this authority.[36] Simpson gleaned from these teachings, also teaching on "the authority of faith."[37] Modern charismatic leader Kenneth Hagin further adapted and popularized MacMillan's teachings.[38]

The Reality of Exorcistic Ministry.

As early as March 1882 Simpson acknowledged, "Christ still casts out devils, and His people should still claim His unchanged power for the wretched victims of Satan when God brings to us."[39] An 1887 issue of his periodical *The Word, the Work and the World* contained an article on casting out demons in China.[40]

The major influence upon Simpson and early Alliance leaders in the area of spiritual warfare and deliverance ministry seems to have been Ethan O. Allen, a descendent of the earlier deist of colonial and furniture fame. Allen launched into a healing and deliverance ministry in the mid 1800s after being healed at a Methodist meeting. Alliance leaders Carrie Judd Montgomery, Sarah M. C. Musgrove, and Edgar K. Sellow were longtime friends of Allen. Simpson associate William T. MacArthur later wrote a short biography of Allen's life and ministry, noting that Simpson held Allen in "very high esteem" and called him the "Father of Divine Healing."[41]

Referring to Genesis 3:15 and Luke 10:19, Allen wrote a tract entitled "Satan Under Your Feet."[42] He operated in the gift of discernment of spirits, and often practiced rebuking, binding the strong man, or "words of castin' out" evil spirits before praying for the sick.[43] He followed what he called the "Old Commission," the words of Jesus in Mark 16:17-18.[44] He prophesied to MacArthur in the 1890s, "Young man, you look like somebody the Lord could use in castin' out devils."[45] His prophecy came true, as MacArthur did indeed engage in deliverance ministry through the years, on at least one occasion teaming up with Simpson in 1912.[46]

Other influences upon Simpson and the Alliance belief and practice of spiritual warfare included Johannes Blumhardt,[47] the German Lutheran pastor who was involved in an extensive, dramatic, and often agonizing two-year process of exorcism of one of his parishioners, and John Nevius, Presbyterian missionary to China who wrote the book *Demon Possession and Allied Themes.* In 1895, Simpson commented on Nevius' book, "The subject fits right alongside of Divine healing and stands or falls along with it." He mentioned that evil spirits can have supernatural knowledge and speak foreign languages.[48] Simpson excerpted articles from Nevius' book, reprinting them the *C&MA Weekly.*[49] Additionally, the deliverance ministry of Hudson Taylor and the renowned Pastor Hsi also had an impact on C&MA theology of spiritual warfare and deliverance.[50] From time to time, Simpson included accounts of casting out demons and other power evangelism encounters in his periodicals.[51]

Demonization of Christians.

Nevius' book did not directly address the issue of demonization of Christians. Nonetheless, early Alliance leaders recognized the problem of demonic attack at various levels upon believers, familiar with the exorcism of believers by Blumhardt and Allen. The July/August 1885 issue of *The Word, the Work and the World* featured an article by Pastor Schrenck, an associate of Swiss Pastor Otto Stockmayer, warning about "transmission of carnal spirits" upon believers through laying on of hands.[52]

Significantly, a major Alliance leader found himself attacked by demons in which he said he had become possessed. Dr. George Peck, one of the Vice Presidents of the Alliance, and his fellow C&MA friend and colleague, C. W. Morehouse, both had earlier been praying for greater power to heal and cast out demons. Being relatively new in the art of spiritual warfare and not realizing the scope of what they were taking on, Peck himself was attacked by demonic forces. In January 1890, he became severely ill with pneumonia, accompanied by insanity and demonic manifestations. Morehouse prayed for his healing and cast out the demons.[53] As a result, Peck launched into a greater ministry, devoting most of his time to healing and deliverance. In August 1895 he spoke at Old Orchard convention on casting out demons.[54]

Another recorded recognition of demonization of Christians occurred during the July 1903 Nyack Convention. Toward the end of the altar ministry led by Minnie Draper, "suddenly the working of demons appeared in a dear and devoted sister." She had a partial deliverance earlier, but this session took about four hours for total deliverance and full victory.[55]

---

1.   A. B. Simpson, *A Larger Christian Life* (Harrisburg, PA: Christian Publications, n. d. [1890]), 29-30.

2.   See Paul L. King, "Holy Laughter and Other Phenomena in Evangelical and Holiness Revival Movements, "*Alliance Academic Review* (Camp Hill, PA: Christian Publications, 1998), 107-122; Paul L. King, "Supernatural Physical Manifestation in Evangelical and Holiness Movements," a paper presented at the combined meeting of Society of Pentecostal Studies/Wesleyan Theological Society, Wilmore, KY, March 2003.

3.   Robert L. Niklaus, John S. Sawin, Samuel J. Stoesz, *All For Jesus* (Camp Hill, PA: Christian Publications, 1986), 7-9.

4.   For an in-depth study of Simpson's beliefs regarding the baptism of the Spirit compared to other views of his day, see Richard Gilbertson, *The Baptism of the Holy Spirit: The Views of A. B. Simpson and His Contemporaries* (Camp Hill, PA: Christian Publications, 1993).

5.   A. B. Simpson, "A Personal Testimony," AW, Oct. 2, 1915, 11.

6.   Walter Turnbull and C. H. Chrisman, "The Message of the Christian and Missionary Alliance," 1927, accessed online at http://online.cbccts.sk.ca/alliance studies/ahtreadings/ahtr_s6.html.

7.   .A. B. Simpson, *A Larger Christian Life* (Camp Hill, PA: Christian Publications, 1988), 42.

8.   A. B. Simpson, *Wholly Sanctified* (Harrisburg, PA: Christian Publications, 1925), 11.

9.   Simpson's Diary, Aug. 9, 1907.

10.   A. W. Tozer, *Wingspread* (Camp Hill, PA: Christian Publications, 1943), 62; Niklaus, *All for Jesus*, 13-14.

11.   Emma Beere, comp., "Simpson Anecdotes," as found in C. Donald McKaig's unpublished *Simpson Scrapbook* (Colorado Springs, CO: A. B. Simpson Historical Library, n.d.), 231; cited in Gary Keisling, *Relentless Spirituality: Embracing the Spiritual Disciplines of A. B. Simpson* (Camp Hill, PA: Christian Publications, 2004), 128-129.

12. Tozer, 79; see also Niklaus, 39-41.

13. Niklaus, 41-42.

14. Ibid., 52-54.

15. Ibid., 55-56.

16. Ibid., 56-57.

17. Ibid., 58-59.

18. Leslie A. Andrews, "Limited Freedom: A.B. Simpson's View of Freedom," *The Birth of a Vision* (Camp Hill, PA: Christian Publications, 1986), 231-233; Niklaus, *All for Jesus*, 63, 64, 70, 269-270.

19. For seven examples, see Adelaide Baldwin, "An Incurable Case of Cancer," *The Word, the Work and the World* (WWW), July 1883, 106-107; G. P. Pardington, *Twenty-five Wonderful Years, 1889-1914: A Popular Sketch of the C&MA* (New York, 1914), 216; Rev. McBride, "Testimonies of Healing," WWW, Sept. 1886,164; Mrs. M. J. Clark, "Testimonies of Healing," WWW, Jan. 1887, 33; Georgia A. Jeffers, "He Said Unto Him, Receive Thy Sight," CAMW, June 10, 1892, 379; C. H. Gootee, "The Miracle of My Healing," *Triumphs of Faith*, Mar. 1926, 62ff.; "The Household of Faith," AW, June 10, 1922, 206; F. G. Wetherspoon, "His Leading," CAMW, Jan. 27, 1893, 59; Mrs. James Gainforth, "Consumption," CMAW, May 31, 1902, 317.

20. Simpson, Editorial, WWW, Aug.-Sept. 1887, 66; "Healing of Miss Ina Moses," CAMW, Jan. 1888, 6; A. B. Simpson, "Old Orchard," CAMW, Jan. 1888, 11.

21. Sophie Lichtenfels, "A Lamb Amongst Wolves," CAMW, Jan. 29, 1895, 70.

22. "The First Impressions of a Friday Meeting at the Gospel Tabernacle," CAMW, Apr. 27, 1894, 461.

23. A. B. Simpson, Editorial, CAMW, Dec. 4, 1896, 517.

24. Simpson, "How to Receive Divine Healing," WWW, July-Aug., 1885, 203.

25. A. B. Simpson, "How to Help the Sick," CMAW, Mar. 13, 1903, 158.

26. Simpson, *The Gospel of Healing* (Harrisburg, PA: Christian Publications, 1915), 175.

27. Ibid., 178.

28. A. B. Simpson, *The Gospel of Healing*, 57. Some may wonder how Simpson regarded the controversy over the genuineness of the end of Mark 16. I have not been able to find anywhere that he discusses it. However, his close friend A. J. Gordon briefly discusses Mark 16 as a "disputed text" in his book *The Ministry of Healing* and concludes, "We believe the evidence in favor of the genuineness of the passage vastly outweighs that against it." A. J. Gordon, *The Ministry of Healing, in Healing: The Three Great Classics on Divine Healing*, comp. and ed. Jonathan L. Graf (Camp Hill, PA: Christian Publications, 1992), 278-279. It is likely that he agreed with Gordon's assessment, and so the matter was settled for him.

29. For a scholarly refutation of the charges against Irving of Christological heresy, see David W. Dorries, *Edward Irving's Incarnational Christology* (Fairfax, VA: Xulon Press, 2002).

30. A. J. Gordon, *The Ministry of Healing, in Healing: The Three Great Classics on Divine Healing*, comp. and ed. Jonathan L. Graf (Camp Hill, PA: Christian Publications, 1992), 184-187.

31. A. B. Simpson, "Worship and Fellowship of the Church," CMAW, Feb. 1898, 125; reprinted in the *Alliance Witness*, Feb. 1, 1967; Simpson, *Christ in the Bible (CITB)* (Camp Hill, PA: Christian Publications, 1994), 5:236. See also A. B. Simpson, "Supernatural Aid in the Study of Foreign Languages," CMAW, Oct. 21, 1892,259-260; A. B. Simpson, *Missionary Messages* (Harrisburg, PA: Christian Publications, n.d.), 31.

32. F. L. Chapell, "The Body for the Lord and the Lord for the Body," CAMW, Oct.-Nov. 1888, 160.; "Field Notes," CMAW, Mar. 23, 1901, 166; T. J. McCrossan, *Christ's Paralyzed Church X-Rayed* (Youngstown, OH: C. E. Humbard, 1937), 310. See also "A Glad Message, *The Christian Alliance*, Feb. 1, 1888, 19; CAMW, Feb.14, 1890, 103; F. W. Farr, "The First and Second Adam," CAMW, Feb. 25, 1892, 137; E. P. Marvin, "A Fraternal Appeal," CAMW, Mar. 3, 1893, 137; A. B. Simpson, "Winged Messengers," AW, May 22, 1915, 116. For a cautionary article about the later teaching of the Catholic Apostolic Church, founded by Irving,, see A. B. Simpson, "The Catholic Apostolic Church, CMAW, Nov. 4, 1899, 365.

33. George B. Peck, *Throne-Life, or The Highest Christian Life* (Boston, MA: Watchword Publishing, 1888),171, 174-175, 177.

34. George D. Watson, *Steps to the Throne* (Cincinnati, OH: Bible School Book Room, n.d.).

35. John A. MacMillan, *The Authority of the Believer* (Harrisburg, PA: Christian Publications, 1980), 93, 96.

36. See my book *A Believer with Authority*, 215ff., for more discussion of these leaders and their teachings.

37. A. B. Simpson, "The Authority of Faith," *AW*, Apr. 23, 1938, 263.

38. Kenneth Hagin, *The Believer's Authority* (Tulsa, OK: Rhema Bible Church, 1984), Preface. See Paul L. King, *A Case Study of a Believer with Authority: The Impact of the Life and Ministry of John A. MacMillan*, Doctor of Ministry dissertation, (Tulsa, OK: Oral Roberts University, 2000), documenting the significant influence of MacMillan's writings on the modern faith teaching on the authority of the believer (pp. 280-286). In particular, Kenneth Hagin made extensive use of MacMillan's material, popularizing the concept in the Pentecostal, charismatic, and modern faith movements (pp. 263-294).

39. "Power over Evil Spirits," Lesson 11, Mar. 12, 1882, WWW, Vol. 1, Mar. 1882, 105.

40. "Miss Cumming on Supernatural Healing," WWW, Mar. 1887, 186-187.

41. William T. MacArthur, *Ethan O. Allen* (Philadelphia, PA: The Parlor Evangelist, c. 1924), 1.

42. Ibid., 4-5.

43. Ibid., 6, 12, 14.

44. Ibid., 7, 10-11.

45. Ibid., 11.

46. William T. MacArthur, "A Reminiscence of Rev. A. B. Simpson," AW, Aug. 21, 1920, 325-326.

47. William C. Stevens, "Divine Healing in Relation to Revivals," CMAW, Feb. 28, 1903, 117, 124.

48. A. B. Simpson, "The Casting Out of Devils," CAMW, Nov. 13, 1895, 311.

49. John Nevius, "Demon Possession," CMAW, July 27, 1901, 49; Aug. 10, 1901, 77.

50. "The Love of Money," AW, July 6, 1946, 418.

51. Sophie Lichtenfels, "A Lamb Amongst Wolves," CAMW, Jan. 29, 1895, 70; "Remarkable Movement on Madagascar," CMAW, Oct. 5, 1901, 194; "Old Orchard Convention," CMAW, Aug. 16, 1902, 95.

52. Pastor Schrenck, "Dangers and Warnings," WWW, July-Aug. 1885, 211-212.

53. "Substance of Dr. Peck's Account of His Healing of Acute Mania," CAMW, Mar. 21-28, 1890, 192ff.

54. George B. Peck, "In His Name," CAMW, Aug. 14, 1895, 102.

55. "Nyack Convention," CMAW, July 25, 1903, 109.

TWO

EARLY C&MA CHARISMATIC MANIFESTATIONS AND THOUGHT

PROPHECIES, VISIONS AND OTHER PHENOMENA
IN THE 19ᵀᴴ CENTURY C&MA

Prophecies, dreams, and visions and other manifestations occurred early on in the fledging movement and were considered as genuinely from the Lord. As early as 1883 Methodist minister John Cookman, a member of Simpson's "Founder's Team," received a healing after seeing a vision of Jesus saying to him: "I am thy Healer, thy Sanctifier, thy Savior, and thy Lord."[1]

In 1889 Simpson wrote of a woman seeing a dramatic vision with symbolic meaning.[2] Simpson was evidently impressed by the vision and its spiritual message. The very next year at the Old Orchard convention of July 1890, Simpson heard a voice crying out in prayer all night long, and it seemed to him like a prophetic of what was to be the result of this convocation.[3] Also in 1890, in writing on sanctification of the mind, Simpson illustrated his teaching by citing another woman who received a vision of an empty skull filled with fire, as symbolic of the Holy Spirit filling the mind with the thoughts and feelings of God.[4]

Simpson thus did not hesitate in accepting such prophetic visions and dreams as from God. Although he sometimes through the years cautioned against taking too much stock in visions and dreams, his mystical bent nonetheless prepared him to be receptive to the possibility that God may genuinely speak through such manifestations from time to time.

Not only for Simpson was the prophetic a reality, but throughout the early Alliance. In 1892 after a series of financial reverses, 37 year-old businessman John Woodberry surrendered to the call to ministry God had place on his life in his early twenties. He and his wife were soon introduced to the C&MA through a prophetic word from a stranger to go to a certain address. His daughter recounts the story:

At the door one morning appeared a stranger, who began with the words, 'I've a message from God for you,' and ended with 'I have faith that you will go.'" When the door closed, queries and ridicule interchanged over such strange guidance as that. What! go to Grand Rapids—85 Baxter Street—and there learn the Way more perfectly? But some one's faith had laid hold on God. By nightfall they were both so uncomfortable that in the morning they were on their way. The greeting they received was alike surprising: "Are you Mr. and Mrs. Woodberry? Captain _____ said you were coming!" And he was right. In that Alliance Home truths were unfolded, such as they had never dreamed of, as Mrs. Dora Dudley, open Bible upon her knee, led them on from salvation to the deeper knowledge of sanctification, divine healing, and the glorious return of Christ.[5]

There they were filled with the Spirit and introduced to the C&MA. They determined to go to the Nyack Missionary Training Institute, miraculously sold their home within two hours, and moved their four children to New York. They eventually became long-term missionaries to China.

SIMPSON CAUTIONS THE FALLIBILITY OF PROPHECY

By 1889 Simpson recognized various strata of divine inspiration in the exercise of the gift of prophecy. He noted that prophecies may range from being mere impressions or they may be deeper convictions more surely from the Spirit, but that these prophecies are imperfect and can be discerned more perfectly over time through experience.[6] Simpson equated "the word of the Lord," that is, a prophecy, with receiving an impression, noting that it can be fallible.[7] He recognized the reality and legitimacy of prophecy, but cautioned against putting too much trust in such words.

Simpson's counsel itself became prophetic the very next year. Predictive prophecy earned a bad name in 1890 when several Christian leaders, including Maria Woodworth (Etter) and C&MA conference speaker Elizabeth Sisson, both friends of Carrie Judd (Montgomery), endorsed and affirmed a prophecy that had been circulating that an earthquake and tidal wave would strike the West Coast, a prophecy that proved to be false (although some claimed that the 1906 earthquake 16 years later was the fulfillment). It is no wonder that Simpson wanted to distance himself from such predictions. Yet it did not destroy Carrie's friendship with Maria. Carrie's new husband George seemed not to be swept up with the prophetic fervor, and evidently became a moderating force during the confusion and disillusionment.[8]

MANIFESTATIONS AT THE ALLIANCE HEALING HOMES

Following the pattern of the faith homes of Johannes Blumhardt in Germany, Dorothea Trudel in Switzerland, and Elizabeth Baxter in England, Simpson and the early Alliance founded healing homes throughout the North America for the purpose of providing an atmosphere of faith, rest, meditation, and prayer, focusing on Scriptures, attitudes, and preparation needed for healing. Healing homes associated with the Alliance included Berachah Home in New York City (later moved to Nyack, New York); Hebron Home in Philadelphia, Bethany Home in Toronto; Sara Musgrove's home in Troy, New York; Mrs. J. P. Kellogg's home in Utica, New York, Kemuel House in Philadelphia; Beulah Home in Grand Rapids, Michigan; and the Alliance Home in Pittsburgh; as well as additional homes in Atlanta, Chicago, Cleveland, Los Angeles, and Santa Barbara, California.[9] While the healing ministry was private and low key, dramatic charismatic manifestations occurred from time-to-time in the healing homes, occasionally being reported in Alliance periodicals. A sampling appears here below.

Berachah Healing Home, Nyack, New York. In March 1891 Julie Boyd was healed as "a divine electricity coursing through my whole body" caused the whole bed to shake.[10] In May 1897 Mrs. A. E. Hester heard an audible voice prophesying, "Go to that Home on the Hudson and stay a few weeks." She had a dream of heaven and the coming of Christ, followed by healing of her tumor.[11]

In July 1899 Mrs. N. S. Dean, who had been bedfast or wheelchair bound for 17 years due to a spinal condition, was dramatically healed. One of the workers spent time with her and hours in prayer for her, what today would be called "soaking prayer." When the worker laid her hand on Mrs. Dean's right leg, Mrs. Dean immediately had a "prickling, tingling sensation." Later she felt a twitch in her back that enabled her to sit upright. Though the worker did not know of the curvature of the spine, she received a prophetic impression from the Lord of Isaiah 55:2, "I will make the crooked places straight." The "impression deepened into a certainty" when she laid her hands on Mrs. Dean again and Mrs. Dean felt the prickling sensation again.

She continued to command the spine to be straightened. The process took about six hours. "I stood upon my feet twice, which I had not done for 17 years." The worker was "wonderfully baptized with a spirit of praise." A light appeared upon the face of Mrs. Dean and her face was transfigured. The worker continued to pray five hours a day for three weeks, resulting in stiff and atrophied muscles being strengthened. One day her ribs creaked "like an old saddle" as they were adjusted into proper place through prayer. Her short leg was lengthened an inch with a grating sound.[12]

Beulah Healing Home, Grand Rapids, Michigan. Dora Dudley, who received healing in 1885 and was influenced by Carrie Judd's book *The Prayer of Faith*, established the Beulah Healing Home in Grand Rapids, Michigan, in 1887. Carrie Judd was the guest speaker at the dedication of the home.[13] Many manifestations of healing took place. Three of the most dramatic are cited here.

Mrs. E. L. McLaine had dislocated her shoulder so that sagged two inches and causing her arm to be lifeless. After several Bible readings and anointing at the C&MA Beulah Healing Home in Detroit, on January 25, 1892, the power of Lord came into her arm and shoulder and it began moving up and down on its own for half an hour, then she was healed.[14] The same year Clay Anderson had a spinal injury that contorted his body. One night he heard an audible voice prophesying to him, "Take thy brother, go to the [Alliance] healing home in Detroit, for thou shalt be healed."[15] He followed the supernatural divine direction, received prayer at the Beulah home and was healed. In 1896 an elderly lady had fallen and fractured several bones. She went to the Beulah Healing Home where Dora Dudley anointed and prayed for her and felt the bones moving back into place.[16]

Alliance Home, Pittsburgh, Pennsylvania. E. D. Whiteside, who himself had experienced a dramatic healing, was asked by Simpson to become the superintendent of the Alliance work in the Pittsburgh and Western Pennsylvania area. He founded the Alliance Home in Pittsburgh as a place of rest and healing. Zolla McCauley had double curvature of the spine and partial paralysis in her body. In 1900 she went to the Alliance Home in Pittsburgh for prayer. When she was prayed over a thrill like an electrical shock went through her body and she was healed.[17]

FALLING UNDER THE POWER OF THE SPIRIT

As mentioned earlier of Simpson's ministry, falling under the power of the Spirit occurred periodically in proto-C&MA and early C&MA meetings. In 1888 E. D. Whiteside testified of receiving a miraculous healing accompanied by unusual physical manifestations such as falling under the power of the Spirit and holy laughter: "Like a flash of electricity, I was instantly thrilled. Every point of my body and nerves was controlled by a strange sensation that increased in volume, until I bowed lower and lower to the floor. I was filled with the ecstatic thrill. My physical frame was unable to stand the strain." He felt he was on the verge of "dying from overjoy."[18]

Also in 1889 Carrie Judd (Montgomery) formed a life-long friendship with holiness and later Pentecostal evangelist Maria Woodworth-Etter, whose meetings included healings, falling under the power of the Spirit, trances, visions, etc., even speaking in tongues in the 1890s.[19] Carrie herself fell under the power of the Spirit several times, and her friend Elizabeth Sisson shook under the power of the Spirit.[20]

Most instances of falling under the power of the Spirit in the Alliance occurred to individuals. However, mass swooning occurred occasionally. In February 1891 at an Alliance-related meeting in Maine, several people fell under the power, some unconscious for hours.[21] In May 1896 at the Washington state Christian Alliance Convention, held at First Baptist Church in Tacoma, a large audience "bowed beneath the wave of Pentecostal power" that filled the room. "Chaplain Stubbs fell before the Lord by a divine impulse . . . with strong cries and tears."[22]

At a combined C&MA / Mennonite campmeeting, in Allentown, Pennsylvania, C&MA General Field Superintendent Dean A. C. Peck preached six services in three days. He described the meetings: "At service after service . . . I saw people fall as dead under the power of God." He affirmed that it was a genuine revival from God and talked about such things happening among the Methodists 50-60 years ago, but were not frequent now because many revivals are of human manufacture.[23]

SIMPSON TEACHES POWER EVANGELISM IN 1890s

Not only did Simpson anticipate tongues for missions, but also supernatural manifestations of God's power to enhance witness. Power evangelism, the concept that God uses supernatural phenomena as an aid to evangelism, has been made popular in recent years by John Wimber, but he was not the originator of the concept. In fact, nearly a century earlier in 1892 Simpson preached on "Signs, Wonders and World Evangelization," declaring, "We believe it is the plan of the Lord to pour out His Spirit not only in the ordinary but also in the extraordinary gifts and operations of power. He will do this in proportion to the zeal of His people to claim the evangelization of the entire world." [24] Simpson preached that all gifts of the Spirit are to be in the church today, including speaking in tongues. He encouraged reawakening and stirring up of the gifts, and believed some missionaries may receive tongues for supernatural proclamation of the Gospel, but not to expect it as God's ordinary course.

Power Encounters Leading to Conversion. Although Alliance leaders did not use the terminology of "power encounters," such encounters did occur through the early ministries of the C&MA. As mentioned earlier, in August 1887 at Old Orchard Convention, when C&MA was first formed, power of God came with a "flash of heat" and sensations like electrical shocks upon schoolteacher on crutches. She was instantly healed, and people were shouting, weeping and singing. Her two sisters were saved on the spot and many more healings followed. This was a strong confirmation of the founding of the C&MA.[25]

Emma Herr received anointing with oil and laying on of hands for healing and baptism in the Spirit, she was overcome and sank to the floor weeping for joy and shouting. Her father, two brothers and a sister were all saved as a result.[26] Alliance periodicals also recorded incidents of power encounters occurring through the ministry of J. Hudson Taylor.[27] In June 1898 C&MA evangelist Frederick Senft reported of a "Pentecostal revival" that a man was saved and fell under the power of the Spirit unconscious. His mother came to look upon him, and she began to weep, tremble and fall to the floor, then was saved and filled with the Spirit. [28]

In May 1903 missionary Laura Gardner gave an address at the Nyack Missionary Training Institute commencement on "Supernatural Work in the Ministry of the Gospel," in which she declared that signs shall follow, and spoke of power encounters of healing, deliverance and miracles accompanying the gospel.[29] In the same year, Zella McAuley, a missionary in India, had smallpox and intense pain. After united prayer, the pain was gone and she testified, "I was thrilled through and through with sensations." She witnessed in the hospital and a Jewish woman was saved.[30]

PRAYING FOR "MISSIONARY TONGUES"

Not only did Simpson and the early C&MA generally expect supernatural manifestations of God's power to enhance witness, but also specifically the gift of speaking in tongues especially for missions, or what is sometimes called *xenolalia* or *xenoglossa*, known languages as opposed to unknown tongues. In February 1892, Simpson wrote, "But does the Bible really warrant the expectation of the gift of tongues for the purpose of preaching the Gospel to the heathen? We must frankly say that we are not quite clear that it does, and yet we would not dare to discourage any of God's children from claiming and expecting it if they have the faith to do so and can see the warrant in His word. . . . He that is able to receive it, let him receive it."[31]

C. T. Studd and the Pohill-Turners of the famous Cambridge Seven had gone to China believing they would receive the gift of speaking Chinese, but they were not able to receive, and were duly chided by J. Hudson Taylor. Similarly, in the summer of 1892, W. W. Simpson and William Christie went to Western China and the Tibetan border under the auspices of the C&MA missions, and "they anticipated receiving Mandarin as well as the Tibetan language as gifts from God in fulfillment of Mark 16." But they did not receive either, although they were able to acquire the language rapidly.[32]

However, these failures did not dissuade Simpson and the Alliance from believing that *xenolalia* was possible and that it might well be God's will. "Responding to the interest in missionary tongues, but wishing to avoid the 'dangers of Irvingism,'" at the Alliance convention in October 1892 Simpson issued an urgent call for the faithful to pray for "the special outpouring of the Spirit in connection with the acquiring of foreign languages and the resistance of the climatic difficulties of Africa, India, and China. We are sure that God has it in His heart to specially signalize His promise in this connection."[33]

SIMPSON AND OTHER HOLINESS LEADERS PROMOTE
THE SUPERNATURAL

At Old Orchard in the summer of 1894 Simpson was urged by Stephen Merritt to write a "book on the Holy Ghost." From 1894 to 1896 Simpson taught a series of messages on the pneumatology of the Old and New Testaments, compiling them together into a book entitled *The Holy Spirit or Power from on High*. He wrote that the reason the Church does not have the gifts of the Spirit today in the same measure as the early church is "the whole body is mutilated and severed, so that it is not possible for the Spirit to flow with undivided and unhindered fullness through the whole." He affirmed that the church may expect all the gifts of the Spirit.[34] At the C&MA convention in October 1897 Simpson preached a series of messages entitled "Present Truths or the Supernatural," stressing that the present truth the Lord was restoring to the Church at that time was truth about the reality of the supernatural.[35]

Anticipation of the reality of supernatural power was burgeoning among many evangelical leaders at this time. J. Hudson Taylor and Andrew Murray were similarly teaching about the supernatural nature of the church and Christian life.[36] Another friend of Simpson, A. T. Pierson, who was interim pulpit successor to Spurgeon, also affirmed the reality and importance of supernatural power: "A supernatural gospel is meant to accomplish supernatural results, and needs a supernatural power behind it and its messengers."[37]

SPEAKING IN TONGUES SIMPSON'S CHURCH BEFORE 1897!

Simpson further illustrated his support for exercising tongues and prophecy by reminiscing about a black woman who evidently spoke in "some simple form" of tongues at Simpson's Gospel Tabernacle some time earlier:

> I remember a dear old black saint, now in heaven, who used to accentuate the most important periods and passages in the sermon, or the meeting, by sometimes springing to her feet with a burst of ecstatic overflow that no language could express. It was a sort of inarticulate cry, while her face literally blazed in ebony blackness with the light of glory. She was simply beating time to one of God's great strains, and while the ear of exquisite taste was sometimes offended, I believe the Holy Spirit was pleased, and the true heart of His Church ought always to make room for the artless freedom of the Spirit's voice. There are no monopolies in the Church of Jesus Christ, and reverent faith will always say, "Let the Lord speak by whom He will."[38]

Even though this outbreak of a primal form of tongues was apparently not accompanied by interpretation, Simpson recognized it as a genuine overflow of the woman's expression of prayer and praise to God. He wanted others to be free to speak out whatever God might be placed in a person's heart.

ANOTHER EXPRESSION OF TONGUES

In 1898 Lizzie Elledges testified that she heard an audible voice prophesying to her, "The Lord hath given the healing faith." The voice also sounded like an unknown tongue and a cloud of glory filled the room. She fell to the floor and could not speak or move, then her body was "shaken by the power of God." A fire went through her body and she recounted that she "felt a new life coursing through my veins." Even as she was writing this testimony, she wrote, power like an electrical shock was coming upon her.[39]

SIMPSON FURTHER ENCOURAGES TONGUES AND PROPHECY

Simpson encouraged the exercise of prophecy and speaking in tongues. He recognized that some genuine tongues have been restored today, but have been tainted by some abuse, exaggeration and excess. After the failed expectations of Studd, the Polhill-Turners, and the Alliance's own W.W. Simpson and Christie, he no longer believed it that it was proper to send out missionaries, expecting them to be given tongues to preach in the native language, though he still believed it might be possible.

However, now he recognized the value of tongues for the local church and the individual. Referring to the operation of spiritual gifts in the assembly in 1 Corinthians 14:26, Simpson encouraged people to speak a word of prophetic utterance or tongues:

> Come out with your simple testimony of some truth, that has helped you, and that you have been told to pass on for the help of others. Fear not to speak the message which the Holy Spirit has burned into your soul for the quickening and the rousing of your soul. It will be a word in season for some weary soul. And if you have, in some simple form, the old gift of tongues welling up in your heart, some Hallelujah which you could not put into articulate speech, some unutterable cry of love or joy, out with it!"[40]

RETURN FROM DEATH

Incidents of apparent resurrection from the dead were rare in C&MA ministry, as they were in the early New Testament church, but there are records of at least two raisings from death in pre-Azusa Street Alliance history. In the March 1889 issue of the *Christian Alliance and Missionary Weekly* an article appeared, giving testimony of woman pronounced dead in 1882 by a doctor, who in that state saw a vision of angels and heaven and heard beautiful music, a bright light and Jesus telling her to go back. Then she came back to life and was gradually healed over two years.[41]

About a decade later, it was reported that a missionary with cholera appeared to be dead after a death-rattle, blood left his face, and his eyes were glazed over. Another missionary, Mr. McGlashan, laid hands on him and prayed, "Lord, give me back his life." Instantly, blood returned to his face, he regained consciousness, and was healed.[42]

SUPERNATURAL DIVINE PROTECTION

Alliance periodicals recorded numerous dramatic incidents of supernatural divine protection including protection from poisonous snake spider and tarantula bites, scorpion stings, being struck by lightning, spells and curses of sorcery, accidental and deliberate poisoning.[43] Among the many incidents, in August 1896 at the Old Orchard Convention, W. A. Cramer reported that a young convert in Congo C&MA was forced to drink poison along with a non-believer. The non-believer died in a few hours, but the young convert never got sick.[44]

"HOLY EMOTION" IN THE EARLY C&MA

The expression of emotion is characteristic of the Pentecostal and charismatic movements—shouting, crying, raising hands, laughing, clapping, emotional praise and worship, dancing, etc. Such emotional expressions became a common part of the early Christian and Missionary Alliance as well, although probably not to the degree and frequency found in the Pentecostal and charismatic movements.

Some have questioned whether Simpson and the Alliance accepted emotional outbursts. Dramatic holiness evangelist Maria Woodworth-Etter visited one of Simpson's services in 1885 and found it rather formal, reporting: "We attended Rev. Simpson's meeting, but was surprised to see it so cold. Not one saved or healed, and no signs of the Holy Ghost baptism."[45] Wayne Warner comments that Simpson "would probably have felt as out of place in Maria's meetings as she did in his in 1885."[46] Warner's observation is undoubtedly true. Compared to her revival meetings where many dramatic manifestations such as falling under the power of the Spirit, visions, trances and emotional experiences were taking place in the months just prior to her visit at Simpson's church,[47] his meetings at this time would have seemed rather tame and tepid. This was early in Simpson's healing ministry, not long after leaving the Presbyterian Church. Warner points out that "as early as 1883 he was cautioning ministers about making a 'public parade' out of praying for the sick."[48] Simpson had written then:

> It is very solemn ground and can never be made a professional business or a public parade. Its mightiest victims will always be silent and out of sight, and its power will keep pace with our humility and holiness. . . . We greatly deprecate the indiscriminate anointing of all who come forward. . . . We hope the wonder-seeking spirit will not be allowed to take the place of practical godliness and humble work for the salvation of men.[49]

Warner concluded that Simpson "abhorred emotional camp meeting styles that were associated with many services where prayer for the sick was offered."[50] While that was true to a degree, as we will see shortly, Simpson became more receptive to much more expression of emotion in his meetings, yet continuing to avoid sensationalism. No doubt some of the formalism of Presbyterian structure may have continued for some years, but, as we will see, that began to change significantly. Additionally, although Simpson never fully embraced Quietism, he was influenced by some of the proponents of Quietist theology and practice such as Francois Fenelon, Madame Guyon and Thomas Upham. He wrote an article entitled "The Power of Stillness" which was re-published again and again through the years, both in pamphlet form and in his periodicals.

However, Simpson's own preaching would sometimes become emotional and dramatic, to the point that some of his critics called him an "enthusiast," what we would today call "emotionalism" or "fanaticism." The grandson of Alliance leader William Christie told me that when his grandfather first encountered the Alliance, he was uncomfortable with the free expression of emotion in Alliance meetings, but eventually adapted. In reality, Simpson developed an appreciation for both quiet contemplation and unreserved (but not unbridled) expression of emotion. All of this being said, Simpson still would have been quite uncomfortable with the extent of emotional demonstration allowed in Woodworth-Etter's meetings.

In September 1885 (probably soon after Woodworth-Etter visited his meeting), Simpson traveled to England to visit William Boardman's Healing Convention. He described the conference as "times of the latter rain" and remarked that the meetings are not as quiet as in America.[51] This may have been the occasion that influenced him to encourage greater exercise of emotion in his meetings. Yet, we can also see earlier experiences in his life that may have begun to influence and change his traditional Presbyterian way of thinking.

As mentioned earlier, in the 1870s before Simpson knew about divine healing, he personally witnessed holy laughter or "the power of divine joy to heal disease."[52] Not long after Simpson began his healing ministry, in February 1884, Mrs. George Ford experienced vision of Jesus and heaven for hours, and healing with what she described as "sensations like powerful shocks from an electrical battery . . . many times, . . . ecstasy of delight . . . wave after wave . . . floating in an ocean of joy."[53] This kind of experience was not an isolated incident.[54]

By the founding of the Alliance at Old Orchard Convention in August 1887, emotional expression had loosened up considerably in Simpson's meetings. People were shouting, weeping and singing. Other than the absence of speaking in tongues, the scene would have reminiscent of a Pentecostal camp meeting.[55] After that time, Simpson and other leaders of the newly formed "Christian Alliance" often reported their meetings as being filled with "holy enthusiasm."[56]

As Simpson's healing ministry expanded, more and more instances of joyful and ecstatic experiences occurred. In 1891 Simpson spoke quite positively of holy laughter and shouting in a C&MA meeting in Columbia, South Carolina.[57] By 1897, Simpson had observed enough of the manifestations to believe they were genuinely from God, writing in his devotional book *Days of Heaven and Earth* about holy laughter as a result of the baptism in the Spirit.[58]

An article by Alliance-affiliated Baptist pastor F. W. Farr in January 1895 entitled "The Function of Emotions in Religion" summed up the Alliance belief and practice regarding emotion. He counseled to avoid repressing emotions altogether, on one hand, and expressing them extravagantly, on the other. He acknowledged that the Alliance had been criticized "as affording scope for and encouraging the use of the emotions," but added, "This criticism is a high commendation."[59] Such emotional expressions continued to spread through that same year, perhaps stimulated by Farr's encouragement.[60]

Though seemingly not a common occurrence, dancing in worship was not frowned upon by Simpson and Alliance circles. In April 1895, Simpson visited a black church associated with the Alliance. He recounted with enthusiasm, "We witnessed a sacred dance by about fifty of the women." They swayed and moved arms and feet, keeping time to the music. Simpson was greatly impressed at the meaningful, dramatic demonstration of worship, remarking, "The effect was truly grand."[61]

In June 1895 Simpson described the Alliance meeting in Los Angeles as a "ceaseless flood of blessing, joy and praise. The tidal wave often swept away all bounds and broke out in shouts of praise."[62] The "tidal wave" continued to crescendo, for it was reported that during the C&MA convention at the Wesleyan church in Wheaton, Illinois in 1898, "The tide of holy enthusiasm [was] rising higher with each service. . . . wave after wave of holy delight rolled over us. . . . waving of handkerchiefs, shouts of praise and tears of rejoicing."[63] By the turn of the century, such expressions of "holy enthusiasm" had become fairly common in the Alliance. It is clear that aside from speaking in tongues in the upcoming Pentecostal revival, pre-Azusa Street C&MA services were quite similar to later Pentecostal worship services, though avoiding many of the excesses.

TRUE AND FALSE PROPHECY IN THE C&MA

Simpson associate Carrie Judd Montgomery became seriously ill in 1898 and received prophecies from two women who said that she would die. Another woman, however, prophesied that she would recover. Carrie testified at the 1898 C&MA convention of the third woman: "The Lord spoke to her and told her that I would be raised up speedily and that I would be able to attend the Christian Alliance [C&MA] convention, which would take place in a few days. I was so very weak and ill that her prophecy seemed incredible, but, praise God, it came true." Of the two other women she commented, "Two Christian women thought they had it from the Lord that I was going to die. . . . How this shows us that we must not depend on *impressions* that do not harmonize with the word of God. . . . Dear readers, always stand firmly upon God's Word, and not upon the *impressions* of those around you (italics mine)."[64]

By the turn of the century, apparently receiving revelations, impressions, and prophetic word had become fairly common in C&MA circles. Simpson discerned problems with the rising manifestations of prophecy and in 1900 cautioned believers to test prophecy or inward visions and revelations by the Word of God (esp. 1 John 4:1-3), righteousness and holiness. He exhorts, "Let us be prepared for false spirits and let us not fear to try them, for if God is giving us any message or revelation, He will always give us ample time to be quite sure that it is God."[65]

CHARISMATA CONTINUE INTO THE NEW MILLENNIUM

The new millennium brought an increase both in the expectation of charismatic phenomena and also in the occurrences of such manifestations like pulsations or electrical shocks, visions and prophecies in C&MA circles, especially in conjunction with healing.[66] Although in the majority of hundreds of healings reported over the years in the *C&MA Weekly* did not mention such manifestations, the fact that such phenomena were reported periodically, without negative cautions, demonstrates the widespread acceptability of such charismatic manifestations. Thrills and chills, swooning, prophecies, holy laughter, and the like were not sought, but sometimes did occur and were accepted by Alliance people and Simpson himself as from God.

1. G. P. Pardington, *Twenty-five Wonderful Years, 1889-1914: A Popular Sketch of the C&MA* (New York,1914), 216.

2. A. B. Simpson, *The Gentle Love of the Holy Spirit* (Camp Hill, PA: Christian Publications, 1983), 61. Originally entitled *Walking in the Spirit*, this was first published in 1889.

3. Simpson, *A Larger Christian Life*, 20.

4. Simpson, *Wholly Sanctified*, 64-65.

5. Ora Woodberry, "John Woodbury," AW, Oct. 22, 1938, 677. For another example of such prophetic direction, see CAMW, Dec. 9, 1892, 370-371.

6. Simpson, *The Gentle Love of the Holy Spirit*; see also CITB, 4:581, where Simpson expounds on this further.

7. A. B. Simpson, *Days of Heaven on Earth* (Camp Hill, PA: Christian Publications, 1984), Nov. 17.

8. Wayne E. Warner, *The Woman Evangelist: The Life and Times of Charismatic Evangelist Maria B. Woodworth-Etter* (Metuchen, N.J. and London: The Scarecrow Press, Inc., 1986), 99-109.

9. Nancy A. Hardesty, *Faith Cure: Divine Healing in the Holiness and Pentecostal Movements* (Peabody, MA: Hendrickson Publishers, 2003), 64-65.

10. Julia C. Boyd, "A Recent Healing," CAMW, Mar. 27, 1891, 202.

11. Mrs. A. E. Hester, "The Lord's Doings," CMAW, Feb. 9, 1901, 84.

12. Mrs. N. S. Dean, "Testimony," CMAW, Jan. 26, 1901, 56.

13. For more on Dora Dudley and the Beulah Healing Home, see Hardesty, *Faith Cure*, 65-67.

14. Mrs. E. L. McLaine, "The Lord's Own Healing," CAMW, Mar. 16, 1894, 303.

15. Clay Anderson, "My Blessed Deliverance," CAMW, Jan. 20, 1893, 42.

16. "Field Notes," CAMW, June 5, 1896, 547.

17. Zolla McCauley, "Testimony," CMAW, Nov. 17, 1900, 284.

18. Irene E. Lewis, *Life Sketch of Rev. Mary C. Norton: Remarkable Healings on Mission Fields* (Los Angeles, CA: Pilgrim's Mission, Inc., 1954), 27; see also Shuman, "A God-Touched Man," AW, May 1, 1957, 3-4.

19. Warner, *The Woman Evangelist*, 82-83.

20. Ibid., 95, 105, 148. Elizabeth [Lizzie] Sisson was an early Alliance convention speaker and sister of C&MA Vice President Charlotte [Lottie] Sisson. They had served as missionaries in India and had worked with Elizabeth Baxter at Bethshan Healing Home in London. For additional examples, see N. C. Smith, "Experience," CAMW, Jan. 15, 1892, 42-43; "My Testimony," CAMW, Jan. 22, 1892, 59; Emma H. Herr, "How I Received the Three-fold Blessing," CAMW, July 13, 1898, 35; Lizzie Elledges, "To His Glory," CAMW, Aug. 17, 1898, 154.

21. "Meetings in Maine," CAMW, Apr. 17, 1891, 241-242; C. S. Carter, "An Explanation," CAMW, May 1, 1891, 274. But Alliance leaders also cautioned against seeking such manifestations, citing false prophecies given in similar conditions (probably referring to the false West Coast predictions).

22. R. S. Stubbs, "At Home," CAMW, May 22, 1896, 499.

23. Dean Peck, "Field Notes," CAMW, Aug. 11, 1897, 137.

24. A. B. Simpson, "Signs, Wonders and World Evangelization," *Communicate* (Camp Hill, PA: Christian Publications), 3:1:7. See also A. B. Simpson, "The New Testament Standpoint of Missions," CAMW, Dec. 16, 1892, 389.

25. A. B. Simpson, Editorial, WWW, Aug.-Sept. 1887, 66; "Healing of Miss Ina Moses," CAMW, Jan. 1888, 6; A. B. Simpson, "Old Orchard," CAMW, Jan. 1888, 11.

26. Emma H. Herr, "How I Received the Three-fold Blessing," CAMW, July 13, 1898, 35.

27. CAMW, Oct. 30, 1896, 390.

28. Frederick Senft, "Alliance Notes: A Pentecostal Revival," CAMW, June 1, 1898, 520. For other examples of power evangelism see Mrs. J. C. St. John, "Saved and Healed, or The Touch of Faith," CAMW, July 20, 1898, 59-59, 71; "A Remarkable Incident," CMAW, Sept. 27, 1902, 180; William C. Stevens, "Divine Healing in Relation to Revivals," CMAW, Feb. 28, 1903, 117, 124.

29. Laura A. Gardner, "Supernatural Work in the Ministry of the Gospel," CMAW, May 16, 1903, 271.

30. Zella Z. McAuley, "The Lord My Healer," CMAW, Aug. 29, 1903, 172-173; see also CMAW, May 7, 1904, 343.

31. A. B. Simpson, "The Gift of Tongues," CAMW, Feb. 5, 1892, 98-99.

32. Gary B. McGee, "The Debate over 'Missionary Tongues' Among Radical Evangelicals: 1881-1897," 28th Annual Meeting, Society of Pentecostal Studies, Mar. 11-13, 1999, 7-8. See William W. Simpson, "Letter from Shanghai, China," CMAW, July 1, 1892, 13-14.

33. McGee, "The Debate over 'Missionary Tongues,'" 8. See A. B. Simpson, "Supernatural Aid in the Study of Foreign Languages," CMAW, Oct. 21, 1892, 259-260.

34. A. B. Simpson, The Holy Spirit or Power from on High: New Testament (Harrisburg, PA: Christian Publications, n.d. [1894]), Vol. 2, 82-84.

35. A. B. Simpson, Present Truths or the Supernatural (Harrisburg, PA: Christian Publications, reprint 1967), 10.

36. Andrew Murray, Key to the Missionary Problem, contemporized by Leona Choy (Ft. Washington, PA: Christian Literature Crusade, 1979), 88. See also J. Hudson Taylor, "The Source of Power," CMAW, June 23, 1900, 416.

37. A. T. Pierson, The Acts of the Holy Spirit (Harrisburg, PA: Christian Publications, 1980), 92.

38. A. B. Simpson, "The Worship and Fellowship of the Church," CMAW, Feb. 1898, 125, reprinted in the Alliance Witness, Feb. 1, 1967; see also Simpson, CITB, 1994), 5:236. Keith M. Bailey, "Dealing with the Charismatic in Today's Church." A paper presented at the District Superintendent's Conference of The Christian and Missionary Alliance, Feb. 28-Mar. 2, 1977, Nyack, New York. Bailey's paper says before 1887, but this may be a typographic error as Simpson wrote this in 1897.

39. Lizzie Elledges, "To His Glory," CAMW, Aug. 17, 1898, 154.

40. Simpson, "Worship and Fellowship of the Church," CMAW, Feb. 1898, 125.

41. Lillie H. Mayhew, "Testimony of Miss Mayhew," CAMW, Mar. 1889, 40.

42. Robert D. Bannister, "The Wonder-Working God," CAMW, Sept. 21, 1898, 274-275.

43. Mrs. V. I. Soner, "Bitten by a Tarantula," CAMW, Aug. 31, 1894, 211; Julia B. Boyd, "Praise to Him," CAMW, May 8, 1895, 302; Mrs. Charles Hagg, "A Testimony of Healing," CAMW, July 31, 1895, 78; A. B. Simpson, "The Story of Dr. Paton," CAMW, Nov. 5, 1896, 409; G. Cooper, "Was It a Cobra Bite?," CMAW, May 5, 1900, 293; Dogmar Rasmussen, "Testimonies of Healing," CMAW, May 19, 1900, 329; Sarah S. Wagner, "Leaves from the Life of John G. Paton," CMAW, July 6, 1901, 3; Annie A. Seasholtz, "God's Protection and Care in a Heathen Land," CMAW, Feb. 22, 1902, 107.

44. "Convention Reports," CAMW, Aug. 14, 1896, 134-135.

45. Maria Woodworth-Etter, Acts of the Holy Ghost (Dallas, TX: John F. Worley Printing Co., n.d.), 118. By tracing her travels, I have determined that this may have been in the late summer of 1885.

46. Warner, The Woman Evangelist, 31, 154.

47. See Woodworth-Etter, Acts of the Holy Ghost, 105-117.

48. Warner, The Woman Evangelist, 149.

49. A. E. Thompson, *A. B. Simpson, His Life and Work* (Harrisburg, PA: Christian Publications, 1960), 140, cited in Warner, *The Woman Evangelist*, 149.

50. Warner, *The Woman Evangelist*, 149.

51. Simpson, "The Conferences in Great Britain," WWW, Sept. 1885, 236.

52. Simpson, *A Larger Christian Life*, 1890, 29-30.

53. Mrs. George W. Ford, "Testimony of Divine Healing," WWW, May 1887, 267.

54. See G. P. Pardington, *Twenty-five Wonderful Years*, 216; John Cookman, "Divine Holiness," WWW, Dec.1885, 336; John E. Cookman, "A Testimony of Healing, WWW, Sept. 1886, 160-162.

55. Simpson, Editorial, WWW, Aug.-Sept. 1887, 66; "Healing of Miss Ina Moses," CAMW, Jan. 1888, 6; A. B. Simpson, "Old Orchard," CAMW, Jan. 1888, 11.

56. "Round Lake Convention," CAMW, July 15, 1892, 34; "Secretary's Report of the Christian Alliance," CAMW, Oct. 26, 1894, 401; A. B. Simpson, "New York Convention," Oct. 16, 1895, 248.

57. A. B. Simpson, "Editorial Correspondence," CAMW, Apr. 10, 1895, 232.

58. Simpson, *Days of Heaven on Earth*, June 27.

59. F. W. Farr, "The Function of the Emotions in Religion," CAMW, Jan. 1, 1895, 5.

60. Mrs. Alfa V. Freeman, "All-Day Meeting, Seattle, Wash.," CAMW, May 1, 1895, 284.

61. A. B. Simpson, "Editorial Correspondence," CAMW, Apr. 17, 1895, 248.

62. A. B. Simpson, "Editorial Correspondence," CAMW, June 12, 1895, 377.

63. "Convention in the Northwest," CAMW, Mar. 23, 1898, 281.

64. Carrie Judd Montgomery, *Under His Wings*, (Oakland, CA: Triumphs of Faith, 1921), 159-161.

65. Simpson, CITB, 6:374-375.

66. Dean, "Testimony," CMAW, Jan. 26, 1901, 56; E. B. Burt, "Testimony of Healing: The Lord My Healer," CMAW, Jan. 13, 1900, 23; Emma McCrary, "Testimony," CMAW, Mar. 3, 1900, 151; Mary Smith, "Testimony," CMAW, July 14, 1900, 30; "Testimonies of Healing," CMAW, Sept. 22, 1900, 172; Zolla Mc-Cauley, "Testimony," CMAW, Nov. 17, 1900, 284; Mrs. E. Drake Norton, "Divine Healing: Testimony," CMAW, May 25, 1901, 287.

THREE

NEW CENTURY ANTICIPATES SUPERNATURAL REVIVAL

In the June 1900 issue of the *C&MA Weekly* J. Hudson Taylor wrote, "We are a supernatural people born again by a supernatural birth, kept by a supernatural power, sustained on supernatural food, taught by a supernatural Teacher from a supernatural Book. We are led by a supernatural Captain in right paths to assured victories."[1] Taylor's remark aroused anticipation for supernatural to break out early in the new century.

By January 1901 revival showers had began to fall upon the C&MA. The Alliance convention in Seattle featured "a baptism of the Holy Ghost and great joy, evidenced by tears and shouts all over the church. . . . Strong men wept for joy." The C&MA convention in Tacoma also experienced "a baptism of holy emotion."[2] Setting the tone for the year and the decade in January 1901, Simpson wrote an article entitled "Apostolic Christianity," advocating becoming an apostolic church of the power of the Holy Ghost.[3]

GREATER EXPECTATION OF THE SUPERNATURAL

In January 1901, Simpson featured an article by Thomas Erskine stressing the need of the supernatural gifts in the church: "Had the faith of the Church continued pure and full these gifts of the Spirit would never have disappeared."[4] In the same year Simpson intimated that something supernatural occurs in the act of Holy Communion. He considered the Lord's Supper as a "channel of grace" for blessing, health and healing, not merely a memorial.[5]

Alliance theologian George P. Pardington, in reference to the day of Pentecost, wrote that tongues may be given today for those preaching in foreign lands, commenting, "A few fully attested instances where the gift of speaking a foreign language has been received." He cited Mrs. Michael Baxter, founder of the healing home in London, saying that she "bears a strong personal testimony, to having at one time addressed a heathen audience in their own language of which she knew nothing from personal study."[6]

In 1903 William C. Stevens wrote of "incomplete effusions of the Spirit," which he defined as "effusions that leave out of sight those demonstrations which marked 'the early rain,' demonstrations of gifts and powers in the Spirit, which belong to Him in the church permanently."[7] The Alliance also showed an emerging awareness of spiritual warfare and the victorious life of the Spirit, featuring an article by Jessie Penn-Lewis entitled, "Satan Under Your Feet," on the believer's position and authority in Christ according to Ephesians 1:20-22.[8]

MORE ON SIGNS, WONDERS AND POWER ENCOUNTERS

In the C&MA Weekly Simpson interspersed encouragement of supernatural power with actual instances of power encounters.[9] The Alliance Weekly reported a "New Testament miracle" of multiplication in Alliance friend Pandita Ramabai's work in India. During a famine the wells dried up, but "God gave us water for more than 1900 people, besides over 100 cattle."[10] The Weekly also gave testimony of a miracle supply of fish similar to Jesus and the disciples casting nets,[11] and miracles of supernatural protection of missionaries.[12] Another article reported the experience of Reuben A. Torrey falling under power of the Spirit after he was baptized with the Holy Spirit.[13]

MORE "HOLY ENTHUSIASM"

By the turn of the century, such expressions of "holy enthusiasm" as described in the last chapter had become fairly common in the Alliance:

- December 1901—Union City, Tennessee—"How the waves of holy emotion rolled over us again and again as we sang, prayed, preached and shouted." Also holy laughter and crying.[14]

- September 1902—Richmond, Virginia—emotional praise, waving handkerchiefs and shouting "Hallelujah!"[15]

- April 1903—nine-week revival in Tennessee—a woman was caught up in the Spirit and spontaneously sang a new song on the Second Coming of Christ. She walked all around the congregation singing, then stopped, lifted her hands to heaven and remained silent and motionless. The congregation "sat spellbound," then one man began shouting praises, and then the whole congregation burst forth in shouting and praises spontaneously. Testimonies "were like artesian wells," people were convicted, saved, and filled with the Spirit.[16]

- November 1903—Findlay, Ohio—"high spiritual tide . . . the spirit of praise reigned, and the hallelujahs and amens were frequent. . . . Hearts were moved to rapturous praise."[17]

- March 1904—New Castle, Pennsylvania, "wave after wave of Holy Ghost power swept over the room and sobs and Hallelujahs mingled together" with the altars filled.[18]

IMPACT OF THE WELSH REVIVAL

The years of 1904-1906 were days of seeking and preparing for revival in the wake of the 1904 revival in Wales. The Welsh revival broke out on September 29, 1904, under the spontaneous leadership of Evan Roberts. Charismatic manifestations such as prophecy, discernment of spirits, proto-glossolalia (groanings or unutterable sounds), visions, and trembling accompanied the revival. After reports of the revival reached America, it brought on days of seeking and preparing for revival in the C&MA and many other ministries.[19]

The January 1905 C&MA Weekly featured an article on "Gifts of the Spirit," urging readers to wait diligently on the Lord, seeking His face for manifestation and exercise of all nine gifts of the Spirit.[20] In February Simpson expressed his desire for the Alliance: "We simply aim to help God's people back to primitive piety, back to Christ and to Pentecost. We have no fads, no mysteries, no complex system. We do not deal in fanciful interpretations, fanatical notions, nor sensational novelties. We emphasize Scriptural simplicity in life, doctrine and world-wide evangelism."[21]

Ripple Effects in Los Angeles. Los Angeles Baptist Pastor Joseph Smale, who had close connections with the C&MA, visited the Welsh revival early in 1905 and in May returned to Los Angeles, sharing with his congregation about the remarkable events. As he was speaking, a wave of revival broke out. Descriptions of the revival included numerous conversions, dreams, visions, groaning, crying, "inarticulate prayers," "torrents of prayer," "breaking out in laughter," "wave upon wave of Holy Ghost power," and "heavenly lights shining on their faces." Miss Gumbrell, who had served in the Alliance Homes in Nyack and New York City, witnessed the revival and described in *The C&MA Weekly* the outpouring at Smale's church as "this is that" from Joel 2.[22] The revival continued in fall 1905 and into the next year, setting the stage for the Azusa Street revival. But not all of the members of this Baptist congregation were receptive to the revival manifestations, thus in September Smale founded a new church called the "First New Testament Church of Los Angeles."[23]

Ripple Effects in India. Shortly after this American awakening, on June 29, 1905, revival broke out at Mukti (meaning "Salvation") Mission, an independent mission founded by Pandita Ramabai in India, closely associated with the C&MA. Alliance missionary William Franklin, who had been editor of the monthly India Alliance periodical 1904-1905, had been asked to teach at Mukti in 1905, and witnessed the revival firsthand. Among the manifestations that occurred, reported by Franklin and others, were visions, dreams, a spirit of prayer, baptism of fire, shaking and trembling. Some girls "were stricken down under the power of conviction of sin," "some for hours at a time . . . are insensible to their surroundings," weeping, praying with hands outstretched, united vocal prayer erupted "like the roaring of many waters or the rolling of thunder, dancing for joy, discernment of spirits." It was criticized by some, but by most was considered "so evidently the work of the Spirit." Some imitation in the flesh was inevitable, but for most people it was a genuine work with changed lives and a love for God, His Word, prayer, and preaching the Gospel.[24] Spontaneous, unsought tongues also occurred later in the revival in 1906.[25]

One of the secretaries of Ramabai recalled a remarkable incident of divine protection from many cobra bites during this time as a fulfillment of Mark 16: "So wonderfully did the Spirit of the Lord impart faith for the emergency, that instead of groans and cries of anguish, there arose to heaven a great shout of victory and praise. Not a girl died from the deadly bites! Every one was healed."[26]

In the fall of 1905 revival spread to the C&MA's Kaira Orphanage, resulting in the transformation of many girls.[27] In October the movement of the Spirit spread to the missionaries and national workers at the C&MA annual conference in India. There was a strong spirit of prayer described as "torrents of prayer," much weeping, anguish, and confession. Manifestations such as dreams, visions, dancing for joy, holy laughter, shaking violently, discernment of spirits, and "heavenly light shining on their faces" continued through 1905 and later in 1906 in the Alliance and other missions. The revival continued to mushroom through 1908.[28]

Outbreak at Nyack in January 1906. In January 1906 revival broke out at the Missionary Training Institute in Nyack for three weeks. Preachers, teachers and students were lying on their faces before the Lord in deep conviction and confession. It was described as a "holy atmosphere," and was reported that "thunder rolls of intercession" could be heard a mile away, everyone praying loudly in unison with all their might.[29] Alliance scholars George Pardington and William C. Stevens were teaching "that the Church was soon to receive the 'Latter Rain.' Dr. Simpson stressed the need for an enduement of power, which he termed the 'Advent Baptism.'"[30] Unknown to them at the time, it would become a prophetic prelude to Azusa Street Revival three months later and the snowballing effect of revival over the next three years.

Prophetic Insight Regarding Coming Revival. As we have already seen, Alliance people were quite aware of the occurrence of visions, revelations, and prophecies long before the Azusa Street Pentecostal revival. In fact, such manifestations appeared to be accepted as standard fair in the C&MA and other evangelical holiness communities. Yet they also cautioned uncritical acceptance of all such revelations. In the February through April 1906 issues of the *C&MA Weekly* May Mabette Anderson, a frequent contributor, counseled regarding the fallibility of visions, revelations, voices and impressions, and cautioned of mistaken judgment or regarding them too highly. Alliance leaders believed that some prophecies may not be from God or Satan, but a mistaken impulse or impression of the flesh. Anderson presented the typical

C&MA cautions against "an undue exaltation given to personal "impressions" and "assurances" believed to be from God."[31]

Writing seemingly prophetically two months *before* the Azusa Street Pentecostal revival, Anderson continued to maintain strongly and clearly what Simpson had taught for seventeen years about the fallibility of prophecy, impressions, revelations, visions, and "inner voices," and their possibility of being expressed as a mixture:

> Beloved, let us understand and admit . . . that we are exceedingly *fallible* creatures. So very *fallible*, in fact, that, though our Father may be very desirous of imparting to us some truth and though He may breathe into the soul in all His Divine purity, yet when we undertake to give it voice and pour it out in verbal phrase to others, we are more than apt—unless we lie low at His feet in deepest humility—to so tarnish and becloud it by our clumsy touch and exaggerated language, as will place it beyond the Divine recognition.
>
> A revelation may be truly from God. Yet, being such imperfect transmitters and interpreters of the Divine thought as is true of each one of us, one may easily be mistaken in the interpretation given to such revelation. . . . Such persons either misinterpreted God's revelation, or have mistaken the voice of the Adversary for that of the Holy Spirit.[32]

It would seem that God was giving Anderson, Simpson, and the Alliance leaders divine prophetic foresight just as the Azusa revival was about to break forth, anticipating the controversies over supernatural utterances that would occur during the next several years, and preparing people with sound counsel.

Just before the Azusa Street revival was about to break out, in another prophetic insight portending the spread of the tongues-as-initial evidence doctrine, Simpson asserted, "We do not for a moment believe that these special enduements [spiritual gifts] are really essential to the baptism of the Holy Spirit. That we may have without any of the supernatural gifts of power. These are additions to our special enduement for service."[33] Such gifts could be "our full equipment for the ministry" or "an additional experience, or a special ministry," but not an essential part of Spirit baptism. Though some have claimed later dates for the C&MA position on evidential tongues, Simpson had drawn the line in the sand and established the characteristic Alliance stand even before the doctrine would propagated and become popular.

---

1. J. Hudson Taylor, "The Source of Power," CMAW, June 23, 1900, 416. Also cited in Andrew Murray, *Key to the Missionary Problem*, contemporized by Leona Choy (Ft. Washington, PA: Christian Literature Crusade, 1979), 88.

2. CMAW, Jan. 13, 1901, 25.

3. A. B. Simpson, "Apostolic Christianity," CMAW, Jan. 26, 1901, 46.

4. Thomas Erskine, "The Supernatural Gifts of the Spirit" CMAW, Jan. 26, 1901, 48.

5. A. B. Simpson, "The Significance of the Lord's Supper," CMAW, May 18, 1901, 270.

6. G. P. Pardington, "International Sunday School Lesson: The Holy Spirit Given," CMAW, May 18, 1901, 262. For more articles on the supernatural, see A. B. Simpson, "The Practical Use of the Tongue," CMAW, June 8, 1901, 312; F. L. Chapell, "Signs Following," CMAW, June 29, 1901, 357.

7. William C. Stevens, "Divine Healing in Relation to Revivals," CMAW, Feb. 28, 1903, 117, 124.

8. Jessie Penn-Lewis, "Satan Under Your Feet," CMAW, Feb. 10, 1906, 74.

9. G. Cooper, "Was It a Cobra Bite?," CMAW, May 5, 1900, 293; "Missionary Incidents," CMAW, May 5, 1900, 300; Dogmar Rasmussen, "Testimonies of Healing," CMAW, May 19, 1900, 329.

10. "God's Faithfulness to Ramabai," CMAW, Jan. 19, 1901, 41.

11. "Their Nets Were Filled: An Answer to Prayer," CMAW, Mar. 2, 1901, 118.

12. Sarah S. Wagner, "Leaves from the Life of John G. Paton," CMAW, July 6, 1901, 3.

13. "Dr. Torrey's Personal Experience," CMAW, Feb. 10, 1906, 84.

14. Wilbur F. Meminger, "Field Superintendent's Report," CMAW, Dec. 7, 1901, 319.

15. W. McBain, "Richmond, Va.," CMAW, Sept. 20, 1902, 165.

16. Mrs. J. E. Ramsayer, "A Great Revival in Northwest Tennessee," CMAW, Apr. 25, 1903, 230-231.

17. F. W. Davis, "The Findlay Convention," CMAW, Nov. 14, 1903, 333.

18. E. J. Richards, "New Castle," CMAW, Mar. 12, 1904, 220.

19. For more on the Welsh revival, see James A. Stewart, *Invasion of Wales by the Spirit through Evans Roberts* (Asheville, NC: Revival Literature, n. d.).

20. Harriett S. Bainbridge, "Gifts of the Spirit," CMAW, Jan. 7, 1905, 2.

21. A. B. Simpson, Editorial, CMAW, Feb. 11, 1905, 81.

22. "Revival Notes," CMAW, Apr. 7, 1906, 212.

23. Ibid.

24. William Franklin, "Work at Mukti," *The India Alliance*, Feb. 1906, 89, 96; Stanley H. Frodsham, *With Signs Following* (Springfield, MO: Gospel Publishing House, 1941), 105-111.

25. J. Edwin Orr, *The Flaming Tongue* (Chicago, IL: Moody Press, 1973), 182.

26. Charles S. Price, *The Real Faith* (Pasadena, CA: Charles S. Price Publishing Co., 1940, 1968), 90-91.

27. Annie Seasholtz, "God's Reviving Work," *The India Alliance*, Nov. 1906, 32-33.

28. William F. Smalley, comp., *Alliance Missions in India 1892-1972* (no publisher or date), 2:898-899.

29. Herbert H. Cox, "Obedience and Disobedience to the Voice of God Contrasted," *The Latter Rain Evangel* (LRE), Aug. 1919, 8.

30. Carl Brumback, *Suddenly . . . From Heaven* (Springfield MO: Gospel Publishing House, [1961]), 88-89.

31. May Mabette Anderson, "The Prayer of Faith," CMAW, Feb. 17, 1906, 98.

32. May Mabette Anderson, "The Prayer of Faith: Part II," CMAW, Feb. 24, 1906, 106-107.

33. A. B. Simpson, Editorial, *Living Truths*, Apr. 1906, 198.

PART TWO

———◆◆◆———

THE 1906–1909 C&MA REVIVAL:
RESPONSE AND REACTION
TO AZUSA STREET

F O U R

The 1906 Revival

On April 9, 1906 revival broke out in a cottage on Bonnie Brae Street in Los Angeles with outbursts of tongues and other manifestations. Meetings for worship and seeking the Lord continued for two weeks, led by African-American preacher William Joseph Seymour. On April 18 in the midst of the prayer meetings a great earthquake rocked the Pacific Coast. The next day the Bonnie Brae meetings moved to Azusa Street where two more incidents of tongues occurred.[1] The revival continued to spread to the New Testament Church pastored by Joseph Smale and other locations in Los Angeles. This was the beginning of what would mushroom into the Pentecostal movement worldwide.

In May Simpson commented on the California earthquake as a sign of the times—"God is shaking."[2] Since he said nothing said about the Azusa revival, word about the events probably had not yet spread to the east coast. In the May issue of *Living Truths* Simpson wrote about revivals taking place, but again not mentioning Azusa Street in particular. However, he seemed to anticipate prophetically the coming controversy, writing with perception, "In these days of genuine revival and intense reaching after higher things, it is especially necessary to guard against excess even in that which is good. . . . We must be prepared to expect delusions and counterfeits at such a time as this and not discredit the true because of the false." He advised "all seekers after truth to 'try the spirits' and 'discern the things that differ.'"[3] Though he apparently little or knew nothing of the events of Azusa at that time, Simpson's cautions prophetically set the stage for all that would occur the next several years.

PENTECOST COMES TO SMALE'S CHURCH

Smale's New Testament Church, already having experienced supernatural revival phenomena in 1905, was open to the full orb of charismatic gifts, including speaking in tongues. The first Pentecostal experience came to the New Testament Church on April 15, days after the initial Bonnie Brae outbreak, when a black woman spoke in tongues in the Sunday morning service.[4] The manifestation was evidently accepted by Smale and the church as genuinely from God. Later in June, full Pentecostal revival broke out in the church. Frank Bartleman, who had received tongues at Azusa on June 15, was present and described the events:

— 55 —

The New Testament Church received her "Pentecost" yesterday. We had a wonderful time. Men and women were prostrate under the power all over the hall. A heavenly atmosphere pervaded the place. Such singing I have never heard before, the very melody of Heaven. It seemed to come direct from the throne. . . .

A young lady of refinement was prostrate on the floor for hours, while at times the most heavenly singing would issue from her lips. It would swell a way up to the throne, and then die away in an almost unearthly melody. She sang, "Praise God! Praise God!" All over the house men and women were weeping.[5]

Smale and his church continued to be open to the new Pentecostal revival. In September, however, a split took place at the New Testament Church with about a dozen people leaving. They apparently were insisting on tongues as the evidence of the baptism in the Spirit, while Smale insisted that it was not necessarily the evidence.[6] Smale also objected to some of the extreme manifestations such as animal sounds and the disunity that resulted from the "strife of tongues."[7] From Bartleman's perspective, "Both 'Azusa' and the New Testament Church had by this time largely failed God."[8] He believed, "Brother Smale was God's Moses, to lead the people as far as the Jordan, though he himself never got across."[9]

From Smale's viewpoint, however, "The blessing was deified, and not a few who previously were among the most excellent of Christians fell into the snare of the devil."[10] Even so, by October Smale reported, "The New Testament Church is on its face before the Lord in daily protracted intercession, and the former cloud of glory is blessedly and wondrously returning upon its people. Conversions and the reclaiming of backsliders are becoming again the joyous scenes in our midst."[11] Some people who had received the gift of tongues continued to remain in the church, and were described by Smale as "living beautiful Christlike lives."[12] He believed that though the movement started in the Spirit, the divisions and dissension proved that the movement was not truly remaining in the Spirit, but reverting to the flesh, being immature and imbalanced:

As it was in Corinth, so it is in Los Angeles. The excellencies of the Spirit of God have been replaced by a careless attitude to the Word of God as a whole; errors of doctrine; eccentricities; touchiness; fault-finding; presumptuous criticisms; a disposition to riot in the house of God, and other manifestations of the flesh life. The effect, in the main, of the tongues in our city, instead of precipitating Pentecost as we had hoped, has been to remove what hopeful signs of Pentecost were known during the fall of 1905 and the early spring of 1906. It broke the unity of the Lord's intercessors. . . .

It has been made very evident during this year of 1906 that not even the Lord's people can be trusted with gifts to use themselves, and we are crying that the Lord will withhold the gifts of the Spirit until His people become so filled with God that there will be no danger of the flesh rising to glory in His blessings."[13]

Significantly, Charles Parham, Seymour's mentor, had even a harsher assessment of the fledging movement, though it appeared to be tinged with racial prejudice as well.[14] Smale's experiences with these early Pentecostals and his subsequent viewpoint were published in the Alliance periodical *Living Truths*, and thus became quite influential and foundational for Simpson and the C&MA stance.

SIMPSON'S INITIAL RESPONSES TO THE AZUSA REVIVAL

In July 1906 Alliance theologian George Pardington's book *The Crisis of the Deeper Life* was published as an exposition of the doctrine of the baptism or filling of the Spirit from the C&MA point of view—a sanctifying experience subsequent to conversion, called a crisis of sanctification.[15] According to Richard Bailey, it was the C&MA's response to the developing Pentecostal movement.[16] However, since it took months to prepare a book for publication and the Alliance at this time did not seem to be aware of much of the Azusa Street happenings, the chronological timing indicates that this could not be so. The book itself does not address the issues of the new Pentecostal movement, so was evidently written before Azusa Street or at least without awareness of or reference to the revival.

The initial C&MA responses began with sporadic references and articles in the Alliance journals, with the book *Signs of the Times* in summer 1907 being the initial book publication to respond to the new Pentecostal revival. Bailey also asserted, "Dr. Simpson responded to the Azusa Street manifestations by preaching and writing about the cross (*The Cross of Christ*)."[17] In actuality, *The Cross of Christ* was a collection of Simpson's sermons from 1903-1909, published in 1910. The cross was a consistent theme of Simpson both before and after Azusa Street. So while some of Simpson's messages on the cross from later 1906 through 1909 could be considered an indirect response to Azusa Street (because to Simpson the cross overshadowed everything), its publication in 1910 would be a *later* response, and nothing in the book addresses the issues of Azusa Street directly, although some of his later messages may address the Pentecostal movement implicitly. Both *The Crisis of the Deeper Life* and *The Cross of Christ* indicate the ongoing emphasis of the C&MA. Simpson sums up the overarching Alliance view that was applied to the Azusa Street manifestations: "Our religious experiences must have the mark of the cross on them."[18]

Simpson's first clear response to the Azusa revival appeared in September 1906, and was both positive and cautious. He had probably received reports from his friends and colleagues on the West Coast—George and Carrie Judd Montgomery, Joseph Smale, and J. Hudson Ballard. Calling the movement "a remarkable manifestation of spiritual power," Simpson cautioned against two opposite extremes:

First, there is the danger of credulity and fanaticism. God will not be displeased with us if we are conservative and careful in investigating all such alleged facts and guarding against fanaticism, human exaggeration, or spiritual counterfeits. . . . But on the other hand, let us also guard against the extreme of refusing to recognize any added blessing which the Holy Spirit is bringing to His people in these last days.[19]

This statement of Simpson set the stage for the C&MA response to the Pentecostal movement during the next several years. The first thing we notice is that Simpson recognized the polarities of the issue and tried to maintain a dynamic tension between the two poles. He would maintain this dynamic tension throughout the next decade, sometimes in one issue of the *C&MA Weekly* cautioning against fanaticism, and in the next issue encouraging open expectancy toward supernatural manifestations.

What was occurring on the other side of the continent seemed to inspire Simpson's heart as in September he preached on revival and stirring up the gift within.[20] Further, Simpson affirmed that gifts and tongues are all for today and that God has gifts for each of us, but he also counseled not to seek after "the strange and wonderful gifts of the Spirit." Rather, we should let the Holy Spirit choose His fitting gifts for us. At the same time, he also counseled "readiness of mind to receive what God is ever truly sending." [21]

By November, still relatively early in the revival, although tongues had apparently not yet reached the C&MA in New York, Simpson warned against exaggeration of tongues and insistence of tongues as the indispensable sign of the baptism of the Spirit.[22] Contrary to some who claim that the Alliance waited until some time later to oppose the initial evidence doctrine, Simpson spoke out early on against the emerging doctrine.

Pentecostal Revival in the India C&MA Breaks Out

Reports in the *India Alliance* from William Franklin in February 1906 regarding the revival in Mukti whet the spiritual appetites of the Alliance missions in India, stirring anticipation of the Spirit's moving in the missions.[23] The prayers and expectations of the missionaries and Indian believers were soon answered dramatically.

Revival at the Alliance Boys Orphanage in Dholka broke out August 26 and spread throughout the C&MA missions in India. It was characterized by "awful cries of repentance, . . . a strong spirit of conviction," groaning and sighing, changed to praise after several hours, and meetings continued every night went on for hours. A vision of Satan and Jesus Christ, as well as healings, gifts of tongues, more visions and dreams, discernment of spirits, and prophecy were all reported in the Indian revival.[24] These appear to be the earliest occurrences of tongues in the C&MA, and they do not seem to have been directly influenced by Azusa Street.

Missionary Maude Wiest, editor of *The India Alliance*, declared that this was the beginning of the "latter rain." Wiest also cautioned about dangers of attaching too much importance to visions, revelations, and ecstasies, exalting them above the Word of God, and warned of spiritual pride and deception by Satan as an angel of light. She counseled a Gamaliel stand, neither opposing the movement nor promoting it excessively.[25]

On September 19, another wave of revival swept over the Alliance orphanage in Khamgaon. The awakening began with a period of silence and hands lifted prayerfully seeking the Lord for blessing, followed by overwhelming conviction, people swooning, confessing, shouting, praising, and groaning in agony of spirit. The noise was heard a block away. It was reported that there was no confusion, but a "wave of divine harmony." One girl, known for being quiet and reserved, stood for two and a half hours with her hands raised unconscious of her surroundings.[26]

Another outbreak burst forth in the Dholka boys orphanage on September 30. The whole mission felt an intensity of concerted prayer. One boy shrieked in agony over conviction of sin, and "two more were so overpowered as to become unconscious of their surrounding and rolled over on the floor in agony." Revival continued into November. There were several cases of healing and "some almost dance for joy."[27]

During September and October revival continued to be poured out upon other areas of the C&MA in India. Among the orphan girls at Kaira, many girls were praying aloud all at one time, singing, laughing, and crying. Alliance periodicals reported that the Kaira girls' orphanage was experiencing an even greater revival than the year before at Ramabai's Mukti Mission. One report dramatically recounted, "The room seemed charged with the Spirit's power. Some shrieked and writhed in anguish, numbers fell unconscious, some had to be held. . . . struggle between powers of light and darkness." Meetings went on almost day and night for three weeks, punctuated by weeping and wailing, and breaking forth into singing "like the melody of heaven."

On October 2, a bright light appeared and girls saw "visions of Christ laboring under the weight of His cross; of His agony in Gethsemene and on Calvary's hill." All day long students had visions and scores fell unconscious under the power of the Spirit. A "roaring of spontaneous prayer" was heard throughout the mission, often with uplifted hands or people falling prostrate, agonizing in prayer, especially in the Khassia Hills. Singing like angelic choirs, visions, dreams and revelations from God, and healings all characterized the revival. Missionaries Sarah Coxe, Christian Schoonmaker, Violet Dunham (who later married Schoonmaker), and Eunice Wells were among those who received the baptism in the Spirit with tongues during this time, and eventually almost all of the missionaries.[28] Dunham commented of these happenings, "Some may call this hallucination, mania, hysteria; but we who saw it knew it was God because of its purifying effect on these lives."[29]

REVIVAL BREAKS OUT AT NYACK AND NEW YORK CITY C&MA

On the other side of the world revival rained upon the Alliance at its home bases in New York City and Nyack. From October 5th through 15th, the renowned Welsh revivalist Seth Joshua visited Nyack and preached at the

C&MA convention held in Simpson's Gospel Tabernacle in New York City. He stirred a longing among the people for revival like that in Wales and created great expectation of the Spirit's moving.[30]

In the midst of this anticipation, Thomas B. Barratt, a Cornish minister from Norway, was staying at the Alliance Guest Home in New York City. After being stirred by hearing Seth Joshua speak on Saturday evening, October 6, the next day he participated in a communion service led by Dr. Henry Wilson. Following the service, he was seeking the Lord in prayer and received the baptism in the Spirit at the Alliance guest house, with shouting and physical manifestations of sensations to his body of warmth, shaking, and swooning. He called for Evangelist James Lyall, another speaker at the convention, who found Barratt lying stretched out over a chair on the floor. At first Lyall was concerned that it was the devil, but became assured that it was the Holy Spirit. Lyall helped him up to a bed as the manifestations continued. He left and returned with Simpson's associate F. E. Marsh, finding Barratt sitting in a chair filled with the peace of God. They rejoiced together, as Barratt called this experience his Pentecost.[31]

After corresponding with people from the Azusa Street revival about his experience, they encouraged him to seek the Lord about tongues. Five weeks later, on November 15, he spoke in tongues and sang in the Spirit, calling it "the seal of my Pentecost." Simpson fully accepted his experience as genuinely from God and published his testimony in the December issue of his periodical *Living Truths*.[32] Barratt soon returned to Europe, sharing his testimony and spreading the Pentecostal movement throughout England, Norway, Sweden and Denmark. The C&MA thus actually became the launching pad for the European Pentecostal movement.[33]

Nearby at Nyack during the same period of time, revival was breaking out, continuing for more than three weeks. Beginning October 28, after a letter was read about the outpouring of the Spirit at Azusa Street, students broke down in "heart sobs, Holy Ghost groans, prostrations. . . . The Spirit alone was leader in the meetings." Occasionally there were "indiscreet remarks," but it was reported that they weathered the storm and the meetings were righted by the Spirit's influence. Spiritual conflict, conviction of sin, confession, cleansing, repentance and restoration all marked the spontaneous meetings. The hymn, "The cleansing stream I see, I see, I plunge, and oh, it cleaseth me!", "was sung over and over for hours."

There were no recorded occurrences of tongues at this time, but there were manifestations of "proto-*glossolalia*," or "groanings which cannot be uttered." Leaders testified of a "marvelous and unprecedented visitation of the Holy Spirit in our midst."[34] The meetings went on for three weeks, but the hunger for the moving of the Spirit continued through the rest of the school year.

While speaking about what the Holy Spirit was doing at Nyack, Simpson's associate F. E. Marsh had a vision "of the need of the Lord's people, as I saw them in their dissatisfied lives, their unrest, worldliness, unbelief, sin and unkind feelings toward each other." He began sobbing, falling over the pulpit Bible. The whole congregation responded with "heart cries." One woman who was under conviction, but was resisting, finally came forward to the altar and fell unconscious for about ten minutes.[35]

Missionary G. W. Batman, who had received the baptism in the Spirit with tongues at Azusa, was passing through New York City on his way to Liberia. Alliance leader Stephen Merritt asked him to speak at the Gospel Tabernacle on a Sunday afternoon late in November. He shared his experience and eyewitness account of the revival in Los Angeles. It further stirred Alliance people to seek more of the Spirit.[36]

PENTECOST FOR A C&MA PASTOR IN OHIO

While the Spirit was being poured out in Nyack, New York City, and India, a spontaneous outpouring took place in the life of Alliance pastor David Wesley Myland. Myland was a member of the famed Ohio Quartette (along with D. W. Kerr, E. L. Bowyer, and James Kirk) and pastor of the United Gospel Tabernacle, the Alliance work in Columbus. He had also served as Secretary and Superintendent of the C&MA work in Ohio. He had been fascinated by the revival in Los Angeles and was corresponding with some of the leaders from Azusa Street.

In October Myland and his friend George D. Watson were preparing for the beginning of the C&MA Convention in Columbus. Myland was lighting a gas furnace that suddenly exploded, burning him severely. Later he also contracted blood poisoning and nearly died. On November 3, at a point when he felt he could not live, he received his Pentecostal baptism, speaking in tongues, which he described as the "residue" or "full measure" of the "beginning of his Pentecost" seventeen years earlier. He saw a vision of Jesus and a heavenly choir and orchestra, and then sang in tongues. Immediately, as interpretation of the tongues, he began to write a song on the "Latter Rain" with his burned and swollen hand, and as he wrote, he was healed. He testified of his amazing experience:

> Presently as they seemed to come to a pause in the singing, at the end of a strain. He turned around so gracefully to me, and looked at me and said, "Well, My child, what would you like to have?" And I said, "Oh, Lord, I would like to join Your choir," and then I seemed to tremble at what I had said, "join that choir!" He turned and looked toward the choir, and then at me and said, "My child, you may," and then all the strength left me, and I said, "Well, I can't now, I wouldn't dare." But He made a motion to me with His baton, and it seemed I was lifted right up and was set down in the choir. I began to sing with them a little and what do you suppose? I was singing the "latter rain" song in "tongues," which I afterwards interpreted, and wrote into English. They all seemed to join in with me and after it was all over they sang another great chorus. I listened, and the great Leader, my glorified Christ, motioned to me and I sat down, and I thought, Oh, what singing! The old Ohio Quartette never could sing like that

and I found myself singing also. The glory died away and I came to myself singing in "tongues." It passed away and immediately I began to reach for my Bible. I took out a piece of blank paper and began to write with my left hand, tried to write with my pencil between the first and second finger. I could not get along very fast and involuntarily took it over into my right hand, the hand that had been so badly swollen, and I found I was healed; the sores were there but I was healed. There wasn't a particle of pain or stiffness, and I wrote the words of the Latter Rain Song, word for word, as fast as I could write; never changed a word, wrote the melody, tried it on the piano, and found it a beautiful melody. . . .

Oh, what glory I was in for an hour. I took out my watch and saw that for just an hour I was lost to this world. Oh, what a vision of Jesus and of heaven! Indescribable! I have just sketched the outline. Oh, what glory there was in my soul.[v]

This is the song that he wrote as an interpretation of singing in tongues, called "The Latter Rain Song" and also "Pentecost Has Come":

There's a Pentecost for all the sanctified.
Heaven's Witness true, which cannot be denied,
And the Spirit's gifts are being multiplied
In God's holy church today.

CHORUS:
Oh, I'm glad the promised Pentecost has come,
And the "Latter Rain" is falling now on some;
Pour it out in floods, Lord, on the parched ground,
Till It reaches all the earth around.

There's a Pentecost for every trusting soul,
Of your life the Spirit now will take control.
Filling, sealing, quickening, healing, making whole,
By God's holy pow'r today.
There's a Pentecost for every yielded heart,
And the "holy fire" God's Spirit will impart;
To obey His will you gladly then will star
In God's holy work today.

There's a Pentecost for those who wait and pray
With surrendered will, O seek it then today;
Christ will baptize all His saints who will obey
With the Spirit's tongues of fire.[x]

PENTECOST FOR FUTURE ALLIANCE LEADERS AT ZION CITY, ILLINOIS

In the fall of 1906 Charles Parham visited Alexander Dowie's church at Zion City, Illinois, testifying of the Pentecostal revival. Many received the baptism in the Spirit with tongues at that time, including F. F. Bosworth and E. N. Richey, who would later serve in the C&MA. More than a decade later, Bosworth testified of his experience:

> Let it not be supposed that I am depreciating God's glorious gift of tongues, because I do not believe that this one manifestation always accompanies the baptism in the Spirit. God graciously gave me this gift eleven years ago and nearly every day in prayer and worship I still speak in tongues, and it is one of the sweetest things in my Christian experience. . . . To me the greatest phase of the baptism in the Spirit is the spontaneous life of intercession.[39]

Bosworth visited Azusa Street and became acquainted with William Seymour. After itinerant ministry for a period of time, Bosworth founded a church in Dallas in 1910 loosely affiliated with the Alliance. He then became a charter member of the Assemblies of God when it was founded in 1914. But he later left in 1918 due to the evidential tongues doctrine, and rejoined the C&MA. Richey likewise joined the Assemblies of God, but then served in the Alliance for a decade in the 1920s and 30s.

BOARD OF MANAGERS MEMBER RECEIVES TONGUES

Minnie Draper, a member of the C&MA Board of Managers and close friend of Simpson, had heard about the events at Azusa Street and other places and was cautious, but also desired more of God in her life. One night in her room late in 1906 while she was seeking God she saw a vision of the Lord and "hours elapsed wherein she saw unutterable things, and when she finally came to herself, she heard her tongue talking fluently in a language she had never learned."[40] Draper continued to serve in the Alliance, speaking and ministering frequently in Alliance meetings on the themes of the Holy Spirit and of divine healing until 1913 when she began independent Pentecostal ministry.

PENTECOST IN THE AKRON C&MA IN OHIO

Ivey Campbell, who received the baptism in the Spirit with tongues at Azusa Street, returned to her home state of Ohio, and began a series of meetings on December 5 at the Union Gospel Mission in Akron, pastored by C&MA leader Claude A. McKinney, a former missionary to Africa. It is not clear if it was her home church, but there she gave her testimony, and, as a result, McKinney's mother and another woman first received the baptism in the Spirit with tongues, and then McKinney himself and several others in the congregation. Some men visiting from Hawaii remarked that "Grandmother McKinney spoke in their native tongue."[41]

Thomas K. Leonard from Findlay, Ohio, attended meetings led by McKinney and was baptized in the Spirit with tongues.[42] He founded a Pentecostal church that later affiliated with the Assemblies of God and a Bible school, both of which no doubt had impact upon the well-established Alliance work in Findlay, which soon became charismatically-oriented.[43] Levi Lupton, a Quaker minister who also attended the meetings in Akron, began an independent Pentecostal work in nearby town of Alliance in conjunction with McKinney and Campbell, which included an annual camp meeting that became the headquarters for the Pentecostal movement in the East.[44]

SIMPSON'S RESPONSE TO THE REVIVALS OF 1906— OPENNESS AND CAUTION

In December Simpson wrote, "Some very wonderful manifestations are being reported in various places. It behooves us to watch these developments at once in a spirit of candor and as spirit of caution." Simpson also cautioned to "try the spirits" and expressed concern about misuse, misunderstandings, excessive emphasis or pride regarding the gift of tongues, and the dangers of seeing false visions or dreams from excessive prayer, fasting, and asceticism.[45] He published the testimony of Thomas Barratt receiving tongues, saying, "All who know him bear witness to his uprightness and sincerity."[46] Through the next several years a few such testimonies were sprinkled in Alliance writings. Simpson began the new year on a positive note, writing in the first 1907 issue of the *C&MA Weekly*, "The manifestations of the Holy Spirit's working during the past months have been truly Pentecostal, and those who watch and pray for His appearing are stirred as never before with the signs that the Lord is near."[47]

SMALE'S ASSESSMENT—THE GENUINE AND THE FALSE

As mentioned above, Pastor Joseph Smale of the New Testament Church in Los Angeles witnessed the Azusa Street revival first hand as tongues and other manifestations occurred in his own church. Being a friend of the C&MA, his observations and views significantly helped to shape the Alliance position and responses to the burgeoning Pentecostal revival. His article "The Gift of Tongues" appeared in the January 1907 *Living Truths*, published by Simpson. In the article, Smale affirmed the reality of gift of tongues, but refuted Pentecostal teaching that all should speak in tongues and that tongues is the Bible evidence for the baptism in the Spirit.

Writing against the need for seeking after tongues, Smale reported that some people who did not want to speak in tongues, and even opposed tongues, have themselves received the gift. He also noted that it is possible to have tongues and not to have genuinely been baptized in the Spirit. Ironically, that is virtually the same position that Azusa Street leader William Seymour himself would later declare: "If you get angry, or speak evil, or backbite, I care not how many tongues you may have, you have not the baptism with the Holy Spirit."[48]

Smale affirmed that "there are in our city [Los Angeles] and church those gifted with the tongues living beautiful Christlike lives," but at the same time many others who speak in tongues have lost their sweetness, love, meekness, and reverence. He also observed some spiritualist-like manifestations and imitations of animal sounds like a dog, coyote, cat and birds, discerning that some such phenomena came from the flesh, others from the devil. He warned that in many cases, "the blessing was deified."[49]

Both Smale and Carrie Judd Montgomery addressed the C&MA convention at Trinity Methodist Church in Los Angeles January 8-11, 1907, regarding experiences of the revival, again advising both openness and caution.[50] The pastor at Trinity Methodist Church had likewise been both receptive and cautious to the revival, commenting, "Here on the Pacific Coast, where the sons of men meet from every quarter of the globe, prophetic souls believe the greatest moral and spiritual battles are to be fought—the Armageddon of the world."[51]

BALLARD'S PRONOUNCEMENT—EVERY CHURCH SHOULD HAVE TONGUES

In the same issue of *Living Truths* appeared an extensive article by J. Hudson Ballard's on "Spiritual Gifts with Special Reference to the Gift of Tongues." As superintendent of the Alliance work in Los Angeles, he had first hand contact with the movement. He concluded, "(a) The church of Christ today may receive the Gift of Tongues. (b) Every local church of Christ should have, in some of its members, the manifestation of this gift. (c) Every Christian should be willing to receive this gift if it please the Spirit to bestow it upon him. (d) It is a dangerous thing to oppose or despise this, one of the immediate manifestations of the Blessed Spirit of God."[52]

He also noted that tongues is one of the least of the gifts, that it is not a necessary evidence of the baptism of the Spirit, that it is not for all Christians, that it needs to be carefully controlled, and that its primary use is devotionally alone with God. His counsel became a key policy statement of the C&MA and would be reprinted again several times in book, periodical, and booklet formats. Especially significant are his statements that *every* local church should have some who speak in tongues, and that *every* believer should be willing to receive the gift if the Spirit desires it. He also warned against forbidding tongues. This counsel became adopted as the Alliance position.

MACARTHUR'S APPRAISAL—MIXTURE OF BLESSING AND DISAPPOINTMENT

In January 1907 William T. MacArthur began a series of articles in the *C&MA Weekly* entitled "The Promise of the Father and Speaking with Tongues in Chicago." In this first installment he wrote that tongues "has brought much real blessing to many, and possibly only fancied blessing to others, which will yet eventuate in sorrow and discouragement. Like so many widespread movements, it is a mixture of good and evil, for Satan has not been asleep." He spoke supportively of four genuine blessings of the Pentecostal movement: "There is a hunger and thirst after God, a joy in His service, a yearning for the lost, and a delight in Bible study."[53]

---

1. Bartleman, *Azusa Street* (1980), 43, 46-47.

2. A. B. Simpson, Editorial, CMAW, May 5, 1906, 255, 269; see also Simpson, Editorial, *Living Truths*, May 1906, 261.

3. Simpson, Editorial, *Living Truths*, May 1906, 257-258. Likewise, Alliance scholar George Pardington wrote an article identifying tests for detecting demons. George P. Pardington, "A Fierce Demoniac Healed," CMAW, May 5, 1906, 255.

4. Bartleman, *Azusa Street* (1980), 43.

5. Ibid., 61.

6. Ibid., 84; Joseph Smale, "The Gift of Tongues," *Living Truths*, Jan. 1907, 35-40.

7. Smale, "The Gift of Tongues," 39. Parham also opposed animal sounds and actions when he visited Azusa Street, considering them to be demonic in nature.

8. Bartleman, *Azusa Street* (1980), 85.

9. Ibid., 62.

10. Smale, "The Gift of Tongues," 40.

11. Ibid.

12. Ibid., 38.

13. Ibid., 38, 40.

14. Parham wrote:

> Hear this: three-fourths of the so-called Pentecosts in the world are counterfeits, the devil's imitation to deceive the poor earnest souls. . . . Many hundreds, in seeking Pentecost, were taught to yield to any force, as God would not permit them to be misled; under those conditions they were ripe for hypnotic influence. . . . Two-thirds of the people professing Pentecost are either hypnotized or spook-driven, being seized in the first place with a false spirit or coming under the control of one afterward. We cannot be too careful to try or test the spirits and any person unwilling to have their experience tested by going to God for themselves or with the brethren, reveal the fact that they are demon-controlled. . . . They plead the blood, and claim to be Jesus, giving messages, and imitate every gift of the Holy Spirit and Pentecostal tongues. Charles Parham, *The Everlasting Gospel* (Baxter Springs, KS: n. p., 1911), 55, 72, 120-121; see also pp. 71-73, 118-119. Parham believed that the only genuine tongues were *xenolalia*, tongues expressed as a genuine language. He also believed that manifestations where blacks and whites were mixing together were not of God.

15. CMAW, July 21, 1906, 33. See George P. Pardington, *The Crisis of the Deeper Life* (Camp Hill, PA: Christian Publications, 1991). Pardington presented this as a paper at the Alliance conference at Nyack in May 1906. A. B. Simpson, Editorial, CMAW, June 2, 1906, 329.

16. Editor's Note, Hartzfeld and Nienkirchen, *The Birth of a Vision*, 164.

17. Ibid. See A. B. Simpson, *The Cross of Christ* (Camp Hill, PA: Christian Publications, 1994).

18. Simpson, *The Cross of Christ*, 34.

19. A. B. Simpson, Editorial, CMAW, Sept. 22, 1906, 177.

20. A. B. Simpson, "Revival," CMAW, Oct. 6, 1906, 229.

21. A. B. Simpson, "All the Blessings of the Spirit," CMAW, Sept. 29, 1906, 198.

22. A. B. Simpson, Editorial, CMAW, Nov. 17, 1906, 305.

23. Franklin, "Work at Mukti," *The India Alliance*, Feb. 1906, 89, 96.

24. "God's Grace in Dholka," *The India Alliance*, Oct. 1906, 38-39; Margaret Ballentyne, "Dholka Revival," *The India Alliance*, Jan. 1907, 76-77.

25. "Editorials," *The India Alliance*, Sept. 1906, 30-31. Wiest soon married missionary Walter Turnbull, and died a few years later. Turnbull later became a Vice President of the C&MA.

26. "Awakening in Khamgaon, India," CMAW, Dec. 8, 1906, 361.

27. Ballentyne, "Dholka Revival," *The India Alliance*, Jan. 1907, 76-77.

28. I. Woodward Bach, "Revival Signs in India, CMAW, Oct. 6, 1906, 216-217; Annie Seasholtz, "God's Reviving Work," *The India Alliance*, Nov. 1906, 32-33; Violetta Dunham, "God at Work in India," CMAW, Jan. 19, 1907, 30; CMAW, Dec. 8, 1906; Frank J. Ewart, *The Phenomenon of Pentecost* (St. Louis, MO: Pentecostal Publishing House, 1947), 68-69; Montgomery, *Under His Wings*, 182. For more accounts of the Indian revivals, see Violet Schoonmaker, *Light in India's Night* (Springfield, MO: Gospel Publishing House, 1957), 23-24, 37-40, 187-192.

29. Schoonmaker, *Light in India's Night*, 191.

30. A. B. Simpson, Editorial, CMAW, Oct. 13, 1906, 225; "Report of the New York Convention, Oct. 13, 1906, 236-237. (see here a summary of Seth Joshua's message).

31. Thomas B. Barratt, "How I Obtained My Pentecost," CMAW, Nov. 3, 1906, 275-276; Thomas B. Barratt, "When the Fire Fell and an Outline of My Life," *The Work of T. B. Barratt* (New York & London: Garland Publishing, 1985), 113-114.

32. Thomas B. Barratt, "The Seal of My Pentecost," *Living Truths*, Dec. 1906, 735-738.

33. Orr, *The Flaming Tongue*, 179-182.

34. F. E. Marsh, "Revival in the Missionary Institute at South Nyack on Hudson," CMAW, Nov. 17, 1906, 316, 318; F. E. Marsh, "The Emphasis of the Holy Spirit in the Revival at Nyack and New York," CMAW, Dec. 1,1906, 338-339; Fred R. Bullen, "Among the Nyack Students," CMAW, Dec. 8, 1906, 363; Mary E. Lewer, "50 Years of Pentecostal Blessing," *Pentecostal Evangel*, Jan. 26, 1958, 7.

35. F. E. Marsh, "The Overturning Work of the Spirit," CMAW, Nov. 24, 1906, 323-324.

36. *The Apostolic Faith*, Dec. 1906, 3.

37. D. Wesley Myland, *The Latter Rain Covenant* (Springfield, MO: Temple Press, [1910]), 174-177. Nienkirchen (p. 121, note 92) states that this took place during the Alliance convention in Columbus, Ohio, but it actually occurred about two weeks later, twenty-one days after he was burned on the first day of the convention.

38. Myland, *The Latter Rain Covenant*, 178.

39. F. F. Bosworth, *Do All Speak in Tongues?* (New York, NY: Christian Alliance Publishing Co., n. d.), 18-19.

40. C. J. Lucas, "In Memorium," *Full Gospel Missionary Herald*, Apr. 1921, 3; cited in G. B. McGee, "Draper, Minnie Tingley," *The New International Dictionary of Pentecostal and Charismatic Movements* (NIDPCM) Stanley M. Burgess, ed. (Grand Rapids, MI: Zondervan, 2002), 588; Gary B. McGee, "Three Notable Women in Pentecostal Ministry," *Assemblies of God Heritage*, Spring 1985-86, 4.

41. R. M. Riss, "Women, Role of," *Dictionary of Pentecostal and Charismatic Movements* (DPCM), ed. Stanley M. Burgess and Gary B. McGee (Grand Rapids, MI: Zondervan Publishing House, 1988), 895; Frodsham, *With Signs Following*, 45. See also Gary B. McGee, "Levi Lupton: A Forgotten Pioneer of Early Pentecostalism, "*Faces of Renewal*, Paul Ebert, ed. (Peabody, MA: Hendrickson, 1988), 197; Gordon F. Atter, *The Third Force* (Peterborough, Ontario: The College Press, 1962), 31; "How Pentecost Reached Ohio in Dec. 1906, "*Assemblies of God Heritage*, Spring 1988, 4.

42. Roger L. Culbertson, "A Glimpse of the Old Central District and the Emerging Ohio District," *Assemblies of God Heritage*, Spring 1988, 4.

43. Faupel mistakenly wrote that Leonard pastored the Alliance Church in Findlay and that he led as many as 26 pastors out of the C&MA in 1912. Faupel, *The Everlasting Gospel*, 236. Faupel later checked his notes and told me that it was probably Myland or Kerr who led the pastors out of the Alliance in 1912.

44. McGee, "Levi Lupton," 197-200.

45. A. B. Simpson, Editorial, *Living Truths*, Dec. 1906, 706-710. Likewise, Simpson preached on the characteristics of true and false fire—true and false tongues and other manifestations. A. B. Simpson, "True and False Fire," CMAW, Dec. 22, 1906, 391.

46. Simpson, Editorial, *Living Truths*, Dec. 1906, 706-710.

47. A. B. Simpson, Editorial, CMAW, Jan. 5, 1907, 1. We note that here and for several years the word "Pentecostal" is used positively by Alliance leaders to indicate genuine supernatural revival from the Lord like the day of Pentecost and following. Later on, Alliance leaders would avoid the term in order not to be identified with more radical elements and the evidential tongues doctrine.

48. Cited in Douglas Jacobsen, *Thinking in the Spirit: Theologies of the Early Pentecostal Movement* (Bloomington, IN: Indiana University Press, 2003), 76.

49. Smale, "The Gift of Tongues," 32-43.

50. C. M. Robeck, Jr., "Smale, Joseph," DPCM, 791.

51. Frank Bartleman, *Azusa Street* (New Kensington, PA: Whitaker House, 1982), 64.

52. J. Hudson Ballard, "Spiritual Gifts with Special Reference to the Gift of Tongues," *Living Truths*, Jan. 1907,23-31; reported by Simpson in Editorial, CMAW, Jan. 26, 1907, 1.

53. William T. MacArthur, "The Promise of the Father and Speaking with Tongues in Chicago," CMAW, Jan 26, 1907, 40.

FIVE

The Revival Surges On into 1906

The year of 1907 exploded with Pentecostal-like revivals throughout the C&MA, beginning with several churches in Ohio, Pennsylvania and Indiana. They were received positively along with cautions for discernment. The Alliance was receptive to tongues and other charismatic phenomena, but also struggled with conflict over excesses and evidential tongues teaching.

In the early part of 1907 other Alliance meetings and leaders encouraged openness to the gifts of the Spirit with moderation and discernment. At the Boston Convention January 29-31, Minnie Draper, Board of Managers member who is believed to have received tongues late in 1906, spoke on the need of a baptism of love, "as far greater than the gift of tongues." Rev. Morton Plummer, an Alliance worker who later became a Pentecostal leader, gave a discourse on Mark 16 regarding tongues, casting out demons, and binding Satan. He commented that tongues is "a foretaste of the time when our 'unruly members' shall be wholly controlled by the Holy Spirit."[1]

Pentecost Continues in Ohio

In January 1907, Warren A. Cramer, pastor of the Alliance church in Cleveland, visited the meetings led by fellow Alliance pastor McKinney in Akron. Cramer returned to Cleveland, sharing with his congregation what he observed. They began to seek the Lord in prayer and about ten days later while praying, he fell under the power of the Spirit and began to speak in tongues. A woman who came to request prayer for healing also fell under the power of the Spirit, received a revelation from the Lord, and was healed. Cramer recounted that another young woman "began singing in English a hymn she had never heard before, the music of which she had never learned." More workers from Akron visited, and "one after another of our people began to receive the baptism."

Then Cramer invited Ivey Campbell to speak at his church beginning February 13. Meetings continued for four weeks to mid-March and perhaps more than fifty received the baptism in the Spirit accompanied by speaking in tongues. Reporting in the C&MA Weekly, Cramer called it "Pentecost at Cleveland." It was viewed by Alliance leaders as a positive and genuine move of God.[2] Cramer's lay associate L. S. Grant spoke in tongues during this time, identified by two people as "good Latin" though he had no knowledge of the language.[3]

Also in January two ministers who had received the experience of tongues came to the Quaker church and Training School in Cleveland, sharing their experiences. As a result, several spoke in tongues, including Bertha Pinkham Dixon, a teacher in the Training School whose husband pastored another Quaker church. She testified, "Out from my innermost being rolled a volume of language unknown to me, while my soul was filled with 'joy unspeakable and full of glory,' which found vent in this new operation of the Spirit. I was literally drunk with 'new wine.' This 'weight of glory' remained for days, while the consciousness of the divine presence within was greater than I had ever dreamed possible in this life."[4]

On May 12 her husband, W. T. Dixon, had a similar experience: "Tuesday morning before he finished dressing, for about two hours he spoke in a tongue that sounded like Chinese. Tears rolled down his cheeks while a vision of the Chinese came before him."[5] After fifteen years of Pentecostal ministry, eventually the couple, believing that tongues was not necessarily the evidence of the baptism in the Spirit and seeing excesses in the Pentecostal movement, found a compatible home with the C&MA and became involved in church planting in California.

Beginning about mid-May through early June 1907, Frank Bartleman, who personally witnessed and participated in the Azusa Street revival, spoke at Alliance churches in Cleveland, Youngstown, and Akron, and across the border in nearby New Castle, Pennsylvania. At Youngstown, they spent several hours each day and night seeking the Lord in prayer in "soul-travail." In some of the earlier meetings, proto-glossolalia in the form of "suppressed groans" occurred. Bartleman described the meetings:

> No two services were alike. In one meeting the very silence of Heaven took possession of us for about four hours. Scarcely a sound was uttered. The place became so steeped in prayer and sacred that we closed the door softly, and walked the same, scarcely speaking to one another, and then only in whispers. Another night we were held in adoration and praise for hours. We seemed to be looking into the very face of God. There was no boisterousness in these meetings, but a subdued spirit throughout. Another night we were all broken up by the love of God. We could do nothing but weep for a whole hour. Every meeting was different, and each seemed to go deeper.[6]

One night the Spirit fell "like an electric shower," and several people fell under the power of the Spirit. He recounted, "Such singing in the Spirit, the 'heavenly chorus,' I have seldom heard. A number came through speaking in 'tongues.'" The leader's wife fell under the power, but according to Bartleman the leader resisted, and "carried on in the 'flesh.'"[7] The Alliance church in nearby Warren also experienced the revival, as Pastor John Waggoner received the baptism in the Spirit with tongues.[8] Other Alliance churches in Ohio continued to be touched by the revival over the next several months.

On the other side of the state, the "large influential" Alliance Church in Findlay, also was impacted by the revival, probably through T. K. Leonard's Pentecostal church and Bible school, as well as the outpourings in Cleveland and in August at Beulah Beach. Sometime in 1907 some people from the church received the baptism in the Holy Spirit "in latter rain manifestation" (tongues).[9] The church became charismatically-oriented, and D. W. Kerr, who received the baptism in the Spirit with tongues at Beulah Beach in August 1907, was asked to become pastor of the church in 1908. Even after Kerr left the church and the Alliance, the church remained charismatic in orientation.

Mrs. Etta Wurmser, who had supervised the planting of the Alliance works in Sandusky and Norwalk and founded a Bible school in Norwalk, moved her Bible school to Findlay in 1914, as well as serving as superintendent of the Alliance work. Alone in her room waiting on the Lord in the early days of the revival (in 1906 before it had spread in Ohio), she came into the Pentecostal experience. She testified, "I was taken up with my God, but I found I was speaking Chinese and other tongues. Oh such days! Such weeks! Such months I never had before in all my days!"[10] "A great part of the flocks" to whom she ministered (the Alliance works in Sandusky, Norwalk, Findlay, and other locations) "received the baptism in the Holy Ghost with signs following. . . . , one would have the gift of healing, another the gift of interpretation, and we would be amazed at the wisdom given. Children began to open the Scriptures and old men and old women received the Holy Ghost." Her Bible school became a training ground for Pentecostals, though she continued to remain associations with Alliance throughout her life, even when involved in independent Pentecostal ministry. Eventually she returned as pastor of the Alliance church in Findlay years later, while continuing to maintain her Pentecostal connections.[11]

PENTECOST IN IOWA AND MINNESOTA C&MA

The Western District of the C&MA also was impacted by the Pentecostal movement. The World's Faith Missionary Association (WFMA), a non-denominational organization in Shenandoah, Iowa, created as a fellowship of workers, credentialing body, and training school, was in close association with the C&MA. The WFMA "offered fertile soil for the Pentecostal movement."[12] Charles Crawford, who was pastor of the Alliance work in Boone, Iowa, director of a Bible school affiliated with the Alliance, and superintendent of the C&MA's Western District, was also a leader in WFMA. Other evangelists who were members of the WFMA and friends of Crawford and the Alliance included George L. Morgan, from Windom, Minnesota, who directed conventions and camp meetings in the region, and H. L. Blake, from Ruthton, Minnesota. Another close friend and associate of Crawford, Blake, and Morgan, was Emma Ladd, wife of prominent Iowa State Supreme Court Judge Scott M. Ladd. She was an evangelist in WFMA who operated a mission in Des Moines called "The Four Lights Mission" after Simpson's fourfold gospel. These all became players in the Pentecostal drama unfolding in Iowa and Minnesota.[13]

Blake and Chicago evangelist William Durham, also a member of WFMA, visited Azusa Street in February, both receiving the baptism in the Spirit with tongues. Blake, who would later join the C&MA, acknowledged in the Azusa Street paper *The Apostolic Faith* that he was initially skeptical, but "became convinced that God was there in mighty power and that this is indeed the work of the Holy Spirit." He testified that since receiving the baptism in the Spirit and tongues on February 25, "I have far greater liberty and Divine unction on me in dealing with souls, and there has come into my life an overflow of love and joy with a deep settled peace planted in the depths of my soul, a something that is inexpressible and indescribable."[14]

Although we do not have details of the impact of the Pentecostal revival upon the C&MA there, we do know that Crawford, Blake, and Morgan were actively involved in the revival. In fact, one WFMA camp meeting with Ladd, Durham, Blake, and Morgan was described as a "grand victorious pentecostal meeting."[15] By 1909 Morgan and Blake had joined the C&MA. Morgan ministered as an evangelist in the C&MA for three decades into his 80s, and served as Assistant Superintendent of the Western District for a time. Affectionately known as "Uncle Morgan," he was honored for his "spiritual stature and capacity for bringing blessing to those with whom he came in contact. He claimed large areas of the district by prayer, and then went forth to take the land for his Lord." He also had vision for a training institute in Minnesota, which eventually was fulfilled by establishing St. Paul Bible Institute (now Crown College).[16]

PENTECOST IN INDIANA C&MA

The Alliance had a strong and large work in Indianapolis. In January 1907 Glenn A. Cook from Azusa Street visited the C&MA Gospel Tabernacle in Indianapolis sharing about Pentecostal experiences. Pastor George Eldridge was out of state, but wired back to his church not to host the tarrying meetings. So they moved to another location with many people from the Alliance church attending.[17] Many people continued to seek the Lord over the next three months.

At one of these special evening services, on Easter Sunday, March 21, a seventeen year-old girl by the name of Alice Reynolds received the baptism in the Spirit: "The power of God fell upon her, and according to observers she uncoiled like a spiral and sank to the floor." She began "speaking and singing in the Spirit in three or four distinct languages, one of which was recognized as Hebrew by a Jewish Christian, Louis Schneiderman, who knelt nearby." Schneiderman had been a Nyack student, later marrying an Alliance girl and becoming a missionary to South Africa. He translated her tongues in Hebrew as "This is the bread of life. This is for you."

Then she sang, "At the Cross," in High German, although she knew no German.[18] A week later she experienced singing in tongues with others, which she described as a "heavenly choir"—"a low humming that gradually rose in harmonious crescendo as six individuals in different parts of the audience rose spontaneously to their feet and a full tide of glorious melody poured forth in ecstatic worship and praise. . . . from my innermost being heavenly music poured forth like strains through the pipes of some great organ. . . . the flowing forth of celestial harmony like a foretaste of divine rapture."[19]

Some of the older Alliance friends criticized her experience, but when A. B. Simpson came to the city (probably during his visit in June), he told her, "I've heard about you, Alice, and about your experience. I believe it and I want you to write me all about it."[20] Nearly two years later she testified of her experience, "The most blessed thing of all was the reality of Jesus Himself and the conscious knowledge that He, whom my weary soul had needed so long, was now reigning within me. Since then, what a tender, patient guide He has been. . . . He has given me many wonderful outward manifestations of His presence, and I truly thank and praise Him for them, but oh! I long that Christ might give me the ornament of a meek and quiet spirit, and a mind to know none other but His will."[21]

Also, sometime during 1907, probably related to this outpouring, Samuel H. Stokes, pastor of the Alliance church in nearby Anderson, received his "latter rain" baptism with tongues, along with some of his church members. The 1907-1908 C&MA Annual Report reported that "the work is in splendid condition, all working together with God in the love of the Spirit."[22]

PENTECOST IN PENNSYLVANIA ALLIANCE CHURCHES

Early in the new year a Methodist elder who had been baptized in the Spirit with tongues at McKinney's meetings in Akron traveled to the Alliance church in Homestead (east of Pittsburgh), beginning meetings on January 11. The first week focused on self-examination, repentance, reconciliation, and restitution. An outpouring of the Holy Spirit occurred on January 18, as "the walls began to fall, and people fell under the power of God."[23] Many of the congregation spoke in tongues. The wife of black Alliance pastor Peter Robinson from Pittsburgh was the first to receive the baptism in the Spirit with tongues, lying under the power of the Spirit for a time. The next evening Peter sang and spoke in tongues at his home.[24]

Homestead Alliance pastor J. E. Sawders reported that on January 21, J. T. Boddy, Alliance pastor in Lincoln Park "lay for hours under the power, then began to speak clearly and fluently in a new tongue," which someone identified as Hebrew. A spiritualist woman who attended the meetings was dramatically delivered from demons and was saved. In the same meetings, George Bowie, who later became a Pentecostal missionary to Africa, also received the baptism with tongues. Boddy's daughter later sang and spoke in tongues at his church.[25] Ivey Campbell was subsequently invited to share in many of the other Alliance missions and homes.[26] Sawders later distributed a tract entitled "The Latter Rain," which was advertised in Pentecostal periodicals.[27]

The South Side Mission of the C&MA in Pittsburgh reported that as they held meetings nightly for three weeks, the Spirit was poured out and four people had spoken in tongues: "One boy twelve or fourteen years old, speaks Italian very distinctly and interprets in English. The sisters speak sentences and quote texts of Scripture, and sing in the language they received, and interpret. Two of the sisters have the same tongue and when one begins to sing some hymn, the other starts in and voices the same words."[28]

Also early in 1907 Scottish C&MA missionary to Palestine Mrs. George (Annie) Murray received baptism in Spirit with tongues in the Pittsburgh area, perhaps at one of Campbell's meetings.[29] Boddy reported in April that many were being baptized in the Spirit with tongues, including teenagers and children, and that the work was spreading to other locations in Pittsburgh, Allegheny, Braddock, and McKeesport, among others.[30] In McKeesport alone a dozen had received tongues by early February.[31]

Controversy also reared its head as Alma White's anti-Pentecostal paper from Colorado, the *Rocky Mountain Pillar of Fire*, was circulated throughout the Western Pennsylvania area. One article published in May 1907 featured a man who had been attending Alliance meetings in the Pittsburgh/Braddock area and had been encouraged by a "Rev. W" (probably E. D. Whiteside) to attend the revival meetings in Homestead. While there he fell unconscious for ten hours, speaking in tongues. Rev. W then took him to various meetings to share his testimony. Later, under the influence of the Pillar of Fire ministry, he repudiated his tongues experience at the Alliance church in Homestead as being of the devil, and went around the Western Pennsylvania area renouncing the movement. He reported, "The *Pillar of Fire* paper is breaking up things here. The meetings at McKeesport and Homestead [also C&MA] have been broken up by the Pillar of Fire."[32]

In the spring of 1907 a special visitation of the Spirit was poured out with speaking in tongues at the C&MA Tabernacle in New Castle, Pennsylvania, pastored by Herbert Dyke. While speaking to congregation on March 10, John Coxe, pastor of the Alliance church in nearby Butler, fell under the power of the Spirit on the platform and began speaking in tongues.[33] A Methodist businessman described the Alliance meetings:

> The strange gift usually comes toward the close of the service while the audience is engaged in earnest prayer. . . . Suddenly one under the power begins to make gestures. The hands move back and forward, the eyes close, a light breaks on their countenance and they pour forth the unknown tongue. They are apparently in a state of trance, and when this ends do not know what they have said or done. The interpretation of what they have said comes later.[34]

Simpson associate F. E. Marsh reported positively of the outpouring, remarking that it was "one of the most sane and simple manifestations of the Spirit's operation in the gift of tongues."[35] He cited a report in a secular newspaper about the Alliance meetings in New Castle:

> Bursting out in song, prayer or sermon, in languages entirely distinct, yet all unknown to the speakers or their hearers, even the most

skeptical and hardened have yielded before the strange manifestation of what seems certainly divine power, and turned in terror from
their sins.

People of all denominations attracted by the manifestations are
flocking to the Alliance Hall. Clergymen have witnessed the demonstrations and come away profoundly impressed. Scores entering out
of curiosity or to laugh and scoff have come away awed and unable
to explain the manifestations, except as the Alliance people assert,
that the prophecy of Joel is coming true and that in the latter days
many shall speak with tongues.[36]

It is particularly significant that the newspaper reported that Alliance
people asserted that the prophecy of Joel was being fulfilled through speaking
in tongues. Marsh and other Alliance leaders were actively supporting the
manifestation of tongues and other Pentecostal phenomena. Further, Marsh
reported that the newspaper gave a fascinating, unusual account of a woman
by the name of Miss Wink who spoke in tongues for thirty minutes, accompanied, not by verbal interpretation, but interpretation through sign language or
gestures as the story of the crucifixion of Christ. Marsh called it "the acme of
the revival."[37]

Dyke and Coxe began to share the Latter Rain revival at New Castle with
other Alliance churches in Pennsylvania and surrounding states. Several other
Alliance churches continued to become active and enthusiastic advocates of
the burgeoning movement. Following preaching at the Alliance churches in
Youngstown and Akron, early in June Bartleman held five services at the C&MA
church in New Castle, in which "God greatly blessed."[38]

PENTECOST IN SPOKANE, WASHINGTON

Following months of prayer for revival, in the spring of 1907 a band of people from the Alliance branch in Spokane gathered together for ten days of
prayer and fasting. As they were seeking the Lord, they asked Him to send
the right person to share the good news of the moving of the Spirit. On the
tenth day,

M. L. Ryan, a holiness evangelist and editor from Portland who had received the baptism in the Spirit with tongues, arrived in Spokane as an answer
to their prayers. He began meetings, and the power of God was manifested, as
people were saved, healed, sanctified and baptized in the Spirit. Ryan reported
that "some of the most remarkable case of speaking in tongues occurred there.
. . . About thirty members of the Christian Alliance [C&MA] have endorsed the
movement and many of them have received their Pentecost."[39]

PENTECOST IN SAN ANTONIO

In the spring of 1907, San Antonio Alliance pastor L. C. Hall, attended several
Pentecostal tent revival meetings. One day Hall spent two hours praying and

praising God alone in the tent. While he was worshiping the Lord with a loud voice, rapt in praise, unknown to him a group of people gathered around. Without any instruction or assistance from anyone else, Hall spontaneously broke out in tongues. Like a fireball, the power of the Spirit spread through the tent, and everyone else who had gathered to seek God also began speaking in tongues. Hall eventually left the Alliance and became known as "The Prince of Evangelists" in the Pentecostal movement.[40]

HENRY WILSON'S TRIP TO OHIO AND THE C&MA CONVENTIONS

Henry Wilson was sent by Simpson from the C&MA headquarters to visit the Alliance Missionary Convention in Cleveland March 25-29 as well as at other Alliance works in Ohio, and report on the Pentecostal revival. Cramer reported of his visit, "Our State workers and field superintendent, Dr. Henry Wilson, were all in perfect accord with the testimony given by those who received their Pentecost, and expressed themselves in thorough sympathy with the experiences as wit-nessed in our midst." The meetings continued to be "modest and steady."[41] Another periodical, *The New Acts*, reported Wilson as concluding "that this work is of God, and no man should put his hand on it."[42]

Simpson also reported on Wilson's appraisal of the Ohio Conventions, writing, "We have been delighted to hear from our good brother, Dr. Wilson, who has just returned from the Ohio conventions, that a deep spirit of revival appears to be resting upon the work and the workers in that district, and that our beloved people are being kept to a great extent from fanaticism and excess and are receiving all the fulness of blessing which the Lord is waiting to bestow without the counterfeit." On the other hand, Simpson also elaborated further about an extreme form of "abandonment" that opens oneself up to deception, thinking one is abandoning himself unreservedly to God.[43]

A later third-hand report of Wilson's visit to Ohio by A. W. Tozer appears to contradict the statements by Cramer and Simpson, who recorded Wilson's approval. According to Tozer, after Wilson visited the Pentecostal meetings in Alliance, Ohio, he concluded, "I am not able to approve the movement, though I am willing to concede that there is probably something of God in it somewhere."[44] This statement, for which the source is unknown and appeared to be uncorroborated, has incited controversy among Pentecostals and Alliance scholars sympathetic to the Pentecostal and charismatic movements, even to the point labeling Tozer as a revisionist.[45]

However, the apparent discrepancy may be solved by recognizing that the town of Alliance was not a site of C&MA activity, thus Wilson was approving what he observed in C&MA meetings in Cleveland, and probably Akron and other C&MA sites, but not the Pentecostal meetings he observed in Alliance.[46] Significantly, a recently discovered first hand report seems to confirm that Wilson had dual viewpoints of the new movement. Bertha Pinkham Dixon, the Quaker pastor's wife who received tongues and later joined the C&MA, recalled that when Wilson was speaking at an Alliance convention in Ohio at that time, he proclaimed "that in a time of upheaval, the scum floats to the top;

also that mountain climbing is lonely work; the farther you go up the mountain the more people you leave behind you." He indicated that there are three classes of people: those who seek restoration of apostolic faith, those who hold back, and those who become fanatics.[47] Wilson's differentiation would be consistent with both positive and negative assessments of different segments of this revival movement. He warned against both holding back and becoming too extreme.

Wilson's assessment of Pentecostalism in the city of Alliance seems to have been a prophetic harbinger of the even more serious problems that would eventually emerge. A year later Azusa Street leader Frank Bartleman preached nine times at the Pentecostal camp meeting there. His evaluation confirms Wilson's earlier appraisal: "It was much a harder fought battle than the year before. There had been much fanaticism and lawlessness developed. The 'flesh' tried to run the meetings."[48] If some in the Alliance thought that Bartleman had been too fanatic, how much more these meetings must have been for Bartleman to make that statement.

Things would get even worse, however, especially the immorality of Levi Lupton, the Quaker minister who was a leader in the Pentecostal movement in the town of Alliance (along with former C&MA pastor C. A. McKinney). F. E. Marsh, who was usually positive about charismatic manifestations in the C&MA, cautioned in 1911 about false prophets who were "pandering to lusts." He wrote, "There are many today, who under the name of great spirituality, seize the opportunity to feed their lust by taking advantage of guileless women, like the leader of the Pentecostal movement in Alliance [Ohio]."[49] The reference is to Lupton, who disgraced his ministry in December 1910 due to a sex scandal.[50]

PENTECOST IN PORTLAND

The Pentecostal movement in Portland, Oregon, began in December 1906 when Florence Crawford from Azusa Street visited the city and conducted meetings. Crawford had worshiped for a time in the Alliance Church in Los Angeles, as well as at Smale's New Testament Church before her baptism in the Spirit with tongues at Azusa Street.[51] M. L. Ryan, holiness evangelist who had friendships with the C&MA, had received the baptism in the Spirit with tongues as a result of those meetings with Crawford in Portland. The Alliance was impacted, and in June a camp meeting resulted in dozens of people baptized in the Spirit with tongues. The Apostolic Faith reported, "The Christian and Missionary Alliance in Portland came into the work in a body. God is working there in mighty power today."[52] This is not to say that the group left the Alliance, but that they had accepted the Pentecostal message en masse.[53]

When Florence Crawford established her Apostolic Faith mission in Portland, it evidently caused some disruption and difficulty in the Alliance work, but the church apparently continued to be charismatically-oriented for many years, calling pastors who had been involved in the revival, including T. A. Cullen, who had been a part of the Nyack revival, John Fee, from the revival in China, and Orville Benham, formerly from the Assemblies of God.

PENTECOST IN CANADA

A. G. Ward served as a field evangelist for the Alliance in Western Canada and was Director of the Alliance Mission in Winnipeg. One of the earliest to receive tongues in Canada, he had heard about the Azusa Street revival and other out-pourings of the Spirit, and according to his own testimony, "My heart was very hungry for God's best in my life." He sought the Lord, praying, "Oh Lord, make me as holy as a pardoned sinner can be made, and fill me as full of Thyself as Thou art willing to fill me." He testified that the Holy Spirit came upon him and "Waves of glory swept through my soul and my lips uttered His praise in an unknown tongue." Others identified that he spoke in German, Indian, Scandi-navian and Polish. The Bible came alive to him and he exercised a more power-ful faith in God as a result of his Pentecostal experience.[54] On one occasion he was preaching with an interpreter to the Indians of the Fisher River reservation about two hundred miles north of Winnipeg. As he was preaching under the anointing of the Spirit, he began to speak in tongues. His interpreter exclaimed, "Why, you are now speaking to us in your own language!"[55]

A. H. Argue, a friend of George Watson, was healed from "a chronic inter-nal trouble" through the ministry of A. B. Simpson in Winnipeg in the winter of 1906.[56] He received the baptism in the Spirit with tongues in April 1907 while visiting William Durham's mission in Chicago.[57] Later, he was praying in the home of George and Annie Murray, Scottish C&MA missionaries to Palestine who had received tongues months earlier in the Pittsburgh area. Suddenly, he burst out speaking in tongues. The Murrays understood him and revealed that he was speaking in Arabic, which Argue had never learned.[58]

PENTECOST AT C&MA NYACK ANNUAL COUNCIL

Simpson spent time in prayer and fasting and waiting on God during the weeks before the annual General Council of the C&MA May 28-31 at Nyack, both for the Council and for a special fresh anointing of the Holy Spirit for himself.[59] To this point tongues had not been manifested at the Missionary Training Institute. He thus approached Council with an anticipation of an outpouring of the Spirit, accompanied by signs and wonders: "Surely we may expect quite as mighty and glorious a fulfilment in these last days as in apostolic times." Students like-wise had been praying daily for an outpouring of the Holy Spirit.

On Sunday, May 26, the day before commencement, one student, Alice Rowlands (who later married Assemblies of God leader Stanley Frodsham) re-called:

> The students were all gathered in the chapel to hear the Baccalau-reate sermon preached. Many had spent the night in prayer and a marvelous feeling of expectancy was on most of us that God would do something out of the ordinary. There was a quiet sobbing going on in several hearts as we bowed in prayer. . . . we all felt like going through with God, cost what it might. Then a student got up sobbing

under the power of the Spirit of God telling how powerless he felt, how the burden of souls was on him, how clean he felt, but oh, *so* powerless. He must have power to go out and win souls for Christ, he must have the Baptism of the Holy Spirit. This was the cry of numbers there, and as he ended the spirit of weeping fell on us and we fell on our faces pleading with God to baptize us."[60]

Then one of the ministers on the platform, probably Warren Cramer from Cleveland, "suddenly burst out in an unknown tongue, and what awe came upon us all as for the first time we heard this manifestation of the power of God." He gave an interpretation, saying that "he believed he had the mind of the Lord and it was that we should listen to the sermon which Brother Ira David would preach. How we listened as he talked of the Holy Spirit, taking the verses, 'Grieve not the Spirit,' 'Quench not the Spirit,' 'Resist not and lie not to the Holy Spirit.' The meeting closed with confession and a healing service and we all kept praying for God to continue in our presence."[61]

Many of the students remained for Council and continued seeking the Lord in prayer meetings, along with ministers, missionaries, and other Council delegates who had gathered. The outpouring fell upon students and Council delegates alike, as many fell under the power of the Holy Spirit and some spoke in tongues. One student made confession of a sin and was filled with joy. She exhorted the others, "Oh girls, confess where you have failed God. It feels so good to know you are forgiven." Alice recalled, "She had no sooner said this than the power of the Lord fell upon her and she began speaking in other tongues."[62]

A black delegate from Pittsburgh, Peter Robinson (who had received tongues in January), prayed with such great fervency and power that the Council leaders did not know how to proceed or control the meetings. Alliance pastors John Coxe from Butler, W. A. Cramer from Cleveland, and Thomas A. Cullen from Springfield, Massachusetts, who had all received the gift of tongues, were asked to moderate the proceeding to make sure every thing was done decently and in order. This "seemed to heighten the already supercharged atmosphere." Alice Wood, a C&MA missionary from Venezuela (who later joined the Assemblies of God), reported that Cramer and Mrs. Murray spoke in tongues publicly there. According to another account, "When Cramer saw the extent to which the Spirit of God was moving upon the people, an utterance of praise in another language leaped to his lips. It was just a sentence, but so powerful that one of the students, David McDowell, fell to the floor as though struck by a sledge hammer."[63]

One night about 2-3 a.m. in the all night prayer meetings, one young woman named Sally Botham, who was planning to go to the mission field in Congo, "sat on the floor before a large map of the world and began praying in tongues. It seemed that as she prayed for each country the Lord gave her a different language." When she prayed in tongues for the Congo, two Alliance missionaries, Lucy Villars and Mary Mullen, recognized the language as "Kefonti," one of the dialects of the Congo. One of them spoke up, saying, "Why, she is speaking in the Congo language! She is telling people to get ready, for Jesus is coming soon!"

They translated further utterances as, "the fountain of blood is flowing from Calvary, sufficient for all our sins, and sufficient for a world of sinners." Botham later became a missionary with the C&MA in West Africa for about forty years, but apparently did not preach in tongues.[64]

Another person testified, "Meetings ran on day and night for nearly a week without human leadership, no thought of time, trains, meals, sleep, etc. The Holy Ghost did wonderfully quicken and strengthen physically all those who thus fasted and waited upon Him." Among the manifestations reported were "agony for sin and self-life," "visions of the cross, blood, throne," and "deep whole-souled shouts of glory and praise, all testifying 'Jesus is coming soon.'" Blumhofer notes, "Most remarkable to some was the fact that tongues speech was interpreted, thus giving the faithful 'messages from the throne direct.'"[65]

Though he had some concerns, Simpson's public response to the events at Council was affirming: "The attitude of the Council upon this important matter was one of great unity, the brethren fully accepting as genuine such manifestations as are characterized by the 'spirit of power and of a sane mind,' while at the same time standing together against various forms of false teaching and wild excitement which are abroad on every side."[66] Privately, Simpson recorded in his diary:

> I noted first a quiet but real quickening in my own soul, and great blessing in the Council. God kept us united, and at the close manifested Himself in some of the meetings in a very unusual way. There were several cases of the Gift of Tongues and other extraordinary manifestations, some of which were certainly genuine, while others appeared to partake somewhat of the individual peculiarities and eccentricities of the subjects, so that I saw not only the working of the Spirit, but also a very distinct human element, not always edifying or profitable. And God led me to discern and hold quietly to the divine order for the gifts of the Spirit in 1 Cor. 12-14. At the same time I could not question the reality of the gifts, and I was led to pray much about it, and for God's highest will and glory in connection with it.[67]

Simpson's private notations were consistent with his public pronouncements, both receptive to the exercise of tongues and other gifts, but cautioning against fleshly demonstrations and demonic influence. H. E. Nelson later reported that in the initial stages the revival was "pure as the morning sun."[68]

---

1. Florence A. Atwater, "The Boston Convention," CMAW, Feb. 23, 1907, 92.

2. W. A. Cramer, "Pentecost at Cleveland," CMAW, Apr. 27, 1907, 201.

3. George E. Davis, "Has the Latin Language," Word and Work, June 1907, 182.

4. Bertha Pinkham Dixon, A Romance of Faith (n.p., 193-?), 73.

5. Ibid., 74-75.

6. Bartleman, *Azusa Street* (1980), 105-106.

7. Ibid., 106; Frank Bartleman, *Another Wave of Revival* (Springdale, PA: Whitaker House, 1982), 112-114.

8. Waggoner left the Alliance probably in 1912 along with several others, and joined the Assemblies of God in 1914.

9. In February 1908, it was reported of the Alliance convention in Findlay that "more received the baptism of the Holy Spirit in latter rain manifestation" (tongues). "Notes from the Home Field," CMAW, Mar. 7, 1908, 389. This indicates that sometime in 1907 there had been a similar outpouring with tongues in the Findlay church, either as a result of Leonard's contact with McKinney and the Alliance, or as a result of the outpouring in Cleveland or Beulah Beach.

10. Etta Wurmser, "Chosen in the Furnace of Affliction," LRE, Jan. 1917, 21.

11. "More About the Findlay School," *Assemblies of God Heritage*, Spring 1990, 20; "Everywhere Preaching," AW, Nov. 7, 1951, 701; W. A. Cramer, "Conventions in Ohio," AW, Apr. 6, 1912, 114; "Work and Workers," AW, Dec. 16, 1933, 797.

12. Ibid., 24.

13. For more on Emma Ladd, see Edith Blumhofer, "Emma Cormer Ladd: Iowa's Pentecostal Pioneer," *Assemblies of God Heritage*, Fall-Winter 1998-99, 21ff.

14. H. L. Blake, "A Minnesota Preacher's Testimony," *The Apostolic Faith*, Vol. I, No. 6, Feb.-Mar. 1907, 5.

15. Ibid., 48. Mrs. Woodward-Back, C&MA missionary on furlough from India where revival had broken out in 1906, was working with the small Alliance work in Des Moines trying to maintain openness to the working of the Spirit in balance, but evidently due to the Pentecostal controversy there was "much distraction and difficulty." Eventually the work in Des Moines became well established with Crawford's cousin J. H. Mintier serving as pastor of the church and Iowa State Superintendent, headquartered in Des Moines. A. B. Simpson, CMAW, Sept. 14, 1907, 121; "Who and Where," AW, Aug. 10, 1912, 302.

16. "Work and Workers," AW, Jan. 13, 1945, 13, 16.

17. Lewis Wilson, "The Life and Legacy of George N. Eldridge," *Assemblies of God Heritage* 21, Spring 2001, 7; Nienkirchen, 83; Menzies, *Anointed to Serve*, 66.

18. Brumback, *Suddenly . . . From Heaven*, 77-78; see also Wayne Warner, *Revival! Touched by Pentecostal Fire* (Tulsa, OK: Harrison House, 1978), 33-35; Alice Reynolds Flower, "My Day of Pentecost," *Assemblies of God Heritage*, Winter 1997-98, 17.

19. Warner, *Revival!*, 35. Alice Reynolds Flower, "Pentecostal Recollections," Jim Corum Interview with Alice Reynolds Flower, Flower Pentecostal Heritage Center, Springfield, MO.

20. Brumback, *Suddenly . . . From Heaven*, 77-78.

21. Alice Marie Reynolds, "All for Jesus," *The Pentecost*, Dec. 1908, 15. In a ceremony conducted by David Myland in 1911, Reynolds married J. Roswell Flower, who became an early leader in the Assemblies of God. Menzies, *Anointed to Serve*, 66.

22. C&MA Annual Report 1907-1908, 68.

23. "Many Witnesses to the Power of the Blood and of the Holy Ghost," *The Apostolic Faith*, Vol. I, No. 7, Apr. 1907, 1.

24. Ibid.

25. Frodsham, *With Signs Following*, 45-46; "Pentecostal in Middle States," *The Apostolic Faith*, Vol. I, No. 6, Feb.-Mar. 1907, 3; "Demons Cast Out," *The Apostolic Faith*, Vol. I, No. 6, Feb.-Mar. 1907, 3; "Pentecostal Testimonies," *The Apostolic Faith*, Vol. I, No. 6, Feb.-Mar. 1907, 6; Ann Taves, *Fits, Trances, and Visions* (Princeton, NJ: Princeton University Press, 1999), 333. Boddy later became an Assembly of God leader.

26. Ivey Campbell, "Report from Ohio and Pennsylvania," *The Apostolic Faith*, Vol. I, No. 6, Feb.-Mar. 1907, 5.

27. *The Pentecost*, Sept.-Oct. 1910, 8.

28. Pentecost in Middle States," *The Apostolic Faith*, Vol. I, No. 6, Feb.-Mar. 1907, 3.

29. Frodsham, *With Signs Following*, 46; P. D. Hocken, "Murray, George A. and Annie," DPCM, 631. The Murrays were speaking at Alliance meetings on March 17, in Greensburg, Pennsylvania, an eastern suburb of Pittsburgh. It is likely that this was the setting and time in which she received tongues. "Greensburg, Pa., "CMAW, Apr. 6, 1907, 166.

30. "Many Witnesses to the Power of the Blood and of the Holy Ghost," *The Apostolic Faith*, Vol. I, No. 7, Apr. 1907, 1.

31. S. F. Black, "In McKeesport, Pa.," *Word and Work*, May 1907, 149.

32. Larry E. Martin, *Skeptics and Scoffers* (Pensacola, FL: Christian Life Books, 2004), 191-192.

33. Frodsham, *With Signs Following*, 46. Though we have no documentation, it is probable that Dyke himself also spoke in tongues, for he continued to teach on the Latter Rain, was involved with Pentecostal activities, and pastored charismatically-oriented Alliance congregations for many years. For Coxe's testimony of his experience, see John Coxe, "The Church and World," *Word and Work*, Apr. 7, 1917, 167-168.

34. F. E. Marsh, "The Gift of Tongues," *Living Truths*, May 1907, 262-263.

35. Ibid., 261-262.

36. Ibid., 262.

37. Ibid.

38. Bartleman, *Another Wave of Revival*, 114; Bartleman, *Azusa Street* (1980), 112-114.

39. M. L. Ryan, "Pentecost in Spokane, Wash.," *The Apostolic Faith*, Vol. I, No. 7, Apr. 1907, 2. See also Marjorie Stewart, "A Story of Pentecost in the Pacific Northwest," *Assemblies of God Heritage*, Spring 1987, 4; Rose Pittman Downing, "The Pentecostal Revival at Latah," *Assemblies of God Heritage*, Spring 1987, 5.

40. Howard A. Goss with Ethel E. Goss, *The Winds of God* (New York, NY: Comet Press Books, 1958), 60-62.

41. W. A. Cramer, "Pentecost at Cleveland," CMAW, Apr. 27, 1907, 201.

42. "An Influential Endorsement," *The New Acts*, Apr. 1907, 3, cited by McGee, "Levi Lupton," 207n41.

43. A. B. Simpson, Editorial, CMAW, Apr. 6, 1907, 158.

44. Tozer, *Wingspread*, 133.

45. Nienkirchen, 136-138.

46. Nienkirchen casts doubt on the authenticity and accuracy of Tozer's report, but this clears up the confusion. See Nienkirchen, 136-138. McGee mistakenly states that Levi Lupton pastored the Alliance church in Alliance, Ohio, when, in fact, there was no C&MA work there. He evidently confused the (Christian and Missionary) Alliance with the town of Alliance, Ohio. See Gary B. McGee, "Pentecostal Awakenings at Nyack," *Paraclete* 18 (Summer 1984), 24-26. 26.Tozer's first C&MA pastor as a teenager (about 1915-1918) was S. M. Gerow, who was involved in the Pentecostal revival in the C&MA church in Akron, Ohio (see "Notes from the Home Field," CMAW, Apr. 11, 1908, 33; S. M. Gerow, "Report of Annual Convention of Akron, O. Branch of the C&MA," CMAW, Apr. 17, 1909, 48). Gerow became a mentor to young Tozer, and according to Tozer's biographer, "Much of his spiritual growth he attributed to the ministry of this godly man." [David J. Fant, *AW. Tozer: A Twentieth-Century Prophet* (Harrisburg, PA: Christian Publications, 1964), 16.] Tozer's early exposure to a man who had ridden out the storm of controversy surrounding the early Pentecostal movement in Eastern Ohio, and particularly in Alliance circles likely shaped his thinking toward Pentecostalism. Gerow had been McKinney's assistant pastor before he left the C&MA for the Pentecostal work in Alliance, Ohio. In spite of McKinney's departure, Gerow had been quite positive about Pentecostal developments within the C&MA, but may

have possibly been the source of Tozer's knowledge of Wilson's negative assessment of Pentecostalism in nearby Alliance, Ohio.

47. Bertha Pinkham Dixon, *A Romance of Faith*, 128.

48. Bartleman, *Azusa Street* (1980), 119.

49. F. E. Marsh, "Here and There: False Prophets," CMAW, July 29, 1911, 284.

50. G. B. McGee, "Lupton, Levi Rakestraw," DPCM, 561-562; McGee, "Levi Lupton," 203 ff.

51. Larry Martin, ed., *The True Believers, Part Two: More Eyewitness Accounts* (Joplin, MO: Christian Life Books, 1999), 95.

52. "In These Last Days," *The Apostolic Faith*, Vol. 1, No. 9, June-Sept. 1907, 1.

53. See the clarification in *The Apostolic Faith*, Vol. 1, No. 12, Jan. 1908, 2.

54. Thomas William Miller, *Canadian Pentecostals: A History of the Pentecostal Assemblies of Canada* (Mississauga, Ontario: Full Gospel Publishing House, 1994), 46.

55. Frodsham, *With Signs Following*, 56-57.

56. Miller, *Canadian Pentecostals*, 73.

57. Thomas William Miller, "The Canadian/American Pioneer Evangelist: A. H. Argue," *Assemblies of God Heritage*, Spring 1995, 6.

58. Frodsham, *With Signs Following*, 57-58.

59. A. B. Simpson's Diary, May 1907.

60. Stanley H. Frodsham, *Jesus is Victor: A Story of Grace, Gladness and Glory in the Life of Alice M. Frodsham* (Springfield, MO: Gospel Publishing House, 1930), 38.

61. Ibid., 38.

62. Ibid., 40.

63. A. B. Simpson, Editorial, CMAW, June 8, 1907, 205; Frodsham, *With Signs Following*, 47, Brumback, *Suddenly. . . from Heaven*, 89-90; McGee, "Pentecostal Awakenings at Nyack," 24-26.

64. Frodsham, *Jesus is Victor*, 40; Frodsham, *With Signs Following*, 47; Brumback, *Suddenly. . . from Heaven*, 89-90; Simpson, Editorial, CMAW, June 8, 1907, 205. The accounts vary a little in the details, but I have attempted to reconstruct and harmonize the accounts. Alice Frodsham has her sitting on the floor before a map; McDowell has her prostrate on the rostrum. Probably both occurred at some point.

65. A. W. Vian, "Further News from Nyack, New York," *Household of God*, Nov. 1907, 6, cited in Edith L. Blumhofer, *Restoring the Faith*, 77.

66. Simpson, Editorial, June 8, 1907, 205.

67. Simpson's Diary, May 1907.

68. Keith M. Bailey, "Dealing with the Charismatic in Today's Church." A paper presented at the District Superintendent's Conference of The Christian and Missionary Alliance, Feb. 28-Mar. 2, 1977, Nyack, New York.

Summer Cloudbursts
of the Spirit

Simpson's Report—Don't Depreciate the Genuine Gold

In Simpson's Annual Report for 1906-1907 at Council he had affirmed that in the current revival there were genuine tongues, but also some extravagance and error. He counseled, "Do not allow the counterfeit to depreciate the genuine gold. Our attitude is both openness and caution."[1] After the outpouring at Nyack, Simpson affirmed that the Alliance "stands for supernatural tongues and all."[2] At the same time, in response to those claiming that tongues is the evidence of the baptism in the Spirit, Simpson assured that the greatest evidence of genuine spiritual gifts is humility and acceptance of the authority of the Word.[3] Simpson's positive attitudes stirred greater anticipation of more to come through the moving of the Holy Spirit.

Pentecost at C&MA Convention in Toronto

Pentecostal revival in the Alliance in Canada continued in June as C&MA Vice President John Salmon received two visions at Toronto C&MA convention being held at his church, where Annie Murray was speaking. He recounted of the experience:

> While engaged in prayer at one of her meetings and kneeling in a lowly attitude there appeared to me like, a sea of glory coming toward me, but just before it reached to where I was kneeling there came a black cloud between it and me. Then God gave me a view of dark Calvary. I seemed to see Jesus laid in His tomb as the bleeding victim taken down from the cross. Then there came an overwhelming sense of my own sinfulness, as if some One had said to me: "John Salmon, your sins brought our Saviour to that cruel death on the cross," I never before seemed to realize such a degree of blood guiltiness on my part in having Jesus Christ crucified for me and I felt as if I would like to lie down in that grave beside that dear Friend who

died on account of my sins having been committed against a holy and righteous God, my best Friend.

A few days after that in the same place God gave me another vision of Jesus Christ my adorable Saviour. While engaged in silent prayer there appeared a curtain before me which was slowly drawn aside, when lo! The Lord Jesus appeared with a crown of gold on His head and arrayed in priestly robes and holding in His two hands a basin. He moved towards me and my wonder was what that basin contained. Before I was aware of it He emptied its contents on my head. I was covered all over with a substance resembling a fleecy white cloud. The moment it touched my head I shook and trembled for some time with great force. he one thought occupying my mind just then was the wonderful condescension of my Lord in giving me such a view of Himself and of His kindness in putting this unction of glory on my head, whose sweet fragrance stilt abides with me. '

Several other people received tongues or other manifestations of the Spirit. Simpson commented that the Pentecostal revival in the Alliance work in Toronto had occurred "without serious strain." He noted that the experience of those who had spoken in tongues had been "accepted frankly as genuine, modest and entirely Scriptural, but the balance of truth has been carefully guarded. The work has been preserved from extravagance and excess and the 'spirit of love and power and a sound mind' has been poured out upon the work and the workers."[5]

MORE OUTPOURINGS IN PITTSBURGH

In June at "at a meeting surpassing all former occasions of power" led by evangelist J. M. Humphrey at one of the Alliance churches in Pittsburgh, four hundred people sought the Lord at the altar for salvation, sanctification and the baptism in the Spirit. It was reported, "Great numbers found what they sought; some from East End, Braddock, Oakmont, and Springdale, received their Pentecost." A young black girl who worked in a Jewish home spoke in Hebrew, amazing them and arousing conviction in their hearts. On a street car, a woman named Sister McGuire was able to speak to Russian Jews in their language. Another young man was able to preach in the Italian language.[6]

PENTECOST AT MCARTHUR'S ALLIANCE TABERNACLE IN CHICAGO

For months, as W. T. MacArthur had reported in the C&MA Weekly, his church had been seeking all that God had for them, including His gifts and graces. They had set aside one evening a week to pray that they "might receive all that God was willing to bestow; and also that we might be delivered from all the deceptions of Satan, and the workings of the flesh." On June 12th nine people remained after the midweek-service at the Alliance Tabernacle in Chicago to wait upon the Lord. Pastor MacArthur shared that one of the leaders, "a man of undoubted reliability and Christian experience," had been praying earnestly and broke out speaking in tongues. He related that there was no hysteria or hypnotic influence, but that "several were strongly convulsed." Another church leader also spoke in tongues after intense supplication. Less than a week later two more spoke in tongues. MacArthur reported positively:

> Those who speak in tongues seem to live in another world. . . . (It) seems to be a means of communication between the soul and God. They do not speak in tongues in the assembly, but when in prayer; they become intense in their supplication; they are apt to break out in the unknown tongue, which is invariably followed by ascriptions of praise and adoration which are well nigh unutterable. . . . There is no shadow of doubt left in our minds as to the Scripturalness of the experience, and we feel sure that no honest heart could find anything to criticize.[7]

PENTECOST IN NEW ENGLAND

The Alliance works throughout New England were swept by the Pentecostal renewal, especially during the summer of 1907. On June 20 at the Alliance meeting led by Superintendent Ira David at the Wesleyan Hall in Boston several spoke in tongues. Three days later at his church in Brockton with Minnie Draper and E. J. Richards as featured speakers eight more people received the baptism in the Spirit with tongues. In July at an Alliance afterglow meeting in Boston led by Morton Plummer, several fell under the power of the Spirit, saw visions regarding the Second Coming, and spoke and sang in tongues. It was reported that the meetings of the C&MA "are being permeated with teaching and testimony" of the Pentecostal baptism in the Spirit.[8]

RESPONSE TO PENTECOSTALISM IN INDIANAPOLIS

Simpson attended the Indianapolis C&MA convention in June, remarking in his diary that he had "much concern on the unity of our work. It was the first of the summer conventions and in a sense a sort of earnest of the others. The work here had been much split over the Tongues, and I had prayed much about it. God answered graciously and gave much blessing."[9] According to the 1907-1908 Annual Report, half of the members had left and joined "The Apostolic Faith Movement,"[10] but he was still encouraged about the moving of the Spirit.

This was probably the time Simpson talked with Alice Reynolds about her experience of speaking in tongues, telling her he believed it was genuine. It was also a personal time of spiritual searching and inspiration for Simpson. While in prayer, he was reminded of "God's meeting with me in this place in a remarkable way in 1881 and before." At that time the Lord had given him a special message from 2 Kings 13:18, 19. This was about Elisha's prophesying to the king of Israel to strike the ground many times with arrows to obtain victory, but the king had struck the ground only three times, and did not gain full victory. In his diary Simpson wrote, "I again claimed it, and with it *all* His best will for me. I smote with *all* the arrows and asked in faith that nothing less than His perfect and might fullness might come into my life."[11] His understanding of this biblical event was so significant an insight he continued to teach years later two years later at the C&MA Convention in Chicago, which was also published in the Pentecostal periodical *The Latter Rain Evangel*.[12]

At the end of June Simpson published an article on "Gifts and Grace," explaining the supernatural gifts of the Spirit, especially tongues.[13] This was probably the message he preached at the Alliance convention in Indianapolis. It would be republished in pamphlet countless times as Simpson's personal response and position on the gifts of the Spirit. In July the book *Signs of the Times* was issued as the first Alliance book addressing the new Pentecostal or Latter Rain movement.[14] It included the earlier January articles by Ballard on tongues and Simpson on "Gifts and Grace."[15]

REVIVAL AT BEULAH HEIGHTS ORPHANAGE

During the summer, revival swept through the Beulah Heights orphanage operated by Carrie Judd Montgomery in San Francisco. Many children gave their lives to Christ. One of her "trusted and respected" children's workers received the baptism in the Spirit, accompanied by speaking and singing in tongues. Carrie and her husband George were impressed with her deepened dedication and spiritual walk with God. Though it would be another year before they received tongues, the example of her life prepared them to desire what God might have for them.[16]

REVIVAL AT TULLY LAKE CONVENTION

The convention at Tully Lake, New York, south of Syracuse was described by Simpson as "a season of quiet but very deep spiritual blessing." He remarked, "There were many unusual manifestations of the Spirit's presence and sanctifying and healing power."[17] He did not elaborate on the nature of the "unusual manifestations," but it is likely that they included speaking in tongues, falling under the power of the Spirit and other such phenomena as in other Alliance conventions.

PENTECOST AT MAHAFFEY CAMP

In its early days Mahaffey Camp in Pennsylvania was not owned by the C&MA, but hosted Alliance camp meetings. Keith Bailey talked with early Mahaffey attendees in those days. They shared with him the occurrence of tongues at Council and also a significant incident at Mahaffey that summer. Two women were singing a duet and got so caught up in the Spirit that they ended by singing in tongues.

PENTECOST AT C&MA ROCKY SPRINGS, PA, CONVENTION—JULY 12-21

Simpson reported on "special manifestations of power of God" and gifts at the Pennsylvania Eastern District Convention at the Rocky Springs Campgrounds near Lancaster.[18] Those manifestations included falling under the power of the Spirit and speaking in tongues. Four evenings of all-night prayer were led by E. D. Whiteside, G. V. Brown, and E. J. Richards, with more than twenty people receiving the baptism in the Spirit, many of them accompanied by tongues.[19]

David McDowell, who had fallen under the power of the Spirit at the Nyack Council, was one of many who received tongues. When McDowell was filled with the Spirit and spoke in tongues, J. R. Kline, pastor of the C&MA church in Grove City, Pennsylvania (later in Tottenville, Staten Island, New York), exclaimed, "I see a fire over his head!" Kline also was filled with the Spirit, speaking in tongues. McDowell's hands were raised high over his head in worship for more than an hour, "and when he lowered them, his hands fell, unexpectedly, on the heads of the wives of two Alliance leaders, and these women promptly burst forth speaking in tongues!" E. F. M. Staudt, the pioneering pastor of the Alliance work in Baltimore, also spoke in tongues.

That night, after returning to the campground from other meetings, he would reach out to lay hands on someone, and again and again, "invariably, everyone he approached—before he could place his hands upon their heads—suddenly began to speak in tongues." Thirty-two people spoke in tongues that night.[20] Simpson reported of the convention, "The meetings were under wise and cautious oversight, and all excess and foolishness were carefully guarded against."[21]

PENTECOST AT NEW YORK STATE C&MA CONVENTION JULY 21-28

Following on the heels of the outpouring at Rocky Springs, the Spirit continued to move at the New York State C&MA Convention at Nyack. The *C&MA Weekly* reported, "Often as the altar was made ready the people would rise almost en masse and press forward and there remain for hours. God was pleased to manifest Himself to many in much power, prostrating them with joy and glory. . . . these are the days of 'the latter rain.'"[22]

At the convention, Alfred Snead, later Foreign Secretary of the C&MA, fell under the power of the Spirit and "lay under the library table, speaking in tongues." The leaders asked McDowell to speak to the youth meeting of about a thousand and share a testimony of his fresh experience from the week before. About a hundred spoke in tongues as a result of his testimony.[23]

Frank Bartleman visited Alliance leader Stephen Merritt in New York City and attended a C&MA service, then spoke at two services at the Nyack Convention. Afterward, E. D. Whiteside asked him to preach two services at the Alliance church in Pittsburgh, where he recounted, "I was to take the train the same night for Cincinnati, but could not stop my message in time. The people were so hungry. I preached for two hours."[24]

On the closing Saturday of the convention, Simpson experienced what he described as a spiritual breakthrough as he was waiting on the Lord:

> I received, as I waited in the aftermeeting a distinct touch of the mighty power of the Holy Spirit—a kind of breaking through, accompanied

by a sense of awe and a lighting up of my senses. It was as if a wedge of light and power were being driven through my inmost being and I all broken open [sic]. I welcomed it and felt disappointed when the meeting was abruptly closed by the leader, for I was conscious of a peculiar power resting upon us all and continuing to fill me. I carried it home with me, and for several days the deep sense remained as a sort of "weight of love," in addition to the ordinary and quiet sense of God I have felt so long.[25]

Pentecost at Old Orchard Convention—August 2-12

At the beginning of the Old Orchard Convention in Maine, Simpson was not reticent about the manifestations in recent conferences, but approached this convention with anticipation, saying that they were "waiting on the Lord—expecting gifts and graces."[26] The convention was indeed marked by supernatural gifts and graces—speaking in tongues, visions, prophecy, falling under the power of the Spirit.

Early in the convention, Mary G. Davies, a missionary to Africa, spoke on "The Ninety-first Psalm," sharing a prophetic word God had given her in a time of danger and fear: "My child, it is about time you practice what you preach. Don't you remember what you told the people in the meeting this morning, how I spoke to you in the night, and showed you how very secure God's children are when abiding in the secret place of the Most High? . . . Don't you remember I showed you how I had given My angels charge over you, to keep you in all your ways? . . . Don't you remember how I said, you shall not be afraid of the 'terrors' by night?"[27]

An all-night prayer meeting took place on Monday night of the convention (August 5), according to the C&MA Weekly, by "a large number of persons on the grounds who were earnestly seeking some deeper manifestations of the Holy Spirit." Leaders "who have learned to know the voice of the Spirit" were concerned about "conflicting elements of an unusual character" and "cross currents of spiritual influence," "but before morning the strain ended in victory and blessing, and a better understanding." The leaders also expressed concern about "many influences on the grounds tending to distract simple and earnest seekers and to lead to the dangerous counterfeits" and "outside parties, and extreme teachings and experiences, yet the last few days became intensely harmonious, sweet and heavenly, and a spirit of love, power and a sound mind overshadowed all hearts and rested upon all the services in mighty blessing."[28]

Bartleman was evidently one of those "outside parties" who attended the Old Orchard convention. Though he was not invited to speak, the Scottish preacher who was speaking (probably Rev. A. Allen) asked Bartleman to join him on the platform. "A score of hungry souls" wanted Bartleman to have tarrying meetings in the camp, but they were not permitted to meet on the grounds. A group of over a hundred gathered outside the camp in the woods. There an unidentified Nyack faculty member received the baptism of the Spirit with tongues.[29]

Alice Belle Garrigus from Newfoundland in Canada had been seeking for more of the fullness of God's power. After a "nine-month period of soul travail," she attended the Old Orchard camp meeting. There she met Minnie Draper, the Board of Managers member who had received the baptism in the Spirit with tongues several months earlier. As a featured speaker on Wednesday morning on the subject of "The Spirit-Filled Life," Draper encouraged those desiring the Holy Spirit to "stick to the honey."

"One night, Minnie Draper had a vision of an old barn located on the outskirts of Old Orchard. She believed it was an authentic vision inspired by God, for He made it plain that this barn would be where the saints would tarry in prayer." Although she had never seen the barn, she discovered that it really existed. So there this group of hungry souls, which included missionaries, local church workers, and young men who had just entered the ministry, sought the Lord, laying prone on the hay and crying out for the "promise of the Father." "As the barn seemed to glow with the heavenly glory," Alice's biographer recounted, "it seemed as if even the words and music being emitted from them, were supernatural." Tongues occurred in many languages, along with interpretations, holy laughter, and victory shouts, all "blended in one harmonious song of praise."

Alice described the occasion with great fervor: "What heart-searchings! What confessions! What separations! What humblings seekers passed through; till one being asked what the new experience was, replied: 'It is the new death.' The Shekinah glory burned as a flame in the heart of the baptized one, and holiness was the atmosphere in which he lived." She left the convention to return to her home and pioneer the first Pentecostal movement in Newfoundland, which became known as the Pentecostal Assemblies of Newfoundland.[30]

PENTECOST AT BEULAH BEACH CONVENTION—AUGUST 9-18

At the Beulah Beach Convention in northern Ohio, many were falling under the power of the Spirit and scores of people were receiving tongues. It was reported in the C&MA Weekly as "the greatest and most marvelous convention in the history of the Alliance."[31] Warren Cramer, who had spoken in tongues some months earlier, was in charge.[32] Among the speakers was David Myland, who had received tongues several months earlier. E. D. Whiteside was in charge of the prayer room and encouraged people not to be afraid of manifestations or fanaticism.[33]

Among the people who spoke in tongues at this convention were John Salmon, head of the C&MA in Canada, Mrs. W. T. MacArthur, wife of a future Board of Managers member, and Rev. and Mrs. D. W. Kerr, who later were leaders in the Assemblies of God. At an all-night prayer meeting, Salmon "received another gracious visitation of the wonderful power of the Holy Spirit":

About three o'clock in the morning one said to me that we had better retire to rest. I replied to the effect that I would remain till four o'clock. Shortly after that a power came upon me as I was bended lowly in prayer and praise, and straightened me upright and in this attitude I continued for a length of time repeating over and over again: "Glory to Jesus, Glory to Jesus," till by and by I got down on the straw covering the ground of the Tabernacle. There I remained conscious all the time, but shaking a good deal and uttering a few words in a tongue to me unknown."[34]

Reflecting on the experience later, Salmon testified:

Sometime afterwards I asked my precious Lord what the difference was between the unction on my head and the remarkable power manifested at Beulah Park, Ohio. He graciously replied: "The power was your enduement; the latter I authenticated it." I said, "All right, Lord; I am satisfied." Yes, I am satisfied—not with myself—but with my exalted and glorified and condescending Master, the Lord Jesus Christ, and can exclaim with Thomas, "My Lord and My God." [35]

Mrs. MacArthur also spoke in tongues during this convention. She enthusiastically related her experience of tongues to the wife of Dayton Alliance pastor D. W. Kerr, saying, like Myland, that "this was like the 'residue of the oil' (Leviticus 14:18, 25) that flowed down upon the hem of Aaron's robe, and that God was doing this thing for all who would receive."[36] Mrs. Kerr's daughter, who was present, described what happened next:

"But," mother parried with her, "we have had the Holy Spirit, God has used us all these years, and I don't know why we should expect to receive anything more."

Just then someone came running into the hotel parlor, and said, "Mrs. Kerr, do you know your husband has gone into the prayer room? And God is filling him with the Holy Spirit!" . . . . So now she arose to the occasion, and ran over to the place of prayer, as she put it, "to see that my husband is not going to receive something he should not have."

Into the prayer room she went, with a somewhat belligerent spirit, but feeling the presence of God, she at least got down on her knees, and spreading her fingers over her face, she "watched and prayed." Rev. Whiteside . . . was in charge of the prayer room that night. Noticing my mother, he came to her and said, "Sister Kerr, this is holy ground. You are filled with fear. Get down to real prayer or get out."

In a moment, as she tells it, she felt as though she were handcuffed and held by a force stronger than herself, and she began to cry out to God to forgive her, and to seek Him with all her heart. By two o'clock in the morning, both father and mother side by side, came

through to a beautiful baptism of the Holy Spirit, speaking and singing in other languages, as the Spirit gave them utterance.[37]

The Kerrs would leave the Alliance several years later, eventually becoming leaders in the Assemblies of God, while Salmon, Whiteside, Cramer and the
MacArthurs stayed in the Alliance.

A. S. Copley, who had ministered in the Alliance mostly in Ohio for more
than a decade and who had at one time served alongside the famed Ohio Quar-
tet along with Kerr and Myland, was another who received his Pentecostal baptism just a month or two earlier earlier at Levi Lupton's camp meeting.[38] He
soon left the Alliance for the Pentecostal movement, relocating to Kansas City
to pastor a Pentecostal church, and then working as a printer with J. Roswell
Flower on his Pentecostal paper, *The Pentecost*.

Two women evangelists who also worked with the Kerrs in Dayton, Ella and
Cora Mae Rudy, may have received their Pentecost at this time or earlier. Unlike
the Kerrs and Copley, they remained in the Alliance. Ella became an Alliance missionary to South China in 1911 and preached in both Alliance and Pentecostal
circles. Cora Mae eventually married Walter Turnbull, who had been involved
with the Pentecostal revivals in the Alliance and Mukti Mission in India.[39]

The *C&MA Weekly* later reported on the Beulah Park Convention, saying it
was "God's new thing," with full restoration of gifts, tongues, healings, and exorcisms, and proclaiming with enthusiasm, "The hosts of darkness which gathered about the camp of the saints were repulsed and driven back, and the glory
of the Lord shown out of His temples. . . . It was a Pentecostal convention. . . . It
is the time of the latter rain."[40] Simpson summed up the summer conventions,
saying that while concerned about "cross currents of both mingled good and
evil," he affirmed that God had "averted the threatened strain in many cases
and given both liberty and unity in the Spirit."[41] He assured readers that "there
was a careful avoidance of unnecessary excitement an extravagance."[42]

Combined with the Pentecostal outpourings in Ohio in the spring, it would
appear that speaking in tongues became common and well accepted within the
Alliance. Nancy Hardesty related that her grandmother, a member of the Alliance church in Lima during this time, "surreptitiously confessed" of the C&MA
in northern Ohio, "In the early days, everyone spoke in tongues."[43]

SIMPSON'S EXPERIENCES OF THE SPIRIT

During this time when the Spirit was being poured out in special ways and
many Alliance leaders were speaking in tongues and experiencing other supernatural manifestations, in the midst of the cautions he was giving, Simpson
was also seeking the Lord for all that God wanted to give him. On August 9,
toward the end of the Old Orchard Convention, in spite of the "mixed spiritual
conditions" and "cross-currents of good and evil" of which Simpson spoke, he
continued to press on for all that God had for him, writing in his diary:

On this Friday afternoon I retired, as I have done for so many years, to the place in the woods were God healed me in August 1881 and renewed my covenant of healing again as I have done every year since.

At the same time I pressed upon Him a new claim for a Mighty Baptism of the Holy Ghost in His complete Pentecostal fullness embracing all the gifts and graces of the Spirit for my special need at this time and for the new conditions and needs of my life and work. He met me as I lay upon my face before Him with a distinct illumination, and then as the Presence began to fade and I cried out to Him to stay, He bade me believe and take it all by simple faith as I had taken my healing 26 years before. I did so, and was enabled definitely to believe and claim it all and rest in Him.[44]

He went on to describe a prophetic sense he received from God:

Then He gave me distinctly Is. 49:8, "In an acceptable time have I heard thee, etc.;" also Acts 1:5, "Ye shall be baptized with the Holy Ghost not many days hence." I knew that I had been baptized with the Holy Ghost before but I was made to understand that God had a deeper and fuller baptism for me and all that day and evening I was as sure of the Coming of His Spirit to me in great power as if I had already received the most wonderful manifestation of His presence.

I was accustomed at Old Orchard to spend hours every night waiting upon Him and praying about the meetings, and He often rested upon me in mighty realization and wondrously guided and blessed the work, but I felt there was MORE.[45]

"More" continued to come to Simpson as he wrote in his diary about "three remarkable seasons of prayer, fellowship, and blessing" on August 23, 27, and 30. The first occasion he received a new revelation of the power and glory of the name of Jesus:

While waiting on God on my lawn at night as I have often done this summer, I had a special season of mighty prayer, in which God revealed to me the NAME of JESUS in special power and enabled me to plead it within the veil for an hour or more until it seemed to break down every barrier and to command all that I could ask. He also let me plead at great length Jer. 33:3 in the fullness of its mean as God saw it, and to ask for "great and mighty things which I KNEW NOT." An utterly new revelation of His power and glory. He has let me know something of Himself, and for 26 years Christ has been in my bodily senses and members, but He has *much more*.[46]

Of the August 27 occasion he wrote:

> While waiting upon the Lord on my veranda, late at night, I ven-
> tured to ask Him for a special token of His giving me Matt. 6:17-18
> and soon after He did give it in the form I asked, viz., a very mighty
> and continued resting of the Spirit down upon my body until it was
> almost overpowering and continued during much of the night. I ac-
> cepted it and told Him I would take the promise in simple faith and
> not hesitate to believe that it was all for me. I had been timid at times
> about dictating to the Holy Spirit who is sovereign in the bestowal of
> His gifts, but now I fully take all that is promised in HIS NAME.[47]

His experience of the "resting of the Spirit down upon my body" sounds
like the description that charismatic leader Francis McNutt gives for falling under the power of the Spirit, namely, "resting in the Spirit."[48] It would seem that
Simpson himself, on this occasion, did experience a type of falling under the
power of the Spirit.

Just a few days later, in early September Simpson awoke from a deep sleep
and suddenly saw a vision of "a mighty being, like some glorious angel, who
seemed to be standing at a desk in the midst of intense business affairs and who
suddenly turned around for a moment and uttered one word, 'Listen.'" It was to
him a prophetic word for himself and the Alliance. He shared at the New York
convention in October his experience and how "it seemed as if that one word
gathered up all that God had to say and since that hour how constantly he has
been listening to the voice of the Master and unwilling to speak a single word to
God's people which he has not caught from the Heavenly Teacher, or take a step
without the confidence of divine direction and command."[49]

About the same time as this vision he recorded in his diary a vision of seeing himself seated with Christ in heavenlies: "One afternoon it seemed as if
heaven was opened and I was permitted to see myself seated with Christ in the
heavenlies within the veil and having the right to use His name in victorious
faith and prayer even as He."[50]

On September 12, the 42nd anniversary of his ordination, Simpson prayed
for God to renew his ordination afresh. He recorded in his diary that he experienced "a baptism of holy laughter for an hour or more."[51] This was a fulfillment
of the prophetic word he had received from God a month earlier that God had a
deeper and fuller baptism for him. At the same time, he was continuing to wait
upon the Lord for more of all that God wanted to manifest in his life. The next
day Simpson noted that a sense of warmth and "penetrating fire" filled his body
for about six hours like a fever, but he knew it was the Holy Spirit. He thanked
the Lord that He was ordaining him in a new way with a new power.[52]

Three weeks later Simpson wrote that 1907 was "a great missionary year"
with the outpouring of the Holy Spirit in tongues and other supernatural manifestations both in the homeland and foreign fields. He anticipated that these events
"may have in it the beginning of a great Pentecostal missionary movement which

will speedily carry to the unevangelized nations the Gospel in their own tongue by a direct supernatural movement of the Holy Ghost."[53]

By the end of the year Simpson's thinking about the purposes of tongues had broadened to recognize that God might bestow tongues for personal blessing and worship as well as for evangelism.[54] Alluding to "inexpressible longings" in Romans 8:26, he wrote that God sometimes has to give a new tongue to adequately express the burden of the Holy Spirit's prayer.[55] For another year or so he continued to believe that God would work through "missionary tongues," but eventually recognized, along with most Pentecostal leaders, that it was not apparently God's ordinary purpose to do so.

1. "Annual Report of the President and General Superintendent of the C&MA, 1906-1907," CMAW, June 15, 1907, 222.

2. A. B. Simpson, Editorial, CMAW, July 6, 1907, 313.

3. A. B. Simpson, Editorial, CMAW, July 13, 1907, 13.

4. John Salmon, "My Enduement, " CMAW, Oct. 26, 1907, 54-55.

5. A. B. Simpson, Editorial, CMAW, July 6, 1907, 313.

6. "Work at Home and Abroad," Word and Work, June 1907, 179.

7. W. T. MacArthur, "The Promise of the Father and Speaking in Tongues in Chicago," CMAW, July 27, 1907, 44.

8. "Work at Home and Abroad," Word and Work, June 1907, 177, 180; "Work at Home and Abroad," Word and Work, Aug. 1907, 210, 212.

9. Simpson's Diary, June 1907.

10. 1907-1908 C&MA Annual Report, 67.

11. Simpson's Diary, June 1907.

12. A. B. Simpson, "The Double Portion: Striking Lessons from the Life of Elisha, " LRE, Nov. 1909, 12-13.

13. A. B. Simpson, "Gifts and Grace," CMAW, June 29, 1907, 302.

14. Signs of the Times (New York, NY: Alliance Press Co., 1907).

15. A. B. Simpson, Editorial, CMAW, July 20, 1907, 25.

16. Richard M. Riss, A Survey of 20th-Century Revival Movements in North America Peabody, MA:Hendrickson, 1988), 77; Daniel E. Albrecht, "Carrie Judd Montgomery: Pioneering Contributor to ThreeReligious Movements," Pneuma: The Journal of the Society for Pentecostal Studies, Vol. 8:2 (Fall 1986), 117.

17. A. B. Simpson, Editorial, CMAW, July 20, 1907, 25.

18. A. B. Simpson, Editorial, CMAW, July 27, 1907, 37; "Convention of the Eastern District, Rocky Springs, Park, Lancaster, Pa.," CMAW, Sept. 7, 1907, 116.

19. "Convention of the Eastern District, Rocky Springs Park, Lancaster, Pa.," CMAW, Sept. 7, 1907, 116. Richards was the C&MA Superintendent for New York State and had given a message on the Holy Spirit.

20. Frodsham, With Signs Following, 49-50; Brumback, Suddenly. . . from Heaven, 89-91; see also Nienkirchen, 110. Mary Lewer recounted that at an unnamed Alliance camp meeting that summer in which on the last evening of the camp thirty people, including herself, were prostrated under the power of the Spirit and broke out speaking in tongues. Since 32 spoke in tongues on this occasion, this may have been the same incident. On the other hand, the Beulah Beach convention could have been the occasion since

scores of people fell under the power of the Spirit and spoke in tongues there. See Lewer, "50 Years of Pentecostal Blessing," 7.

21. Simpson, Editorial, CMAW, July 27, 1907, 37.

22. "Notes from the Home Field: New York State Convention," CMAW, Aug. 10, 1907, 70.

23. Brumback, Suddenly . . . from Heaven, 91; McGee, "Pentecostal Awakenings at Nyack," 26.

24. Bartleman, Azusa Street (1980), 107-108.

25. Simpson's Diary, July 28, 1907.

26. A. B. Simpson, Editorial, CMAW, Aug. 3, 1907, 49.

27. Mary G. Davies, "The Ninety-first Psalm," CMAW, Aug. 17, 1907, 78; see also "Notes from the Home Field: The Old Orchard Convention," CMAW, Aug. 31, 1907, 116.

28. "Old Orchard Convention," CMAW, Aug. 31, 1907, 106; "Notes from the Home Field: The Old Orchard Convention," CMAW, Aug. 31, 1907, 116.

29. Bartleman, Azusa Street (1980), 108-110.

30. Burton K. Janes, The Lady Who Came: The Biography of Alice Belle Garrigus, Newfoundland's First Pentecostal Pioneer (St. John's, Newfoundland, Canada: Good Tidings Press, 1982), Vol. 1, 100-107. See also Burton K. James, "Walking in the King's Highway: Alice Belle Garrigus and the Pentecostal Movement in Newfoundland," Assemblies of God Heritage, Summer 1986, 3.

31. "Notes from the Home Field: Beulah Park Convention," CMAW, Sept. 14, 1907, 128.

32. Frodsham, With Signs Following, 46.

33. Brumback, Suddenly . . . from Heaven, 79-80.

34. John Salmon, "My Enduement," CMAW, Oct. 26, 1907, 54-55.

35. Ibid.

36. Brumback, Suddenly . . . from Heaven, 79-80. A C&MA Convention was held at the MacArthur's church in Chicago August 29-September 1. (See A. B. Simpson, Editorial, CMAW, Aug. 17, 1907, 73). Undoubtedly, Mrs. MacArthur shared her experience, and it is likely that more people spoke in tongues at that time. Her husband probably also spoke in tongues at some point, for in future years he would cooperate with Pentecostals and speak in some of their meetings.

37. Brumback, Suddenly . . . from Heaven, 79-80.

38. W. E. Warner, "Copley, Albert Sidney," DPCM, 226. At the C&MA Convention in Bowling Green, Ohio, in March 1907, David Myland shared his testimony of his Pentecostal experience. Copley, who was leading singing at the meeting, was described as "filled with the glory light" on his face, so it is possible he may have received a foretaste of his Pentecostal baptism at this time. "Notes from the Home Field," CMAW, May 18, 1907, 236.

39. See Ella Rudy, "Perilous Days in China," LRE, Jan. 1927, 6; where Ella preached in the Stone Church. Walter Turnbull's first wife, who was in the India revival, died on the mission field.

40. "Notes from the Home Field: Beulah Park Convention," CMAW, Sept. 14, 1907, 128.

41. A. B. Simpson, Editorial, CMAW, Aug. 24, 1907, 85, 92.

42. Ibid., 85.

43. Hardesty, Faith Cure, 107.

44. Simpson's Diary, Aug. 9, 1907.

45. Ibid.

46. Simpson's Diary, Aug. 22, 1907. Here in his diary he gives a date of August 22, but later he says that August 23 was the first remarkable season of prayer. They appear to be the same occasion. He may

have confused the dates, or perhaps the season of prayer continued past midnight of the 22nd, thus encompassing both dates.

47. Simpson's Diary, Aug. 28, 1907.

48. Francis MacNutt, *Healing* (Notre Dame, IN: Ave Maria Press, 1974, 1999); 246; see also Francis MacNutt, *Overcome by the Spirit* (Grand Rapids, MI: Chosen Books, 1990).

49. "Notes from the New York Convention," CMAW, Oct. 12, 1907, 33.

50. Simpson's Diary, Sept. 3-5, 1907.

51. Simpson's Diary, Sept. 12.

52. Simpson's Diary, Sept. 13.

53. A. B. Simpson, "A Great Missionary Year," CMAW, Oct. 5, 1907, 4, 10.

54. A. B. Simpson, "The Holy Spirit and Missions," CMAW, Oct. 26, 1907, 57, 66.

55. A. B. Simpson, "Golden Censers," CMAW, Jan. 4, 1908, 233-234.

Autumn Drenchings — 1907

Pentecost Continues at Nyack

W. C. Stevens, principal of the Missionary Training Institute at Nyack, reported that when classes resumed for the fall semester many manifestations and tongues occurred. He spoke of them positively, assuring, "Never has the Faculty had to sit in council over the matter; the usual oversight has sufficed to temper and guide tractable hearts, so that regular routine has been undisturbed and spiritual freedom has had its unhindered operation. The result has been a deepened mutual confidence, love and respect in all our body."[1]

Pentecost in New Jersey and New York Conferences

At the New Jersey Prayer Conference on September 9 it was reported, "The blessed Holy Spirit had been graciously manifested in several branches. Some spoke of the purifying and empowering the Pentecostal filling had brought to them."[2] Field evangelist and superintendent W. F. Meminger reported that meetings in Rochester "were full of conviction, confession and victory," and rousing music punctuated by shouts.[3]

At the New York State Prayer Conference in Binghamton October 1-3, "Much prayer was made for discernment and wisdom in these trying days, believing and accepting the truth of the 'Latter Rain' outpouring of the Holy Spirit, but deploring the fleshly extravagances which are bringing reproach on the name of Jesus."[4] Minnie Draper, who had received the gift of tongues nearly a year earlier, was a featured speaker. She spoke on Mark 16:16-18, testifying that she had "seen with her own eyes and heard with her own ears the literal fulfillment, this summer, of every one of these signs."[5] Meminger reported of one particular service that the altar was filled three times for healing, and everyone who came for prayer was healed. People were praying fervently, shouting, and singing with "holy delight," and several spoke in tongues. A 73-year old man was converted and "shouted aloud with great joy." Meminger declared, "This service will never be forgotten. On and still on swept the power of God. . . . [This] was not merely a wave of passing emotion."[6]

Bartleman at Alliance-Related Ministries in Carolinas

In September Bartleman visited Rev. J. M. Pike in Columbia, South Carolina, preaching several times at his Oliver Gospel Mission.[7] Pike was a long-time friend of the Alliance, as the Alliance work in South Carolina was founded in conjunction with his Oliver Gospel Mission. He was editor of *The Way of Faith*, a holiness periodical that became Pentecostal. In his journal, Pike featured news about the Azusa Street revival and other outpourings of the Spirit, especially from Frank Bartleman.[8] Pike reported of Bartleman's visit, "His presence was a benediction to us and our home. . . . None who have intercourse with him can doubt his absolute abandonment to God, and the fullness of the Spirit within him. He lives, moves and has his being in the will of God. We commend him to all who are seeking God's highest and best."[9]

In spite of his Pentecostal inclinations, the Alliance continued friendship with Pike for several years, inviting him to speak at Alliance conventions. Bartleman also visited Dunn, North Carolina, where the Alliance had an active work open to Pentecostal manifestations. After G. B. Cashwell had received the baptism in the Spirit with tongues in December 1906 at Azusa Street, he returned to his home in North Carolina and spread the Pentecostal message, especially among holiness groups. Dunn then became known as "Azusa Street East."[10]

Respected Missionary Shares Her Testimony

In October Mary B. Mullen, a former C&MA missionary to Africa who founded a school for African-Americans in the Carolinas, testified in the *C&MA Weekly* of her experience of holy laughter, trembling, falling, and speaking in tongues. She had been seeking a "deeper death to self" and was waiting on the Lord for a deeper revelation of Himself. As she was lying on her bed one night, she recounted, "It seemed as if a strong hand passed like a fluttering dove from my head down, and was felt in every part of my being. This was followed by an unspeakable joy and holy laughter." For more than an hour the Spirit seemed to move over her body. She sat and tried to write, but her hand trembled, so she lay down again. Mullen described what happened next:

> The joy of the Lord flooded my entire being, until it seemed I could not stay in this world. Then the Spirit seemed to say, "Now I am ready for the tongue," and I said, "Lord I covet the best gifts, please answer my prayer for love, wisdom and power to intercede for others." This seemed to check the outpouring of the Spirit, and I said, "Lord, if you want my tongue to speak an unknown language, take it, take it, and the third 'take it' was spoken in another language, and for a few minutes I talked to Him in a tongue unknown."[11]

She began to travail in prayer for locations around the world, beginning with Jerusalem and the language seemed to change with each country.

Because of confusion about tongues, she felt she should keep her experience private, but sensed that the Spirit was leading her to tell Simpson. He thought positively enough about her experience to share it publicly in his periodical. He also entrusted her to help lead seeker meetings for the outpouring of the Holy Spirit, because she also cautioned believers to "seek Him, not gifts or even graces, but Him, Him alone."[12]

PENTECOST AT GOSPEL TABERNACLE NEW YORK CONVENTION

At the C&MA New York Convention in October, all night meetings were led by E. D. Whiteside and Mary Mullen. Conversions and other manifestations of the Holy Spirit took place during this time.[13] On October 11 John Salmon shared his experience of shaking and receiving tongues at the Beulah Beach Convention in August and his visions and experiencing of the Spirit's empowering at the Toronto convention two months earlier. He affirmed that tongues authenticated his earlier enduement.[14] The next day Simpson recounted his own experience of seeing a vivid vision of an angel in his mind a few weeks earlier.[15]

In early October Frank Bartleman visited Nyack, preaching three times. Then he attended the C&MA Convention at Simpson's Gospel Tabernacle in New York City. He spoke in the nearby Pentecostal Glad Tidings Hall, where "workers kept coming in from the Alliance convention, after the meeting closed there." The next night he preached again with many falling under the power of the Spirit. The evangelist in charge of the C&MA convention meetings came in after the Tabernacle service had ended.

The next evening Bartleman attended an all night meeting held at the Alliance convention. He recalled,

> A young girl came under the power and her spirit was caught up to the throne. She sang a melody, without words, that seemed to come from within the veil, it was so heavenly. It seemed to come from another world. I have never heard its equal before or since. A. B. Simpson was there himself that night and was tremendously impressed by it. He had been much opposed to the "Pentecostal" work. Doubtless God gave it as a witness for him. Several were slain under the power.[16]

According to Bartleman, several more people spoke in tongues that night. Bartleman's claim that Simpson was opposed to the Pentecostal work must have been based on hearsay from others. An examination of both Simpson's public and private words shows that he was not opposed to Pentecostal manifestations or the movement as a whole, only that he was opposed to the evidential tongues teaching and excesses.

Harold Moss, who later served as principal of Beulah Heights Bible and Missionary Training Center, also gave an amazing eyewitness report of the same incident:

People were slain everywhere under the mighty power of God, including the ministers on the platform. The case of one young lady, Miss Grace Hanmore (who since has become my wife), was quite remarkable. She was caught away in the Spirit and rendered wholly oblivious to anything natural. A sweet spirit of holy song came forth in notes like that of a nightingale and it filled the whole building. The power of God took hold of the physical and she was raised bodily from the floor three distinct times. she afterwards stated that she had a vision of a golden ladder and had started to climb it.[17]

This may be the same occasion as reported in the C&MA Weekly of the Thursday night meeting with Whiteside and Mullen presiding: "It seemed as if the very gates of heaven were opened for a little while to the ears of mortals."[18]

During the convention a former student of the Nyack Missionary Training Institute who was a Baptist pastor's wife from Newark, New Jersey, became ill. When Whiteside and another Alliance leader prayed for her, she was healed, falling unconscious under the power of the Spirit. Then she began praising God in tongues, identified as German, which she had never learned. A few nights later in one of the all-night meetings of the convention she gave a prophetic word under the anointing of the Holy Spirit. When she returned to her home in Newark, she met a German washwoman and understood her even though not knowing German. Simpson affirmed the genuineness of the incident, commenting, "We are glad in the midst of so many confused and mingled currents of truth and error to be able to give to those who are waiting upon the Lord to fully know His will in these strange times any light as clear and well-authenticated as this."[19]

Immediately following this remarkable convention Simpson published the record of Salmon's testimony,[20] and encouraged readers to expect the Latter Rain, a greater outpouring of the Holy Spirit than at Pentecost.[21] Writing that the Alliance should expect more manifestations of Holy Spirit power,[22] at the same time, he also cautioned Alliance branches not to open their doors to irresponsible leaders, perhaps referring to people like Bartleman or Lupton.[23]

It is noteworthy that Whiteside, one of the most notable and respected leaders in the C&MA, was actively involved in the Pentecostal outpourings. He was in charge of the prayer rooms in both the Beulah Beach and New York Conventions, encouraging supernatural manifestations of the Spirit and exhorting people not to be afraid of fanaticism.[24] People for whom he prayed received tongues under his ministry, such as the Kerrs and the Baptist pastor's wife. Further, he repeatedly invited Pentecostals like Frank Bartleman (and later in the 1910s and 1920s Hardy Mitchell, F. F. Bosworth, and Raymond Richey) to speak at his church. His active involvement with Pentecostal people and his open encouragement of Pentecostal experiences provide a great deal of circumstantial evidence that it is likely Whiteside himself had spoken in tongues.

Also at this convention Henry Kenning, instructor of music at the Missionary Training Institute and an associate and song leader of Simpson received his Pentecost, testifying that he did not seek gifts but God Himself:

> There came over me a sense of God's overshadowing presence, and I felt there was nothing to do but to bend lower and lower under the weight of His overshadowing. . . . by the blessed constraint of the Spirit, I was prostrated at His feet. . . . from the very inner springs pf my being there began to well up a wordless melody of praise and thanksgiving to God. After a little while, without any conscious effort of my mind or will there flowed sweetly and calmly utterances in another tongue, in perfect cadence and rhythm. My whole being was vibrant with rapturous response. . . I was satisfied, satisfied, satisfied, not with the new song in a new tongue, not with the ecstacy [sic], but with God, with Himself.[25]

An Alliance missionary to India confirmed that he was speaking in pure Tamil. Kenning eventually went on to pastor the charismatically-oriented Alliance church in Springfield, Massachusetts, vacated by T. A. Cullen when he was appointed to take over the work in Oregon.[26]

PENTECOST IN CENTRAL AND SOUTH CHINA ALLIANCE

Simultaneously with the Pentecostal outpouring in the C&MA in Eastern United States, the Spirit was also moving in the Alliance on the other side of the world. In July missionary Philip Hinkey reported on spiritual awakening in South China in which there were "marked manifestations of the Spirit's presence and power," much conviction of sin and weeping aloud, and "a veritable tempest of confession and supplication." He also recounted demonic attacks on three people.[27] Although speaking in tongues did not occur at this time, this awakening primed the pump for Pentecostal revival to break forth in just a few months.

In August some of the South China C&MA missionaries were vacationing at Macao, and there heard Mr. and Mrs. T. J. McIntosh from the revival in North Carolina share their Pentecostal experiences. As a result, Rosa Edwards and Frank Hamill received the baptism in the Spirit with tongues, as well as some of the Chinese Christians, and returned to the Alliance mission, enthusiastically sharing their experiences with the other missionaries.[28] This set the stage for the moving of the Spirit in the South and Central China Alliance missions through the fall of 1907. On September 21, missionary L. Bowring Quick fell under the power of the Spirit and began speaking in tongues, along with several more Chinese Christians in Wuchow. During the next several weeks many more manifestations occurred. Missionary Ethel Landis experienced holy laughter, falling under the power of the Spirit for two and a half hours. Several missionaries and Chinese had visions, including Rose Edwards, who shouted through the night when she saw Jesus with the scars in His hands and feet. Other missionaries, Mrs. Quick, Mr. and Mrs. Thomas Worsnip, and Robert Jaffray, all spoke in tongues. Hamill sang in tongues for a long time on various occasions with L. B. Quick interpreting.[29]

Missionary Philip Hinkey, who had been extremely ill and was planning to leave the field, received a miraculous healing and the baptism in the Spirit with tongues, along with the gift of interpretation. A healing anointing also flowed through him as he prayed for others. One of the other missionaries remarked, "Before, . . . everyone had to be quiet to let him sleep. Now he keeps everyone awake! He shouts and sings and praises God continually."[30] Missionary Mabel (Dimock) Oldfield, who was hesitant about the manifestations, recalled:

> Mr. Hinkey was really blessed, and though apparently from what I hear he went to greater excesses than some others, he has been honestly seeking after God; and when he realized he had in some respects been deceived, he acknowledged it. And God has led him, healed him, blessed him, and made him a blessing. All along he has declared that "tongues" are not the evidence of the baptism of the Spirit, and he has gradually come to see that manifestations are not necessary. He has truly been a great blessing here in Kweilin, and we do praise God for the influence of his life here.[31]

Ethel Landis also reported to *The Apostolic Faith* about this outpouring and Hinkey's healing, remarking, "A good many of the Chinese have received their Pentecost, and are singing, praying, and praising in new tongues."[32] Eventually, fourteen missionaries, probably including Landis and John Fee, and nearly sixty Chinese spoke in tongues.[33]

Simpson also reported this remarkable revival, yet writing that "there also appear to have been some strange manifestations. We must not accept everything that occurs even in a deeply spiritual meeting, without trying the spirits by the Word which the Holy Spirit Himself has given."[34] Quick and other missionaries encountered demonic manifestations, even in the middle of prayer meetings, and were actively involved in exorcism.[35] Robert Jaffray, C&MA Field Director in South China, noted in his 1907-1908 South China report that "quiet" manifestations of tongues occurred, proclaiming that this is the "latter rain." He testified of his experience of tongues in a later article in the *C&MA Weekly*:

> Personally I have never received such a spiritual uplift as when I received this blessed Baptism and spoke in tongues. The anointing then received "abideth" unto this day. These are a few of the many benefits that I would mention: (1) A deeper love for, and understanding of, the Word of God than ever before. (2) A knowledge of my utter strengthlessness and of the power of the Name and the Blood of Jesus in prayer as never before. (3) An unction in witnessing and preaching greater than ever before. (4) A control of the "unruly member"

in daily life since the Lord took peculiar charge of my tongue. (5) A clearer understanding of the mighty works of the Holy Spirit and of evil spirits, in these last days of the Present Age.[36]

MORE OUTPOURINGS IN INDIA

In July 1907, Amy Carmichael, famed Keswick Anglican missionary, had written in *The India Alliance* about revival in India. She cautioned critics of the revival not to "tell God how to work," or insist on a "quiet revival." She noted that Tamils are not naturally an emotional people, so that expressions of emotion, weeping, and prayer "like the roar of the sea," are God's doing. Though she was startled by the manifestations, Carmichael said she heard from the Lord, "Do nothing. . . . Hands off." She commented, "There is more to fear from stagnation than from excitement where the things of God are concerned."[37]

At the request of a reader, in August *The India Alliance* published an article by A. T. Pierson, giving an exposition of 1 Corinthians 14. The editor, Mrs. Walter Turnbull, presented a caveat to the article, saying that Pierson's viewpoint, while pointing out dangers in the exercise of the gift of tongues, was too negative. She encouraged the readers with a kind of "seek not, forbid not" response similar to those given by Simpson and other Alliance leaders: "Let us not despise the least of God's gifts. But let us seek God Himself, not manifestations or gifts, and He will divide severally to every man as He will. Not the gift but the Giver should occupy our attention."[38]

Pierson's negative evaluation did not prevent a Pentecostal outpouring at the fall Alliance Convention in Bombay. The revival was accompanied by visions, swaying, tongues, laughter, singing in tongues, interpretation, and falling under power of Spirit. The Holy Spirit was poured out on the C&MA mission station at Gujarat with mighty waves of prayer, sometimes lasting all night. Many missionaries and workers received tongues at that time.[39]

William Franklin had left Mukti in February 1907 to establish a new Alliance training school in Akola. He returned to the United States in August to care for his aging father, but the movement of the Spirit he had been a part of continued to snowball. In November the revival was extended at the Annual Convention at Akola, with people breaking out in holy laughter.[40] The revival continued in the Alliance work in Bombay, including manifestations as a vision of Jesus, swaying and shaking and holy laughter. Missionary Kate Knight's experience of holy laughter and singing in tongues was reported in the *C&MA Weekly*.[41]

PENTECOST CONTINUES AT FALL AND WINTER MEETINGS

Whatever reticence Simpson or some Alliance leaders may have had about Bartleman, other Alliance leaders welcomed his ministry. In late October, Whiteside invited Bartleman to preach again at his church in Pittsburgh, with the result that several people received the baptism of the Spirit with tongues. Bartleman then went to the C&MA church in Beaver Falls and preached twice at special request from Pastor F. H. Rossiter, his second visit there as well.

From there he went to Chicago, preaching four times at the C&MA church pastored by William T. MacArthur, whose wife had received tongues during the summer.[42]

This Pentecostal outpouring of the Spirit continued to swell throughout the Alliance during the fall and winter, especially in New York. In Syracuse State Superintendent E. J. Richards taught on the "Latter Rain baptism" and the gifts of the Spirit in 1 Corinthians 12-14, which "deepened the longing in our hearts for all the fullness of God."[43] In Corning Pentecostal revival broke out when local Baptist pastor Lewis J. Long invited evangelists from Canada who burst forth in tongues while praying. Alliance evangelist Wilbur F. Meminger, who attended the meetings, reported supportively, "The congregation was greatly moved, sinners cried out for mercy, believers were sanctified, much blessing came to many hearts."

However, some church officers and members forced the evangelists out. The evangelists continued meetings at the home of a prominent local businessman, and Pastor Long continued prayer meetings every night at the Baptist Church. The Alliance, which had a branch but not an official established church in Corning, held a convention during this time. Pentecost was poured out as some prayed in tongues. Meminger testified that when praying for the sick, "wave after wave of holy emotion rolled over us, and shouts of victory arose as the sick were healed." Some who were assisting in praying for the sick themselves fell under the power of the Spirit.[44] Meminger himself, as he finished preaching a message, suddenly saw a vision of the doom of the lost and cried out, "My God, an open Hell!," startling the congregation. He fell to the floor in tears and groanings for twenty minutes.[45]

Pastor Long, who participated in the Alliance convention, evidently soon left his Baptist church (or perhaps was asked to leave) and became the founding pastor of an official Alliance church in Corning, as Long testified, for "those in the city that were anxious to accept the full gospel."[46] The Alliance evidently became the center of Pentecostal activity, unpopular with many churches as he recounted later: "The persecution at this time from the various churches in the city, and from other sources, was something dreadful, because the enemy was bound not to have such a church here. But God was with us and we have prospered very much."[47] The church grew rapidly, and within three years Long was appointed pastor of Bethany Church in Toronto and Eastern Canadian District Superintendent, replacing John Salmon, who retired to California to be more involved with the Pentecostal movement.[48]

In another prayer council of the Alliance in December, skeptical Episcopalian rector C. E. Preston heard C&MA worker Miss Bird speak in tongues. Describing her as a "devout Presbyterian," his impression was that "if Miss Bird speaks in tongues, surely God must be in it." Eventually he accepted the validity of the movement, testifying, "Today I am free in this wonderful experience of this Latter Rain."[49] Sisters Ella and Emma Bird were official C&MA workers in Baltimore, Maryland. The Alliance work in Baltimore became Pentecostally-oriented, but remained with the Alliance until 1923.

"YEAR OF THE HOLY GHOST"—ALLIANCE RESPONSES

"It has been a year of the Holy Ghost."[50] So declared Simpson at the end of 1907, in spite of the controversies and excesses of the Pentecostal movement and losses of people. Throughout the year, Simpson and other Alliance leaders maintained the C&MA's openness to all that God has to give, but also cautioned against "the undue magnifying of any one gift or the seeking of any kind of power apart from Christ Himself." [51] He wrote that "some sincere and zealous friends are unduly sensitive about even the extremely gentle and moderate words of caution that have been expressed."[52] Simpson focused on the need for trying the spirits,[53] and warned about the dangers of counterfeit gifts and "a kind of 'abandonment' urged by certain spiritual leaders that would throw our whole being open to any powerful influence and hypnotic control which the enemy might wish to exercise."[54]

Simpson and other Alliance leaders warned against over-reaction toward excesses in the movement: "The way to meet and overcome fanaticism is not to oppose all unusual spiritual manifestations, but to accept that which is truly of the Lord and then from the standpoint of a friend gently and wisely correct the spirit of extravagance which you can never do if you take your place among the critics and the enemies of 'spiritual gifts.' The only way to meet error is to go all the way with truth."[55]

MacArthur warned against exalting the gift above the Giver and agonizing to receive a gift the Spirit may not have intended the person to receive. Such can result in counterfeit tongues inspired by evil spirits. Like Smale and Parham, he was concerned about strange animal-like behavior, stating that some have crowed like a rooster and manifested other animal sounds.[56] MacArthur also counseled to seek God, not manifestations, but to wait expectantly upon Him without fear of fanaticism. He recommended "seeking the fullness of God in a way that is acceptable to Him."[57]

Simpson associate F. E. Marsh discussed the blessings, regulations and limitations of tongues according to 1 Corinthians 12-14. He affirmed, "There have been counterfeits of this manifestation, but the counterfeit only proves the genuine coin." He mentioned, "We have seen some apeing the gift of tongues for self-glorification," and cited a woman claiming to speak Arabic who was exposed by one who really knew the language. Yet he also strongly supported the positive manifestations of tongues in the Alliance meetings.[58]

While warning of counterfeits and lack of discernment, Alliance leaders affirmed the genuineness of the movement in the Alliance as a whole: "There is no doubt but that God graciously inaugurated this 'revival.'"[59] Another Alliance leader verified to Simpson during the year, "It is the river of God, but not yet as clear as crystal."[60] Significantly, Pentecostal historian Edith Blumhofer remarked of this time, "Alliance spokespersons had an almost uncanny way of discerning potential difficulties that enthusiastic Apostolic Faith adherents seemed prone to overlook. Within several years, some Pentecostals would echo Alliance appeals for prudence and balance. For the moment, however, the cautions seemed to go largely unheeded."[61]

1. A. B. Simpson, *11th Annual Report of the Christian and Missionary Alliance* (May 27, 1908), 82.

2. "Prayer Conference in New Jersey," CMAW, Oct. 12, 1907, 32.

3. W. F. Meminger, "Notes from the Home Field: Touring New York State," CMAW, Nov. 30, 1907, 153.

4. "New York State Prayer Conference," CMAW, Nov. 16, 1907, 117.

5. Ibid., 118.

6. Wilbur F. Meminger, "Touring New York—Binghamton, N.Y.," CMAW, Dec. 21, 1907, 204.

7. Bartleman, *Azusa Street* (1980), 110-111.

8. C. M. Robeck, Jr., "Pike, John Martin," NIDPCM, 988.

9. Bartleman, *Azusa Street* (1980), 111. The Oliver Gospel Mission eventually broke up over the Pentecostal movement and perceived excesses. See Steve Thompson and Adam Gordon, *A 20th Century Apostle: The Life of Alfred Garr* (Wilkesboro, NC: Morningstar Publications, 2003), 104-105.

10. Synan, *The Holiness-Pentecostal Tradition*, 114.

11. Mary B. Mullen, "A New Experience," CMAW, Oct. 5, 1907, 17. Her testimony was published as a tract, and advertised in Pentecostal publications. See "Pentecostal Tracts," *The Pentecost*, Sept.-Oct. 1910, 16.

12. Mary Mullen, "Some Danger Lines," CMAW, Nov. 2, 1907, 75.

13. A .B. Simpson, Editorial, CMAW, Oct. 19, 1907, 37.

14. "Notes from the New York Convention," CMAW, Oct. 19, 1907, 48; John Salmon, "My Enduement," CMAW, Oct. 26, 1907, 54-55.

15. "Notes from the New York Convention," CMAW, Oct. 12, 1907, 33.

16. Bartleman, *Azusa Street* (1980), 111-112.

17. Harvey Cox, *Fire from Heaven* (Reading, MA: Addison-Wesley Publishing Co., 1995), 68; Nienkirchen, 84-85.

18. "Notes from the New York Convention," CMAW, Oct. 19, 1907, 48.

19. "A Remarkable Testimony," CMAW, Nov. 9, 1907, 98; see also Frodsham, *With Signs Following*, 240; Barratt, *The Work of T. B. Barratt* (New York and London: Garland Publishing, 1985), 170. This woman was probably Clair Switzer, a member of the "Nyack Gleanings" editorial board and the wife of Rev. S. H. Switzer, Baptist pastor in Newark suburb of Harrison who was also affiliated with the C&MA.

20. John Salmon, "My Enduement," CMAW, Oct. 26, 1907, 54-55.

21. A. B. Simpson, "What Is Meant by the Latter Rain?," CMAW, Oct. 19, 1907, 38.

22. A. B. Simpson, "Our Wonder-working God," CMAW, Oct. 19, 1907, 42.

23. A. B. Simpson, Editorial, CMAW, Oct. 19, 1907, 37.

24. Brumback, *Suddenly . . . from Heaven*, 79-80.

25. For Kenning's lengthy testimony, see Henry Kenning, "After He Has Come . . . Ye Shall Be Witnesses, "*Word and Work*, Jan. 1910, 10-13.

26. A. B. Simpson, Editorial, CMAW, Jan. 23, 1909, 280.

27. Philip Hinkey, "Spiritual Awakening in South China," CMAW, July 6, 1907, 318.

28. D. H. Bays and T. M. Johnson, "China," NIDPCM, 59, 60.

29. Ethel F. Landis, "Pentecost in South China," *The Bridegroom's Messenger*, Mar. 1908, 2.

30. Mabel Dimock Oldfield, *With You Alway, the Life of a South China Missionary* (Harrisburg, PA: Christian Publications, 1958), 88.

31. Ibid., 89.

32. "Chinese Filled with the Holy Spirit," *The Apostolic Faith*, Vol. II, No. 12, May 1908, 2.

33. T. J. McIntosh, "Macao, China," *Apostolic Faith* (Houston), Oct. 1908, 4. Landis continued Pentecostal connections and involvement and Fee later pastored the charismatic Alliance church in Portland, Oregon.

34. Mr. & Mrs. Joseph Cunningham, "A Loving Tribute," CMAW, Dec. 21, 1907, 193. A. B. Simpson, Editorial, CMAW, Dec. 21, 1907, 198.

35. Transcript of audiotaped interview with Rev. L. B. Quick, Apr. 18, 1962. C&MA Archives.

36. Robert Jaffray, "Speaking in Tongues—Some Words of Kindly Counsel," *Alliance Weekly*, Mar. 13, 1909.

37. Amy Wilson-Carmichael, "Need We Tell God How to Work," *The India Alliance*, July 1907, 7-9.

38. Editorial, *The India Alliance*, Aug. 1907, 19; Arthur T. Pierson, "Speaking with Tongues," *The India Alliance*, Aug. 1907, 19-21.

39. Frodsham, *With Signs Following*, 111-113.

40. "The Annual Convention," *The India Alliance*, Dec. 1907, 68.

41. Kate Knight, "For His Glory," CMAW, Jan 25, 1908, 274.

42. Bartleman, *Azusa Street* (1980), 112-113.

43. "Notes from the Home Field," CMAW, Dec. 21, 1907, 203.

44. Wilbur F. Meminger, "Touring New York," CMAW, Dec. 7, 1907, 168.

45. Mrs. Wilbur F. Meminger, *The Little Man from Chicago: The Life Story of Wilbur F. Meminger* (New York, NY: Alliance Press Company, 1910), 154-155.

46. Meminger, "Touring New York," 168; L. J. Long, "Corning, N. Y.," CMAW, June 12, 1909, 185. See also C&MA 1907-1908 Annual Report, 61.

47. Long, "Corning, N. Y.," 185.

48. Reynolds, *Footprints*, 296.

49. C. E. Preston, "Some Manifestations of the Spirit Thirty-five Years Ago," LRE, Feb. 1909, 23.

50. A. B. Simpson, "Thanksgiving Thoughts," CMAW, Nov. 30, 1907, 140.

51. A. B. Simpson, Editorial, CMAW, Mar. 2, 1907, 97.

52. Ibid.

53. A. B. Simpson, Editorial, CMAW, Feb. 2, 1907, 99.

54. A. B. Simpson, Editorial, CMAW, Mar. 16, 1907, 121.

55. A. B. Simpson, Editorial, CMAW, May 4, 1907, 205; William T. MacArthur, "The Promise of the Father and Speaking with Tongues in Chicago," CMAW, Feb. 16, 1907, 76.

56. William T. MacArthur, "The Promise of the Father and Speaking with Tongues in Chicago," CMAW, Feb. 9, 1907, 64.

57. MacArthur, "The Promise of the Father and Speaking with Tongues in Chicago," CMAW, Feb. 16, 1907, 76.

58. F. E. Marsh, "The Gift of Tongues," *Living Truths*, May 1907, 259-264.

59. May Mabette Anderson, "The 'Latter Rain,' and Its Counterfeit, Part IV" *Living Truths*, Sept. 1907, 535.

60. Jones, *The Lady Who Came*, 103.

61. Edith L. Blumhofer, *The Assemblies of God: A Chapter in the Story of American Pentecostalism, Volume 1 – To 1941* (Springfield, MO: Gospel Publishing House, 1989), 185.

CHARISMATIC WAVES ROLL ON INTO 1908

In 1908 and following, charismatic manifestations continued in C&MA, but many divisions over the evidence doctrine and other practices continued to plague the Alliance, with the result that many people left C&MA churches to be more Pentecostal, and some C&MA churches left C&MA to become Pentecostal. At the same time, others withdrew from the Alliance because they were too accepting of Pentecostal phenomena.

STIRRINGS IN ST. LOUIS

At the St. Louis Alliance convention January 2nd, J. T. Boddy spoke on the Latter Rain of the Spirit." Boddy had fallen under the power of the Spirit and received the baptism in the Spirit with tongues at the Alliance church in Homestead, Pennsylvania a year earlier. It was reported by John Gormer, "Some who were skeptical were convinced that God was in the present movement, and that there are at least some genuine cases of the gift of tongues."[1]

REVIVALS IN THE NORTHEAST

The reverberations continued into the New Year as revivals were reported in Alliance works in Monongahela, Pennsylvania, with shouting and praises and in Schenectady, New York, with shouting and laughing.[2] The Eastern District Prayer Conference was called a "full gospel" meeting, punctuated with shouts and tears. Several Alliance leaders—Senft, George W. Davis and Whiteside—all spoke on Latter Rain themes with signs following. John Coxe from Butler shared the blessings of his Pentecostal baptism. Herbert Dyke from New Castle taught that "the baptism of the Spirit does not discount previous experiences."[3] F. H. Senft gave a positive report of many speaking in tongues at the Alliance church in New Castle, Pennsylvania.[4]

At the New Jersey Prayer Conference in Jersey City in March, "several received the 'latter rain filling' with the gift of tongues."[5] As a result of this outpouring in this New Jersey Alliance convention, as well as the previous

September, most of the New Jersey branches of the C&MA thus became charismatically-oriented. In the Jersey City branch, a teenage girl by the name of Lillian Merian experienced the baptism in the Spirit with tongues, eventually becoming a missionary to South Africa.[6]

PENTECOST IN WAYNESBORO, PENNSYLVANIA

In January 1908, young David McDowell, fresh out of the Nyack Missionary Training Institute with his new experience in the Spirit, moved to Waynesboro to pastor the Alliance church. He recalled, "I found a small company of sincere believers. Some had come in contact with Pentecost, and many were hungry for God." He began cottage prayer meetings where several people received healings and the baptism in the Spirit with tongues.

In one incident, a father had been severely ill with one of the worst cases of asthma McDowell had ever seen and his four-year son was disabled and had never been able to walk. After being anointed with oil and prayed over by McDowell and the elders, the father abandoned his medicines and actually became worse, in danger of death. McDowell hurried to house where he laid hands on him and "began a powerful rebuke in tongues as the Spirit moved me." Instantly, the man was healed and began running around the house breathing freely as he raised his hands and praised God and sang. All of a sudden the little boy who had never walked let out a shout and began running around with his father. Twenty years later McDowell met the son, now grown and still testifying of his healing.[7]

On May 5, McDowell was traveling by train from Harrisburg to New York City, where he had been invited to speak at a new Pentecostal mission, which became the Glad Tidings Tabernacle. He was led by the Spirit to talk with a man on the train, noting that he was reading a Jewish newspaper. As they were conversing, all of a sudden felt himself led to raise his arms and speak in tongues for several minutes. The man was shocked and surprised, asking, "Why didn't you tell me you were a Hebrew?" McDowell replied that he was not. The man responded, "You are not a Hebrew. Where did you get this language? You speak to me in purest Hebrew. You tell me more about my people than I know. We don't speak that language anymore; we speak Yiddish." He was puzzled how McDowell could know Hebrew. McDowell told him of how he came to Jesus and how was he baptized in the Spirit, reading to him Acts 1 and 2. The train reached the station and they had to part, but the man left with tears in his eyes as McDowell told him to buy a New Testament and seek his Messiah.[8]

PENTECOST IN THE C&MA IN SCOTLAND

In January 1908 Alliance-affiliated believers in Scotland were waiting on God for revival.[9] Alliance representative S. A. Renicks had testified of the Latter Rain outpourings in the C&MA work in America. The Pentecostal outpouring broke forth within two months. Renicks recounted that "the power fell" and about forty people were speaking in tongues. He made a point of the fact that the first speaking in tongues in Scotland had occurred through the C&MA work. The leader, Mr. Bell, who was described as an "out and out Alliance man," also received the gift of tongues.[10]

PENTECOST IN THE C&MA CONVENTIONS IN THE SOUTH

In March W. F. Meminger reported that the Bowling Green convention was attended by the "Latter Rain" and a "Pentecostal outpouring . . . with signs following." In April the C&MA Missionary Conference in Nashville was held "under the auspices of the Pentecostal Mission."[11] At this point, cooperation existed between the Alliance and Pentecostals.

Meminger also recounted of the Atlanta convention February 7-16, "a cloud burst of glory. . . . The fire came down—who will describe the scenes . . . a great volume of prayer." One of the featured speakers, along with Simpson and Wilson, was J. M. Pike from Columbia, South Carolina, who continued to report Pentecostal happenings in his *Way of Faith* periodical.[12] However, this revival did not go smoothly because of the more radical Pentecostal elements. It was reported in September that the C&MA work in Atlanta had been "broken up over new religious movements," but the Alliance convention was "united and enthusiastic."[13]

At the Fall convention (October 10-26) in Atlanta, along with Simpson and Wilson, one of the featured speakers was again J. M. Pike.[14] In spite of the conflicts with Pentecostal excesses, District Superintendent R. A. Forrest felt comfortable in inviting Pike to speak and Simpson and Wilson evidently had no problem sharing the platform and speaking ministry with Pike.

The Alliance meetings in Dunn, North Carolina, were held in the Free Will Baptist Church, which became a center for the Pentecostal movement in the area. H. H. Goff, pastor of the Free Will Baptist Church, received the baptism in the Spirit with tongues early in 1907.[15] It is evident that the Alliance remained open to Pentecostal manifestations and maintained cordial relationships with Pentecostals by continuing to meet at this church.

REVIVAL AT C&MA CHURCHES IN THE NORTHWEST

On Christmas Day, 1906, Florence Crawford and seven others from Azusa Street had begun a series of meetings in Portland, Oregon, establishing a Pentecostal work there and going on to Seattle, Washington.[16] The Alliance was impacted by the movement as well. Pastor C. D. Sawtelle, Superintendent of the Northwest District, was receptive to the Pentecostal movement and may have even spoken in tongues himself, but he had mixed reactions to some of the Pentecostal activities, writing in the 1907-1908 Annual Report of the C&MA:

> It has been a year of peculiar trials. . . . The new movement struck us
> a few months ago with its evils and with its greater blessings. It came
> with such force and authority as to refuse absolutely to be ignored.
> We knew not what to do with it, and knew less what it would do with

us. We nestled up a little closer to Jesus. . . . He has made us in some little measure a blessing to the movement and has made it a great blessing to us.[17]

Sawtelle was not dismayed by the Pentecostal movement, however, for in March 1908, he asked Frank Bartleman to speak at the C&MA church in Portland. On his way north from Los Angeles, Bartleman visited Carrie Judd Montgomery's Healing Home, in Beulah, near Oakland. When he arrived in Portland, he preached there 24 times. According to Bartleman's account, "God blessed preciously, but we did not break through fully. There was too much opposition and conservatism. Altogether however, much good was accomplished, and the saints especially were greatly benefited and blessed."[18] He went on to preach ten times at the C&MA in Tacoma, Washington, with several receiving the baptism in the Spirit with tongues.[19]

PENTECOST AGAIN IN SOUTH CHINA

In South China revival broke out again in March. The regular order of a meeting was set aside to seek the Lord. No leaders were appointed, but the Holy Spirit was in charge. The Spirit fell in a quiet Saturday night meeting, and many began to speak in tongues spontaneously without seeking. They exercised a spirit of discernment, and determined that this was not a "temporary joyous ecstasy." They testified that speaking in tongues was just the beginning of God's work; there is much more and greater to come. One confessed to stealing, was baptized in the Spirit with tongues, and returned the money. A ten-year-old blind girl saw a vision of Jesus. This was described as a "genuine Holy Ghost revival."[20]

REVIVAL CONTINUES IN OHIO

C. A. McKinney left the C&MA early in 1908 to pursue involvement in the Pentecostal movement in nearby Alliance, Ohio, and start a Pentecostal church in Akron. It would appear that McKinney was one of the first pastors to leave the Alliance over the Pentecostal controversy.[21] S. M. Gerow, McKinney's young assistant pastor from Nyack who replaced McKinney, reported in April regarding the C&MA convention in Akron, "We praise Him for a clearer vision and conception of a Pentecostal plain to which His church is being lifted. . . . Praise God for the 'Latter Rain' Pentecost with signs and wonders following."[22]

McKinney's departure did not dampen the enthusiasm and expectation of the Spirit's moving in Alliance circles. The Alliance works in Toledo, Bowling Green, and Findlay, and other locations had all experienced Pentecostal outpourings of the Spirit since the Cleveland convention the prior March, and many people had been converted. At the convention of Gospel Mission of the Alliance in Findlay in February, under the teaching of Kerr of Dayton, Cramer of Cleveland, Chandler of Wheaton, Wurmser in Norwalk, and Hosler of Bowling Green, people were saved and healed, and "more received the baptism of the Holy Spirit in latter rain manifestation" (meaning tongues).[23] The Findlay church eventually invited D. W. Kerr to pastor the church.

Leaders had prayed that the "Spirit of Pentecost" be poured out again at the 1908 Cleveland convention as at the convention, and Kerr spoke on the latter rain and the Pentecostal outpouring, sharing from his own experience at Beulah Beach. Cramer reported that "they were not disappointed" and a "cloudburst of holy joy" broke out at the convention, resulting in generous giving and missionary pledges.[24] Reporting later in the month on the four C&MA conventions in Ohio, L. A. Harriman recounted that one person was prostrated by the power of God and many were healed and received the Holy Spirit.[25] W. F. Meminger reported that at the C&MA convention in Cincinnati some spoke and sang in tongues. "All were deepened in God. Everything was done decently and in order."[26]

PENTECOST IN JERUSALEM

Lucy Leatherman of the American Consulate in Jerusalem had been called to the mission field to Arabs in Jerusalem in 1898 while as student at Simpson's Missionary Training Institute at Nyack. She had visited the Azusa Street mission in 1906 and was baptized in the Spirit with tongues, testifying of her experience everywhere she went on her journey back to Jerusalem.[27] She reported in 1908 that Elizabeth Brown, an Alliance missionary in Jerusalem, had received tongues and other manifestations: "She had the real old-fashioned manifestations like many had at Azusa Street. . . . She felt waves of fire passing through her head and face and then began to speak in tongues. She sings the heavenly chant. It is precious to hear her."[28]

POSITIVE REPORTS OF EUROPEAN PENTECOSTALISM

Simpson published in the C&MA Weekly affirming reports of Pentecostal outpourings in Europe. An article by Baron Uxkull, a Pentecostal speaker at Alliance conventions, reported that believers in Russia "are seeking holiness in the daily life. They don't seek special supernatural gifts; they receive them with awe if God gives them."[29] Simpson again published T. B. Barratt's testimony of tongues, along with the resulting Scandinavian Pentecostal revival in Sweden, Norway, and Northern Europe. Manifestations included demons being cast out, quaking and trembling, and falling under the power of the Spirit. European Pentecostal leaders Alexander Boddy and Jonathan Paul, friends of Simpson, were mentioned. Another visitor to the Alliance home, Andrew Johnson, took the Pentecostal revival to his home country of Sweden.[30]

PENTECOST CONTINUES IN INDIA

Barratt was traveling the world, sharing his experience of the baptism in the Spirit and his subsequent gift of tongues. He ministered in India from April to August and was welcomed at the Alliance Missionary Home in Bombay, where he shared his testimony with the Alliance missionaries. He went on to Ramabai's Mukti Mission and was well received there as well.[31]

In May A. C. Snead reported tongues and interpretation in India: "We are seeing the mighty workings of the Spirit here, in the gracious outpouring of the 'Latter Rain,' and are being so burdened for souls that the other things seem of small moment. Nearly all the missionaries at Dholka have received the baptism of the Spirit, new tongues being given." Many native Christians were also baptized in the Spirit, speaking in tongues, with some interpreting.[32] Simultaneous audible prayer, visions, revelations, healing, speaking and singing in tongues, interpretation, discernment, and prophecy all continued to occur in the Alliance mission stations and ministries.

Satan tried to bring wildfire, fanaticism, and counterfeits, Walter Turnbull reported, but they were rebuked.[33] "They learned to be careful to try the spirits, lying signs and wonders," then demons were cast out, healings were manifested, and many were speaking in tongues while others interpreted.[34]

The India Alliance also reported on the revival at Dholka, which included visions and revelations, speaking and singing in tongues, interpretation of tongues, discernment of spirits, prophecy and exhortation, even occurring among a few of the children. There were a few instances of counterfeits, or people getting carried away with excitement or a "spirit of self-importance," but overall the revival resulted in a general atmosphere of peace and love and unity.[35]

Another report in *The India Alliance* described boys in the Akola orphanage prostrated under the power of the Spirit, speaking in tongues, interpreting, and seeing visions. One boy woke up one night with a message in tongues, preaching repentance for two hours in a language he did not know to an Islamic boy who understood him perfectly. Some boys had visions of the Cross and of Christ. The editorial acknowledged that some manifestations are of the flesh and some are of the Enemy, but can be expected in any revival. The editor cautioned not to be "hasty and unwise" in criticizing the whole "tongues movement." On the contrary, many have genuinely grown deeper in their faith and Christian love.

A ten year-old boy gave a message in tongues to another boy who wanted to be baptized. A third boy interpreted, saying, "The Spirit says you are not to be baptized today." Later, it was revealed that the boy's motive for being baptized was that he believed it would result in him getting the gift of tongues.[36] Missionary Frances Bannister reported about a boy falling under the power of the Spirit, who was speechless and could not talk, but spoke in tongues.[37]

Christian Schoonmaker had a vision of Christ, and exercised a ministry of healing and discernment of spirits. In Khassia Hills a woman with a horrid skin disease had been cast out of her village and left to die. While hearing the preaching of the gospel, she exclaimed, "God has given me medicine!" As she rubbed her body with her hands, she shouted, "I am well." It was a power encounter that left the unbelievers in awe of God's power.[38]

PENTECOST FOR GEORGE AND CARRIE JUDD MONTGOMERY

In 1907 George Montgomery had visited the Pentecostal revival in Los Angeles, returning to Carrie with glowing reports. Nevertheless, Carrie remained more cautious.[39] Carrie had been desiring more of God and all He had to give, but was unsure about the Pentecostal movement because of excesses and abuses she had seen:

> I watched the so-called Pentecostal work carefully and prayerfully. There was much that did not appeal to me. People who claimed to have received the baptism seemed to get in the way of the Spirit. Beginning in the Spirit, they often seemed to fail to walk in the Spirit. They became lifted up, or let self get the ascendancy. Many of the manifestations did not seem at all like the work of the calm, majestic Spirit of God. In many meetings there was much confusion, and God tells us He is not the author of confusion, but of peace. (1 Cor. 14:33, 40). The people often failed to walk in Scriptural lines in regard to unknown tongues, using them in the general assembly, "the whole church," where there was no interpreter, contrary to the Word of God.[40]

Further, she had an experience with the Holy Spirit when "a power to testify came into my soul, and the Word of God was wonderfully opened to me" that she had always considered her baptism in the Spirit

> until a few months ago, when I began to watch what God was doing in pouring out His Pentecostal fulness upon some of His little ones. At first I was perplexed. I knew my experience, above referred to, was real and lasting in its effects. How could I cast it away? Then I came to understand that I was not to depreciate His precious work in the past, but to follow on to receive the fulness of the same Spirit. Before Pentecost, Jesus "breathed" on His disciples and said unto them "Receive ye the Holy Ghost" (John 20:22). I believe they then received a foretaste, or earnest, of what they afterwards received in fulness, at Pentecost.[41]

Several of her C&MA missionary friends had also written her from various mission fields about the blessedness of their experiences of speaking in tongues.[42] It was then that she began to seek the Lord for what more He might have for her as she observed some godly friends who had received the experience:

> One lady I had known for years as a sanctified and anointed teacher of God's Word. She was not satisfied, and pressed on by faith into the fulness of the Holy Ghost. Her experience was most satisfactory, such appreciation of the blood, such power to witness, increased intercessory prayer, such a baptism of divine love. She spoke with tongues but kept the gift in its proper place. Other dear friends, whose lives I had fully known, pressed on by faith and received their baptism.

While speaking at the Alliance convention in Chicago in the summer of 1908, Carrie met together in the home of one of those old friends to pray and wait on the Lord. She described how she received her Pentecostal baptism at that time:

On Monday, June 29, less than a week from the time I first took my stand by faith, the mighty outpouring came upon me. I had said, "I am all under the blood and under the oil." I then began singing a little song. "He gives me joy instead of sorrow," etc. To my surprise, some of the words would stick in my throat, as though the muscles tightened and would not let me utter them. I tried several times with the same result. My friend remarked that she thought that the Lord was taking away my English tongue, because He wanted me to speak in some other language. I replied, "Well, He says in Mark 16:17, 'They shall speak with new tongues,' so I take that, too, by faith." In a few moments I uttered a few scattered words in an unknown tongue and then burst into a language that came pouring out in great: fluency and clearness. The words to come from an irresistible volume of power within, which seemed to possess my whole being, spirit, soul and body. For nearly two hours I spoke and sang in unknown tongues (there seemed three or four distinct languages). Some of the tunes were beautiful, and most Oriental. A "weight of glory" rested upon my head, which I could distinctly feel, and even see in the Spirit. I was filled with joy and praise to God with an inward depth of satisfaction in Him which cannot be described. To be thus controlled by the Spirit of God and to feel that He was speaking "heavenly mysteries" through me was most delightful. The rivers of living water flowed through me and divine ecstasy filled my soul. I felt that I drank and used up the life and power as fast as it was poured in. I became weak physically under the greatness of the heavenly vision, but my friend asked the Lord to strengthen me, which He did so sweetly, letting His rest and healing life possess my whole frame. Passages from the Word of God came to me with precious new meanings. Not long after this I had a vision of the work of His Cross as never before.

The blessing and power abides and He prays and praises through me in tongues quite frequently. When His power is heavy upon me, nothing seems to give vent and expression to His fulness like speaking or singing in an unknown tongue.

Several times the Holy Spirit spoke through her in tongues understood by missionaries as Indian and Chinese dialects. Harriette Shimer, a Quaker missionary to China who was also speaking at the convention, heard her praying and singing in Chinese throughout the week. She did not know much about the

Pentecostal movement and was really somewhat opposed to it. Her experience with Carrie changed her mind. On one occasion, a couple from China and their two sons, heard her speak in Chinese, and readily understood what was said. Carrie further testified, "At other times, in my private devotions, or with some friend of the same mind, I have been given sweet, ecstatic utterances which seemed indeed like the tongues of angels."[43]

Shortly after Carrie's experience she returned to the West Coast and her husband also received the baptism in the Spirit with tongues. They "both realized a greater power for service, and increased fellowship in prayer and praise." Interestingly, Carrie, who was more cautious, received tongues first, while George, who was more open, received tongues later. George and Carrie remained in the C&MA for several more years, and frequently shared their testimony of their "fuller" baptism in the Spirit in C&MA circles. The following summer, William T. MacArthur invited Carrie to speak at the Chicago C&MA convention. She commented that MacArthur "is in sympathy with the deepest teaching, when on Scriptural lines, so he gladly welcomed our own testimony as to our Pentecostal baptism."[44] Carrie shared that more than a year after her Pentecostal experience there was a great increase in many areas of her spiritual life: holy joy, holy stillness, love, power to witness, teachableness, love for the Word of God, spirit of praise, her sense of "nothingness," health, revelation of Christ and His finished work, and communion with God.[45]

Carrie was invited by Simpson to preach and share her testimony of her Pentecostal experience even in 1918, the year before his death.[46] Simpson and the C&MA leaders always appreciated their ministry, and George continued to be reelected yearly as an honorary Vice President of the C&MA (even after they joined the Assemblies of God in 1917) up until his death in 1930.

SUMMER MEETINGS CONTINUE REVIVAL

In June Meminger reported at the C&MA Convention in Flushing, Ohio, "The waves of Holy Emotion rolled higher and higher."[47] In July Bartleman was invited back again for the third time to Whiteside's church in Pittsburgh, preaching there in four meetings, then went on to preach at Salmon's church in Toronto.[48] In July the Southeastern District Prayer Conference featured teaching from A. J. Ramsey on the "latter rain."[49]

Simpson advised for the upcoming Old Orchard Convention to maintain order and to try the spirits of "wild self-asserting and unsafe voices." But he also encouraged receptivity to the genuine moving of the Spirit: "At the same time there is ample room for the fullest and freest testimony and all the messages which the Spirit has for the churches."[50]

Salmon reported on the Beulah Park Convention in August: "There was perfect freedom for each speaker to give forth all that was in his heart regarding the Latter Rain, or Pentecostal movement now spreading over the earth. While there was divergency of views in this matter, yet there was no confusion and the meetings closed daily with altar services where numbers of people were seeking an enduement of power for service in the Lord's vineyard."[51] W. A. Cramer further reported of the convention, "The clear scriptural presentation of Pentecostal or 'Latter Rain' truth, dispelled the mists and fogs of human reasonings, leaving the spiritual atmosphere of the convention permeated with the invigorating ozone of the full Gospel."[52]

Also in August Bartleman spoke eight times at the Falcon Camp Meeting in North Carolina, which had been C&MA-related, but was rapidly becoming Pentecostal. Bartleman recounted, "We had some great altar services and many souls were wonderfully helped. Sinners were saved, and saints filled with the Holy Ghost. Some were healed."[53] The Falcon camp meeting had been founded in 1900 by the C&MA, but became a bastion for the burgeoning Pentecostal movement in the South, eventually being turned over to the Pentecostal Holiness Church in 1943.[54]

The Northwest C&MA Convention in Chicago included charismatically-oriented speakers. One was William Franklin, who had been an Alliance missionary in India and also teacher of English at Pandita Ramabai's mission. He later became superintendent of the New England District of the C&MA, replacing Ira David, another tongue-speaking Alliance leader. Also, William H. Piper, pastor of the Pentecostal Stone Church in Chicago, and his wife were featured speakers.[55] The friendly relationship between the Alliance and the Stone Church continued for nearly two decades.

REVIVALS CONTINUE IN THE FALL

During the fall of 1908 Bartleman spoke three times in the Alliance church in Springfield, Massachusetts, where Tom Cullen, a former missionary to South America who had received tongues, was pastor. He visited with Springfield Alliance member Mrs. Albert Weaver, who supported his ministry financially. He was invited by Pastor Rossiter for the third time to the C&MA church in Beaver Falls, Pennsylvania, where he preached five times.[56]

As an overflow of the fall New York City Convention, R. A. Forrest, E. D. Whiteside, and Ira David, all of whom encouraged charismatic manifestations, spoke to the students of the Missionary Training Institute at Nyack October 12-14. Then Frank Bartleman was invited by a faculty member who had received tongues to speak to the students and faculty. Although there was apparently some opposition at the school and several of the faculty gave him guidelines as to what he could and could not say, he was given opportunity to speak during Dr. George Pardington's "Quiet Hour" on October 15, as well as the next morning.[57]

The Alliance Weekly reported the occasion, describing Bartleman as "a man filled with the Holy Ghost and love for the brethren," and commenting that he preached a "message from the heart of God, the burden of which was the exaltation of Jesus." He shared a conciliatory message that "people who zealously endeavor to maintain some doctrine, experience or truth in and for itself, grieve the Spirit, hurt the heart of Jesus and wound themselves," but when Christ is exalted everything else falls into its place and there is perfect harmony.[58]

Evidently Simpson did not feel as negatively toward Bartleman at this time or else he would not have included the positive praise of Bartleman in his periodical. Bartleman's message would have sounded a sympathetic chord with Simpson's Christo-centric emphasis. For Pardington to allow Bartleman to speak during his designated time indicates openness on the part of Pardington to Bartleman and his message. The presence of Whiteside and David, who were already favorably disposed to Bartleman's message, probably gave assurance to Simpson as well.

Also in October Peter Robinson, the black tongue-speaking pastor from Pittsburgh, was invited by Pastor L. J. Long to speak at the Alliance convention in Corning, New York, where Pentecostal revival had broken out the year prior. L. A. Harriman, the Alliance pastor from Bridgeport, Connecticut, enthusiastically reported that the "Spirit was pleased to manifest Himself more than once in unusual power."[59]

MORE OUTPOURING IN INDIA

In October came a report of tongues in many places in the India Alliance missions, "To whatever station we go we . . . hear praises to our blessed Lord and Master sung and shouted. And not only in the Gujerat tongue but in 'new tongues.'"[60] In October and November the annual C&MA Akola Convention in India featured teaching and personal testimonies about the baptism in the Spirit and the "Latter Rain" throughout the year. The emphasis of the conference and teachings was that the true results of the baptism in the Spirit are "a more intense prayer-life," "a deeper love to God and to all His children," and "holy boldness."[61]

Over all, in 1908 the Alliance continued to maintain openness to all charismatic phenomena, and many such manifestations were welcomed and experienced. At the same time the Alliance struggled with excesses, immature exercise of the gifts, teaching on evidential tongues, and defections both to the Pentecostal movement and to those opposing the movement.

---

1. John Gormer, "The St. Louis Convention," CMAW, Feb. 15, 1908, 337.

2. "Notes from the Home Field," CMAW, Jan. 4, 1908, 236.

3. "Notes from the Home Field," CMAW, Jan. 11, 1908, 253.

4. "Notes from the Home Field," CMAW, Jan 25, 1908, 284.

5. M. H. Cromwell, "N. J. Prayer Conference," CMAW, Apr. 4, 1908, 16.

6. Merian made a decision to serve the Lord in 1912 at the age of 17, and then attended the Pentecostal Beulah Heights Missionary Training School in North Bergen, New Jersey. As a missionary in South Africa, she worked with Nyack graduate George Bowie, and married a young missionary named Ralph Riggs. Riggs would eventually become General Superintendent of the Assemblies of God in 1953. Glenn Gohr, "Now You Will Know. . . Whatever Happened to Lillian Riggs?", *Assemblies of God Heritage*, Spring 1988, 7.

7. David H. McDowell, "Father and Son Healing Together," *Revival! Touched by Pentecostal Fire*, ed. Wayne E. Warner (Tulsa, OK: Harrison House, 1978), 93-95.

8. Warner, *Revival!*, 155-157. McDowell later affiliated with the Assemblies of God in 1914 and eventually became Assistant General Superintendent of the Assemblies in 1927. He continued to have contact with A. B. Simpson and Alliance leaders through the years.

9. "Notes from the Home Field: From Scotland," CMAW, Jan. 18, 1908, 269.

10. S. A. Renicks, "Notes from the Home Field: From Scotland," Mar. 14, 1908, 404. This is probably the same person as Andrew Bell of Dumferline, Scotland, mentioned in the Pentecostal periodical *Confidence.* See "The Latter Rain in Scotland," Supplement to *Confidence,* May 1908, 4; "Scotland: A Report from Glasgow, *"Confidence,* Oct. 1908, 16.

11. "A Missionary Conference," CMAW, Apr. 11, 1908, 33.

12. W. F. Meminger, "Touring Southern Cities," CMAW, Mar. 14, 1908, 405; "Notes from the Home Field: Special Notices," CMAW, Jan. 11, 1908, 254.

13. Editorial Notes, CMAW, Sept. 5, 1908, 380.

14. A. B. Simpson, Editorial, CMAW, Sept. 14, 1907, 121.

15. Vinson Synan, *The Holiness-Pentecostal Movement in the United States* (Grand Rapids, MI: Wm. B. Eerdmans, 1971), 124-125.

16. D. William Faupel, *The Everlasting Gospel* (Sheffield, England: Sheffield Academic Press, 1996), 214-215.

17. A. B. Simpson, Annual Report of the Christian and Missionary Alliance, 1907-1908, 75.

18. Bartleman, *Azusa Street* (1980), 116-118. According to Bartleman, Sawtelle was eventually transferred to the Alliance work in Texas, but later left the Alliance for secular work because "he became discouraged because he could not go on with God in the Alliance, and so quit the work entirely." (pp. 117, 124). Bartleman seemed to imply that Sawtelle was being exiled to Texas. However, he was transferred in October 1908 as a pioneering District Superintendent of the newly formed Southwestern District, comprised of Alabama, Arkansas, Louisiana, Mississippi, New Mexico, Oklahoma, and Texas, likely because of his success in the Northwest District. But as it was a pioneer work, it was apparently an unfruitful field at that time. It is likely that his discouragement was over the lack of response and fruit, not Bartleman's opinion that "he could not go on with God in the Alliance." If that were so, he would not have left the ministry altogether but rather just left the Alliance to minister in the Pentecostal movement as several other Alliance leaders did. Several years later, Sawtelle did return to evangelistic ministry in the Alliance.

19. Bartleman, *Azusa Street* (1980), 117-118.

20. "South China," CMAW, Aug. 1, 1908, 287-289; Orr, *The Flaming Tongue,* 162-163, 182.

21. G. W. Gohr, "McKinney, Claude Adams," DPCM, 567-568; Atter, 31.

22. "Notes from the Home Field," CMAW, Apr. 11, 1908, 33.

23. "Notes from the Home Field," CMAW, Mar. 7, 1908, 389.

24. "Cleveland Convention," CMAW, Apr. 4, 1908, 17.

25. L. A. Harriman, "Four Conventions in Ohio," CMAW, Apr. 26, 1908, 65.

26. W. F. Meminger, "Touring Ohio Cities," CMAW, May 2, 1908, 85.

27. "Pentecostal Experience," *The Apostolic Faith,* Nov. 1906, 4.

28. *The Apostolic Faith,* May 1908, Vol. II, No. 13, 1.

29. Baron Waldemar Uxkull, "Experiences of God's Grace in Russia," CMAW, Jan. 11, 1908, 245. Brumback spelled his name "Uxhall," noting that F. B. Meyer also reported on the ministry of Baron Uxhall, noting many instances of speaking in tongues in the Russian Baltic province of Estonia. Cited by Carl Brumback, *What Meaneth This?* (Springfield, MO: Gospel Publishing House, 1947), 94-95.

30. T. B. Barratt, "God's Working in Norway, Sweden and Northern Europe," CMAW, Jan. 11, 1908, 245-246.

31. Barratt, "When the Fire Fell. . .", 186.

32. A. C. Snead, "Gleanings from Nyack: India," CMAW, May 16, 1908, 116. See also in report "Fires Are Being Kindled," *The Apostolic Faith,* Vol. II, No. 12, May 1908, 1. *The Apostolic Faith* reported that five missionaries at Dholka received tongues at this time. There were six missionaries stationed at Dholka at

that time in addition to Schoonmaker, who had received earlier. This indicates that only one of the six had not received tongues at that time.

33. W. M. Turnbull, "Another Chapter about Dholka," CMAW, July 4, 1908, 222-223; see also M. B. Fuller, "The Heathen for Thine Inheritance," *The India Alliance*, July 1908, 2.

34. Mrs. Walter Turnbull, "Showers of Blessing," CMAW, Aug. 8, 1908, 307.

35. Mrs. W. M. Turnbull, "Another Chapter about Dholka," *The India Alliance*, May 1908, 130-132.

36. O. Lapp, "Akola Orphanage," *The India Alliance*, June 1908, 136; S. P. Hamilton, "More About Revival, "*The India Alliance*, June 1908, 136-137; "Editorial." *The India Alliance*, June 1908, 138-139; see also Frances Bannister, "The Work of God in Bhusawal," CMAW, June 6, 1908, 153-154.

37. Frances Bannister, "A Hindu Boy's Testimony," CMAW, June 6, 1908, 158.

38. "The Pentecostal Revival," *The Apostolic Faith*, Vol. II, No. 12, May 1908, 2. See also additional reports in this issue of *The Apostolic Faith*.

39. Daniel E. Albrecht, "Carrie Judd Montgomery: Pioneering Contributor to Three Religious Movements, "*Pneuma: The Journal of the Society for Pentecostal Studies*, Vol. 8:2 (Fall 1986), 109, 116-117.

40. Carrie Judd Montgomery, "The Promise of the Father," *Triumphs of Faith*, July 1908, 1. See also Montgomery, *Under His Wings*, 166.

41. Montgomery, "The Promise of the Father," 1-2.

42. Albrecht, "Carrie Judd Montgomery," 117.

43. Frodsham, *With Signs Following*, 234-237; Montgomery, *Under His Wings*, 168-170; Riss, *A Survey of 20th Century Revival Movements*, 77.

44. Carrie Judd Montgomery, "Letter from Mrs. Montgomery," *Triumphs of Faith*, Sept. 1909, 208.

45. Carrie Judd Montgomery, "A Year with the Comforter," *Confidence*, Nov. 1909, 249ff.

46. Albrecht, "Carrie Judd Montgomery," *Under His Wings*, 231.

47. W. F. Meminger, "Touring Ohio," CMAW, June 13, 1908, 185.

48. Bartleman, *Azusa Street* (1980), 120.

49. Edgar E. Johnson, "Annual Prayer Conference," CMAW, Aug. 15, 1908, 335.

50. A. B. Simpson, Editorial, CMAW, July 25, 1908, 278.

51. W. A. Cramer, "Beulah Park Convention," CMAW, Sept. 12, 1908, 402.

52. Ibid., 403.

53. Bartleman, *Azusa Street* (1980), 121.

54. D. Chris Thompson, "From the Superintendent," *Evangel*, Vol. 56, Num. 7. (July 2001), 2; Synan, *The Holiness-Pentecostal Tradition*, 121.

55. Isabella M. Fisher, "The Chicago Convention," CMAW, Sept. 12, 1908, 403.

56. Bartleman, *Azusa Street* (1980), 124, 126-129.

57. Ibid., 129; "Gleanings from Nyack: Overflow from the Convention," CMAW, Oct. 31, 1908, 80.

58. "Gleanings from Nyack: Overflow from the Convention," CMAW, Oct. 31, 1908, 80.

59. "Notes from the Home Field," CMAW, Nov. 28, 1908, 147.

60. F. H. Back, "Has It Been Worth While?," CMAW, Oct. 3, 1908, 2.

61. "Convention Notes," *The India Alliance*, Dec. 1908, 65.

CURRENTS AND
CROSS CURRENTS — 1908

THE BARMEN DECLARATION

In February 1908, Simpson wrote an editorial about the Barmen Convention in Germany with Stockmayer and others discussing the tongues movement. Simpson agreed with the Barmen declaration taking a "Gamaliel" position not to oppose or promote the movement. The five points of the Barmen declaration proclaimed: 1) the gifts of the Spirit are for today, 2) Some tongues and prophecy are not of the Holy Spirit, 3) There has been lack of discernment and failure to try the spirits, 4) We the Church are guilty for not discerning, 5) We need to warn not to be carried away.[1]

Pentecostal historian Roberts Mapes Anderson erroneously claimed that Simpson "hailed the condemnation of the 'Tongues Movement' in Germany by resolution of a Holiness convention in Barmen (now Wuppertal)."[2] However, the Barmen Convention did not oppose the Pentecostal movement. Anderson confused the Barmen Convention of December 1907 with the Berlin Declaration of September 1909.[3] The Berlin Declaration opposed manifestation of the gifts, whereas the Barmen Convention affirmed the gifts with discernment, taking a Gamaliel position on the Pentecostal movement by neither opposing nor actively promoting the movement. Simpson supported the Barmen Convention, but not the Berlin Declaration. The Berlin Declaration also opposed Pentecostal Pastor Jonathan Paul whom Simpson supported and later invited to speak at his Gospel Tabernacle in 1912.[4]

C&MA BOARD RESOLUTION ON THE LATTER RAIN MOVEMENT

In March the C&MA Board of Managers composed a "Resolution of the Board of the C&MA regarding the 'Latter Rain Movement.'" The resolution stated that the C&MA was not adding new doctrinal statements as authoritatively binding concerning the Latter Rain and other related doctrines such as baptism, church government, footwashing and particulars about sanctification.[5] The resolution did not mention speaking in tongues specifically, but the Alliance position regarding the doctrine of tongues as the indispensable evidence of the baptism in the Spirit had already been established and was being maintained.

CONCERNS AND CAUTIONS

May Mabette Anderson wrote that some who claim "full Pentecost" with tongues need a circumcised tongue because of their judgmental spirit toward those who do not speak in tongues.[6] Mrs. Michael Baxter of London, who had preached in tongues on one occasion many years before Azusa Street, wrote on a personal Pentecost, affirming that some manifestations have been of God, but there are also dangers of fleshly or demonic ecstasy.[7]

Pastor C. J. Moon reported that many have received the Holy Spirit with "some mighty manifestation, violent shaking of the body, extreme agony and travail four souls, tongues, etc." He affirmed, "While we are not to seek outward manifestations, yet it is evident from God's Word that we have a right to expect them (Mark 16:20)."[8]

A. J. Ramsey, who participated in the great Beulah Beach convention in 1907, nonetheless cautioned, "There are reliable records of many instances of 'tongues' proceeding from other spirits. . . . 'Tongues' may, or may not, accompany baptism."[9] Ramsey declared that "all of theses signs do not necessarily follow every believer." He laid down the guidelines of 1 Corinthians 12-14, saying that tongues is not the evidence and not to seek after tongues. He exhorted readers to pursue love, not gifts.[10]

While Alliance leaders affirmed the reality of prophetic utterances, they also felt a need to deal with excesses in following revelatory impressions and misuse of the gift of prophecy. Anderson warned about deceptive leadings. She cautioned that some in the current movement are ignoring 1 Corinthians 14 or saying it does not apply to the present movement, and that some are claiming authority to their inner leadings over Scripture. She also warned that there are dangers to prolonged fasting not controlled by the Holy Spirit.[11]

Simpson counseled, "Let us not run after men or women who seem to have supernatural gifts and power."[12] He warned about danger of too much dependency and direction on prophecies: "True prophecy is a perpetual ministry in the New Testament church. It is nothing less than receiving the Spirit of God and giving forth the messages of God to men under His inspiration and power. This does not mean new messages of authority in addition to the Holy Scriptures, but it does mean the Holy Scriptures themselves interpreted and applied under the quickening touch of the Spirit of God." Simpson cautioned of the danger of prophets and prophetesses claiming they are authorized by the Holy Spirit to reveal secret sins and direct the decisions of others. Paul refused to listen to voices dissuading him.[13] Alliance leaders further cautioned that Satan will attempt to duplicate signs and wonders and tongues in the last days, and thus we need to discern the true and the false, and counseled regarding how to discern false powers, inward voices and leadings, counterfeit voices.[14]

From this sampling, we can see that a pattern appears to have been emerging in the Alliance periodical. One article would encourage the supernatural gifts of the Spirit; another article would caution extremes in doctrines and practices. Simpson evidently was attempting to maintain a dynamic tension between the two extremes of opposition to the gifts, on one hand, and undiscriminating acceptance of such phenomena, on the other. Through the next several years Simpson would continue repeatedly to alternate between encouragement of the gifts and discerning caution.

To use a driving analogy, at times, it seems, he would step on the accelerator, and at other times on the brake. To many Pentecostals, the Alliance seemed to be riding the brake all the time. To non-Pentecostals both within and outside of the Alliance, its foot seemed to be too much on the accelerator. To Simpson and early Alliance leaders, they were trying to shift gears smoothly without burning out the clutch.

MacArthur's Article on Supernatural Utterances

In October W. T. MacArthur wrote an article on supernatural utterances, maintaining that tongues, interpretation and prophecies are sometimes a mixture of flesh and spirit—that they are fallible, but not necessarily demonic. He warned against those who consider tongues as a Satanic delusion, saying that they "have gone a long way toward blasphemy in their denunciations," because thousands of devout Christians have spoken in tongues.

From intimate familiarity of his wife's experience of tongues (and perhaps his own), he described the "blessedness of the experience" as "the heavenly intoxication of supernatural song, or the blissful agony of supernatural intercession." Yet, on the other hand, he also warned against believing that messages in prophecy, tongues, and interpretations are direct messages from God, and especially against putting such utterance on par with Scripture.

Rather, MacArthur understood the experience of tongues as "not God speaking through them, and it is not Satan deluding them, but it is their being strengthened with might by His Spirit in the inner man." It was his conclusion that because "the unknown speech is simply the result of the human spirit having been quickened and empowered by the Holy Ghost," that is why some manifestations may be tainted with human fallibility. While the Holy Spirit may be empowering the speech, the utterance comes through an imperfect human channel. The words may "have been prompted by the Holy Ghost," but never had the infallibility of Scripture. He acknowledged that there many times a speaker may have uttered words "unmistakenly dictated" by the Holy Spirit, "and yet they had a human coloring and inherent fallibility." Many times, MacArthur concluded, such manifestations may be neither from God or the devil, but simply human.

MacArthur affirmed that speaking in tongues is valuable "in proportion as the speaker communes with God." He acknowledged the benefit of tongues or other supernatural gifts, admitting, "It seems to us that is not possible to reach the highest and best of our heavenly inheritance apart from them," yet noting that such manifestations need to be balanced by our understanding.[15]

INCIDENCES OF GENUINE AND DEMONIC TONGUES IN CHINA

In February 1908, W. W. Simpson reported that his Chinese prayer partner in Tibet, spoke in tongues in beautiful English, even though he knew little English.[16] The veteran missionary was impressed by the change in his prayer partner. This then began Simpson's quest for the baptism in the Spirit with tongues (which he received in 1912). In June A. B. Simpson reported in his annual report that in Wuchow, South China, many began to speak in tongues in a "heavenly baptism."[17]

On the other hand, an April article by W. W. Simpson and William Christie described a Chinese man at the C&MA Conference in China in January 1908 who was shaken violently, spoke in tongues, prophesied strangely, then impersonated Jesus, and seemed to be in a trance. He became angry and began cursing when the missionaries sang "Nothing But the Blood of Jesus." Christie discerned demonic presence and ministered deliverance. Simpson and Christie commented that this was "positive proof that demons as well as the Spirit cause speaking in tongues."[18]

APPEAL FOR WISDOM AND WATCHFULNESS

Simpson's annual report for 1907-1908 acknowledged many genuine instances of tongues and other extraordinary manifestations with deep humility, earnestness, soberness, and free from extravagance and error, and deepening of spiritual life. He reaffirmed that the Alliance position is one of "candor and caution," open to all that God wants to give, with watchfulness for counterfeits. He also expressed concerns about divisiveness of the evidence doctrine, seeking after manifestations, and claiming of prophetic authority almost like fortune-tellers.[19] He counseled that there is need for "wisdom and watchfulness" by the leaders against unscriptural excitement, false manifestations, seeking tongues rather than the Lord Himself. He concluded that the Alliance had been "guided safely through the crisis," and permanent blessing resulted.[20]

Further, Simpson wrote, "Revival has been the keynote of the year," citing outpourings of the Spirit in Congo, China, and India with many missionaries and native workers receive tongues and healing. There were "some manifestations that needed careful guarding." The "final results of this visitation were a remarkable deepening of the spiritual life of all the workers and churches."

SIMPSON COUNSELS TRUE FIRE VS. FALSE FIRE

In several articles in September Simpson wrote about distinguishing the genuine from the false or fleshly. He preached on "Fire-Touched Lips" from Isaiah 6, saying, "The baptism of the Holy Ghost is a baptism for our tongues, and if it does not bring us a new tongue it should bring us a new message, a new unction, a new mighty power, to be silent from the voices of earthly folly, clamor and sin, and charged with heavenly might to witness for Jesus Christ to the uttermost part of the earth."[21] Simpson advised, "The way to fight false fire is by the true fire."[22] He further counseled not to pursue tongues nor to criticize or oppose it, but "Jesus is the only true object of pursuit."[23] In yet another editorial

Simpson declared, "It matters little what gifts and manifestations we possess if we have not the spirit of gentleness and love that will at least let your brother alone and if you cannot agree with him will love him and pray for him in silence. We believe that in almost every instance the test of spiritual health will be found by applying the simple rule which the physician usually first applies to his patient, 'Put out your tongue.'"[24]

CRISIS AND GROWTH

In May William MacArthur, then the Northwest District Superintendent, reported of his district:

> This has been a crisis year in our history. The 'Tongues manifestation' has somewhat revolutionized the work, but we rejoice to report that nothing fanatical or extreme has resulted. Our members have been slightly depleted on account of our determination to hold everything strictly to Pauline order, and a few have withdrawn, feeling that the phenomenon was of Satanic origin. Our congregations, however, in the aggregate, are larger, and notwithstanding the financial strain the actual cash remitted exceeds that of last year.[25]

F. H. Senft reported that in Washington, D. C. that the Alliance work had lost members through the Pentecostal movement.[26] An account of the difficulties in the mission work in India reported that in spite of some hindrances in the Gospel work in India, "We are glad for Pentecost and for what we know of it in our souls."[27] Simpson affirmed that there is much that is "holy and divine" in the supernatural manifestations, but also along with "wild waves of fanaticism and bitter strife of tongues leading to some cases of division and dismemberment of some branches." Yet he assured that the crisis had passed, and that there is room in the C&MA "for all the height and depths of the Holy Spirit's grace and power along with the simple and practical trust."[28]

1. A. B. Simpson, Editorial, CMAW, Feb. 29, 1908, 366.

2. Robert Mapes Anderson, *Vision of the Disinherited*, 146.

3. See P. D. Hocken, "Berlin Declaration," DPCM, 55.

4. A. B. Simpson, Editorial, AW, July 6, 1912, 210.

5. A. B. Simpson, Editorial, CMAW, Mar. 28, 1908, 432.

6. May Mabette Anderson, "Who Shall Abide?", CMAW, Jan. 11, 1908, 244.

7. A. B. Simpson, Editorial, CMAW, Jan. 18, 1908, 264.

8. C. J. Moon, "The Receiving of the Holy Ghost," CMAW, Feb. 22, 1908, 344.

9. A. J. Ramsey, "The Receiving of the Holy Spirit and the Baptism in the Holy Spirit—Identical or Different?," CMAW, Feb. 22, 1908, 345.

10. A. J. Ramsey, "Speaking in Tongues: An Exegetical Study," CMAW, Apr. 4, 1908, 7, 17.

11. May Mabette Anderson, "Deceptive Leadings," CMAW, Apr. 11, 1908, 25.

12. A. B. Simpson, Editorial, CMAW, May 23, 1908, 128.

13. A. B. Simpson, "The Anointing," CMAW, May 23, 1908, 130.

14. J. Hudson Ballard, "Delusions of the Last Days," CMAW, July 18, 1908, 259; "The Difference between the True and the False," CMAW, Aug. 22, 1908, 343, 344, 352.

15. William T. MacArthur, "The Phenomenon of Supernatural Utterance," CMAW, Oct. 31, 1908, 72-73.

16. W. W. Simpson, "A Miracle of Grace in Tibet," CMAW, Feb. 22, 1908, 341; Gordon F. Atter, The Third-Force (Peterborough, Ontario: The College Press, 1962), 65.

17. A. B. Simpson, "Annual Report of the C&MA 1907-1908," CMAW, June 20, 1908, 193.

18. W. W. Simpson and William Christie, "Demon Possession in Our Mincheo Native Conference, Jan. 1908," CMAW, Apr. 18, 1908, 38-39. For other descriptions of this same incident see also William Ruhl, "Western China," CMAW, May 9, 1908, 9; and "Deliverance from Demons," "Demon Possession," China's Millions, Sept. 1908, 102-103; A. B. Simpson, "Annual Report of the C&MA 1907-1908," CMAW, June 20, 1908, 193.

19. A. B. Simpson, "Annual Report of the C&MA 1907-1908," 155-56.

20. Ibid. , 193.

21. A. B. Simpson, "Fire-Touched Lips," CMAW, Sept. 12, 1908, 404.

22. A. B. Simpson, Editorial, CMAW, Sept. 19, 1908, 414.

23. A. B. Simpson, "Side Issues and the Supreme Object of Life, CMAW, Sept. 19, 1908, 416.

24. A. B. Simpson, Editorial, CMAW, Sept. 26, 1908, 430.

25. William T. MacArthur, "Excerpts from Annual Reports," May 28, 1908.

26. "Notes from the Home Field," CMAW, Mar. 27, 1909, 437.

27. "Some Hindrances in Gospel Work in India," CMAW, Mar. 28, 1908, 425.

28. A. B. Simpson, Editorial, CMAW, Apr. 4, 1908, 10.

RIPPLE EFFECTS IN 1909

There were not as many or as frequent reports of charismatic manifestations in Alliance periodicals in 1909. Like the Azusa Street revival, which lasted about two years, the Alliance revival was beginning to wind down. Yet revival outpourings and charismatic phenomena and practices continued to occur.

ANOTHER REVIVAL OUTBREAK AT NYACK

In February another revival outbreak occurred at Nyack with "frequent spontaneous burst of song from the audience."[1] Several students continued to receive the baptism in the Spirit, some with tongues. Agnes Beckdahl, who was a student at the Missionary Training Institute and later a missionary to India with the Assemblies of God, recalled that five male students spent a night in a basement in prayer, and three of them received the baptism in the Spirit with tongues. "The next day," she reported, "in the Grammar Class, one of the brothers was so filled with the Spirit . . . that we could hardly work, and we ended by going on our knees in prayer."[2]

MORE REPORTS OF LATTER RAIN OUTPOURINGS

In January missionary Violetta Dunham reported that the father of a dying baby received the baptism in the Spirit with a vision of heaven. The baby had a death rattle, but was miraculously healed.[3] In February an article by C&MA missionary E. O. Jago recounted a dream from God.[4] Jago was quite open to Pentecostal phenomena and later preached in Pentecostal meetings while continuing leadership in the Alliance.

At the opening of the New Jersey C&MA Prayer Conference in Jersey City in March, everyone was aware of a special manifestation of the presence of the Holy Spirit. They fell on their knees, let the Spirit take charge, and ended up praying for two hours. Several delegates remarked that it was the best Prayer Conference they ever had. Although they had experienced some disruption for about three months due to opposing poles of skepticism and fanaticism, the conference was marked by joyful fellowship and unity.[5] Local Baptist pastor Rev. Switzer, whose wife evidently had spoken in tongues, fully supported the

Alliance, bringing his church into full affiliation with the C&MA. A decade later in his obituary his Alliance church was hailed by A. B. Simpson as "indeed a Pentecostal church of the Lord Jesus Christ."[6]

In April, S. M. Gerow, in his report of the annual Alliance convention at Akron, testified again about "the 'Latter Rain' which has been falling during the last two years."[7] In the April convention at Cleveland, Pastors Kerr and Stokes and District Superintendent Patterson all spoke on Pentecostal revival themes.[8] The ministry of David McDowell and others at the Alliance church in Waynesboro, Pennsylvania, brought report in May that "the Latter Rain outpouring of the Holy Spirit was taught and sought and received" at the C&MA convention there and many were healed.[9]

Alliance missionary to China, Mrs. Woodbury, reported in May that a missionary named Mrs. Hansen was "speaking in the Mandarin tongue," preaching on a street corner in Shanghai, but she did not know what she was saying. As a result, a man was converted.[10] Blanche Hamilton, an Alliance missionary to India, recounted that many of the native Indians were speaking in tongues in English and that, "Nearly all of the missionaries are baptized here, and have the gift of tongues also."[11]

Simpson reported that there is "revival in almost every field."[12] He commented that the power of God had fallen in India upon missionaries, orphans, native Christians and native workers. In many cases they were accompanied by tongues, but the special feature was a spirit of intercession.[13] In July, the *C&MA Weekly* recorded a dream from God, in which a woman saw Jesus speaking a prophetic word, and peace came upon a troubled child she held in her lap.[14]

Rev. Archibald Forder, a C&MA missionary to Palestine and Arabia, had become involved in the Pentecostal movement and left the C&MA for a time, ministering independently. However, in 1909, while continuing Pentecostal activities, he returned to missions work with the C&MA, especially in Jerusalem, where Pentecostal revival had broken out the year before.[15]

OTTO STOCKMAYER'S VISIT

In February German healing leader Otto Stockmayer spoke at a series of meetings in Simpson's church. Simpson affirmed that Stockmayer's position on tongues agreed with the C&MA, upholding the reality of the supernatural gifts, but opposing evidence doctrine and advising the exercise of discernment.[16] Simpson associate F. E. Marsh remarked that Stockmayer believed that the false may be mingled with the true.[17]

REVIVAL IN WASHINGTON

The Full Gospel Mission of the C&MA in Everett, Washington, as well as the Alliance mission in nearby Mukilteo, had grown through the ministry of Pastor A. C. York and his wife and another couple, Brother and Sister McNab. Alliance conventions in both locations had resulted in conversions, healings, and people filled with the Spirit. At Mukilteo, new District Superintendent Wilbur F. Meminger, who had encouraged charismatic manifestations in New York and other Alliance conventions, reported, "Each session the Holy Spirit ploughed deeper: young, middle aged and old were swept into the kingdom." At Everett, he testified as he did so many times before, "Wave after wave of holy emotion rolled over us. We were all deepened in God."[18]

PENTECOSTAL TERMINOLOGY CONTINUES

Alliance leaders continued to use Pentecostal language and share Pentecostal experiences in the third year of the Alliance revival. J. Benjamin Lawrence wrote on the baptism of the Spirit, calling it "the Chrismatic baptism" and "Pentecostal baptism."[19] John Boyd counseled readers to seek their "personal Pentecost," but not to seek tongues. He exhorted, "Forbid not the exercise of the least of the gifts by those who have the genuine." He cautioned that some may say they are not seeking tongues, "perhaps not with the lips, but may not the desire for tongues or some other manifestation be the dominant thought and thus the prayer of the heart?" Then he warned that it is possible to receive a tongue from Satan under those conditions, and one needs to seek in prayer the protection and guidance of the Bridegroom.[20] Here is a clear instance of the typical Alliance "Seek Not, Forbid Not" position.

The *C&MA Weekly* referred to the "Cleveland Pentecost" of two years ago, noting that those who received tongues continue to have "temperate testimonies of Pentecostal experience" and "quiet and rich Pentecostal experience."[21] Another *C&MA Weekly* article on "A World-Wide Present Day Pentecost," exhorted that the church needs "extraordinary powers" and the "necessity of the Pentecostal baptism."[22]

SIMPSON CONTINUES TO ENCOURAGE GIFTS WITH DISCERNMENT

Simpson himself continued to use Pentecostal language in his articles and sermons, speaking of the early and latter rain receiving a "Pentecostal enduement."[23] In March, Simpson announced a C&MA Easter Week convention in Cleveland on "Pentecostal Revival themes."[24] Throughout 1909 Simpson continued to promote the exercise of all the gifts and manifestations of the Spirit, yet also encouraging discernment. Early in the year, Simpson asserted that some manifestations and movements are not wholly scriptural, calling them "Satan's scarecrows." Citing Matthew 7:9-11, he exhorted that we should not fear because "if a son asks bread . . ." God our Father will not give a stone.[25] Simpson wrote of two extremes—some so centered on gifts and manifestations that it has made others afraid. He assured those who are afraid that "God knows how to give without a counterfeit."[26]

CONTROVERSY OVER MISSIONARY KATE KNIGHT

Kate Knight, missionary to India, had received the baptism in the Spirit with tongues in the fall of 1907. In January 1909, Simpson announced that she was retiring from the C&MA to be released to minister freely to teach and pray for people for the baptism with the Spirit. Simpson assured that she was not being asked to leave because of her experience with tongues, but affirmed that the C&MA has "entire openness" to the gift of tongues.[27] Rumors were circulating in Pentecostal circles that Knight had been dismissed from the C&MA for speaking in tongues. The next month Simpson responded that these reports were false, affirming, "More than a score of our missionaries received tongues as Miss Knight and are continuing in the Alliance work in perfect harmony."[28]

In March Simpson wrote that Kate Knight asked to be received back into the Alliance and "in a very sweet Christian spirit has expressed her regret for what she believes was a mistake in withdrawing." She was received back without a problem.[29] However, Brethren writer G. H. Lang later condemned her beliefs and practices in his publication *Modern Gift of Tongues: Whence Is It?*[30] Lang, whose writings were popular in Alliance circles, may have had a negative impact upon some in the C&MA, influencing some to question the experience of Knight.

JAFFRAY ON TONGUES AND THE PENTECOSTAL MOVEMENT

A March issue of the *C&MA Weekly* featured an article by Robert Jaffray, South China Field Director entitled "Speaking in Tongues—Some Words of Kindly Counsel." He recounted the benefits of his experience of tongues and warned against considering supernatural utterances as infallible, but not to be afraid of receiving them.[31] On the issue of whether it is appropriate to desire tongues, he counseled:

> There is a great danger of fear of the works of the devil to such an extent that we shall lose all courage to seek earnestly for the true and full endowment of the Spirit for which our souls hunger. I have met some who are so prejudiced on account of why that have seen that they say they have no desire to ever speak in tongues, forgetting that tongues is one of the gifts of the Spirit. Let us not allow the enemy so to drive us away from, and cheat us out of, the real blessings of the Spirit because he has counterfeited in some cases the gift of tongues. We have no business to be afraid of evil spirits, for His has given us "power over all the power of the enemy," and He can give supernatural discernment of spirits.[32]

Significantly, he believed, evidently with the support of Simpson, that speaking in tongues often is the initial manifestation:

> May it not be that the Spirit usually gives the "tongues" first to test us and see whether or not we may be trusted with greater gifts of the Spirit which may be indeed of more value in the Christian ministry. There may be this reason also, that if the Spirit can get hold of a man's tongue He has what corresponds, according to James, to the bit in the horse's mouth and the rudder of the ship, and so in turn the whole body may be bridled by the Spirit of God.[33]

Pentecostal historian Edith Blumhofer concludes of Jaffray's positive and negative assessments, "Jaffray considered Pentecostal experience meaningful in his personal life but disappointing on his mission station."[34]

Exhortations for Balance and Discernment

C&MA Weekly articles in 1909 featured many appeals both for openness to the Spirit and for discernment and avoidance of excess. May Mabette Anderson wrote on the need for discernment, unwise attitudes, and the exercise of calm authority over Satan.[35] M. A. Dean reaffirmed that any gift of the Spirit can be as much an evidence as any other. He spoke positively of speaking in tongues, saying that "blessed as the experience of tongues is," it is not the only evidence. He cited William MacArthur that doctrine is not founded on experience, but on teaching of Christ and the apostles. Affirming that this revival is indeed the "latter rain," he exhorted that we can look for even greater manifestations, but not get our eyes on gifts. He encouraged readers to get a larger vision of the baptism of the Spirit than tongues.[36]

Dealing with those who were claiming authoritative prophetic revelation from God, Simpson cautioned that no man, whether he claims to be an apostle, prophet or saint has any right to proclaim a message whether in known or unknown tongues with a claim that it possesses authority over their consciences. There is no new revelation, he avowed, only illumination of Scripture.[37]

With summer conventions approaching, Simpson counseled both sides of the issues regarding supernatural manifestations, on one hand, not to be deceived, nor, on the other hand, to be afraid of counterfeits.[38] Midsummer, again addressing the rhetoric and attitudes of both opponents and proponents of Pentecostal teaching, Simpson wrote on the need for a wholesome tongue, noting that "the first effect of the outpouring of the Holy Ghost on the day of Pentecost was fire-touched tongues."[39]

L. A. Harriman, who pastored charismatically-oriented Alliance churches, especially in Bridgeport, Connecticut and in Indianapolis, averred, "No feeling, manifestation or voice is absolute evidence." Rather, the "true Bible evidence" is the fruit of the Spirit.[40] Significantly, this is precisely what Azusa Street leader William Seymour would later say when he recanted the evidential tongues doctrine.[41] Edgar Sellow wrote that some who have received the much-coveted gift of tongues are still not satisfied, and "He whose mind is stayed on God will no longer seek the gifts."[42]

Why Not Tongues without Controversy?

In August, just before the annual Old Orchard Convention, Simpson expressed the yearning of his heart, "Why may we not have all the supernatural ministries of the early church . . . even tongues, without making them a controversy?"[43]

In conjunction with the Old Orchard Convention, Simpson counseled not to be afraid of counterfeits because God is able to save us from them. He expressed concern that people might miss what God has for them because of fear. Simpson,

Jaffray, and Carrie Judd Montgomery all gave messages at the Old Orchard Convention on the moving of the Spirit.[44] Simpson preached in his address that all the gifts are to equip for ministry, including tongues, as God wills. He exhorted that floods of blessing will come to the church, not just individuals.[45]

Though no details were given, according to Simpson, the Holy Spirit was present at the camp meeting in all the fullness of His offices and operations. All the gifts of the Spirit were present, but there was no extravagance, excess, or strife of tongues.[46] At the end of the convention Simpson remarked, "In some respects this has been one of the most wonderful camp meetings we have ever held at Old Orchard."[47]

Simpson wrote that the effects of the baptism of the Holy Spirit are not necessarily tongues or prophecy, but don't limit the sign or method.[48] Through this he was telling those who were insisting on tongues as the evidence not to limit the evidence to tongues only. To those who were opposing manifestations, he was telling them not to limit God but to allow tongues. To those who were fearful of spurious manifestations, Simpson counseled not to be afraid of counterfeits because God is able to save us from them. To the over-cautious, he cautioned that they might miss what God has for them.[49]

MONTGOMERYS MINISTER IN ALLIANCE CONVENTIONS

Even though she was active in Pentecostal circles, Carrie Judd Montgomery was invited to speak several times at the Nyack convention in July.[50] Her experiences and teaching were well accepted by Simpson and the leaders of the convention. At Old Orchard, even though not on the schedule, Simpson invited her to speak with "great liberty" on the Holy Spirit each evening in the main meeting.[51] Her messages were described as "quiet, sober, and yet deeply spiritual teaching about the baptism of the Holy Spirit, removing difficulties and harmonizing conflicting views."[52] Her husband George also shared his testimony and personally ministered to "seeking souls."[53]

On their way back to California after the Old Orchard Convention, George and Carrie Montgomery were invited to share and minister in other C&MA conventions as well. At the Beulah Beach Convention in Ohio, along with D. W. Kerr and Vice President John Salmon, they prayed for many people to receive the Pentecostal baptism. She recalled, "The meetings were precious beyond description. He we met many dear ones who had received the 'Latter Rain' fullness of the Holy Spirit, and our fellowship with them was so sweet and perfect, it seemed a little foretaste of Heaven's own joy." They also went on to minister at the Alliance convention in Chicago, probably at William MacArthur's church. Undoubtedly, she testified of her blessed experience of speaking in tongues the summer before when she was in Chicago speaking at another C&MA meeting.[54]

SIMPSON SHARES PROPHECIES AT CHICAGO CONVENTION

While preaching at the Alliance Convention in Chicago, Simpson shared with the congregation prophetic words he had received from the Lord many years earlier. He recalled a time more than thirty years earlier in which he was traveling around the country "trying to get hold of other people's blessing." The conviction of the Holy Spirit was so heavy upon him, that he felt like the pounding in his heart would crush him. Rushing out into the woods, he heard the Lord saying to him, "Child, haven't you got Me? What more do you want? I am all these things."

On another occasion he traveled five hundred miles to get a blessing at one of Moody's meetings. After being there just a few hours, God said to him, "Go back home." So he obeyed. When he got home, he threw himself face down before the Lord, then God said, "You have Me and I am the whole Convention, now use Me."[55] By sharing these prophetic words of admonition from the Lord to him, Simpson was both affirming the gift of prophecy as a message from God and at the same time encouraging people to seek Jesus Himself, not the manifestations, gifts or blessings.

A DEATH AND A VISION

After preaching a youth street service during the New York Convention in October, Wilbur F. Meminger remarked, "My heart is breaking for souls." A few minutes later, he collapsed and soon died. After his wife had grieved for him during the night, at 4:00 a.m., she recounted, "the Spirit of God took hold of me and led me to pray in the Holy Ghost." She prayed around the world for two hours, and then became still before the Lord while another woman, Miss McFedries, prayed for her. Suddenly, she saw a vision of her husband dressed in a beautiful robe. Then "suddenly like a flash Jesus appeared—The King, so wonderful, so beautiful, words cannot express." Her husband picked up jewels (that represented souls) from a pure, transparent mound, filling his arms again and again, laying them at Jesus' feet. Jesus responded, "Well done, good and faithful servant." This dramatic vision gave Mrs. Meminger peace and victory in the midst of her sorrow.[56]

MODERATION BRINGS LOSS ON BOTH SIDES

In spite of Simpson's efforts to encourage openness to the gifts with discernment, conflicts still arose, and many people left the Alliance. In March Frederick Senft reported "some loss of members through the Pentecostal movement."[57] In September, A. E. Funk wrote about the "true faithful bands of full gospel believers" in the C&MA, both affirming that the Alliance still believed in the "full gospel" and also encouraging people to remain loyal to the Alliance and not leave or cause division.[58] Northwest District Superintendent W. T. MacArthur conveyed in his annual report:

> We feel that we have passed successfully through the crisis occasioned by the "speaking in tongues" though we have lost a considerable number on account of it. Quite a few left us because we entertained the subject for even a moment, believing it all to be of

the devil, while a much larger number have lost interest in us because we insisted upon holding everything strictly to the Pauline regulations. . . . We have not deviated from our first position, viz. that anything that was not Pauline was not of God, there we expect to remain.[59]

By trying to maintain a middle-of-the-road position, the Alliance lost people on both sides.

1. Lubelle Patrick, "Gleanings from Nyack, CMAW, Feb. 27, 1909, 362.

2. Agnes N. T. Beckdahl, *A Witness of God's Faithfulness* (by the author, n.d.), 38; cited in McGee, "Pentecostal Awakenings at Nyack," 27.

3. Violetta Dunham, "The Healing of Little Ruth," CMAW, Jan. 23, 1909, 275.

4. E. O. Jago, "The Man in Plain Clothes: A Dream," CMAW, Feb. 20, 1909, 343.

5. M. H. Cromwell, "New Jersey Prayer Conference," CMAW, Apr. 10, 1909, 34.

6. "The Late Rev. S. H. Switzer," AW, Jan. 19, 1918, 251.

7. S. M. Gerow, "Report of Annual Convention of Akron, O. Branch of the C&MA," CMAW, Apr. 17, 1909, 48.

8. CMAW, Mar. 27, 1909, 431.

9. "Notes from the Home Field," CMAW, May 15, 1909, 116.

10. Rev. and Mrs. J. Woodberry, "Report of Beulah Chapel," CMAW, May 22, 1909, 134, see also Frodsham,*With Signs Following*, 241-242.

11. Blumhofer, 428.

12. A. B. Simpson, "Summary of Year's Work of the C&MA," CMAW, May 22, 1909, 137.

13. A. B. Simpson, "Report of the Work of the C&MA for the Year 1908-1909, 155.

14. "A Dream," CMAW, July 17, 1909, 261.

15. A. B. Simpson, Editorial, CMAW, Jan. 30, 1909, 296. For Forder's Pentecostal activities, see A. Forder, "And Ishmael Will Be a Wild Man," LRE, Aug. 1909, 2.

16. A. B. Simpson, Editorial, CMAW, Feb. 27, 1909, 364.

17. F. E. Marsh, "Pastor O. Stockmayer on the Gift of Tongues," CMAW, Mar. 13, 1909, 397.

18. CMAW, May 15, 1909, 116.

19. J. Benjamin Lawrence, "The Baptism of the Spirit," CMAW, Jan. 16, 1909, 260.

20. John Boyd, "Seated with Christ," CMAW, Jan. 16, 1909, 261ff.

21. "Notes from the Home Field, CMAW, Jan. 16, 1909, 268-269.

22. William Phillips Hall, "A World-Wide Present Day Pentecost," CMAW, Jan. 23, 1909, 276-277.

23. A. B. Simpson, "Editorial," CMAW, Jan. 16, 1909, 264; A. B. Simpson, "Editorial," CMAW, Jan. 23, 1909, 297.

24. Simpson, Editorial, CMAW, Mar. 27, 1909, 432.

25. Simpson, "Editorial," CMAW, Jan. 23, 1909, 280.

26. A. B. Simpson, "A Week of Prayer," CMAW, Feb. 6, 1909, 314.

27. A. B. Simpson, "Retirement of Miss Kate Knight," CMAW, Jan. 23, 1909, 291.

28. A. B. Simpson, Editorial, CMAW, Feb. 20, 1909, 348.

29. A. B. Simpson, Editorial, CMAW, Mar. 27, 1909, 432. Knight later retired from the field due to health. By1915 she apparently had more fully embraced the Pentecostal movement and teaching, becoming involved withthe Pentecostal Shiloh House in Fredonia, New York. See Kate Knight, "The Baptism in the Holy Spirit,*Confidence*, June 1915, 109ff.; Kate Knight, "The Baptism in the Holy Spirit, *Confidence*, July 1915, 129ff; Kate Knight, "The Baptism of Fire," *Confidence*, Dec. 1915, 230ff.

30. G. B. McGee and S. M. Burgess, "India," NIDPCM, 121.

31. Robert Jaffray, "Speaking in Tongues—Some Words of Kindly Counsel," CMAW, Mar. 13, 1909, 395-396, 406.

32. Ibid.

33. Ibid., 395.

34. Blumhofer, *Restoring the Faith*, 104. For more on Jaffray's charismatic life and ministry, see Louise Green,"Robert Jaffray: Man of Spirit, Man of Power," *His Dominiion*, Vol. 16, No. 1 (March 1990), 2-14.

35. May Mabette Anderson, "An Unwise Attitude—Part I," CMAW, Feb. 6, 1909, 309; May Mabette Anderson, "An Unwise Attitude—Part II," CMAW, Feb. 20, 1909, 343.

36. M. A. Dean, "Some Bible Evidences of the Baptism of the Holy Ghost," CMAW, Apr. 3, 1909, 7-8.

37. A. B. Simpson, "The Holy Ghost," CMAW, Apr. 24, 1909, 48.

38. A. B. Simpson, Editorial, CMAW, June 12, 1909, 180.

39. A. B. Simpson, "A Wholesome Tongue," CMAW, July 31, 1909, 302.

40. L. A. Harriman, "The Sure Criterion," CMAW, Oct. 2, 1909, 6.

41. See Emile Hugo Hawkins, Sr., "The Real Bible Evidence According to William Joseph Seymour," Masters thesis, Oral Roberts University, May 1995.

42. Edgar K. Sellow, "I Am Not Satisfied," CMAW, Oct. 23, 1909, 60.

43. A. B. Simpson, "Christian Altruism," CMAW, Aug. 7, 1909, 322.

44. A. B. Simpson, Editorial, CMAW, Aug. 7, 1909, 314.

45. A. B. Simpson, "Floods of Blessing," CMAW, Aug. 14, 1909, 333.

46. Simpson, Editorial, CMAW, Aug. 14, 1909, 332.

47. Montgomery, *Under His Wings*, 187.

48. A. B. Simpson, "The Preparation," CMAW, Nov. 6, 1909, 91.

49. Simpson, Editorial, CMAW, Aug. 7, 1909, 314.

50. A. B. Simpson, Editorial, CMAW, July 31, 1909, 296-297, 302.

51. Montgomery, *Under His Wings*, 186-187.

52. "Report of the Old Orchard Convention," CMAW, Aug. 21, 1909, 352.

53. Montgomery, *Under His Wings*, 187.

54. Ibid.

55. A. B. Simpson, "The Double Portion: Striking Lessons from the Life of Elisha," LRE, Nov. 1909, 12.

56. Meminger, *The Little Man from Chicago*, 148-152.

57. F. H. Senft, "In the Sunny South," CMAW, Mar. 27, 1909, 437.

58. A. E. Funk, "On the Way," CMAW, Sept. 4, 1909, 392.

59. William T. MacArthur, "Excerpts from Annual Reports," May 25, 1909.

PART THREE

C&MA RESPONSE TO THE
PENTECOSTAL MOVEMENT
1910-1919

ELEVEN

REVIVAL REVERBERATIONS AND REACTIONS 1910–1911

The first thing that we notice about this next decade is that the controversy over the Pentecostal movement did not completely stifle manifestations in The Christian and Missionary Alliance, although they were less frequent and less emphasized in succeeding years. Unlike some evangelicals who branded the whole movement as not of God due to its excesses, Simpson and early Alliance leaders continued to maintain and encourage an attitude of both openness and caution. Contrary to some Pentecostal claims, they did not reject charismatic manifestations. Rather, they desired to have all of the gifts of the Spirit, including tongues, in active operation in the C&MA without controversy, as Simpson had urged in 1909.

TONGUE-SPEAKER APPOINTED DISTRICT EVANGELIST

The Alliance continued to be open toward its ministers who had Pentecostal experiences. Myland, whose ministry was broadening rapidly throughout Pentecostal circles as well as in the Alliance, was appointed in 1910 as an Ohio District Evangelist.[1] Though his message and ministry were unabashedly charismatic in nature, he was given a greater platform and freedom to preach and teach the Latter Rain in Alliance churches. Because of the many requests for his ministry, he was not able to attend to them all, so he anointed and prayed over handkerchiefs in the name of Jesus Christ. He testified of many powerful results occurring through this method, including healings from cancers, palsies, rupture, gallstones, tuberculosis, and fevers, and deliverance of drunkards, liars, gamblers, and more.[2]

ANOTHER OUTPOURING AT NYACK

The year of 1910 brought more revival manifestations at Nyack. During another Pentecostal outpouring, Reuben E. Sternall from Canada received the baptism of the Spirit with tongues, later becoming a charter member of the Pentecostal Assemblies of Canada.[3] Other classmates at Nyack who received the baptism in the Spirit with tongues included Frank Boyd and William Evans, among others. Sternall married another student, Ella (Sunshine) Hostetler, and began Pentecostal ministry in Canada in 1911.[4] William Evans pastored the Alliance work in Richmond, Virginia, through 1914 before joining the Assemblies of God. Frank B. Collitt, another student experiencing the revival, remained in the Alliance, serving in more charismatically-oriented Alliance churches.

MORE OUTPOURINGS IN NORTHEAST

Alliance leaders Frank Casley, J. T. Boddy, and Annie Murray participated in a Pentecostal convention in Wilkinsburg, Pennsylvania, near Pittsburgh.[5] The *C&MA Weekly* reported in March 1910 that the Latter Rain had started to fall on the Alliance work in Dover, New Jersey.[6] Collitt soon was called to pastor the church. The same month featured a report of the Alliance Convention in Haverhill, Massachusetts in which Pentecostals were welcomed and the pastor of the local Pentecostal church greeted the convention. New England Superintendent Ira David, a tongues-speaker, spoke on the Holy Spirit. The C&MA announced meetings to follow at the Pentecostal church. There appeared to be close friendship at this time between Alliance and Pentecostal people.[7]

DISTRICT SUPERINTENDENTS RECEIVE TONGUES

New York C&MA leader John W. Welch had moved to Oklahoma to become state superintendent and establish the Alliance work there. He received baptism in the Spirit with tongues while conducting a C&MA revival service in Muskogee, Oklahoma. The fledging Alliance work quickly became Pentecostal, and Welch eventually joined the Assemblies of God, becoming chairman in 1918.[8]

After touring California in evangelistic work in 1907 George Eldridge had become Superintendent of the Southern Pacific District. George and Anna Eldridge had initially been reticent about the Pentecostal revival, even warning his church back in Indianapolis not to hold Pentecostal meetings. But by 1910 George recounted, "Our hearts were open to anything new God was doing, yet we moved in that direction very cautiously."[9] George's wife Anna set aside time to seek the Lord, and subsequently received the baptism of the Holy Spirit with tongues at a Pentecostal home meeting led by Alliance Vice President John Salmon in Los Angeles: "There, under the prayerful instruction of old Pastor Salmon, she was enabled to yield herself more fully than ever before, to praise and adore her Lord so wholeheartedly that the blessed Spirit came upon her as He did upon the early disciples, and she, too, magnified the Lord Jesus in other tongues, and was filled to overflowing."[10]

George visited the Azusa Street mission and was prayed for by William Seymour, but with no manifestations. At a later time, late one night while in prayer alone he was filled with the Spirit, speaking in tongues, and as a result his attitude toward Pentecostals changed.[11] Eldridge had experienced entire sanctification many years earlier after the Lord spoke to him in an audible voice, saying, "I am what you need and want, not 'it' but Me!"[12] He said that "from that time I never sought an experience, but I sought Him."[13] Yet he believed that his baptism in the Spirit with tongues was something different, something more—a "full baptism" that he described as "like the outflowing of water from my inmost being according to Jesus' words in John 7:37, 38."[14] As a result, Eldridge led much of the Southern Pacific district into Pentecostal experiences.[15]

TESTIMONIES OF CHARISMATIC MANIFESTATIONS

Charismatic manifestations such as dreams, visions, prophecy, tongues, exorcisms, and supernatural protection continued to occur and continued to be reported in the *C&MA Weekly*, though less frequently.[16] This shows that the C&MA continued to encourage charismatic manifestations with discernment, but the revival was beginning to wane and the controversy was taking its toll on the C&MA.

Among the incidents, Walter Jenson testified of receiving the baptism in the Spirit with tongues and being delivered from the errors and deception of Christian Science.[17] In July Carrie Judd Montgomery was welcomed to speak at the Beulah Park Convention on the "Latter Rain," which shows a continuing openness to teaching on Pentecostal themes by the leadership of the C&MA at that time.[18] At the Minneapolis-St. Paul C&MA Convention, it was reported in October, "waves of glory passed over the place."[19]

One particular highlight of the year was a testimony of a teenage girl in Pennsylvania who had been in severe pain from a spinal injury. She heard an audible voice from God speaking prophetically to her. She was healed and received a gift from the Holy Spirit to compose poetic songs from the Lord spontaneously for nine hours.[20]

MORE MANIFESTATIONS ON MISSION FIELDS

Not only in North America, but also on Alliance mission fields, various charismatic manifestations continued to be reported. In Congo, ten people were poisoned because they wanted to attend a C&MA convention. They were all miraculously healed—like a page out of the book of Acts and Mark 16.[21] The *C&MA Weekly* reported on revivals in Africa, especially a Pentecostal outpouring in South Africa.[22]

Missionary Mrs. W. S. Smith reported on "the Lord's blessing at Kwaiping Station in South China," saying, "The words of Jesus, 'These signs shall follow them that believe' have been fulfilled in many cases," especially healings and exorcisms.[23] Mrs. Worsnip reported that in the South China mission during the winter term of 1910 at the women's school, "one of our former students was praying for healing. But instead of being healed, the Spirit came upon her in convicting power, and she came to the school and confessed wrong thing that were in her life. Then she exhorted her schoolmates, and quite a stir was made in the school. Some of the girls received a great blessing, and a few spoke in tongues. . . . The young girl was healed afterwards and has been teaching school this term.[24]

Missionary Martha Woodworth reported about a woman in India who was struggling over assurance of salvation. The missionary prayed that she would receive a revelation, dream, or vision to encourage her. Her prayer was answered as the woman had dreams of a light and of Christ on the Cross, giving her assurance of salvation.[25] Louis Turnbull reported in October that a young native C&MA leader in India saw a vision of an angel and received a gift of healing to pray for others with power and see them healed. Among the incidents, he cast demons out of a ten year-old girl.[26]

The Bosworth Connection

F. F. Bosworth, who had received the baptism in the Spirit with tongues at Zion City, Illinois, in 1906, founded an interdenominational church in Dallas in 1910 loosely affiliated with the C&MA, yet Pentecostal in nature and practice. According to his biographer, the Alliance work held nightly tent meetings all around Dallas and the surrounding countryside.[27] Working with him was E. G. Birdsall, who also eventually became a C&MA minister after serving in the Assemblies of God. They likely became good friends at this time with long-time Fort Worth Alliance lay worker (and a one-time C&MA Vice President) Warren Collins, who also spoke in tongues.[28]

Early Aimee Semple McPherson Contact

It was also in 1910, Pentecostal historian Edith Blumhofer relates, that a nineteen year-old girl by the name of Aimee Semple McPherson "stood unprepared in a London pulpit before a large, eager congregation (probably at a Christian and Missionary Alliance convention),"[29] invited to speak by Pentecostal leader Cecil Polhill.[30] In her message "Lost and Restored," she spoke spontaneously she spoke of what she would later claim was a prophetic inspiration, an interpretation of the work of God throughout history that would guide her future ministry. Blumhofer comments, "She always claimed that it came to her in an experience strikingly similar to tongues speech: 'My mouth opened; the Lord took control of my tongue, my lips and vocal organs, and began to speak through me in English.' She spoke for seventy-five minutes, and in the course of her speaking she claimed she had a vision that became the basis for the illustration of this sermon."[31]

Simpson Supports Pentecostal Movements in Chile and Argentina

In April 1910 Nyack graduate and C&MA missionary Ana H. LaFevre reported in the *C&MA Weekly* on revival in Chile among Methodists, Presbyterians and the Alliance: "In some cases there is speaking and singing in other tongues. As far as we know we believe it has been genuine and all from the Lord, yet we know errors often accompany this manifestation." Particularly in the C&MA work in Valdivia, she recounted, "We have as blessed times as dear as Nyack." Even children "have had real burdens of prayer for the lost, and pray for hours at a time and have been prostrated under the power of the Spirit, praying and singing in other languages."[32] Evidently, similar manifestations had taken place in her experience at the Missionary Training Institute. Simpson himself had visited Chile and affirmed Ana LaFevre's report.

Simpson also gave an account of the Pentecostal revival he observed in Chile, especially through the ministry of Willis C. Hoover and the Methodist Church. After Simpson spoke on the Holy Spirit in Hoover's Methodist Church, the people "broke loose in such a torrent of prayer as we have seldom heard or seen." Several spoke in tongues, and there were many healings and conversions. Simpson stated that Pastor Hoover did not teach that speaking in tongues is the necessary evidence of the baptism of the Holy Spirit. He supported Hoover even when the Methodist bishop and officials disciplined him and threatened to dismiss him from the Methodist church. Eventually he was dismissed and became known as the father of the Pentecostal movement in Chile.[33] Many months later in an editorial Simpson gave further positive support to Dr. Hoover's ministry in Chile even after he was defrocked from his denomination.[34]

Simpson also wrote of the Argentine C&MA mission seeking the outpouring of the Spirit. At first there was much excitement and considerable confusion when one or two workers "became temporarily unbalanced." However, eventually they experienced a "sound Scriptural baptism of the Holy Spirit."[35]

ADDITIONAL COUNSEL—ENCOURAGEMENT AND CAUTION

Repeatedly, A. B. Simpson assured readers that contrary to false rumors that the C&MA was against tongues, the Alliance did recognize all the gifts of the Spirit including tongues, but was opposed to the teaching that tongues is the evidence and is necessarily for all. He affirmed, "Many of our most wise and honored workers both in the homeland and in the mission field have had this experience."[36] Simpson declared of the mission of the C&MA: "This movement stands preeminently for the supernatural."[37] Again Simpson asserted, "Power, supernatural power. This is perhaps the most unique and impressive feature of the Gospel and is the element most lacking in the average life of the Christian and the Church."[38]

Simpson's encouragements of the supernatural were interspersed with cautions as well. He warned of shipwreck because of not trying the spirits and being cautious in following people who claim special spiritual gifts and powers. He noted that one such person was now in prison and those who followed him are under a cloud of shame and suffering. He counseled that the best evidence that a movement is of God is modesty and humility.[39] Alliance leader Mary McDonough warned of a "strange mixture of spiritual desire, psychical phenomena and demoniacal control" in the Latter Rain movement. She advised, "Keep your eyes away from others. . . . Do not covet their 'manifestations' or 'gifts.' Avoid gatherings where psychical manifestations are much in evidence."[40] Simpson wrote that in the midst of spiritual cross currents and confusion in these days, the gift of discernment is much needed.[41]

J. Hudson Ballard wrote in an article entitled "Unsound Words" that there is some misuse of the term "Pentecost" to refer only to speaking in tongues. "Pentecost" may include manifestations such as tongues, but not necessarily. Being "Pentecostal," Ballard asserted, is much broader than tongues.[42] Up until this point, the C&MA had been freely using the term "Pentecostal" to describe supernatural outpourings of the Holy Spirit. Eventually, C&MA leaders would shun the term Pentecostal as it became more identified with the tongues as evidence doctrine and excesses in practices.

There had been more difficulty and fallout from the movement in 1910, as reflected in a year-end report from Pacific District Superintendent C. H. Chrisman: "On the Pacific Coast we have the greatest collection of self-appointed prophets in the Western Hemisphere. . . . with few exceptions they boast of being special custodians of some phase of the full Gospel." He lamented the fact that as a result the Alliance work had been "hindered and handicapped."[43] Field evangelist Ulysses Lewis reported that almost all of the churches in the district "suffered from divisions as usual," and were "tried and sifted," but "have settled now to bed rock with loyal people."[44] The 1909-1910 Annual Report noted that George Davis had gone to the South Pacific and C. H. Chrisman, to the North Pacific as District Superintendents "to restore the equilibrium."[45] Davis and Chrisman had both demonstrated leadership in guiding churches through the Pentecostal movements with both openness and discernment.

ATTEMPTS TO STEM THE TIDE OF LOSSES

According to Canadian Alliance historian Lindsay Reynolds, because of the inroads of the Pentecostal message of the evidence doctrine, and Simpson's published stand against it in April 1910

> many withdrew from Alliance membership, and took with them an alarming number of church properties that had been committed to the Alliance message. In an effort to stem the tide of the losses, Dr. Simpson and the Board of Managers quite logically took strong steps to acquire or gain control of Alliance Church properties. Pressure was brought to bear on District Superintendents, who, in turn, were expected to exert their powers of persuasion on church boards.[46]

What began as an informal policy became formalized in 1912 through constitutional change at the C&MA's General Council. Through this process begun in 1910, Reynolds notes, "The inexorable metamorphosis of The Christian and Missionary Alliance from its original concept as a fraternity to that of a denomination, took a giant step forward."[47] For the aged Canadian Vice President John Salmon (now nearly 80 years old), both his own reticence toward "ecclesiastical control" and his positive experiences with the Pentecostal movement (including his own experience of tongues) led him to believe that "this new Alliance policy was an unbearable burden" and "he found the New York decision to be repugnant and unconstitutional. He would be unable to represent the new Alliance policy."[48] In September 1911, Salmon announced that he was retiring to Southern California, where he subsequently became more involved with the Pentecostal movement. Yet he also retained his Alliance connections as an evangelist and an Honorary Vice President of the C&MA.

He became actively involved with the Pentecostal movement for a period of time, finding kinship in their mutual experiences of speaking in tongues. However, he encountered extremists in the movement. Reynolds explains, "For a while he tolerated their extravagances; then he tried to restrain and counsel his new-found friends in an effort to bring the movement back to a sound scriptural basis. When they refused to accept his advice or follow his example, he completely withdrew from them and returned his whole attention to his Alliance family."[49] Alliance friends who had been concerned about his Pentecostal ventures were relieved that he had come back into the Alliance fold and avoided the excesses of the movement.

BE WATCHFUL, NOT FEARFUL

Simpson began the year of 1911 by encouraging people not to be afraid of the excesses and counterfeits, because by doing so one can miss the blessing of God:

> It is perhaps true that many earnest and sober Christians have become so much afraid of extreme and unscriptural manifestations in meetings for united prayer that they have not been waiting upon God as earnestly as in time past. This is one of the enemy's snares to frighten us away from the mercy seat. Let us trust God to keep us from the devil's counterfeit and to give us a genuine blessing, even "the spirit of love and power and a sound mind," and let us wait upon Him with confidence for the outpouring of the Holy Spirit.[50]

F. E. Marsh warned against false prophets," listing three signs of a false prophet: 1) heresies like Jehovah Witnesses (then called "Millennial Dawn") 2) love of money, and 3) pandering to lusts. Of the third sign he wrote, "There are many today, who under the name of great spirituality, seize the opportunity to feed their lust by taking advantage of guileless women, like the leader of the Pentecostal movement in Alliance [Ohio]."[51] The reference is to Levi Lupton, the Quaker minister who was a leader in the Pentecostal movement in Alliance, Ohio (along with former C&MA pastor C.A. McKinney), but disgraced his ministry in December 1910 due to a sex scandal.[52]

By the end of the year, Simpson was again warning of delusions, cautioning that even if an angel should speak with the tongues of heaven, it should have no weight until we check it with God's Word and the Holy Spirit. He avowed that there is no new revelation, but rather the illumination of already-inspired truth.[53]

On a positive note, Board of Manager minutes for June 1911 recorded that Eldridge and MacArthur restored harmony in the Southern California District.[54] Apparently there had been some friction over Pentecostal beliefs and practices, but as moderates trying to maintain both openness and caution, Eldridge and MacArthur acted as bridge-builders between Pentecostals and non-Pentecostals. Eldridge was soon appointed as Field Superintendent for the entire Pacific Coast because of his leadership.[55]

MORE DREAMS, VISIONS, TONGUES AND EXORCISMS

In August 1910 Nellie Smith, a Seventh Day Adventist woman, had gone to see Carrie Judd Montgomery in New York City. Spending three hours with her, Carrie counseled the woman about her bondage to the legalism of Sabbatarianism and laid hands on her to receive the baptism in the Spirit. As a result, she was blessed with a vision of Calvary. However, Carrie discerned that she was not yet fully free from her bondage and thus not fully filled with the Spirit. She went to see Carrie's friend Minnie Draper in February 1911 who counseled and prayed with her further. Receiving a special word from the Lord, she was set free from her doubts and legalism. Two days later, after additional prayer and receiving another vision, she was baptized in the Spirit with "joy and peace and billows of love . . . beyond words to describe." She spoke just one sentence in tongues and received the interpretation, "I shall be like Him."[56]

The C&MA Weekly described a boy in the Dholka C&MA orphanage in India who was godly and frequently prayed in tongues in his sleep.[57] A September issue of the *Weekly* reported continuing revivals in Africa: "Sights and signs resembling the scenes which we have read of in India and China" in Tembuland, South Africa. A "celestial and indescribable" ecstasy came upon the believers in praying and singing.[58]

Two issues of *The Alliance Weekly* recounted the testimony of Anna Shipton's vision and dream of heaven.[59] However, many years later Alliance leader Walter Turnbull wrote of how A. T. Pierson had exposed "Mother" Shipton's prophecy as a hoax.[60] This, no doubt, contributed to the later C&MA's increased caution about such phenomena.

In November 1911 the Ohio state C&MA convention, led by W. A. Cramer, was held in the Pentecostal mission at Piqua, Ohio, and was considered successful.[61] So at this time, the C&MA and Pentecostals were still working together cooperatively. Also in November, George Eldridge, as newly appointed Field Superintendent for the Pacific Coast, led the Alliance convention in Spokane, Washington. One of the pastors recounted, "Many received the touch divine that set the joybells of their hearts ringing, and many were made hungry for more of God and His blessed fullness, and everyone seemed to be profoundly conscious that they were standing on holy ground."[62] Anna Eldridge shared her testimony of her baptism in the Spirit with tongues, and many came forward to receive the Holy Spirit.[63] Undoubtedly some of them spoke in tongues.

SIMPSON'S MINISTRY AT PENTECOSTAL STONE CHURCH

The C&MA had a good cooperative relationship with the Pentecostal Stone Church in Chicago and its pastor William Piper. Alliance leaders W. T. MacArthur, E. O. Jago, Ira David, and others were all invited to speak there. In 1911 Simpson was invited to preach at the church. He was asked to visit 17 year-old Alfred (A. N.) Bostrom, who was dying. Simpson prayed for him at his dying bed and A. N. was healed instantly, never taking medicine again throughout his 87 year-old life. After a time with the Assemblies of God, A. N. and his brother John joined the C&MA in the mid-1920s. John eventually returned to the Assemblies of God, but A. N. stayed with the C&MA.[64]

SIMPSON SPEAKS WELL OF BRITISH PENTECOSTAL LEADER

Simpson mentioned that while in England he visited with his old friend A. A. Boddy, pastor of All Saints Church in the Church of England. Boddy had frequently written for the C&MA Weekly. Since 1907 Boddy had embraced Pentecostalism and had become a prominent leader in the British Pentecostal movement. Simpson had no criticism of Boddy's Pentecostal leanings, but spoke of him warmly.[65] Their long friendship was not strained by Boddy's Pentecostal activities and teachings. It should be noted that Boddy and British and European Pentecostals, by and large, did not hold firmly to the initial evidence doctrine.[66] Boddy did believe that tongues was available to all believers, but that did not diminish Simpson's friendship with Boddy.

THE NEGATIVE IMPACT OF DURHAM'S THEOLOGY

During 1910 and 1911, William Durham had shaken up the Pentecostal movement with his teaching refuting the Wesleyan view of sanctification, by claiming that there is no second work of grace that cleanses the believer from sin.[67] Rather, it is accomplished at salvation by the finished work of Christ, and thus it became known as the "finished work doctrine." As Durham's view began to predominate in the Pentecostal movement, it carried with it the idea that the baptism in the Spirit was solely an empowering event evidenced by tongues, not primarily by sanctifying evidences such as the fruit of the Spirit or transformation of character. A bitter opposition arose between Pentecostals who embraced Durham's theology and other Pentecostals who believed that the baptism in the Spirit involved a second blessing of sanctification or a third blessing that takes place after sanctification.

William Seymour was one example of the view maintaining that sanctification was essential to the baptism in the Spirit, and an acrimonious division arose in the Pentecostal movement. In 1911 Seymour even locked Durham out of his church at Azusa Street and prophesied that Durham would die if he turned aside from the will of God.[68] Likewise, in January 1912 Charles Parham claimed that Durham had committed the sin unto death and prophesied Durham's death within six months, praying, "If this man's doctrine is true, let my life go out to prove it, but if our teaching on a definite grace of sanctification is true, let his life pay the forfeit."[69] Durham died July 1912, a seeming fulfillment of both Seymour's and Parham's prophecies, but his teachings continued and became more popular. New movements that developed, such as the Assemblies of God and the Foursquare Church, often adopted much of Durham's viewpoint.

Although the C&MA did not accept the Wesleyan eradicationist view of sanctification or the Keswick suppressionist view, and thus would have agreed with some of Durham's teaching, it nonetheless believed that the baptism in the Spirit was a subsequent work that involved sanctification, what Simpson called "habitation," transformation by the indwelling Christ. Alliance leaders called it "the sanctifying baptism of the Spirit."

So, for the Alliance, the chief evidence of the baptism in the Spirit was a holy life. When those who spoke in tongues did not show such evidences as love, unity, tolerance, C&MA leaders questioned the experience, while many Pentecostals claimed that such evidences are secondary to the experience of tongues. This issue tore at the fabric of the C&MA relationships with Pentecostals, especially as it became divisive. C&MA leaders would point to Scriptures such as John 17:22. If it causes disunity, rancor, or elitism, Simpson and others would cast doubt on the manifestation's authenticity, or at least asserting that what had begun in the Spirit then reverted to the flesh. Smale had pointed this out earlier regarding the Azusa revival. Yet Simpson and Alliance leaders did not dismiss the entire movement, but maintained friendships with Pentecostals who did manifest the fruit of the Spirit and were not dogmatic or elitist about tongues as the evidence.

---

1. C&MA Board of Managers Minutes, June 4, 1910.

2. D. Wesley Myland, "A Personal Word," LRE, Oct. 1911, 11.

3. Gordon F. Atter, *The Third Force* (Peterborough, Ontario: The College Press, 1962), 32. For his testimony, see R. E. Sternall, "The Obedience of Faith," LRE, Feb. 1928, 4.

4. Miller, *Canadian Pentecostals*, 54. Miller lists E. S. Williams and J. Roswell Flower as colleagues of Sternall at Nyack during this time, but other sources indicate this was not so.

5. "Wilkinsburg Convention," LRE, Mar. 1910, 23. All three of them eventually left the Alliance.

6. Mrs. L. C. Baylor, "Dover, N. J.," CMAW, Mar. 5, 1910, 363.

7. "Convention in Haverhill, Massachusetts," CMAW, Mar. 19, 1910, 404.

8. Atter, 66; Menzies, *Anointed to Serve*, 134.

9. Lewis Wilson, "The Life and Legacy of George N. Eldridge," *Assemblies of God Heritage*, Spring 2001, 7; George N. Eldridge, *Personal Reminiscenses* (Los Angeles, CA: West Coast Publishing Co., [1930?]), 41.

10. Wilson, 7; Eldridge, 41.

11. Wilson, 7; Eldridge, 41.

12. Eldridge, 33.

13. Ibid.

14. Ibid., 41.

15. Brumback, *Suddenly from Heaven*, 75-78.

16. For a dream with an appearance of Jesus, see Courtney H. Fenn, "Mary Ashton's Dream," CMAW, Mar. 19, 1910, 396. For testimony of a progressive healing and a vision for two days, and a baptism in the Spirit with a manifestation "like a strong current of electricity," see Mrs. F. A. Gilbert, "Testimony," CMAW, May 21, 1910, 126. For a vision and healing from cancer, see M. Josephine Lazenby, "My Experience of Divine Healing," CMAW, Nov. 19, 1910, 118.

17. Walter Jensen, "How the Lord Miraculously Delivered Me from Christian Science," CMAW, Apr. 16, 1910, 42.

18. "Notes from the Home Field," CMAW, July 16, 1910, 258.

19. Mae E. Frey, "Minneapolis-St. Paul Convention," CMAW, Oct. 29, 1910, 77.

20. India Herlinger, "Testimony," CMAW, Dec. 31, 1910, 215.

21. Annie M. Giles, "Greensburg, Pa," CMAW, May 21, 1910, 132.

22. "Gleanings from Nyack," CMAW, Apr. 30, 1910, 82.

23. Mrs. W .S. Smith, "The Lord's Blessing at Kwaiping Station, South China," CMAW, Feb. 19, 1910, 328.

24. "Fourteenth Annual Report of the Christian and Missionary Alliance," May 30, 1911, 145.

25. Martha Woodworth, "One of India's Suffering Ones," CMAW, July 2, 1910, 217.

26. Louis F. Turnbull, "Punja Mana," CMAW, Oct. 1, 1910, 1. In December, "many manifestations of God's power" were reported in India. Charlotte Rutherford, "India, Ancient and Modern," CMAW, Dec. 3, 1910, 146.

27. I say that it was "loosely affiliated" with the C&MA, because it was not listed among official Alliance works, though his biographers (one of them his daughter) identified it with the C&MA. In those days, the Alliance was more of an interdenominational fraternal fellowship, not a denominational organization, so that many people and churches affiliated with the C&MA informally. Oscar Blomgren, Jr., "Man of God: Fred F. Bosworth, Part IV: Bosworth Begins His Work," Herald of Faith, Jan. 1964, 16-17.

28. Collins held credentials for a short time with the Assemblies of God (1917-1921), but left over the evidential tongues issue and continued to work with the C&MA until his death in 1927.

29. Edith Blumhofer, Aimee Semple McPherson: Everybody's Sister (Grand Rapids, MI: Wm. B. Eerdmans, 1993), 206.

30. Ibid., 88.

31. Ibid.

32. "Gleanings from Nyack: South America, the Neglected Continent," CMAW, Apr. 2, 1910, 9.

33. Willis Collins Hoover with Mario G. Hoover, History of the Pentecostal Revival in Chile (Santiago, Chile: Imprenta Eben-Ezer, 2000), 126-128; see also Frodsham, With Signs Following, 175-187; A. B. Simpson, "Editorial Correspondence," CMAW, Apr. 30, 1910, 71-73, 86.

34. A. B. Simpson, Editorial, CMAW, Dec. 24, 1910, 200.

35. Ibid.

36. A. B. Simpson, Editorial, CMAW, Apr. 30, 1910, 78.

37. A. B. Simpson, "Our Trust," CMAW, May 28, 1910, 145.

38. A. B. Simpson, Editorial, CMAW, July 9, 1910, 240.

39. A. B. Simpson, Editorial, CMAW, July 30, 1910, 288.

40. Mary E. McDonough, "The Harvest Rain," CMAW, Feb. 5, 1910, 297, 305.

41. A. B. Simpson, Editorial, CMAW, Oct. 8, 1910, 24.

42. J. Hudson Ballard, "Papers for Thoughtful Christians IV: Unsound Words," CMAW, Dec. 24, 1910, 195.

43. C. H. Chrisman, "Notes from the Home Field," CMAW, Dec. 24, 1910, 205.

44. Ulysses Lewis, "Sustentation Fund," CMAW, May 21, 1910, 131-132.

45. Annual Report of the Christian and Missionary Alliance, 1909-1910.

46. Reynolds, *Footprints*, 294.

47. Ibid., 293.

48. Ibid., 295.

49. Ibid., 304.

50. A. B. Simpson, Editorial, CMAW, Jan. 21, 1911, 264.

51. Marsh, "Here and There: False Prophets," CMAW, July 29, 1911, 284.

52. McGee, "Lupton, Levi Rakestraw," DPCM, 561-562; McGee, "Levi Lupton," 203 ff.

53. A. B. Simpson, Editorial, AW, Dec. 16, 1911, 161.

54. C&MA Executive Committee Minutes, June 17, 1911.

55. "Notes from the Home Field," AW, Feb. 17, 1912, 317.

56. Nellie Grant Smith, "Delivered from Seventh Day Bondage," LRE, May 1911, 22.

57. H. V. Ludrus, "The Life and Death of a Dholka Boy," CMAW, June 24, 1911, 195.

58. "Gleanings from Nyack: Darkest Africa," CMAW, Sept. 9, 1911, 380.

59. CMAW, Sept. 9, 1911, 378; "A Vision from Heaven," AW, Oct. 21, 1911, 38. (Note that the *Christian and Missionary Alliance Weekly* changed to *The Alliance Weekly* beginning October 1911).

60. Walter Turnbull, "Mother Shipton's Prophecy," AW, Feb. 5, 1927, 90-91.

61. AW, Feb. 17, 1912, 318.

62. "Notes from the Home Field," AW, Feb. 17, 1912, 317.

63. Ibid.

64. As related by Dr. Harvey R. Bostrom about his father.

65. A. B. Simpson, Editorial, CMAW, Apr. 29, 1911, 65.

66. Henry I. Lederle, *Treasures Old and New: Interpretations of "Spirit-Baptism" in the Charismatic Renewal Movement* (Peabody, MA: Hendrickson Publishers, 1988), 47-48. See Mary Boddy, "The Real Baptism of the Holy Ghost," *Confidence*, Nov. 1909, 260-261.

67. See William W. Menzies, "The Non-Wesleyan Origins of the Pentecostal Movement," in Vinson Synan, ed., *Aspects of Pentecostal-Charismatic Origins* (Plainfield, NJ: Logos, 1975), 90-94; Synan, *The Holiness-Pentecostal Movement in the United States*, 147-153.

68. Douglas J. Nelson, "For Such a Time as This: The Story of Bishop William J. Seymour and the Azusa Street Revival: A Search for Pentecostal/Charismatic Roots," (Ph.D. dissertation, University of Birmingham, England, 1981), 39.

69. Edith Blumhofer, "The Finished Work of Calvary: William H. Durham and a Doctrinal Controversy," *Assemblies of God Heritage*, Fall 1983, 9. Other Pentecostal leaders, including A. A. Boddy and former C&MA conference speaker Morton Plummer, endeavored to bring harmony between the opposing camps. See Morton W. Plummer, "The Finished and the Unfinished Work," LRE, Aug. 1912, 2; "Pastor Boddy," LRE, Sept. 1912, 12-13.

1912—Year of Revival and Crisis

Alliance leaders continued openness to charismatic manifestations, but the year would become a critical turning point in the C&MA. Early in the year Simpson continued in his editorials to reaffirm belief in tongues and the gifts of Spirit, but again continued to disavow the evidence doctrine.[1]

Partnership Between the Alliance and Pentecostals

Cooperation between the Alliance and at least some Pentecostals continued in 1912 and following. W. A. Cramer held evangelistic meetings in January in the Pentecostal mission at Piqua, Ohio, after the successful C&MA convention there in November.[2] Gregory Mantle, a British minister and friend of the C&MA, was a speaker at the Pentecostal convention in London in January. He was a personal friend of Cecil Polhill, though acknowledged as not being "in the [Pentecostal] Movement."[3] Mantle, a bridge-builder between Pentecostal and Keswick/Higher Life movements, was a featured speaker at Alliance conventions beginning about 1911, and began pastoral ministry in the Alliance in the United States by 1915, eventually joining the faculty of the Missionary Training Institute at Nyack.

In a Board of Managers meeting on March 30, it was announced that Cecil Polhill of England proposed a cooperative venture in missions between the Alliance and the Pentecostal work of England. The matter was referred to a committee of Simpson, Funk and Glover, and later approved, with the Alliance and the British Pentecostal Mission sharing support of missionaries for several years.[4] During the summer, an annual Pentecostal convention was held at Montwait, Massachusetts, organized by Albert Weaver, a member of the Alliance church in Springfield. Among the speakers were German Pentecostal pastor Jonathan Paul and Dr. Yoakum.[5] The Alliance church was apparently involved with the convention.

In October Dr. Charles Blanchard, president of Wheaton College and an honorary vice president of the C&MA, was a featured speaker at the Pentecostal Stone Church in Chicago, and his sermon was featured in *The Latter Rain Evangel*.[6] Along with frequent visits from William T. MacArthur and another C&MA scholar Ira David, a relationship begun earlier continued to blossom between the Stone Church and the Alliance.

Teaching on the Authority of the Believer and Spiritual Warfare

The C&MA continued to be on the forefront in exorcism and spiritual warfare ministry.[7] MacArthur recounted that during this year he and Simpson discerned and dealt with a demonized woman who ultimately did not want to get rid of her demon companion.[8] In October Simpson published "The Hand Upon the Throne," based on teaching of C&MA leaders George D. Watson and George B. Peck on "throne power" and the authority of the believer. Alliance leader John MacMillan later wrote on this theme.[9] These themes would later be embraced by Pentecostals and charismatics, especially in the Word of Faith Movement.

C&MA/Pentecostal Revival in Dallas

From July 25 to November 1912, Maria Woodworth-Etter carried on a crusade through Bosworth's church. Many were healed, baptized in Spirit with tongues, and fell under the power of Spirit. As representatives of the Alliance, honorary Vice President George Montgomery and his wife Carrie, long-time friend of Woodworth-Etter, attended the meetings.[10] Carrie reported:

> She believes in working for the unifying of all the members of the body of Christ, and therefore she does not preach mere theories, but holds up a living Christ, receiving all who are honest in their hearts and purposes towards Him, even if they do not yet see the truth just as she teaches it. She also avoids laying stress upon certain words or expressions, with which the enemy is trying to cause divisions in the body of Christ. Therefore there is no contention or strife in these meetings, but love and unity.[11]

After this time, however, Bosworth and his church became more aligned with the Pentecostal movement until Bosworth returned to the Alliance in 1918.

Simpson Welcomes European Pentecostal Leaders

At Simpson's invitation, German Pentecostal leader Pastor Jonathan Paul preached at Simpson's Gospel Tabernacle in New York in the summer of 1912. Simpson affirmed that his position on Pentecostalism was moderate and quoted Paul saying that tongues is not a necessary evidence for the baptism in the Spirit.[12] Pastor Paul believed:

> The gift of tongues may be received by any regenerate person. Children readily receive the gift, but I cannot in all such cases say they

have received the baptism of the Holy Ghost. Then there are those also who have received the baptism, but have not spoken in tongues. I knew personally those who have undoubtedly received the baptism. Their lives and power and love show this, and I could not say that they were not baptized with the Holy Ghost. I myself received the baptism twenty years ago, and had all the evidences which I have today though I did not speak in tongues. . . . Later I spoke also in tongues, but I had the baptism twenty years before.[13]

This was compatible with Alliance belief and Simpson welcomed him with open arms. Simpson also invited his friend British Pentecostal leader A. A. Boddy to preach in his church when he was visiting in the United States in the fall of 1912, but Boddy's schedule did not permit him to do so.[14] The fact that Simpson invited these Pentecostal leaders to speak indicates that the Alliance continued to welcome moderate Pentecostals.

PENTECOSTAL OUTPOURING IN TIBET

Revival among C&MA mission stations in West China began in August and September of 1911 through a series of meetings led by Mr. Lultey of China Inland Mission. The revival was accompanied by weeping and wailing, conversions, and simultaneous vocal prayer.[15] The revival continued into 1912 and 1913 with manifestations of tongues, visions, and prophesying "in nearly all our stations," as missionary Martin Ekvall reported, as well as healings and casting out demons.[16]

On May 5, 1912, W. W. Simpson, long-time C&MA missionary to Tibet, received the baptism in the Spirit with tongues. Simpson's wife and children, William Christie's wife Jessie and ten year old son Milton, Mrs. David Ekvall, and, over the next several months, about a hundred people from the mission soon also received Spirit baptism with tongues. Manifestations of holy laughter, visions, prophesying, falling under the power of the Spirit, singing in the Spirit, deliverance and healing also accompanied this revival.[17] According to W. W. Simpson, almost all of the Chinese leaders received the "full baptism" with tongues.[18] This revival continued to be reported in the *Alliance Weekly* as late as November, describing more than thirty receiving the Holy Spirit accompanied by speaking in tongues and prophesying, many healings, and the exorcism of a young woman.[19] W. W. Simpson's testimony and report of this revival was all recorded in the *Alliance Weekly* quite positively and supportively nearly a year later.[20] Ekvall reported in April 1913, "The West China mission was formerly in the hardest and most unyielding field, and it has now become one of the greatest harvest fields in mission work."[21]

However, the positive attitudes at the Alliance headquarters back home began to wither as W. W. Simpson became insistent that tongues was *the* evidence of Spirit baptism. Also, according to W. W. Simpson in a letter to J. W. Welch, William Christie had begun seeking the baptism in the Spirit, and almost spoke in tongues, but after two months concluded that it was not the Holy Spirit, but rather an evil spirit.[22] Both Christie and Simpson had witnessed genuine and false tongues several years earlier in the mission,[23] but they had differing reactions to the appropriateness and spiritual safety of seeking Spirit baptism with tongues. Simpson saw no need to worry about receiving a demonic manifestation, while Christie, though open to tongues (as both his wife and son had received), concluded that a demon might have been influencing his seeking.

Christie's cautionary attitude combined with W.W. Simpson's aggressiveness furthered the rift in the mission, which came to a head in 1914, with Simpson refusing to recant the evidence doctrine. Simpson wanted to continue to maintain his position on the field (which he claimed he had been allowed to maintain in his own station for years),[24] while Christie and the Alliance leaders wanted him to maintain the position that the Alliance had taken all along. Even with the controversy over W. W. Simpson's view of evidential tongues and his subsequent departure in May 1914, supernatural ministry and charismatic manifestations continued. At the end of May 1914, the *Alliance Weekly* reported exorcisms of demon possession in Tibet. People there would wait for spirit-possession like waiting for the baptism of the Spirit. Some who become spirit-possessed were able to foretell the future. Many exorcisms took place after tormented people seeking help from Christians.[25] Likewise, in July 1914 missionary Katherine MacKinnon reported that a Christian woman in West China who was thought to be dead and was dressed in grave clothes by mourners suddenly sat up and was well! The woman related that while she was in that state of apparent death she saw a vision of Mrs. William Christie and her servant preaching to her to trust the Lord and then she regained consciousness.[26]

BALLARD BECOMES SPOKESMAN FOR PENTECOSTAL ISSUES

J. Hudson Ballard, who had penned one of the C&MA's earliest and most-repeated position responses on tongues in 1907, emerged in 1912-1915 as the chief spokesperson to answer questions about the C&MA's beliefs and practices regarding speaking in tongues, writing numerous articles and replies to questions. Simpson apparently had confidence in him to give the most articulate, balanced, and reasoned responses. Possibly responding to the rising "Finished Work" theology of Durham, in Ballard wrote an article entitled "How May I Know I Am Spirit-Filled." In this article he enumerated the evidences of the Spirit-filled life as: 1) the presence of Christ, 2) the preciousness of the Word, 3) the preeminence of heavenly things, 4) progress in grace, 5) power with men, 6) passion for souls, and 7) prayerfulness.[27]

In his question-and-answer column, "The Spiritual Clinic," he fielded readers' questions regarding tongues, reiterating that tongues is not the chief gift or a necessary evidence, but it is a gift for today. Further, he noted, not every seeming manifestation of tongues is genuine, nor are all manifestations of tongues pure.[28] He commented further that the gift of tongues is for all the church, but not necessarily for every individual Christian, yet rather as God wills. He assured, "There is a real place for the gift of tongues in the life of the church." Forbidding tongues, he warned, is fighting against God. Further, he exhorted, "Let us all be sure we are willing to receive any gift, including the gift of tongues; yet let us leave the matter

— 154 —

to the will of the Spirit Himself and be deeply thankful and satisfied with what He chooses to bestow. . . . Let no one dare oppose God's true gift. Let each one make sure he is ready for any gift the Spirit 'wills' to send him."[29]

C&MA Consensus: A Place for Tongues in Every Church

As Ballard continued to speak for the Alliance position in 1913-1915, he commented concerning 1 Corinthians 14, "The chief value [of tongues] is to the inner experience of the person who has that gift. . . . To speak in tongues is quite permissible (vs. 5). Those who deny the right to exercise the genuine gift of tongues are surely going contrary to Scripture. . . . Tongues are not to be forbidden."[30] Most significant, Ballard asserted, "Alliance leaders are quite agreed in believing that speaking with tongues is one of the gifts of the Spirit and should have a place in every Spirit-controlled church."[31] This was the Alliance position for another two decades, but was abandoned in the 1930s.

C&MA Reorganization and Constitutional Revision Causes Fallout

In January 1912, Foreign Secretary Glover reported that due to new works of new spiritual experiences there had been a diversion of missionary funds. He encouraged continuing to give to Alliance missions, assuring, "With regard to variation of belief concerning details of doctrine, as for instance the question of the gift and manifestation of tongues, there is in our Society no rigid lines drawn, but sufficient latitude for all who are moderate and reasonable."[32] However, because of the loss of funds, property, pastors, and congregations, the Board of Managers felt that some kind of action needed to be taken in order to stem the tide of losses.

In February Simpson wrote an editorial of the important upcoming Alliance Easter conference discussing how to be open to the Spirit's moving while avoiding "present dangerous drifts." When the Easter Conference commenced March 31, the Board of Managers planned an agenda to discuss reorganization of the C&MA and revision of the C&MA Constitution, with recommendations to go to General Council in May.[33] One of the proposed changes became known as the "reversion clause," stating that the property of an Alliance work would revert back to the Alliance if the work no longer maintained Alliance beliefs or left the Alliance fold. What began as informal policies implemented in 1910, became formalized in this constitutional change. Nothing in the reorganization and revision specifically named the problem of Pentecostal fallout, but the implications of the reversion clause were not lost on the strongly Pentecostallyoriented of the Alliance, just as on John Salmon a few months earlier.

In an editorial just before the General Council in May, Simpson explained the purpose of the upcoming constitutional changes at General Council to be held at Boone, Iowa, May 27-30. According to Simpson, the proposed changes would strive to be "adjusted to a more perfect harmony between the central authority and executive control on one hand, and local freedom and independence in the various districts and branches on the other. . . . We believe the new order will secure great strength and unity in the center of the work, and perfect liberty in every section and department, and that with perfect order and without friction, 'fitly framed together,' we shall grow up into all the fulness of God's plan for our far-reaching work."[34]

The Annual Council in Boone approved the reorganized organizational structure, including the "reversion clause" to eliminate loss of C&MA buildings and funds to those who leave C&MA and/or its teachings. According to some reports, as many as 24 other pastors eventually left the C&MA as a result.[35] Some writers of Pentecostal history give the impression that there was an immediate mass exodus from the C&MA.[36] However, not all leaders left all at once, but over a period of months, and even years. Some, like C. A. McKinney, L. C. Hall, and A. S. Copley, had left the Alliance years earlier.

Bell Resigns from British Alliance

Even before the Easter Conference started, the most immediate fallout resulted as it was announced at the March 30th Board of Managers meeting that Mr. Bell of Manchester, England, submitted his resignation as treasurer on account of opposition of the Alliance to the doctrine of restorationism. This is probably the same Mr. Bell who received tongues along with about forty others in the Alliance revival in Scotland in 1908, and was at that time described as an "out and out Alliance man." Since Alliance leaders taught some form of restorationism or the concept of the Latter Rain, Bell must have meant the evidential tongues doctrine.

Ironically, it was in the same meeting that the proposal from Cecil Polhill of England for partnership in missions between the Alliance and the Pentecostal work of England was considered and later approved.[37] For some Pentecostals the C&MA was charismatically-open enough to work cooperatively, yet for others the Alliance was not sufficiently or distinctively Pentecostal.

Minnie Draper Resigns Board of Managers

Just a week later on April 6, at the end of the Easter Conference but still nearly two months before the final vote the end of May, Minnie Draper resigned her position on the Board of Managers. Having been a part of the discussions, she apparently became uncomfortable with the action the Board was taking, and evidently felt she could not remain on the Board under those circumstances,[38] just as Salmon several months earlier. She did not leave the C&MA immediately, however, but continued in ministry with the Alliance for a period of time. She was still involved with the healing ministry of the C&MA through the remainder of the year and was a speaker at Alliance conventions in the summer and October. In 1913 Draper still held credentials with the Alliance when she began her Pentecostal ministry in Ossining, New York, but evidently did not renew her credentials later in the year.[39]

Discord in Findlay

Evidently because of the influence of Pentecostal leader T. K. Leonard and D. W. Kerr, former pastor of the Alliance work in Findlay, Ohio, some conflict and loss arose over Pentecostal teachings and practices, even though the church had experienced Pentecostal revival. A new pastor, E. J. Witte, had come in to stabilize the work. By April, according to field superintendent F. H. Senft, "The work has undergone changes that have not been helpful to its growth, but the faithful ones are patiently plodding on and praying for enlargement."[40] Witte himself soon left for the Assemblies of God (and later returned to the C&MA in the 1920s).[41] In 1914, Etta Wurmser moved her Bible school in Norwalk (which was training many Pentecostal ministers and missionaries) to Findlay and took over the church there, until about 1918. After about a decade of directing the school evidentially as an independent Pentecostal ministry (not holding Alliance credentials, but maintaining connections with the C&MA), she returned to pastor the Alliance church in Findlay for nearly two decades.[42]

David Wesley Myland Leaves

As of the end of April 1912, Myland no longer served as a C&MA Ohio District Evangelist, but was still listed as pastor of the Alliance-affiliated United Gospel Tabernacle in Columbus. The spring district Alliance convention was held in his church. However, by July he had resigned his church and soon moved to Plainfield, Indiana, where he founded a new Pentecostal institution, Gibeah Bible School. The school included a number of former Alliance people.[43] It is significant, however, that in his integrity, he did not take the United Gospel Tabernacle out of the Alliance or start a new work in competition with the existing Alliance work in Columbus. Also, he never joined the Assemblies of God, perhaps because he wanted to maintain friendships with the Alliance,[44] or out of "desire to have the freedom to follow his own biblical convictions and avenue of ministry without control or restraint."[45]

Western District Superintendent Resists Constitutional Changes

Charles Crawford, who as Western District Superintendent had experienced and supported the Pentecostal revival in his district, was a member of the constitutional revision committee. Apparently he was unhappy with the decisions of the committee and the C&MA council, for although he continued as a district superintendent and an honorary vice president until 1916, he gradually withdrew financial support and distanced his district from the C&MA, failing to implement the constitutional changes in his district. The Board responded by redrawing the district border lines, leaving him as superintendent only of Iowa, and eventually asked him to resign in 1916. According to the home secretary's 1916 report, "When the Board decided to dispense with the services of Mr. Crawford, there was only one organized branch left in the District."[46]

Eldridge Gradually Withdraws

By the summer of 1912, George Eldridge had resigned his position as California State Superintendent of the C&MA, presumably due to his Pentecostal convictions, yet he remained a District Evangelist as well as pursuing Pentecostal endeavors. He also continued and as a speaker for Alliance conventions for another four years and as an Honorary Vice President of the C&MA for six years.[47] In 1913 he left the Alliance church he was pastoring in Los Angeles and started another church called Bethel Mission, ostensibly to provide a more Pentecostal church (still listed as a C&MA church). In 1916 it relocated (avoiding the reversion clause), was renamed Bethel Temple, and affiliated with the Assemblies of God.

Ira David Departs, But Returns

In March 1912, Dr. Ira E. David, who had served for many years as the superintendent of the New England district, resigned his position, moving to the Chicago area to be near his aging father and to become involved with the Pentecostal movement there.[48] From March through July he had been a frequent guest speaker at the Pentecostal Stone Church in Chicago, along with Bosworth, Myland, and Azusa Street leader William Seymour.[49] Evidently he felt a kinship that drew him into a more active role in the Pentecostal movement, and he became a frequent speaker at the Stone Church. However, like Salmon, disillusioned with excesses in the Pentecostal movement and emphasis on evidential tongues, he returned to the Alliance less than two years later. He became an active leader in the C&MA as a convention speaker, Bible teacher, and eventually a Board of Managers member, as well as continuing his Pentecostal connections, especially with the Stone Church.

First Departure from Tibetan Mission

Fallout began to occur on the mission field as well. After the Pentecostal outpouring upon the Alliance mission on the Tibetan border in May, the first withdrawal from the mission was announced at the November Board of Managers meeting. Grace Agar submitted her resignation from the Tibetan Mission to join the Pentecostal movement.[50] W. W. Simpson and his wife would follow in 1915, and still others by the end of the decade.

Simpson's Alleged Regret

David McDowell, former C&MA pastor who became an Assemblies of God leader, reported that sometime during 1912 Simpson remarked to him, "David, I did what I thought was best, but I am afraid that I missed it."[51] McDowell seems to imply that Simpson was regretting his stand against tongues as the evidence of the baptism in the Spirit. Nienkirchen connects this with Simpson's pensive statement in his diary in October 1912:

> Five years have passed since these mem. were written. Much has come and gone. God has been ever with me and wrought for me.

No extraordinary manifestation of the Spirit in tongues or similar gifts has come. Many of my friends have received such manifestations, but mine has still been a life of [   ] fellowship and service. At all times my spirit has been open to God for anything He might be pleased to reveal or bestow. [52]

Nienkirchen concludes from this statement, "Were it not for the evidence of Simpson's diary, this anecdote preserved in the annals of Pentecostal history might readily be dismissed as obvious triumphalism. The diary's account of Simpson's unsuccessful pursuit of a Spirit baptism with tongues, however, apparently corroborates the revisionist comment attributed by McDowell to Simpson."[53]

Some in the C&MA might dismiss McDowell's claim of Simpson's regret as unreliable and colored by Pentecostal bias. However, there is no real reason to doubt the authenticity of the statement, only McDowell's and Nienkirchen's interpretations of the statement. If we assume that Simpson really made the statement, we need to consider the context of both the events of 1912, and the whole of Simpson's teaching and responses regarding the Pentecostal movement.

Circumstantially, we can acknowledge that there is a connection with the happenings of 1912, but Nienkirchen mistakenly concluded that Simpson had changed his mind about the appropriateness of seeking tongues. A study of the evidence from all of Simpson's statements in context shows that Simpson did not change his mind. (This is discussed in the chapter on "The Early C&MA and 'Seek Not, Forbid Not'").[54] Rather, in the context of the events of 1912 it is most likely that Simpson was referring to the decision to add the reversion clause to the constitution, with the resulting exodus of numerous Alliance leaders and churches into the Pentecostal movement. He and the majority of the other Alliance leaders evidently had thought it was best to stop the financial bleeding through this legislative change.

Even if Simpson eventually concluded that this was not the wisest way to handle the matter, the "water was over the dam" and the decision was never reversed.[55] It did prevent further loss of property and allocated funds, but the ultimate loss of people, and thus additional funds, may have been much greater. Effectively, it began the C&MA on a course to becoming a denomination, even though leaders would disclaim it for decades. C&MA historian Lindsay Reynolds comments, "It was this new policy of gaining control of church properties, that more than anything else so far, advanced denominationalism within the Alliance.[56]

Further, Brumback, an Assemblies of God historian, commented, "Nyack students who managed to see Dr. Simpson alone in his later years (and it took some managing!), declare that he manifested a deep interest in the Pentecostal Revival which he had reluctantly rejected."[57] It is true that Simpson continued to maintain a deep and positive interest in the Pentecostal revival, but Brumback makes two erroneous assumptions: 1) Simpson had rejected the Pentecostal movement, 2) Simpson regretted his stance on tongues as the initial evidence.

Simpson had not rejected the Pentecostal movement. He wanted Pentecostal manifestations in Alliance churches. What he rejected were the evidential tongues doctrine and uncontrolled excesses in the movement. He never retracted his criticism of these elements. In fact, if you look at Alliance writings and especially Simpson's own writings after 1912, they clearly demonstrate he had not changed his position. He was always open to and desirous of Pentecostal manifestations in the Alliance, so long as they were moderate and balanced.

1. A. B. Simpson, Editorial, AW, Jan. 27, 1912, 258.

2. "Who and Where," AW, Feb. 17, 1912, 318.

3. A. A. Boddy, "The London Conference," *Confidence*, Feb. 1912, 37.

4. C&MA Board of Manager Minutes, Mar. 30, 1912.

5. "Pentecostal Items," *Confidence*, Apr. 1912, 90; "Pentecostal Items," *Confidence*, June 1912, 140.

6. Charles A. Blanchard, "The Two Preparations," LRE, Mar. 1913, 2.

7. For a report about a demon being cast out in China, see L. J. Cutler, "A Demon Cast Out," CMAW, Apr. 8, 1911, 19.

8. MacArthur, "A Reminiscence of Rev. A. B. Simpson," AW, Aug. 21, 1920, 325-326.

9. A. B. Simpson, "The Hand Upon the Throne," AW, Oct. 12, 1912, 35; see George B. Peck, *Throne Life, or The Highest Christian Life* (Boston, MA: Watchword Publishing, 1888); George D. Watson, *Steps to the Throne* (Cincinnati, OH: Bible School Book Room, n.d.); George D. Watson, *Bridehood Saints* (Cincinnati, OH: God's Revivalist, n.d.), 117-118, 120-122; John A. MacMillan, *The Authority of the Believer* (Harrisburg, PA: Christian Publications, 1980), 49, 55, 93, 96; King, *A Case Study of a Believer with Authority*, 274, 289-290, 320-321; Paul L. King, *A Believer with Authority: The Life and Message of John A. MacMillan* (Camp Hill, PA: Christian Publications, 2001), 219-220.

10. Maria B. Woodworth-Etter, *Acts of the Holy Ghost: Life and Experience of Mrs. M. B. Woodworth-Etter* (Dallas, TX: John F. Worley Printing Co., n.d.), 350-371.

11. Maria Woodworth-Etter, *Signs and Wonders* (New Kensington, PA: Whitaker House, 1997), 156-157.

12. A. B. Simpson, Editorial, AW, July 6, 1912, 210.

13. Cited in Elizabeth V. Baker, *Chronicles of a Faith Life* (New York and London: Garland Publishing Co.,1984), 142.

14. Alexander A. Boddy, "Transatlantic Experiences," *Confidence*, Apr. 1913, 70.

15. Martin Ekvall, "Revival in West China," AW, Apr. 5, 1913, 8-9.

16. Ibid.

17. W. W. Simpson, "Notes from Kansu," AW, Mar. 1, 1913, 345-346; see also A. Williams, "Tibet: Brothers Williams and Trevitt," *Confidence*, July 1912, 167; Frank Trevitt, "Tibet: News from Bro. Trevitt," *Confidence*, Dec. 1912, 286; W. W. Simpson, "A Revival Near Tibet," *Confidence*, Jan. 1913, 3-5; W. W. Simpson, "A Revival Near Tibet," *Confidence*, Mar. 1913, 52.

18. W. W. Simpson, "Miracles of Grace on the Tibetan Border," LRE, Jan. 1916, 8.

19. W. W. Simpson, "Missionary Department: From Tibet," AW, Nov. 16, 1912, 104.

20. W. W. Simpson, "Notes from Kansu," AW, Mar. 1, 1913, 345-346.

21. Martin Ekvall, "Revival in West China," AW, Apr. 5, 1913, 8-9.

22. Nichol, 50; letter from W. W. Simpson to J. W. Welch, Jan. 26, 1919, Flower Pentecostal Heritage Center, Springfield, MO.

23. W. W. Simpson and William Christie, "Demon Possession in Our Mincheo Native Conference, Jan. 1908," CMAW, Apr. 18, 1908, 38-39. For other descriptions of this same incident see also William Ruhl, "Western China," CMAW, May 9, 1908, 9.

24. Letter from W. W. Simpson to J. W. Welch, Jan. 26, 1919, Flower Pentecostal Heritage Center, Springfield, MO.

25. J. D. Williams, "Our Foreign Mail Bag," AW, May 30, 1914, 141.

26. Katherine MacKinnon, "Mission Life in Chone, West China," AW, July 18, 1914, 264.

27. J. Hudson Ballard, "How May I Know I Am Spirit-FIlled?" AW, Jan. 6, 1912, 211.

28. J. Hudson Ballard, "The Spiritual Clinic," AW, Feb. 24, 1912, 325.

29. J. Hudson Ballard, "The Spiritual Clinic," AW, Mar. 2, 1912, 343. For more of Ballard's teaching on tongues and other gifts of the Spirit see: J. Hudson Ballard, "The Spiritual Clinic," AW, July 20, 1912, 254; J. Hudson Ballard, "The Spiritual Clinic," AW, July 27, 1912, 270; J. Hudson Ballard, "The Spiritual Clinic," AW, Oct. 5,1912, 14; J. Hudson Ballard, "The Old Time Baptism of the Holy Ghost," AW, Oct. 12, 1912, 23; J. Hudson Ballard, "The Spiritual Clinic," AW, Dec. 21, 1912, 190; J. Hudson Ballard, "The Spiritual Clinic," AW, Aug.9, 1913, 302.

30. J. Hudson Ballard, "Studies in I Corinthians," AW, June 20, 1914, 198-199; June 27, 1914, 214-215. Ballard defined the gift of prophecy as: "Prophesying is speaking for God under the unction of the Holy Spirit." J. Hudson Ballard, "The Spiritual Clinic," AW, Mar. 20, 1915, 398.

31. J. Hudson Ballard, "The Spiritual Clinic," AW, Nov. 21, 1914, 126. He also reflected that the current movement does not meet the criteria of 1 Corinthians 14 and proper control of the gifts.

32. R. H. Glover, "The Diversion of Missionary Funds," AW, Jan. 20, 1912, 249-250.

33. AW, Mar. 30, 1912, 401; AW, Apr. 1, 1912, 1.

34. A. B. Simpson, Editorial, AW, May 25, 1912, 113-114.

35. E. B. Robinson, "Myland, David Wesley," DPCM, 632-633.

36. Faupel, The Everlasting Gospel, 236.

37. C&MA Board of Manager Minutes, Mar. 30, 1912.

38. See resignation letter from Minnie Draper, Apr. 6, 1912. She was gracious in her resignation and did not mention any complaint.

39. McGee, "Draper, Minnie Tingley," DPCM, 250.

40. F. H. Senft, "Ohio Convention," AW, Apr. 6, 1912, 114.

41. See Assemblies of God Directory, 1917. For his return to the C&MA, see "The Household of Faith," AW, Dec. 13, 1924, 422, where Witte served as supply pastor for the Alliance church in Muncie, Indiana. Also see C&MA Annual Reports for 1924-1928, where he pastored churches in Mechanicsburg and Dubois in Pennsylvania.

42. "Everywhere Preaching," AW, Nov. 7, 1951, 701.

43. AW, Apr. 27, 1912, 59; E. B. Robinson, "Myland, David Wesley," DPCM, 632.

44. Robinson, "Myland, David Wesley," 632-633.

45. J. Kevin Butcher, "The Holiness and Pentecostal Labors of David Wesley Myland: 1890-1918," unpublished Masters of Theology thesis, Dallas Theological Seminary, 1983, 133.

46. Notes and correspondence in C&MA Archives.

47. AW, July 6, 1912, 223; AW, Aug. 31, 1912, 351; AW, Sept. 21, 1912, 415; Lewis Wilson, "The Life and Legacy of George N. Eldridge," 7.

48 . "Who and Where," AW, Oct. 12, 1912, 29, 31; Ira E David, "God's Directive and Permissive Will," LRE, Oct. 1912, 7; Ira E. David, "A Bible Telegram and the Victory of Praise," LRE, Dec. 1912, 19; Ira E.

David, "Brought Low," LRE, Feb. 1913, 15; "The Cloud of His Glory Upon Us," LRE, June 1913, 2; LRE, Mar. 1914, 13; I. E. D., "Nurturing the Gift," LRE, Mar. 1914, 9.

49. "Notes," LRE, Apr. 1912, 14; Ira E. David, "Christian Development through Trial and Hardship," LRE, May 1912, 2; Mrs. Ira E. David, "Christ Our Example in Holiness," LRE, May 1912, 23; "Not I But Christ," LRE , June 1912, 2; Ira E. David, "Encouragement for Defeated Ones," LRE, July 1912, 19; Ira E. David, "The Hour and the Place of Crisis," LRE, Apr. 1913, 21; Alexander A. Boddy, "Transatlantic Experiences," *Confidence*, Mar. 1913, 59.

50. C&MA Board of Manager Minutes, Nov. 2, 1912.

51. Brumback, *Suddenly . . . from Heaven*, 93-94, cited in Nienkirchen, 106.

52. Nienkirchen, 106, 147. Among Simpson's friends who had received tongues were A. A. Boddy, Willis Hoover, Jonathan Paul, George and Carrie Judd Montgomery, Robert Jaffray, Ira David, W. A. Cramer, Mrs. William T. MacArthur, H. M. Shuman, A. C. Snead, Mr. and Mrs. Albert Weaver, Warren Collins, Rev. and Mrs. George Eldridge, John Salmon, and many others.

53. Nienkirchen, 106.

54. See also Paul L. King, "Seek Not, Forbid Not: The Early Christian and Missionary Alliance Position on Glossolalia," *Wesleyan Theological Journal*, Vol. 40, No. 2 (Fall 2005), 184-219.

55. The 1912-1913 C&MA Annual Report put it in a positive light: "The year has been one of test concerning the new Constitutional and Legislative character of the Council, but most satisfactory results have already been in evidence. The wisdom of the action at the last Council has manifested itself in what we believe to be a larger and more enthusiastic representation from all sections of the field than in any previous years, one hundred and seventy delegates being in attendance." C&MA 1912-1913 Annual Report, 81.

56. Lindsay Reynolds, *Footprints*, 294.57. Brumback, *Suddenly . . . from Heaven*, 95.

THIRTEEN

WALKING THE TIGHTROPE
OF OPENNESS AND CAUTION

BE WATCHFUL, BUT NOT FEARFUL

In February 1912 a Simpson editorial, referring to the Father giving good gifts to His children (Luke 11:13), counseled not to be fearful of special gifts and blessings just because there is some fanaticism. He exhorted, "Let us not be less watchful, but let us be less fearful." Further, he wrote of important upcoming Easter conference discussing issues such as "How to Maintain the Spirituality and Simplicity of the Work in the Midst of the Present Dangerous Drifts," "How to Secure the Largest Measure of the Holy Spirit in the Most Safe and Scriptural Way,"[1] It was Simpson's desire for the Alliance to be receptive of "the largest measure of the Holy Spirit," while at the same time avoiding what he considered to be unscriptural excesses and dangers. Mrs. George (Anna) Eldridge cautioned in The Alliance Weekly against seeking after manifestations, emotions or thrills.[2] It is significant that although the Eldridges were Pentecostally-oriented and would eventually leave the Alliance, they advocated not seeking after manifestations.

WARNINGS OF COUNTERFEITS

In July 1912, The Alliance Weekly referred to an article in The Overcomer (published by Jessie Penn-Lewis) warning to "believe not every spirit," and cautioning that it is possible for a soul "to be surrendering itself to evil spirits, believing it to be surrendering to the Holy Spirit . . . unwittingly."[3] The 1912 annual report of the Congo mission reported a girl who became demon-possessed after her Christian mother died. She was speaking in counterfeit tongues and was wild and abusive in her speech, but she was delivered.[4]

In September 1916 Simpson wrote, "God was not in the earthquake, the whirlwind, or the fire, but in the still small voice. The natural heart is prone to look for signs, wonders, and startling manifestations of the divine presence and power. But we miss the voice of God when we look for these things and often invite the counterfeit of the enemy's demonstrations and delusions."[5]

In November 1916 Frederick W. Farr, another long-time Alliance leader, wrote an article entitled "Satanic Mimicry" on counterfeits and Satanic imitations.[6] An article entitled "Demons Becoming Active" in February 1919 warned of increasing supernatural demonic activity. It specifically reported that demon possession was becoming more common in India, including an apparent resurrection of a dead man by a demon spirit, manifesting with twitching and clairvoyance.[7] In August 1919 an article by Harriet Bainbridge on "Counterfeits" counseled trying the spirits by the Word of God.[8]

Cautions about Prophetic Revelations

There was concern in Alliance circles about imbalance in the exercise and acceptance of prophetic utterances. Cramer, although charismatically-oriented and one of the earliest Alliance leaders to speak in tongues, nonetheless counseled of the fallibility of prophecy and the need for balance in exercise of spiritual gifts.[9] Simpson wrote, "In the life of the Spirit we need not be in bondage and always expecting some strained or supernatural word from the Lord."[10] We see that Simpson's concern about inappropriate seeking extended, not only to tongues, but also to prophecy.

Simpson warned to try the spirits, recounting a young girl being healed at the point of death "through a voice, light filling the room and the face of a beautiful woman appearing to her. The healed girl now speaks with authority on doctrinal questions which are of vital importance to the power of darkness." He further reported that she uses theological language not of her own personality and says she does not believe the whole Bible or in hell.[11] He noted the need for not accepting all supernatural manifestations automatically or indiscriminately as being from God.

Three months later, Simpson mentioned receiving a letter from his friend, A. A. Boddy, about a young woman named Dorothy Kerin in London, who was healed and was supposedly the woman who made the statement that the Bible was not infallible and hell was not real. Boddy sent a statement from Dorothy Kerin saying she was not the woman and did not say or believe those statements. Simpson commented that he was glad the comments did not apply to the woman, but continued to caution that "no word from any human lips, no matter how strongly it may seem to be authenticated by blessing on the speaker, should have the slightest weight as affecting the infallible word of God."[12]

W. W. Newberry, pastor of the Alliance church in Newark, New Jersey, a center of Pentecostal renewal, wrote a book entitled *Untangling Live Wires: Light on Some of the Problems of Divine Guidance*, published by the Alliance. In it he warned about false guidance, dreams, visions, and voices. He affirmed and gave examples of both genuine manifestations of such phenomena as prophecy, word of knowledge, and impressions, but also cautioned that some can come from the soulish realm and also from demonic sources.[13] In October 1917 a missionary reported a problem with false prophets prophesying false things in Chile.[14]

CONCERNS ABOUT HEALING PRACTICES

Concerned about some of the practices of healing evangelists, Simpson exhorted, "We are not professional healers, but simply witnesses of Christ whose business it is to bring men into direct contact with the Lord Jesus and tell them that He is still the same yesterday, today and forever."[15] Further, even though the Alliance believed in acts of faith as a point of contact,[16] they were also concerned about excessive emphasis and almost magical regard for supernatural points of contact.

William T. MacArthur, a friend of Pentecostals, in an article entitled "Fabrics Filled with Power," affirmed that there is some "semblance of truth" to "the charging of clothing with the power of the Holy Ghost" for healing, but warned that those who have gone into the "handkerchief business" are "charlatans and pretenders." Such conduct, MacArthur advised, cannot be reconciled with the "unostentatious behavior of the apostles." It is an "unwholesome love for the spectacular."[17]

On one hand, this Alliance leader affirmed that there is an appropriate place for using such articles as a point of contact of faith and that they could be used by the Lord to transmit the healing power of the Spirit (such as in the ministry of Myland). On the other hand, he stressed that these means were not emphasized by the apostles, nor were they performed in a showy manner. When invited to participate in these activities, MacArthur personally declined.

CORRECTIVES TO PENTECOSTAL THEOLOGY

In 1914 in an article entitled "Baptized in the Name of the Lord Jesus," Simpson affirmed the appropriateness of baptism in the name of the Trinity, countering the "oneness" or "Jesus Only" teaching that was arising in Pentecostal circles.[18] In 1916 another long-time Alliance leader, Edgar Sellow, continued to argue against the Pentecostal "finished work" position derived from Durham: "To expect an inward work to be heralded by signs and wonders is not Scriptural. The effect of the divine indwelling will be manifestations of the divine life." He went on to cite the classic holiness position from Hebrews 12:1, saying that "faith is the evidence."[19] The Alliance continued to maintain that the experience of the baptism or filling of the Holy Spirit involved a work of increased sanctification, though not defined as Wesleyan eradicationism or Keswick suppressionism.

CAUTION AGAINST TOO MUCH CAUTION—
RESPONSE TO *WAR ON THE SAINTS*

Although Alliance leaders repeatedly expressed caution about accepting all apparent supernatural phenomena as from God, they also cautioned against being overly cautious, skeptical, or cynical. For example, in 1912 Welsh revivalists Jessie Penn-Lewis and Evan Roberts published their pivotal book *War on the Saints*.[20] In it, they warned strongly of deception and attack of demonic forces upon believers. They did not condemn all charismatic manifestations, but believed that the church was not mature enough to handle them.

Pastor N. H. Harriman, of Arlington, Massachusetts, presented a seven-part critique in *The Alliance Weekly* that first mentions commendable parts of the book, but then says he is "unable to commend unqualifiedly" some parts of the book. Sadly, he averred, the "atmosphere" of the book is harmful and morbid, canceling out the commendable parts of the book. He agreed with the authors' warning against seeking after tongues, but advised that their view of tongues was too negative. Simpson commented on the series of articles, essentially agreeing with his conclusion even though he respected Penn-Lewis and Roberts. He also cautioned against Roberts' recent claim to date setting for Christ's second coming and supposed revelations.[21]

In January 1915, Simpson wrote an editorial on Penn-Lewis and Roberts and their book *War on the Saints,* saying, "While we have not been able to accept without a little reservation some of the strong statements of these beloved teachers respecting the question of demon possession and kindred topics, yet we profoundly esteem, love and value the personal character and ministry of these true servants of the Lord."[22] In a later issue, Simpson cautioned again regarding the book, advising, "We must distinguish between demon possession and demon opposition."[23]

HOLY AND UNHOLY SUPERNATURALISM

Four months before Simpson's death in 1919, he was still both encouraging and cautioning, "We may, therefore, look for supernatural manifestations in our time of the most seductive and misleading character, but which are not of God, but from the wicked one. There is a true and holy supernaturalism which will always be recognized by its humility, self-control, holiness, love and good fruits. But there is a loud, arrogant, presumptuous and disorderly fanaticism which scoffs at all restraints and scatters its anathemas against all that oppose it and if possible would 'deceive the very elect.'"[24]

---

1. A. B. Simpson, Editorial, AW, Feb. 24, 1912, 322-323.

2. Anna O. Eldridge, "Purified and Tried," AW, Sept. 4, 1915, 357.

3. "Believe Not Every Spirit," AW, July 13, 1912, 229.

4. "24th Annual Report of the Congo Mission," AW, May 17, 1913. 104-105.

5. A. B. Simpson, Editorial, AW, Sept. 30, 1916, 417.

6. Frederic William Farr, "Satanic Mimicry," AW, Nov. 4, 1916, 70.

7. "Demons Becoming Active," AW, Feb. 22, 1919, 331.

8. H. S. Bainbridge, "Counterfeits," AW, Aug. 9, 1919, 315.

9. W. A. Cramer, "Adjustability and Tact," AW, May 18, 1912, 103.

10. A. B. Simpson, Editorial, AW, Aug. 24, 1912, 321.

11. A. B. Simpson, Editorial, AW, Feb. 22, 1913, 322.

12. A. B. Simpson, Editorial, AW, May 10, 1913, 82.

13. William Wisdom Newberry, *Untangling Live Wires: Light on Some of the Problems of Divine Guidance* (New York, NY: Christian Alliance Publishing Co., 1914).

14. Walter Feldges, "Wheat and Tares in Chile," AW, Oct. 20, 1917, 41.

15. A. B. Simpson, Editorial, AW, Nov. 30, 1912, 130.

16. See A. B. Simpson, "According to Your Faith," CMAW, Sept. 8, 1906, 146; George P. Pardington, "Sanctification," CMAW, June 2, 1906, 348ff.; A. E. Funk, "Pittsburgh Convention," AW, Apr. 9, 1921, 57; Walter Turnbull and C. H. Chrisman, "The Message of the Christian and Missionary Alliance," 1927, accessed online at http://online.cbccts.sk.ca/alliancestudies/ahtreadings/ahtr_s6.html.

17. W. T. MacArthur, "Fabrics Filled with Power," AW, Sept. 14, 1912, 390.

18. A. B. Simpson, "Baptized in the Name of the Lord Jesus," AW, May 2, 1914, 66.

19. Edgar K. Sellow, "Receive Ye Holy Ghost," AW, Feb. 12, 1916, 310.

20. Jessie Penn-Lewis with Evan Roberts, *War on the Saints*—Unabridged Edition (Ninth Edition) (New York: Thomas E. Lowe, Ltd., 1973). Because of controversy over Penn-Lewis' frequent and indiscriminate use of the term "demon possession" with regard to demon influence in a Christian's life, a later abridged edition was issued after her death, eliminating that terminology. Roberts had wanted to revise the book about two years after it was released, but Penn-Lewis refused. Brynmor Pierce Jones, *The Trials and Triumphs of Mrs. Jessie Penn-Lewis* (New Brunswick, NJ: Bridge-Logos Publishers, 1997), 204-206, 228-230.

21. N. H. Harriman, "'War on the Saints': An Analytical Study," AW, Dec. 27, 1913, 205-206; Jan. 3, 1914, 219-221; Jan. 10, 1914, 230-231; Jan. 17, 1914, 250; Jan. 24, 1914, 268; Jan. 31, 1914, 283; Feb. 28, 1914, 347; A. B. Simpson, Editorial, AW, Jan. 17, 1914, 241-242.

22. A. B. Simpson, Editorial, AW, Jan. 2, 1915, 210.

23. A. B. Simpson, Editorial, AW, Jan. 16, 1915, 241.

24. A. B. Simpson, "The Church," AW, June 21, 1919, 195.

The Domino After-Effects — 1913–1919

While not all Pentecostal people left the Alliance all at once, more fallout from the crisis year and constitutional revision continued through the end of the decade. And yet, charismatic phenomena continued to occur and be encouraged by Alliance leadership. The claims by some Pentecostal historians that Pentecostal manifestations disappeared from the C&MA simply are not true.

Simpson's Appeal Against Organizing an Evidence Doctrine Movement

In September 1913 Simpson again reaffirmed the reality and acceptance of scriptural manifestations of tongues in the Alliance, but disavowing evidence doctrine as "extreme, uncharitable and unscriptural." He expressed sorrow that extreme leaders in the Pentecostal movement were turning away "godly and useful members of the C&MA from their loyalty to the work and the faithful support of foreign missions workers. . . . In a number of instances our Alliance branches have been disturbed and seriously broken by these extreme teachings and agitations. . . . We believe an effort is being made to establish some kind of religious movement holding to this exclusive doctrine." He affirmed that many of the most blessed and godly people in the Alliance who speak in tongues speak out against this doctrine.[1]

Simpson's apprehension of a possible emerging Pentecostal organization propagating evidential tongues was perceptive, for in December 1913 a letter went out from The Word and Witness, a Pentecostal periodical, calling for Pentecostals to come together for a meeting in April 1914.[2] That meeting to organize Pentecostals convened together at Hot Springs, Arkansas on April 2-12, 1914. On that historic occasion the Assemblies of God was founded, including in its leadership Bosworth, Kerr, Flower, Welch, and many former C&MA leaders and members.[3] The forming of a Pentecostal denomination further eroded relationships in the Alliance with Pentecostals and led to additional loss of people in the Alliance movement.

CLEVELAND CHURCH DEFECTS

In September 1911 W. A. Cramer had resigned the Alliance church in Cleveland to work with the Beulah Park Home. Daniel Kerr moved from Dayton to pastor the church at Cleveland. He found that almost all of the people there had received the baptism in the Spirit with tongues. So it soon voted (by 1914) to become a Pentecostal church and leave the C&MA.[4]

Cramer, though one of the earliest Alliance leaders to speak in tongues and having led the church into Pentecostal revival, apparently did not embrace the full extent of Pentecostal belief and practice and the direction in which the church was going. Undoubtedly, he was disappointed that the church felt it necessary to leave the Alliance.[5] Cramer remained in the Alliance, serving as District Secretary and later pastoring charismatically-oriented C&MA churches in Springfield, Massachusetts, Detroit, and Tulsa, among others.

Later in 1914, Cramer spoke at the New England C&MA Convention, encouraging people to remain in the Alliance. He spoke on "Loyalty to Alliance Principles and Teachings," saying that the C&MA has given "the fullest scope for an exercise of all spiritual gifts promised in the Word of God. . . . We are glad to urge as does Paul to young Timothy, first 'not to neglect the gift that is in thee,' and again, 'stir up the gift of God which is in thee." He warned of two extremes: 1) "failure to yield to the legitimate operation of the Holy Spirit," and 2) "passivity, or so called abandonment of mind and will to the supernatural then giving place to evil rather than good, destroying our usefulness in the work of the Lord."[6]

SALEM CHURCH DISAFFILIATES

Cramer's exhortation to remain loyal to the Alliance was unheeded by the Pentecostal Church in Salem, Massachusetts, which disaffiliated its longtime connection with the C&MA just three months later in February 1915.[7] When the Alliance work was dissolved, the reversion clause kicked in, and the Pentecostal work moved to a new location. The building was put up for sale, stemming the loss of money and property for the Alliance, but losing yet another whole congregation.

TOTTENVILLE CHURCH LEAVES ALLIANCE

The Alliance church in Tottenville on Staten Island, New York, had been a center of charismatic revival ever since Pastor J. R. Kline had received the baptism in the Spirit with tongues in the summer of 1907 at the Rocky Springs Alliance Convention in Lancaster, Pennsylvania. Herbert Cox and G. F. Bender, two pastors of the church after Kline, had also received the baptism in the Spirit with tongues. In May of 1914 it was reported that the church had left the C&MA for the Pentecostal movement.[8] Kline later served on the General Presbytery of the Assemblies of God.

SEVERAL PENNSYLVANIA CHURCHES DEFECT

Many Alliance churches throughout Pennsylvania were impacted by the Pentecostal revival during the 1907 camp meetings at Rocky Springs near Lancaster, at Beulah Beach near Cleveland. According to Assemblies of God professor and historian A. Reuben Hartwick, "The message of Pentecost was preached in the Christian and Missionary Alliance churches in the steel towns of western Pennsylvania by Alliance pastors and evangelists" who had experienced the camp meeting revivals.[9] At least three Pennsylvania C&MA churches that switched allegiance to the Assemblies of God in 1914 were Chambersburg, Clairton, and Waynesboro.

Frank Casley, an evangelist and church planter for more than a decade in the Alliance, and his brother Will, had proclaimed the Pentecostal message openly for several years in the Alliance churches they planted. Rather than stay with the Alliance or join the Assemblies of God, in 1916 these churches established a new organization called The Free Gospel Churches, centered in Export, Pennsylvania.[10]

Alliance Missionaries in China, Venezuela, Congo, and India Resign

Jacob Kistler, who graduated from Nyack in 1909, had served on the Alliance mission field in China until summer of 1912, when he returned for health reasons. In 1914 he was ordained with the Assemblies of God.[11] At the Board of Managers meeting in September 1914 it was reported that Mr. and Mrs. Bailly, Mr. Bullen, and Miss Shigallis resigned from the Venezuelan mission, evidently over Pentecostalism. This was the entire missionary contingent from Venezuela, effectively closing the Alliance field in Venezuela. Mr. Young, missionary to Congo, also left at this time.[12]

After going on furlough from the Alliance mission in India in 1914 Christian Schoonmaker and his wife Violet left the C&MA, returning to India as missionaries for the Assemblies of God in 1915.[13] He had received the baptism in the Spirit with tongues in the Indian C&MA revival in 1908, had a vision of Christ, and exercised a ministry of healing and discernment of spirits. Schoonmaker died in 1919 of smallpox after refusing vaccination, while his wife continued to serve with the Assemblies of God.[14] In 1916 Herbert H. Cox of the India mission resigned from the Alliance to accept the pastorate of a Pentecostal assembly in Newark, New Jersey.[15] Cox then went on to pastor a Pentecostal church in Zion City, Illinois.

Eldridge's Church Departs

George Eldridge continued in Alliance ministry for about four years after the 1912 constitutional change. In 1915 he spoke at the dedication of a new Alliance church building in California, the Pasadena Tabernacle,[16] and in 1916 he was still involved with the C&MA Southern California Convention as a "local worker" and was considered a "beloved brother" in the *Alliance Weekly* in May. However, in November 1916, Eldridge's church, Bethel Mission, moved to a new location, ostensibly to avoid the C&MA reversion clause. The church was renamed Bethel Temple, affiliating with the Assemblies of God, where Eldridge subsequently became a significant leader.[17] In spite of this, he was still listed as an Honorary Vice President of the C&MA until August 1918.[18] He continued to maintain cordial relations with many in the Alliance, but not all held him in esteem. Weeks before Eldridge left the Alliance, Home Secretary E. J. Richards sent to Simpson a letter critical of the negative effects of Eldridge's leadership, speaking of Eldridge's "blunders."[19]

THE TIBETAN MISSION AND THE W. W. SIMPSON CONTROVERSY

In April and May of 1914 one of the most grievous controversies regarding Pentecostalism arose over W. W. Simpson's position on tongues. Simpson was asked to accept C&MA statement that tongues is not the essential evidence of the baptism in the Spirit. He replied that he could not and resigned from the C&MA. Mr. and Mrs. Ivan Kaufman and other C&MA Tibetan border mission workers joined the Pentecostal ranks.[20] In May 1914 Simpson's editorial reported W. W. Simpson's withdrawal from the C&MA:

> Grave differences have arisen between our dear brother and the Executive Committee in West China, chiefly upon how far the extreme views of the Pentecostal movement should be pressed upon the people. The attitude of the Alliance is well-known in giving the fullest liberty to our Pentecostal brethren to receive and exercise all the gifts of the Spirit, while at the same time we claim from them the same liberty for their brethren who have received the Holy Spirit, but have not had precisely the same type of religious experience. We greatly regret if Mr. and Mrs. Simpson have found it impossible to cooperate with us in this extremely reasonable and Scriptural basis, but we are sure that separation of this kind should be accomplished in the spirit of mutual love, confidence, and consideration.[21]

In September 1916, A. B. Simpson wrote a letter to Mrs. M. Albert Weaver (a member of the Alliance church in Springfield, Massachusetts, who was also actively involved in the Pentecostal movement) explaining the position statement Simpson and the C&MA Board presented regarding W. W. Simpson's view of tongues, and subsequent resignation. Mrs. Weaver evidently showed the letter to W. W. Simpson. In reaction, W. W. Simpson wrote a caustic letter to A. B. Simpson the following month, claiming that there was a "great discrepancy" between the statement presented to him in West China by Glover and what A. B. Simpson claimed to have written. He accused A. B. Simpson, Glover, and the Board of Managers of deception and "Tammany Hall politics."

The discrepancy appears to be nothing more than that A. B. Simpson was "substantially" summarizing the position and recalling somewhat fuzzily from memory the intent of what had been written, not a verbatim account or intention to deceive or misrepresent. Responding to A. B. Simpson's concern was that tongues or miracles are not to be sought, W. W. Simpson claimed that "I have always consistently cautioned them against seeking for tongues or manifestations." He ended his letter by telling A. B. Simpson, "If you will only humble yourself to seek the Lord for this mighty baptism you'll get it and then you know what I am talking about."[22] The two Simpsons (not related) obviously had differing views about what constituted inappropriate seeking. To the Alliance W. W. Simpson's attitude appeared to be elitist and arrogant. Anyone who really knew A. B. Simpson knew him to be a humble man, who earnestly desired all that God desired to give him. That attitude toward A. B. Simpson was not found among other Pentecostals such as George and Carrie Montgomery, Willis Hoover, A. A. Boddy, or Jonathan Paul.

Mr. and Mrs. W. W. Simpson and Mr. and Mrs. Ivan Kaufman later returned to the Tibetan border to resume missionary work eventually under the banner of the Assemblies of God. The Kaufmans reported that "the native brethren who had been longing and praying for their coming were overjoyed at their arrival, and pleaded with them not to leave them."[23] Dr. William Conrad, the grandson of William Christie, reported that after W. W. Simpson had left the Alliance, he was attending a Pentecostal mission conference in Pennsylvania when he encountered a woman speaking in tongues, which he recognized as the Gansu language. The woman, who knew not what she was saying, was actually exhorting him to return to the Gansu (or Kansu) province on the border of Tibet.[24]

In 1918 Foreign Secretary Robert Glover expressed his sorrow that some former missionaries of the China-Tibetan border mission had returned to work independently to open an work in the center of the field, stirring controversy and causing defection from native churches on the issue of tongues: "With great evangelized areas in other parts of the province, such action is a violation of universally recognized missionary policy." He further enjoined that it also causes confusion for young Christians and "presents a painful spectacle before the heathen of Christians working out of harmony and at cross purposes."[25] A year later the C&MA mission on the Tibetan border went through trials due to additional people leaving for the Pentecostal movement: "Our mission has passed through a test during the last year. The 'Assemblies of God' have continued their work and, in all, seventy-eight members, five evangelists, and two school teachers have withdrawn from our mission."[26]

From the viewpoint of W. W. Simpson, he was resuming ministry where he felt he was unjustly forced out, but from the viewpoint of the C&MA he was lacking integrity by infringing on their territory and proselytizing their members and leaders. This no doubt had a long-term effect of cooling the cooperative relationship between the C&MA and Pentecostals. The Alliance had been willing to work together with Pentecostals who did not force the evidential tongues issue, but the strong clash caused the Alliance leaders to back away from the Pentecostal movement.

According to William Christie's grandson, Dr. William Conrad, eventually the C&MA and the Assemblies of God agreed to split the field between them, working out an equitable agreement to co-exist peacefully.[27] Christie, however, apparently soured by the divisiveness of the controversy, ultimately concluded that much of the tongues-speaking was "spurious" in spite of the experience of his wife and son.[28] Christie's view may have contributed to the later cooling of charismatic manifestations and cooperation with Pentecostals in the 1930s, when Christie served as Vice President of the C&MA.

ADDITIONAL REPERCUSSIONS—SPRINGFIELD CHURCH WITHDRAWS

Evidently the conflict over W. W. Simpson had caused the Weavers and the majority of the Springfield Church to withdraw from the Alliance by November 1916. Undoubtedly, Cramer and MacArthur, pro-charismatic leaders who had pastored the church, were grieved by the departure. The property was left to the Alliance under the reversion clause, but there were few who wanted to continue the Alliance work. Home Secretary E. J. Richards reported to the Board that it "was unwise to continue any Alliance meetings there under the present conditions." The Alliance meetings with the few left were stopped and the property was leased to those who wanted to continue as a Pentecostal church.[29] Eventually, the work in Springfield was reestablished by R. C. Steinhoff, a charismatically-oriented leader who had pastored the Alliance church in Akron.

AKRON CHURCH EXPERIENCES TURMOIL, BUT RECOVERS

Apparently the Alliance Church in Akron, Ohio went through a trying period of time regarding the Pentecostal beliefs, but Gerow, who had come pastored the church after C. A. McKinney left for the Pentecostal movement, returned to stabilize the situation along with the help of two other tongue-speaking Alliance leaders, W. A. Cramer, Secretary of the Central District, and H. M. Shuman, Superintendent of the Central District. They reported to the Board of Managers in January 1917, "The strain in the work there thro [sic] some Pentecostal wrong teaching is all healed and the work is in good condition."[30]

COXE FAMILY LEAVES

John Coxe, after leaving the Alliance work in Butler, Pennsylvania, had pastored the Alliance church in Wilmington, Delaware, then in New Castle, Pennsylvania, where he had first spoken in tongues. By January 1917, Coxe had left the C&MA to be involved more with the Pentecostal movement, beginning a series of meetings in the Pentecostal church in Zion City, Illinois, pastored by Herbert H. Cox, former C&MA missionary to India. Simpson commented on his departure:

> We have always believed and said that there is ample room in the Alliance for the deepest and highest religious experience and the most spiritual testimony and work. The only limiting condition is conformity to the Word of God. The Alliance is in full accord with every manifestation of the Holy Spirit in His gifts and graces which is consistent with the teaching of the apostle Paul in First Corinthians, chapters 12-14. The writer sincerely

believes that in a great number of cases at the present time the particular manifestation of speaking in tongues has been wholly genuine and in perfect harmony with godly sincerity, simplicity and love. He is as firmly assured on the other hand that in numerous cases it has been abused, exaggerated until allowed to run into fanaticism and error. It was for this reason, no doubt that the Holy Spirit placed the discerning of spirits immediately before the gift of tongues. We trust God will greatly bless and use our beloved brother Coxe and the step which he has taken, we have no doubt in all good conscience may be overruled for good by the God of love and peace.[31]

His angst over Coxe's departure shows in his words. Simpson wanted to welcome the charismatic gifts in the Alliance with both liberty and controls, encouraging people to remain in the Alliance. No doubt Coxe's friend Cramer, who had earlier urged loyalty to the Alliance, was also disappointed with Coxe's decision to leave the C&MA. Coxe ministered for a time independently in Pentecostal circles before he founded a Pentecostal church in Wilmington in 1919.[32] He preached periodically in the Pentecostal Stone Church in Chicago.[33] Coxe's daughter Sarah left the Alliance mission in India in 1918,[34] and his son William, who had pastored in the Alliance in Pennsylvania, New York, and New England, also left for the Assemblies of God about 1920.

The Toll upon Simpson

Combined with the conflicts regarding Western District Superintendent Charles Crawford, culminating in his resignation in the summer of 1916, all of these controversies and defections weighed heavily upon A. B. Simpson. Years later his close friend Kenneth MacKenzie commented,

> I cannot refrain from recording the agony through which he passed. . . . when so many of his most trusted and valued friends withdrew from him because he did not go with them to the limit which was their ideal. He could not say of them as did St. John, "They went out from us, but they were not of us," for they were. Their presence and prayers, their sympathy and service, had been a bulwark to him in times of stress and strain. But he had to let them go from him and trust God with the consummation, whatever that might be.[35]

Notes from Simpson's diary in December 1916 intimately show a glimpse of the anguish that he was experiencing as the disputes and financial situation had worsened:

> This year has been unparalleled in suffering and testing, and in answered prayer. At present I need God as never before. I am older and

need new life, etc. There are new forces and spirits in the work and things are harder. But God has done for me wondrous things this year in financial help, physical strength, and victory over the enemy in men and angels. I never so needed him. I am taking Him now for deliverance from a difficult financial burden so that I shall be set free from financial obligations that tie me up in my freedom. . . . Jesus will see me through. Also prayer for Council, summer conventions and my way plain. Also my head, heart, and life. . .

But O Lord help now in great need upon me. . . . And [   ] give me fullness Spirit to [ ] and overcome and [ ] all situations around me.

Sometime during the year of 1917, according to Simpson's friend Carrie Judd Montgomery, Simpson evidently suffered a nervous breakdown.[36] Very likely the loss of people and funds from The Christian and Missionary Alliance, and especially the exit of his friends Coxe and Eldridge combined with the emotional stress of the W. W. Simpson and Crawford controversies, took their toll upon the emotional and physical health of the usually optimistic, but aging, battle-worn sage. The leader who had preached the value of positive confession had hit a hurdle that challenged his faith more than anything else in his life. Within a year, however, by the fall of 1918 when visited by George and Carrie Montgomery, he had significantly recovered, and was nearly back to his original buoyant self.[37]

Montgomerys Join the Assemblies of God

In 1917 Carrie Judd Montgomery became ordained with the Assemblies of God, eventually pastoring an Assemblies church. Her joining another group may have been due in part to the greater openness of the Assemblies to ordain women to ministry (although the C&MA did license women and several served as pastors), as well as the Pentecostal links.[38] Yet she and her husband also continued their C&MA connections. George Montgomery continued to be reelected yearly as an Honorary Vice President of C&MA until his death in 1930. Carrie spoke at Alliance meetings in 1918 at Simpson's Gospel Tabernacle and at Old Orchard. Articles by the Montgomerys continued to be published by *The Alliance Weekly* in the 1920s and 30s. According to their daughter, Faith Berry, Carrie later wished that she had stayed with the C&MA.[39]

Harry Turner Withdraws, but Later Returns

Nyack student Harry L. Turner had received the baptism in the Spirit with tongues about 1912 and joined the C&MA Mission in Argentina in 1913. His ability and anointing were evident and he was appointed chairman of the C&MA mission in Argentina in 1917. However, embracing Pentecostal teaching in 1918, he left the C&MA, at first ministering independently, then joining the Pentecostal Assemblies of Canada. Noel Perkin, who also had earlier Alliance connections, served with him. Turner would eventually return to the C&MA in 1926, and later become President of the C&MA's St. Paul Bible Institute (now known as Crown College), as well as serve as President of the C&MA.[40]

Others Eventually Withdraw, Yet Still Others Return

A. G. Ward served in the C&MA until 1919 when he was ordained with the Assemblies of God.[41] The Louis Turnbulls continued in C&MA missions until their furlough in 1921, when they returned to the United States and took over Bethel Temple, pastored by his father-in-law George Eldridge. Victor Plymire returned from the Tibetan border mission on furlough in 1920, received the baptism in the Spirit with tongues, and subsequently was ordained by the Assemblies of God.

In the midst of the defections, some charismatically-oriented people, and even complete congregations, eventually returned to the Alliance. The 1915-1916 C&MA Annual Report noted, "A great many friends, who a few years ago were alienated through a divergence of views as to the work of the Holy Spirit, are returning to our fellowship, not only as individuals, but whole branches and assemblies have asked to be recognized, and letters of confession and regret have been received from both leaders and laymen."[42]

1. A. B. Simpson, Editorial, AW, Sept. 6, 1913, 353-354.

2. Menzies, Anointed to Serve, 93.

3. Ibid., 92-105.

4. AW, Nov. 11, 1911, 94; Nienkirchen, 109.

5. AW, Feb. 21, 1914, 335.

6. W. A. Cramer, "Loyalty to Alliance Principles and Teachings," AW, Nov. 7, 1914, 82.

7. William Franklin, "Itinerary in New England," AW, Feb. 13, 1915, 317, 319.

8. C&MA Board of Manager Minutes, May 30, 1914.

9. A. Reuben Hartwick, "Pentecost Comes to the Northeast: A Survey of Early Events and Influential Leaders," Assemblies of God Heritage, Spring 1990, 4.

10. Ibid.

11. "Gleanings from Nyack," CMAW, Oct. 23, 1909, 59; "Missionary Department," AW, Aug. 3, 1912, 281; Assemblies of God Archives.

12. C&MA Board of Manager Minutes, Sept. 1, 1914.

13. AW, Jan. 30, 1915, 287.

14. E. B. Robinson, "Schoonmaker, Christian H.," DPCM, 770-771; Editorial, AW, Apr. 19, 1919, 59.

15. C&MA Board of Manager Minutes, May 13, 1916.

16. "Dedication of Pasadena Tabernacle," AW, Nov. 20, 1915, 126.

17. Lewis Wilson, 7; Nienkirchen, 114.

18. "South California Convention," AW, Apr. 1, 1916, 13; A. B. Simpson, Editorial, AW, May 3, 1916, 98; see AW, Nov. 11, 1916, 95, where Eldridge is no longer listed as a District Evangelist, and Bethel Mission is no longer listed as C&MA; see AW, Nov. 25, 1916, 127, where Eldridge is still listed as an Honorary

Vice President. See AW, Aug. 24, 1918, and following issues where Eldridge is not listed as Honorary VP in the header.

19. Letter from E. J. Richards to A. B. Simpson, Oct. 4, 1916. For other related correspondence, see E. J. Richards, "Report of the Home Dept. to the Board, Nov. 11, 1916. It seems that Richards felt Eldridge had failed to exercise sound leadership over a crisis situation with the Santa Barbara church and its pastor who was in a drunken stupor for a week. Pentecostal sympathizer Ira David was called in to salvage a disastrous situation. Telegram from E. J. Richards to J. E. Jaderquist, Oct. 23, 1916. C&MA Archives.

20. Letter from A. B. Simpson and J. D. Williams to R. H. Glover regarding W. W. Simpson, Apr. 13, 1914. Letter of resignation from W. W. Simpson and his wife, May 12, 1914. The statement from A. B. Simpson and J. D. Williams that W. W. Simpson was asked to accept was:

We believe that the gift of tongues or speaking in tongues did in many cases in the Apostolic Church accompany or follow the baptism of the Holy Spirit. We believe also that other supernatural or even miraculous operations on the part of the Holy Spirit through His people are competent, rightfully belonging and possible according to the sovereign will of the Holy Ghost Himself through all the Christian age. But we hold that none of these manifestations are essentially connected with the baptism of the Holy Ghost, and that the consecrated believer may receive the Spirit in His fulness without speaking in tongues or any miraculous manifestation whatever, and that no Christian teacher has the right to require such manifestations as evidences of the baptism of the Holy Ghost. The teaching of the Apostle Paul in I Corinthians, Chapters 12-14 makes this exceedingly plain."

The response from W. W. Simpson and his wife was as follows:

Your official statement with reference to 'tongues' and the baptism of the Holy Spirit, dated April 13th, has just been handed to us by Dr. Glover, your representative in China. After careful consideration and prayer we have decided that we cannot subscribe to this statement because we consider it contrary to the teaching of Acts 2-4 & 3; Acts 8-17-18; Acts 10-44-46; Acts 19-6. And since we consider the Word of God the only sure guide on this as well as other lines, we are compelled to sever our relations with the Christian and Missionary Alliance. We hereby tender our resignations. Praying the Lord may show you your error on this point and use you for His glory.

21. A. B. Simpson, Editorial, AW, May 30, 1914, 130.

22. Letter from A. B. Simpson to Mrs. M. A. Weaver, Sept. 8, 1916. Letter from W. W. Simpson to A. B. Simpson, Oct. 17, 1916. C&MA Archives.

23. LRE, Apr. 1918, 14.

24. Conversation with Dr. William Conrad, Jan. 20, 2005.

25. Robert H. Glover, "Our Foreign Mailbag," AW, Oct. 5, 1918, 9.

26. Mrs. Phoebe B. Snyder, "Tibetan Border Mission Conference," AW, Oct. 25, 1919, 26.

27. Dr. William Conrad, Christie's grandson, told me that he visited the Gansu province in the 1980s and found descendents of the original Alliance and Assemblies works there. Even through Communist rule the churches had been sustained and had grown to several hundred members. Though no longer affiliated with the C&MA and the Assemblies of God, there were a tongue-speaking church, a non-tongue-speaking church, and a church that had some who had the gift of tongues and some who did not. Conversation with Dr. William Conrad, Jan. 20, 2005.

28. Conrad told me he was surprised to learn that his grandmother and uncle had spoken in tongues, something he never knew, since his grandfather seemed doubt the veracity of much tongue-speaking.

29. E. J. Richards, "Report of the Home Dept. to the Board, Nov. 11, 1916.

30. Report of the Secretary of the Home Dept., C&MA Board of Manager Minutes, Jan 27, 1917.

31. A. B. Simpson, Editorial, AW, Jan. 13, 1917, 225. Coxe remained listed as pastor of the C&MA church in New Castle, PA, for several months, but this is probably due to editorial lack of changing the typeset for the page.

32. Coxe spoke at a Pentecostal camp meeting in August 1917 at New Castle, Pennsylvania, the city where he first received the baptism in the Spirit. LRE, June 1917, 13; LRE, Feb. 1919, 16.

33. Coxe preached in the Stone Church in March, August, and September. John Coxe, "God's Purpose in Pentecost," LRE, Apr. 1917, 2ff.; John Coxe, "Tried in the Fire But No Surrender," LRE, June 1917, 20; "Special Meetings," LRE, Aug. 1917, 12; John Coxe, "The Great Battle of Armageddon," LRE, Nov. 1917, 2ff.

34. AW, June 29, 1918, 207.

35. Nicklaus, et. al., 115.

36. Carrie Judd Montgomery, "An Eastern Trip in the Lord's Work," Triumphs of Faith, Jan. 1919, 15.

37. According to a report in March 1918, Simpson had made progress toward recovery, but was "still subject to sleeplessness and high pressure upon nerves and brain." "Editorials," AW, Mar. 23, 1918, 385.

38. Nancy Hardesty mentions that some people sought ministerial credentials in Pentecostal denominations "in order to continue their ministries outside their previous affiliations and to enjoy such perks as ministerial railroad passes." Hardesty, Faith Cure, 108.

39. Notes of John Sawin from interview with Faith Berry. C&MA Archives.

40. Lindsay Reynolds, Rebirth (Beaverlodge, Alberta: Evangelistic Enterprises, 1992), 206-207; "Missionary Department: The Foreign Secretary's Report," AW, June 15, 1918, 169.

41. B. M. Stout, "Ward, Alfred George," DPCM, 878.

42. C&MA 1915-1916 Annual Report, 61.

FIFTEEN

SIMPSON'S CONTINUING DESIRE:
WHY NOT TONGUES
WITHOUT CONTROVERSY?

Although the defections and controversies caused some Pentecostals to believe that the Alliance response effectively eliminated tongues and charismatic manifestations from the C&MA, such phenomena did continue in the Alliance, though probably with less frequency. Such occurrences were not always openly reported, perhaps to avoid sensationalism. Yet some experiences continued to be shared in Alliance periodicals, as Simpson continued to strive for a charismatic C&MA without chaos.

REVIVALS WITH SIGNS FOLLOWING

Revivals with signs following such as outpourings of the Spirit, healings, visions, tongues, and other manifestations continued to break out from time to time in Alliance circles and were reported in *The Alliance Weekly*.[1] In 1914 Simpson reported a "Pentecostal outpouring" through Paul Rader's meetings in Toledo.[2] New England District Superintendent William Franklin, who had been a part of the Pentecostal revival in both the Alliance mission and Ramabai's Mukti Mission in India, reported in 1915 that in the New England C&MA Convention "the Lord worked with them with signs following."[3]

In 1916 John Coxe from New Castle was invited by fellow tongue-speaker Warren Cramer for a series of evangelistic meetings at the C&MA's United Gospel Tabernacle in Columbus, Ohio,[4] the church originally pastored by David Wesley Myland. It continued to be charismatically-oriented under the leadership of Cramer, but did not embrace the Pentecostal evidence doctrine. The Annual Report of the C&MA for 1916 reported on revivals in India, Africa, Chile, and West China, stressing commitment to the full gospel and the supernatural, ending with a prayer, "God grant . . . a new Pentecost of power and service."[5]

MORE DREAMS, VISIONS, VOICES, AND HEALINGS

The *Alliance Weekly* continued to publish numerous testimonies of supernatural manifestations such as visions, voices, and prophecies throughout the decade.[6] While the reports of such manifestations became fewer in succeeding years, they still continued. During this decade, the *Weekly* featured at least twelve visions, several of Jesus or angels, and six dreams.[7] A sampling of the most significant include the following:

- A wounded soldier having a vision and trance of being transported in Spirit to a prayer meeting.[8]

- A man in Africa involved in witchcraft who was bitten by a poisonous snake. He refused the help of the missionaries and native Christian leaders, so they prayed that hell would be revealed to him. While unconscious and dying, he saw a vision of hell. He regained consciousness, accepted Christ and was healed. He heard a voice from God the next day telling him to go tell others about Jesus and his testimony.[9]

- A C&MA missionary in India reported that a Brahmin mother had hid a believing child's Bibles in a neighbor's home. The boy had a dream of where they were hid and the next day went right to the location and found them.[10]

POWER ENCOUNTERS AND DIVINE PROTECTION

The Alliance Weekly continued to share dramatic incidents of power encounters and supernatural divine protection. A woman testified of healing from eating poisonous mushrooms by claiming Mark 16:18.[11] A Chinese woman who accepted Christ had a dream of a light upon the floor of her room. Idols on a shelf began to move. Jesus came through the doorway and the idols crawled off the shelf. "Where are you going?" she asked. They replied, "When Jesus comes in we must go."[12] A woman in Congo who apparently died had a vision of Jesus and an angel saying she would be healed in four weeks. Then she came back to life and testified and four weeks later she was healed. Her husband and others repented and came to faith in Christ.[13]

HOLY LAUGHTER AND HOLY FIRE

Instances of holy laughter and similar ecstatic experiences like "holy fire" continued to take place among Alliance people. In 1913 an Alliance missionary reported that among several conversions in a revival in Argentina was a young man who experienced holy laughter.[14] Lutheran pastor Louis Henry Zwiemer received the baptism in the Spirit in 1914, accompanied by shouting, a feeling of holy fire, and holy laughter in the Spirit. Revival broke out in his church and he was accused of heresy, defrocked, and forced to resign. Then he became a prominent C&MA pastor.[15]

Mrs. S. P. Hamilton, who had been a part of the 1905-1909 revival in India, reported continued revival in India in 1916 with uplifted hands, tears, confession, holy laughter and crying for joy.[16] More than a year later, E. R. Carner, another Alliance missionary who had been a part of the earlier revival in India, related more incidents of holy laughter in the Alliance mission in India.[17] In 1917 another writer testified of receiving the baptism of the Spirit with "deep emotion," "increasing degrees of intensity" and "waves or billows of fire." After the experience he went to conduct a prayer meeting and a spirit of conviction came upon the people in just a few minutes.[18]

PROPHECIES, TONGUES AND INTERPRETATION

The Alliance continued to believe in and report prophetic utterances, including predictive prophecies. Dr. H. W. Pope related that he had prophesied a new Navy convert would become the chaplain of a warship in less than a month. It came true, as within a few weeks the man was conducting five services each Sunday.[19] British C&MA leader and Simpson associate F. E. Marsh reported that in Silverton, Devonshire, in western England, Mrs. Thomas of Liverpool prophesied that Mrs. Jordan, an invalid who had been bedridden for five years, would be healed. Shortly, Mrs. Jordan was indeed healed and herself received a "divine message."[20] A prophetic dream pictured provision for a debt the writer had one night, which came true the next day.[21] Simpson continued to encourage exercise of the gift of prophecy, exhorting readers, "Let us be willing to speak as the oracles of God and prophesy according to the proportion of our faith."[22]

After the controversy involving W. W. Simpson, it appears that Alliance leaders became more reticent to report specific testimonies of receiving the gift of speaking in tongues, although such manifestations did not cease. One particular testimony was published in *The Alliance Weekly*, however, that stands out significantly.

May Evans gave testimony of her healing from cancer after prayer on September 2, 1914. After prayer she had no pain for ten days. She awoke on September 13 with the power of the Lord on her and she began to praise God in tongues. The Lord gave her an interpretation: "This thing I will cast off from thy being." She then was in pain for five days in which she said that the cancer was being "pushed" out of her breast. Then in weakness she saw a vision of Christ and His presence filled the room. She was lifted up off her bed on her feet with no effort of her own. The pain was gone and a week later the cancer dropped off her chest "like a stone." Confirmation was given by George and Anna Eldridge.[23]

SALMON'S "TELEGRAM FROM GOD"

Although the aged John Salmon had gone into retirement after his worldwide trip to China, his supernatural ministry in the Spirit had not abated in his final years. In December 1917, about six months before his death, Salmon dreamed of vast group of foreigners surrounding a woman pleading for something to eat. She was alone without any help. When he awoke he asked God the meaning of the dream, and the Lord responded, "I want you to help her." He replied, "Well, Lord who is it?" And the Lord said, "It is Mrs. Cole in North China." Then he said, "Well, Lord, how much shall I send her?" "Send her $50." He sent the money the next morning, not knowing that at about the same time Jean Cole had been praying for funds to come in to feed starving people in North China displaced by flooding. Cole called the incident a "telegram from God."[24]

Spiritual Warfare and Deliverance Ministry

Spiritual warfare and deliverance ministry became more common in Alliance circles, especially on the mission field. A series of articles dealing with spiritual warfare, demonization, and deliverance ministry appeared in *The Alliance Weekly* in 1918, including an editorial by Simpson on Luke 10:19 and the authority of the believer.[25] William Christie testified at the Old Orchard Convention in 1917 of exorcisms and healings in the Tibetan region.[26] In spite of not receiving tongues as the evidence of the baptism in the Spirit, Christie nonetheless operated in the supernatural, especially in the ministry of power encounters, supernatural knowledge or discernment, and exorcisms.[27]

In one incident of supernatural knowledge, a former Tibetan lamaistic priest named Dkon-Mchog-Bastan-Adzin, had become severely ill, and had tried to find relief for seven years through sorcery and witchcraft. He was lying on a bed when Christie was summoned by the man's wife to pray for him. Christie "was swept by a strong impression that if this man would forsake heathenish ways, and put his trust in Jesus Christ, the power of God would be manifested, and he would be healed." As a result the man confessed Jesus as his Savior and the family burned all of the lamaistic paraphernalia. Then Christie "rebuked the disease in the name of Jesus" and "suddenly the former priest felt a touch of life, and he arose," and was totally healed.[28]

"The Alliance Is Supernatural, or It Is Nothing"

Considering the conflicts and loss of leaders to the Pentecostal movement, one might think that the Alliance had substantially cut off contact with the movement and abandoned supernatural manifestations. However, the Alliance continued to maintain contact and cooperation with moderate Pentecostals and continued to encourage the supernatural in Alliance churches.

In the spring of 1913, a man named E. H. Garlock, who was an alcoholic and quite sick at the time, went to see A. B. Simpson at Nyack. He was not healed at that time, but someone at Nyack told him about Maria Woodworth-Etter's meetings. He attended and was healed.[29] Evidently, as a result of Woodworth-Etter's connections with Bosworth in Dallas the prior autumn and with Carrie Judd Montgomery's friendship with Woodworth-Etter, at least some at Nyack remained open to her ministry.

In 1916 Pentecostal leader A. W. Orwig wrote that George D. Watson, a close friend of the C&MA, was not opposed to tongues, contrary to reports: "On someone telling me, several years ago, that Dr. Watson did not allow the speaking in other tongues in his meetings, I assured the person that he was in error, for I had heard some thus speak without the slightest protest. Some of the 'Pentecostal' people sometimes attend Brother Watson's meetings because of the high order of Scriptural expositions they receive of the deepest and most blessed themes of the Sacred Oracles, frequently on prophetical subjects."[30]

More recent Pentecostal historians have made a similar mistake, asserting that Watson "rejected 'tongues' as unscriptural and even 'demon-inspired.'"[31] In reality, since Watson was closely associated with the C&MA, he likely held a similar position to that of Simpson and other Alliance leaders—open to tongues and other supernatural manifestations, but not accepting tongues as the evidence of the baptism in the Spirit. Additionally, Watson was a good friend of David Myland, who had spoken in tongues shortly after the Alliance convention in Columbus where they had ministered together. Further, Pentecostal leader John G. Lake testified that Watson and Myland had been influences in his life.[32]

A. E. Thompson wrote a two-part exposition on 1 Corinthians. 12-14. He affirmed that tongues is "one result of an infilling of the Holy Spirit" and is "usually an overflowing spirit of praise." Significantly, he assured, "Tongues are desirable, yet prophecy is preferable," and that tongues should not be forbidden if used as directed in 1 Corinthians 14. Gifts that edify others should be sought and exercised, such as prophecy; "if one has the gift of tongues, he should seek also the gift of interpretation," because it edifies the church.[33] These instructions and guidelines presume the ongoing permission and encouragement of the exercise of the gifts in Alliance worship services.

W. T. MacArthur quipped, "The Alliance is supernatural or it is nothing."[34] In 1917 Simpson asserted, "The Holy Spirit originated the Alliance in order to produce in modern times an attested copy of the Church of the apostolic pattern. The modern Church is far away from the original pattern. The popular Church is not the Church of Pentecost." He cautioned that the C&MA in places has lost the original "flavor" and pattern.[35]

SIMPSON URGES A "FULLER BAPTISM" AND "BACK TO PENTECOST"

Simpson continued to encourage Alliance readers to return to Pentecost and desire a "fuller baptism" in the Spirit. He himself in his 1907 diary had claimed a fuller baptism "with all the gifts and graces." In his 1909 Annual Report, he had written of the hunger of Alliance workers for a "mightier baptism of the Holy Ghost."[36] Again in 1913 Simpson encouraged readers to get "back to Pentecost" and "make our lives Pentecostal too," emphasizing that when the Holy Spirit comes, "all our flippancy, all our smartness, all our frivolity, all our playing with sacred things will wither and die."[37]

In 1914 Simpson wrote an editorial on the baptism of the Spirit, reaffirming that the gifts of the Spirit are fully recognized, but are not the essential evidence. Gifts "are not determined by our wishes but His will." He did acknowledge that "the sealing and baptism of the Spirit does not exhaust the fulness of His gracious manifestation and working." He considered tongues as "the express of divine emotion."[38]

Again in 1914 Simpson encouraged readers to claim a "deeper sanctification" and a "fuller baptism of the Spirit."[39] This was almost identical to terminology used by David Wesley Myland and Carrie Judd Montgomery years earlier to describe their experiences of speaking in tongues as the consummation of their earlier baptism of the Spirit.[40] The fact that Simpson continued to use this terminology indicates that he still believed there was something more in the realm of the Spirit to be experienced.

CORDIAL PENTECOSTAL-C&MA RELATIONSHIPS

In spite of negative feelings over the defection of many people, leaders, and churches from the Alliance to the Pentecostal movement and the W. W. Simpson controversy, Alliance leaders continued to maintain good rapport with more moderate Pentecostal leaders. In 1913 Cecil Polhill of the Pentecostal Missionary Union in England asked the C&MA Board of Managers to accept Mr. and Mrs. McGillivray in the C&MA West China Mission. Alliance leaders agreed to co-sponsor the couple at the Alliance mission by the Tibetan border. By October 1915 they were granted half support by the Board of Managers.[41] This demonstrates continued C&MA openness to moderate Pentecostalism in spite of the contention over W. W. Simpson' departure from the Alliance.

Also in 1913, Kate Driscoll, C&MA missionary to Sudan, spoke at Myland's convention, the Gibeah Pentecostal Assemblies Camp Meeting, in Indiana.[42] There evidently was some concern on the part of Alliance leadership regarding Driscoll and her colleague from the Sudan Alliance mission about their Pentecostal beliefs and practices, but the Board of Managers determined that matters of policy and method regarding them had been resolved.[43]

The same year, E. O. Jago, missionary to Palestine, was a featured speaker at the Pentecostal Stone Church in Chicago.[44] Jago was receptive to recruiting Pentecostals for C&MA Palestinian missions work, affirming, "I care not what society a man belongs to. I simply want to know if he is filled with the Holy Ghost and has sufficient ability to master a foreign language. . . . In these days the supernatural must take place in the foreign field, especially among the Mohammedans, and we need men filled with the Holy Ghost."[45] Also in 1913, it was reported that Mr. and Mrs. Ramsay from the Alliance mission in India were sent by A. B. Simpson to represent the C&MA in the Pentecostal convention at Sunderland, England. Mrs. Ramsay shared her personal testimony at one of the evening meetings of the convention.[46]

Simpson invited his old friend A. A. Boddy, one of the chief leaders of the Pentecostal movement in England, to speak in one of his Friday healing meetings at the Gospel Tabernacle in 1914.[47] Boddy also spent time fellowshipping with Alliance pastor W. A. Cramer and his wife as well as Alliance members Albert and Mabel Weaver in Massachusetts. Cramer was preaching at the Pentecostal convention at Rockrimmon campground. Mrs. Weaver had attended the Pentecostal Sunderland convention in England with Boddy a few months earlier.[48] Also the same year, Simpson's associate Kenneth MacKenzie assisted a Pentecostal Jewish pastor in a Pentecostal convention for friends of Israel.[49]

In December 1914 Simpson spoke warmly of a Pentecostal leader, saying, "our dear brother, Mr. Stewart of the Pentecostal Mission Bands of

Indianapolis."[50] In 1915 the pastor of a Pentecostal church assisted in laying on hands for ordination of a C&MA minister.[51] Professor C. E. Rossignol from the Missionary Training Institute received the baptism in the Spirit with tongues early in 1915 at a Pentecostal convention in Newark, New Jersey. He was then invited to be in charge of the music at the Stone Church Convention in May.[52] In June of the same year, at the Los Angeles C&MA convention it was reported, "Large numbers of our Pentecostal friends joined heartily in the work in their prayer and their giving." George Eldridge was one of the leaders of the convention.[53] Likewise, in 1915, Wesley Myland, now an independent Pentecostal evangelist, assisted with the funeral of a C&MA minister in Illinois.[54]

In 1918, William Fetler, a Pentecostal missionary to Russia, was invited to speak to the students at the Missionary Training Institute in Nyack about the mission work in Russia. As a result several students volunteered to become missionaries to Russia. One Chinese student was inspired to give to the Pentecostal Russian mission work $300 that he had saved up.[55]

C&MA-PENTECOSTAL BRIDGEBUILDING

Simpson reported that in the Los Angeles Alliance convention multitudes of interested people, especially Pentecostals, were "thronging the services . . . and manifested a most cordial spirit."[56] George and Carrie Montgomery, who were hosting Pentecostal conventions in California, also actively participated in the Alliance convention held at First Baptist Church in Oakland in 1915.[57] A few months earlier A. A. Boddy had observed of Carrie's leadership of the Pentecostal meetings he visited, "Mrs. Carrie Judd Montgomery's name was a guarantee against fanaticism or wild fire, and the meetings were controlled by the Spirit."[58] The Montgomerys were able and respected bridge-builders between Pentecostals and non-Pentecostals.

Another example of this bridge-building occurred with J. Narver Gortner, a Methodist pastor who came into the Pentecostal experience through connections with the Alliance and the Montgomerys. In 1911 while he was pastoring in Southern California near the Mexican border, Gortner's wife became so severely ill she had to be taken to a hospital in Los Angeles. While staying in Los Angeles, his son Vernon attended a C&MA Sunday School where he heard that Jesus could heal his mother. Pentecostal medical doctor F. E. Yoakum and the local Alliance pastor visited her in the hospital. Through their prayers and those of a prayer group, she soon recovered completely.

Seeing God's power, he became more interested in the Holy Spirit. In 1914 he attended one of the Montgomerys' Pentecostal conventions. Carrie invited him to her cottage for tarrying meetings in which he recounted, "waves of divine glory, like the billows of the deep, swept across that assembly of saints." He went to bed and the next morning woke up with a Scripture on his mind, "and just then God in a mysterious way opened the heavens and the power of God fell upon me, and my body was quivering from head to foot, and I began to speak in other tongues as the Spirit gave utterance."[59]

Even though George and Carrie Montgomery joined the Assemblies of God in 1917, they continued to have a warm and positive relationship with the charismatically-oriented South California C&MA District Superintendent Herbert Dyke. In the fall of 1917, when Dyke was sick with smallpox, George and Carrie prayed with him, and he was healed as a result of their prayers. Then his wife was hit with sickness, but she too was healed.[60]

A positive relationship continued between the Pentecostal Stone Church and the C&MA in Chicago, even though the church hosted the 1917 Assemblies of God Council. Its earlier pastor, William Piper agreed with the C&MA position on the evidence doctrine. In 1916 and 1917 W. T. MacArthur, then pastor of the Pentecostally-oriented Alliance work in Springfield, Massachusetts, spoke several times at the Pentecostal Stone Church in Chicago. His sermons and tracts were printed in the Pentecostal periodical *The Latter Rain Evangel*.[61]

In 1918 Stone Church pastor Hardy W. Mitchell (ordained with Assemblies of God) preached at Alliance work in Fort Worth, Texas, where Warren Collins had been a lay minister for the C&MA, while also holding credentials with the Assemblies of God. After the Assemblies of God firmed up the evidence doctrine, Collins and Mitchell eventually followed the Bosworths in leaving the Assemblies.[62] In the fall of 1918, George and Carrie Judd Montgomery visited with Mitchell and his wife.[63]

Later on the same trip, the Montgomerys visited A. B. Simpson in New York Simpson had been quite ill, but was recovering. She spoke at his Friday afternoon meeting at his invitation about "the incoming, in all His fullness, of the blessed Holy Ghost." She recalled, "Mr. Simpson feels that the children of God in these solemn days should press on to receive all the fullness of the Spirit."[64] This was consistent with Simpson's urging for a fuller baptism in the Spirit.

Carrie also recorded, "We had a blessed time of prayer and praise together with these dear friends." Simpson invited her to speak in the weekly Friday afternoon meeting. At Simpson's request, she recalled, "I told the dear people present of the great things God had done for me, not only in body but also in mind and spirit through the incoming of the Pentecostal fullness of the blessed Holy Ghost."[65] On their return trip to California in December they stopped by Fort Worth to visit long-time friend Warren Collins, whom she described as a Pentecostal.[66]

Respected Tongue-Speaking C&MA Leaders

The Alliance did not endeavor to keep tongue-speaking ministers out of leadership. Rather, if they showed promise and seemed to be moderate in their views and practices, they were given leadership opportunities and promotion. For example, in 1917 Harry Turner, who had received the baptism of the Spirit with tongues at Nyack in 1912, was named as chairman of the C&MA mission in Argentina.[67] A year later, however, Turner decided to join the Pentecostals. He wanted to still be involved with the Alliance as well, but the leadership was wary about the extent of his Pentecostal beliefs and practices. After about six years of Pentecostal ministry, Turner became disillusioned with the movement and returned to the Alliance. He so gained the confidence of the Alliance that he was later elected president of the C&MA.

Ira David, who had left the superintendency of the New England District in 1912 for the Pentecostal movement, returned to the Alliance about two years later, pastoring a church in Chicago. He was accepted enthusiastically back into Alliance leadership, becoming a featured convention speaker at C&MA conferences in Chicago and Boston in 1917 and 1918.[68] Yet he also continued to be involved in the Pentecostal movement in the Chicago area, frequently speaking at the Pentecostal Stone Church and contributing articles to the *The Latter Rain Evangel*.[69]

Late in 1917 S. H. Switzer, pastor of the Alliance church in Harrison, New Jersey, passed away. Simpson praised his church as "indeed a Pentecostal church of the Lord Jesus Christ," remarking, "It has been a great privilege to many of us to come here, to feel the warm breath of his Spirit-filled soul, to catch the heavenly choruses of song, worship, and the praise of life of the people here." Simpson eulogized him with the words, "Oh, what a heritage he has left us! . . . Oh, how his mantle fell on all his flock."[70]

BOSWORTH RETURNS TO THE ALLIANCE

In the summer of 1918 the Assemblies of God firmed up the evidential tongues doctrine. F. F. Bosworth had tried to convince the Council to back off the position, but when they would not, Bosworth and his brother B. B. left the Assemblies of God graciously without putting up a fight, and left on the next train to a C&MA convention. A. P. Collins, one of the founding leaders of the Assemblies of God, initially supported Bosworth, but shortly recanted his support.[71] F. F. soon was appointed Assistant Superintendent for the Southern District of the C&MA, serving with District Superintendent R. A. Forrest.[72]

Bosworth wrote a booklet directed to his Pentecostal brothers entitled *Do All Speak with Tongues?: An Open Letter to the Ministers and Saints of the Pentecostal Movement*, eventually published by the C&MA publishing company. In it he argues against the evidence doctrine, that all should speak in tongues, and "seeking for a physical manifestation [of tongues] when they ought to be witnessing and laboring for souls."[73] He strongly asserted, "I am absolutely certain that many who receive the most powerful baptism for service do not receive the manifestation of speaking in tongues. And I am just as certain on the other hand, that many who *seemingly* speak in tongues, are not, nor have ever been baptized in the Spirit."[74]

Bosworth was invited to speak at the Alliance General Council in Toccoa, Georgia, in May 1919.[75] He left his other church, which affiliated with the Assemblies of God, and started a new church in Dallas affiliated with the C&MA.[76] In the fall of 1919 Bosworth's first wife died, and about four years later he married a graduate of the Missionary Training Institute at Nyack.[77]

Harry W. Lucas, a young Pentecostal evangelist who had attended the Pentecostal Bethel Bible Training Center in Newark, New Jersey, started preaching in Pittsburgh area in both Pentecostal and Alliance circles between 1914-1917.

By 1918 he had become credentialed with the C&MA as a popular evangelist and began to pastor the charismatically-oriented Alliance church in nearby Washington, west of Pittsburgh. He later pastored other charismaticallyoriented Alliance churches in Akron, Louisville, and Detroit.[78]

Other Assemblies Ministers Follow Suit

Thomas J. O'Neal, who had served as an Assemblies of God presbyter along with F. F. Bosworth, soon followed the Bosworths, leaving the Assemblies of God by October 1918 over the evidential tongues issue and joining the C&MA early in 1919. O'Neal had been a minister with the Pentecostal Church of the Nazarene before receiving the baptism in the Spirit with tongues. Since they did not accept his experience of speaking in tongues, he had joined the Assemblies of God at their founding in 1914, pastoring churches in Kansas and Oklahoma.[79]

Now he found the Assemblies position too rigid and narrow, but was welcomed with open arms by the Alliance.[80] He served as an evangelist, working with B. B. Bosworth mainly in the Southern District, and just two years later was appointed by R. A. Forrest as Assistant District Superintendent after Bosworth left the position for evangelistic work.[81] He served actively in the Alliance as a pastor and evangelist until his death in 1940.[82] Several other Assemblies of God ministers switched to the C&MA by the early 1920s, including E. G. Birdsall, Hardy Mitchell, Warren Collins, C. Orville Benham, Edward Armstrong, Alonzo Horn, A. T. Rape, E. J. Witte, Raymond T. Richey and his father E. N. Richey.[83]

Simpson's Last Years and Transition of Leadership

In his last years, Simpson continued to encourage exercise of all the gifts of the Spirit in Alliance churches and meetings. In October 1917 Simpson wrote an article entitled "The Dynamite of God," saying that the baptism of the Spirit is "especially manifest in intercession. Sometimes it is manifest in ecstatic tongues of praise and special messages of prophetic appropriateness in testimony, warning, comfort, or encouragement. It is the spirit of revival coming down, not only upon individuals, but upon multitudes in mighty floods of Pentecostal blessing."[84]

In December 1917, less than two years before his death, Simpson wrote wistfully as had in 1909, "Why may we not have all the gifts and all the graces of the Apostolic Church blended in one harmonious whole. . . . Why may we not have all the supernatural ministries of the early Church? . . . Why may we not have the ministry of teaching, the gifts of wisdom, knowledge, the faith of primitive Christianity, and even the tongues of Pentecost, without making them subjects of controversy, without judging one another harshly, because each may have all the gifts, and all in such beautiful and blended harmony. . . ."[85] Just a month before his death, Simpson's "Gifts and Grace" article was republished in the *Alliance Weekly*, reaffirming the Alliance position of openness and caution toward the gifts of the Spirit.[86]

As Simpson aged, more responsibilities were shifted to other Alliance leaders, and they began to consider who would succeed Simpson. In January 1919

Simpson suffered a stroke. Though he continued without pain, he became unable to function actively as the leader of the C&MA. On May 31, 1919, Paul Rader, pastor of Moody Memorial Church, was elected Vice President of the C&MA.[87] A year earlier he had preached on "The Vision and the Passion," exhorting, "Have the passion of the Holy Ghost, not the fire of fanaticism."[88] As a dynamic personality, Rader appeared to manifest the vision and passion that Simpson had in organizing the Alliance more than thirty years earlier. After Simpson's death October 29, Rader became acting President of the C&MA.

A few days before Simpson's homegoing, his dear friend Robert Jaffray and other friends and colleagues assembled around him to claim healing and victory over death. Knowing that his time was near and that God had not given him a special faith to claim healing on this occasion, he commented to them, "Boys, I can't go that far with you this time."[89] Yet he confessed, "Jesus is so real." He had assurance that his life's work was done and he had completed his course.

1. "A Revival in Wuchang, China," AW, Aug. 16, 1913, 312; Robert Glover, "Our Foreign Mailbag," AW, Apr. 12, 1919, 44.

2. A. B. Simpson, Editorial, AW, July 18, 1914, 257.

3. William Franklin, "Itinerary in New England," AW, Feb. 13, 1915, 317, 319.

4. AW, Apr. 15, 1916, 46.

5. "Annual Survey of the Christian and Missionary Alliance for Fiscal Year Ending December 31, 1916," AW, June 9, 1917, 136-137.

6. Dr. E. Howard Taylor, "Healing on the Mission Field," AW, June 1, 1912, 135.

7. Eleanor Beard Hatton, "Follow Thou Me," AW, May 2, 1914, 77; "A Dream and Its Impression," AW, July 11, 1914, 247; "The Sunday Morning Dream," AW, July 3, 1915, 214-215; "A Dream," AW, Aug. 14, 1915, 308; E. R. Carner, "Brahmins: A True Story," AW, June 3, 1916, 152-154; "A Chinese Woman's Dream," AW, Mar. 16, 1918, 376; "Answered Prayer," AW, May 31, 1913, 134.

8. "The Prayer Circle," AW, Nov. 16, 1918, 107-108.

9. H. D. Campbell, "The Man Who Saw Hell," AW, June 28, 1913, 200-201.

10. E. R. Carner, "Brahmins: A True Story," AW, June 3, 1916, 152-154.

11. Mrs. William McLatchkey, "Healed from Poisoning," AW, July 11, 1914, 254.

12. "A Chinese Woman's Dream," AW, Mar. 16, 1918, 376.

13. H. L. Pierson, "The Healing of Congolese Woman," AW, Jan. 4, 1919, 218.

14. George Jennings, "Revival at Tapalque, Argentina," AW, Dec. 6, 1913, 152.

15. H. M. Shuman, "Louis Henry Zweimer," AW, Nov. 4, 1953, 11.

16. Mrs. S. P. Hamilton, "Continued Blessings in India," AW, July 22, 1916, 66.

17. E. R. Carner, "Showers of Blessing in India," AW, Oct. 27, 1917, 58.

18. George A. Steel, "The Baptism of the Holy Spirit," AW, June 30, 1917, 199.

19. Dr. H. W. Pope, "Putting Things Right," AW, Aug. 2, 1913, 283.

20. F. E. Marsh, "Here and There," AW, Oct. 11, 1913, 23.

21. "Answered Prayer," AW, May 31, 1913, 134.

22. A. B. Simpson, "Jeremiah, an Example of Faith and Courage," AW, Nov. 14, 1914, 98.

23. Mrs. May Evans, "Healed of Cancer," AW, July 10, 1915, 231.

24. Jean Ratan Cole, "Getting Telegrams from God," LRE, Aug. 1920, 11.

25. A. B. Simpson, Editorial, AW, Mar. 2, 1918, 337; W. G. Colby, "The Gospel and the Devil in Kong Chang," AW, Feb. 23, 1918, 330-331; A. E. Thompson, "Light from the Bible Lands: Demon Possession," AW, Mar. 23, 1918, 397.

26. William Christie, "The Lord's Healing on the China-Tibetan Border," AW, Feb. 9, 1918, 7-8.

27. Howard Van Dyck, William Christie: Apostle to Tibet (Harrisburg, PA: Christian Publications, 1956), 119-131.

28. Lewis, Life Sketch of Rev. Mary C. Morton, 30-32.

29. Warner, The Woman Evangelist, 177-178.

30. B. F. Lawrence, The Apostolic Faith Restored (St. Louis, MO: Gospel Publishing Co., 1916), in Three Early Pentecostal Tracts (New York and London: Garland Publishing, Inc., 1985), 85.

31. Synan, The Holiness-Pentecostal Movement in the United States, 137. Synan may have based his conclusion on an early report by Cashwell, cited by Goff, that Watson would have opposed tongues. See Florence Goff, Fifty Years on the Battlefield for God (Falcon, NC: n.p., 1948), 52.

32. Gordon Lindsay, The New John G. Lake Sermons (Dallas, TX: Christ for the Nations, 1974), 6, 15-16.

33. A. E. Thompson, "The Corinthian Epistles: Spiritual Gifts and Graces," AW, Feb. 12, 1916, 315-316; A. E. Thompson, "The Corinthian Epistles: The Use, Abuse and Value of Gifts," AW, Feb. 26, 1916, 341.

34. W. T. MacArthur, "Watching the Father Work," AW, July 15, 1916, 244.

35. A. B. Simpson, Editorial, AW, May 26, 1917, 114.

36. A. B. Simpson, 1909 Annual Report of the Christian and Missionary Alliance, May 25, 1909, 36.

37. A. B. Simpson, "Back to Pentecost," AW, Mar. 8, 1913, 358.

38. A. B. Simpson, Editorial, AW, Feb. 14, 1914, 305.

39. A. B. Simpson, Editorial, AW, Apr. 11, 1914, 18.

40. Myland, "A Personal Word," LRE, Oct. 1911, 11; Montgomery, "The Promise of the Father," Triumphs of Faith, July 1908, 1.

41. C&MA Board of Manager Minutes, Oct. 11, 1913, Oct. 16, 1915.

42. The Christian Evangel, July 19, 1913, Vol. 1, No. 1, p. 1.

43. C&MA Board of Manager Minutes, July 24, 1913.

44. E. O. Jago, "A Great Crisis!," LRE, Oct. 1913, 2.

45. Ibid., 4.

46. "German Thoughts about the Sunderland Convention," Confidence, July 1913, 134; "Sunderland Convention: A Synopsis of the Meetings and Addresses," Confidence, June 1913, 117-118.

47. A. A. Boddy, "Westward Ho! At the C&MA Tabernacle, New York," Confidence, Oct. 1914, 183.

48. A. A. Boddy, "Westward Ho!," Confidence, Aug. 1914, 145; A. A. Boddy, "Westward Ho! The Conclusion of the Journey, Confidence, Dec. 1914, 225.

49. Word and Work, Aug. 1914, 252.

50. A. B. Simpson, Editorial, AW, Dec. 19, 1914, 177.

51. "Ordination of Mr. George P. Simmonds," AW, Jan. 30, 1915, 286.

52. "Fifteen Days with God," LRE, June 1915, 13.

53. "Report on the Los Angeles Convention," AW, June 1, 1915, 158.

54. "Christian Hettelsater," AW, Aug. 7, 1915, 302.

55. LRE, July 1918, 14.

56. A. B. Simpson, Editorial, AW, May 1, 1915, 65.

57. Ibid.

58. A. A. Boddy, "Westward Ho!," *Confidence*, Dec. 1914, 224.

59. Wayne Warner, "J. Narver Gortner: The Early Life of a Key Figure in the Assemblies of God," Part 1, *Assemblies of God Heritage*, Spring 1988, 15-16; J. Narver Gortner, "The Baptism of Suffering Joins Us into One Body: How a Methodist Preacher Came Into Pentecost," LRE, July 1922, 6-7. Five years after this experience Gortner joined the Assemblies of God.

60. Herbert Dyke, "Healed from Smallpox—A Thanksgiving Note," AW, Nov. 24, 1917, 117.

61. W. T. MacArthur, "What 'Forsaking All' Meant to Abraham," LRE, Apr. 1916, 6; LRE, June 1916, 15; William T. MacArthur, "The Three Companies of Christians," LRE, Jan. 1918, 6-8; William T. MacArthur, "The Translation of the Saints," LRE, Feb. 1918, 2ff.; LRE, Apr. 1918, 23.

62. "Notes," LRE, Jan. 1918, 12.

63. Montgomery, "An Eastern Trip in the Lord's Work," *Triumphs of Faith*, Jan. 1919, 13.

64. Ibid., 15.

65. Montgomery, *Under His Wings*, 231.

66. Montgomery, "An Eastern Trip in the Lord's Work," 16.

67. "Annual Conference in Azul, Argentina," AW, June 16, 1917, 168.

68. A. B. Simpson, Editorial, AW, Sept. 29, 1917, 401; "The Boston Convention," AW, Jan. 19, 1918, 244; AW, Sept. 7, 1918, 366.

69. Ira E David, "God's Directive and Permissive Will," LRE, Oct. 1912, 7; "The Cloud of His Glory Upon Us," LRE, June 1913, 2; LRE, Feb. 1916, 13; "Notes," LRE, July 1916, 12; Ira E. David, "Clean Hands and Pure Hearts," LRE, Aug. 1916, 15; Ira E. David, "The Laws of Soul Winning," LRE, Oct. 1916, 2; Ira E. David, "Lord, Teach Us to Pray," LRE, Nov. 1916, 8; "Notes," LRE, Feb. 1917, 12; Ira E. David, "The Importance of Winning Children for God," LRE, May 1918, 16; Ira E. David, "The Subdued Believer," LRE, Dec. 1919, 2. See also Mrs. I. E. David, "Measuring the Pattern," LRE, Nov. 1916, 22.

70. "The Late Rev. S. H. Switzer," AW, Jan. 19, 1918, 251.

71. "Assemblies of God Superintendents," *Assemblies of God Heritage*, Winter 1981-82, 3.

72. Menzies, 126-130.

73. F. F. Bosworth, *Do All Speak with Tongues?: An Open Letter to the Ministers and Saints of the Pentecostal Movement* (New York, NY: Christian Alliance Publishing Co., [1918]), 13.

74. Ibid., 4.

75. Editorials, AW, May 31, 1919, 146, 156.

76. AW, July 19, 1919, 271; "The Household of Faith," AW, Sept. 14, 1919, 414. Bosworth had asked A. G. Garr to pastor his church for a few months while he traveled in evangelistic ministry. Garr emphasized the evidential tongues doctrine and it split the church. See Thompson and Gordon, *A 20th Century Apostle*, 123-125.

77. Editorials, AW, Nov. 22, 1919, 130

78. "Home Field Notes," AW, May 11, 1918, 94; "Home Field Notes," AW, Apr. 12, 1919, 46; "The Alliance Family, AW, July 31, 1957, 12. Lucas may have been the brother of Christian Lucas, who was an instructor at Bethel Bible Training Center and son-in-law of J. T. Boddy. See Flower Pentecostal Heritage Center website: www.agheritage.org.

79. *Word and Witness*, July 1915, 4; Bob Burke, *Like a Prairie Fire: A History of the Assemblies of God in Oklahoma* (Oklahoma City, OK: Oklahoma District Council of the Assemblies of God, 1994), 51, 54, 57, 62.

80. Letter from Thomas J. O'Neal to J. W. Welch, Oct. 21, 1918. Flower Pentecostal Heritage Center.

81. "Notice!," AW, Apr. 19, 1919, 62; AW, May 22, 1920, 126; "The Household of Faith," AW, June 25, 1921, 237; "The Household of Faith," AW, July 1, 1922, 254.

82. "Obituaries," AW, Dec. 28, 1940, 828, "Dallas and Oklahoma City Districts," AW, Jan. 18, 1941, 45.

83. The Richeys and Mitchell eventually returned to the Assemblies of God years later.

84. A. B. Simpson, "The Dynamite of God," AW, Oct. 20, 1917, 36.

85. A. B. Simpson, "Members of One Another," AW, Dec. 8, 1917, 148; Simpson, "Christian Altruism," CMAW, Aug. 7, 1909, 322.

86. A. B. Simpson, "Gifts and Grace," AW, Sept. 20, 1919, 403.

87. Editorials, AW, May 31, 1919, 146, 156.

88. Paul Rader, "The Vision and the Passion," AW, May 25, 1918, 115.

89. "Grace's Consummation," AW, Dec. 8, 1945, 423.

PART FOUR

CHARISMATIC TEACHING AND
PRACTICE AFTER SIMPSON
(1920-PRESENT)

SIXTEEN

RESURGENCE IN THE RADER ERA —
1920–1924

With the passing of A. B. Simpson, the question arises, what would happen to the existing charismatic theology, phenomena, and practice in The Christian and Missionary Alliance? With the dynamic leadership of Paul Rader, followed by R. H. Senft and H. M. Shuman, along with the Alliance Board of Managers, there appears to have been continued openness to charismatic phenomena and continued cooperation with moderate Pentecostals in the decade following Simpson's death. In fact, there was a resurgence of charismatic life infused in the C&MA during this period of time.

RADER'S AFFIRMATION OF THE SUPERNATURAL

Rader was a man of passionate vision who brought an infusion of life into the Alliance. Rader affirmed his belief in the continued operation of the supernatural in the twentieth century.[1] Less than a year after his installation as president of the C&MA, Rader recounted the vision he had in 1912 at Niagara Falls of people going over the Falls in agony. It gave him a burden for evangelism and led to his experience of being filled with the Holy Spirit.[2]

In his Annual Report at General Council in 1920, Rader prayed for the gift of healing to fall upon younger men and women in the C&MA.[3] Just after the anniversary of Simpson's death Rader was considered by The Alliance Weekly editors as a "real prophet of God."[4] A month later Rader wrote with that pro-phetic voice, "The fight of our day is supernaturalism against materialism. The answer to materialism is a supernatural Christ." He gave an illustration of that supernatural fight, recounting an incident while pastor of Moody Church in which a man came down the aisle barking like a dog. He promptly cast out the demon.[5]

On another occasion, he recalled holy laughter, when a friend laughed for hours after being filled with the Spirit.[6] He also maintained friendships with those involved in the Pentecostal movement such as Aimee Semple McPherson and E. W. Kenyon. During his tenure as President of the C&MA, he appears to have maintained the same openness with discernment to charismatic phenomena and practice and cooperation with Pentecostals as did Simpson.

Due to Rader's independent management and ministry style, however, he eventually came into conflict with the Board of Managers. As Alliance historians note, "Rader, a rugged individualist, preferred going it alone and ruling with an autocratic hand."[7] Being a decisive, driving visionary, he often made decisions and launched ministries independently of the Board of Managers. He wanted to reorganize the Alliance with more control given to him, while the Board insisted on mutual decision-making and teamwork. When the Board of Managers turned down his proposal, he resigned, effective early in 1924. While he never again served in Alliance leadership, he actively supported and promoted Alliance work, especially missions.

One might wonder what might have developed if some mutual agreement could have been reached, for on one hand, as Rader's biographers intimate, later ventures of Rader showed that he needed wise counselors, yet the C&MA could have continued to grow strongly under his passionate, visionary leadership.[8] His departure ultimately resulted in a loss of momentum that had been building, but Alliance leaders continued to maintain encouragement of the supernatural.

CHARISMATIC RESURGENCE WITH FORMER PENTECOSTALS AND OTHERS

During the 1920s cooperation between the Alliance and moderate Pentecostals continued. In addition, several former Pentecostals left the Assemblies of God or other Pentecostal denominations, obtained credentials with the C&MA, and actively ministered in and through the Alliance. These included F. F. and B. B. Bosworth, Edward Armstrong, Alonzo Horn, Warren Collins, Hardy W. Mitchell, Raymond T. Richey and his father E. N. Richey, C. Orville Benham, among others.

F. F. and B. B. Bosworth. In the 1920s the Bosworth brothers launched itinerant evangelistic and healing ministry both inside and outside of the C&MA. The Bosworth revival campaign at Lima, Ohio, in 1920 was marked by many miraculous healings and many receiving the baptism with the Spirit. When prayed for by Bosworth, a woman testified that the power of God went through her body; then she saw a bright light and a vision of Jesus and was healed of cancer. Blindness and paralysis were healed, including restoration of sight to a man blind for more than ten years. Alliance pastor R. H. Moon testified, "Lima has never seen such a deep stirring spiritually." In Bosworth's meetings, it was reported, there was "no fanaticism or carnal emotionalism."[9]

Bosworth held a revival campaign in Pittsburgh in 1920, teaming up with E. D. Whiteside. Many healings and signs followed, and sinners trembled at the power of God manifested and were saved. Whiteside called it "an apostolic revival." *The Alliance Weekly* editors called the Bosworths "deeply spiritual evangelists and teachers of the Full Gospel of Jesus Christ."[10]

In 1921, Bosworth held meetings in Detroit in connection with the C&MA and Pastor W. A. Cramer. There was an outpouring of the Spirit in revival. A blind woman miraculously received her sight and many other testimonies of healing were reported.[11] According to Bosworth, "Paralytics were healed and walked off the platforms, having been carried up. . . . People received the baptism of the Holy Spirit right on the platform, the atmosphere was so charged with the power of God. One night, without any suggestion from anyone, three different ones broke out speaking in tongues."[12] J. D. Williams reported on the Bosworth revival campaign in St. Paul, saying that the Full Gospel was preached, but there was an absence of emotionalism or sensationalism.[13] According to *The Pentecostal Evangel*, Bosworth reported that many people in his mid-America meetings were baptized in the Spirit accompanied by speaking in tongues.[14] Though not reported in Alliance periodicals, this probably continued to be an ongoing characteristic of Bosworth's meetings.

Dramatic healings took place in the Bosworths' campaigns in Chicago, Toronto, and many other places with manifestations and sensations going through the bodies of people from head to foot.[15] Local reporters commented on the Bosworth campaigns: "In striking contrast with many evangelists who have visited Toronto, the preaching of evangelist Bosworth is characterized by an entire absence of sensationalism or any endeavor to excite emotional outburst on the part of the hearers. He is a plain man and preaches the plain old-fashioned Gospel."[16]

However, some tension arose in the Alliance at this time as President Paul Rader "felt that the Bosworths were making a dangerous mistake in giving healing the prominence they did," consequently Rader discouraged Alliance churches in Canada from inviting them back.[17] Likewise, Home Secretary E. J. Richards cautioned at the General Council, "There are possibly a few individuals in our ranks that seek the spectacular and magnify certain phases of truth out of just proportion to the other part of our testimony."[18] Less than two years later, however, Rader's concerns were evidently alleviated and their relationship was reconciled, as Rader welcomed the Bosworths warmly to his new church in Chicago.[19] Rader continued to invite Bosworth to be a speaker at his Chicago Gospel Tabernacle through the end of the decade.

In 1922 F. F. Bosworth married Nyack Missionary Training Institute graduate Florence Valentine, who served as licensed C&MA worker in charge of an Alliance branch in Ohio.[20] In 1924 Bosworth published the first edition of his book *Christ the Healer*, which contained numerous messages and testimonies of healings in Alliance meetings. The book was at one time required for ordination studies in the C&MA, and was expanded in the 1940s to contain additional messages. In the 1970s and following it was used as a textbook at Kenneth Hagin's Rhema Bible Training Center.

Edward Armstrong. Evangelist Edward Armstrong, an associate of Bosworth, had been credentialed with the Assemblies of God, but joined the C&MA with Bosworth. In July 1921 at an Alliance tent meeting in New Jersey led by Armstrong, demons of epilepsy were cast out and the person was healed.[21] In November of the same year, in revival meetings of Armstrong in Baltimore the glory of God filled the room in one instance of a person receiving the baptism in the Spirit. "Some felt the power of God through them like an electrical shock and shouted the praises of God."[22] Evidently many must have spoken in tongues, for by two years later almost all of the church had received tongues.[23]

Warren Collins. Warren Collins from Fort Worth, Texas, had been an early Vice President of the Alliance and lay preacher for many years. He was probably Bosworth's contact with the C&MA in 1910 when Bosworth started his church in Dallas, and likely participated in the great revival with Maria Woodworth-Etter through Bosworth's church in 1912. Collins obtained credentials with the Assemblies of God in 1917, continuing to minister in the Alliance as well during that time, eventually coming back totally into the Alliance in 1921 with full ministerial credentials. In July 1920, he left his business to engage in full-time evangelistic and healing work. When he held meetings in New Orleans, 1000 were converted and 2000 sick were prayed for. Many miraculous healings occurred including six deaf people and a deaf mute.[24] About a month later, Collins held meetings at a Baptist Church in Memphis, marked by many miraculous healings and exorcisms, including a deaf mute who was healed and spoke.[25] In the fall more testimonies were given from Collins meetings telling of signs following. Reports recounted 450 saved, more than twenty deaf mutes healed, and paralysis healed.[26] Though having Assemblies of God credentials, Collins preached a series of meetings with the Alliance in Philadelphia in December, resulting in many conversions and healings.[27]

After he returned fully to the Alliance in 1921, his meetings continued to be "characterized by charismatic worship," and Pentecostals continued to frequent his meetings.[28] In 1922 Collins and the Bosworth brothers held meetings together in many Alliance churches, as well as Pentecostal and other churches and ministries, resulting in conversions, baptisms in the Spirit, and many healings, some of them quite dramatic. Demons were cast out of children at some of Collins' meetings. Several doctors endorsed divine healing in his meetings and were baptized in the Spirit.[29] When Collins died in January 1927, his obituary in *The Alliance Weekly* affirmed that he "learned the secret of drawing divine health for his body from the Lord and had a real ministry of healing."[30] Other Pentecostals who had been involved with Collins' evangelistic ministry also joined the C&MA, including Frederick J. Betts and Lawrence R. Carter.[31]

Hardy W. Mitchell. In December 1921, former Pentecostal Stone Church (Chicago) pastor Hardy W. Mitchell left the Assemblies of God and began ministry in C&MA as itinerating evangelist, holding meetings with the Alliance work in Detroit, pastored by W. A. Cramer.[32] Revivals with Mitchell continued at C&MA churches nationwide, including Sheridan Gospel Tabernacle in Pittsburgh (Whiteside's church), Minnesota, Illinois, New Jersey (in connection with the Bosworths), and Fort Worth, Texas. Apparently the aged Whiteside retired as pastor of Sheridan Gospel Tabernacle and asked Mitchell to take his place in 1922.[33] Mitchell, however, had an itch as an itinerant evangelist, and did not remain at Sheridan Gospel Tabernacle very long.

Raymond T. Richey. *The Alliance Weekly* reported on various occasions that Raymond T. Richey, a friend of Collins and an Assemblies of God evangelist, held many meetings in Alliance circles. In one article, he was referred to as "our [C&MA] worker in Houston," although there was not an official C&MA work there at the time.[34] In 1922 he received C&MA credentials, having left the Assemblies of God.[35] Richey's healing ministry had begun October 1920 when he went to assist Collins in his meetings in Hattiesburg, Mississippi, but Collins could not come due to sickness. Richey carried on the meetings, and the anointing of the Lord came upon Richey, resulting in many conversions and healings.[36]

In 1923 Richey continued evangelistic and healing meetings in conjunction with the C&MA in Fort Worth, Oklahoma City, and Tulsa, as well as at Toccoa Falls Bible Institute. In Tulsa, the C&MA/Richey services resulted in thousands healed and converted. C&MA churches formed in Oklahoma City and Tulsa out of his meetings. *The Alliance Weekly* commented that Richey's meetings "open a very good field for the Alliance in this section of the country." Not long before, Tulsa had experienced a scandalous race riot with many black residents killed and homes burned. Richey's meetings brought revival and reconciliation to a city torn with violence. W. A. Cramer, the veteran tongue-speaking pastor from charismatic Alliance churches, was recruited to pastor the new Alliance work in Tulsa.[37]

In August of that same year Richey ministered at Toccoa Falls Institute and quickly became a close friend of its founder, Southern District Superintendent R. A. Forrest.[38] Forrest sometimes ministered together with Richey and did follow up work from his revival meetings. Forrest seemed to be quite receptive to charismatic phenomena and tongue-speaking Alliance leaders with Pentecostal connections, such as Richey and his father, Collins, Ira David, Glenn Tingley, Bosworth, the Bergs, and Bosworth's associate Thomas J. O. Neal, so much so that one wonders if he may have spoken in tongues himself. T. J. McCrossan, who joined the Alliance in 1923 and ministered with Pentecostal evangelist Charles Price, later spoke well of Richey, along with Bosworth.[39]

C. Orville Benham. Also in 1923 C. O. Benham conducted evangelistic and healing meetings in the C&MA, sometimes ministering together with the Bosworths and Mitchell. Benham had been a minister with the Assemblies of God and an assistant of F. F. Bosworth, but joined the Alliance along with his friends. Through his meetings there were many healings, people baptized in the Spirit, and demons cast out. Benham also served as the interim pastor of the charismatically-oriented Portland Gospel Tabernacle (C&MA) during this period of time.[40]

The Dixons. After fifteen years of ministry and missions in Pentecostal circles, former Quakers W. T. and Bertha Pinkham Dixon found a home with the C&MA, agreeing with the Alliance position that tongues is not necessarily the evidence of the baptism in the Spirit. They were recruited by the Southern California District Superintendent George W. Davis for church planting in the C&MA. [41]

CONTINUED ALLIANCE/PENTECOSTAL COOPERATION

Cordial Relations with the Eldridges. Just two months after Simpson's death, George Eldridge, now an Assemblies of God pastor, nonetheless wrote words of appreciation for Simpson in *The Alliance Weekly*.[42] The next month, Dr. Walter Turnbull of Nyack, a relative of the Eldridges, spoke at Eldridge's Assemblies of God church in Los Angeles.[43] In June 1920 Eldridge preached at the funeral of an Indianapolis Alliance lay leader at the church he had pastored more than 13 years earlier.[44] In 1924 C&MA Financial Secretary W. S. Poling reported that he visited his "old friends" the Eldridges in Los Angeles.[45]

Mattie Perry Ministers in Alliance and Pentecostal Circles. Mattie Perry had been a pioneering superintendent and evangelist for the C&MA in southeastern United States following her graduation from the Missionary Training Institute in 1896.[46] She became quite ill and was an invalid for several years, while at the same time supervising Elhanan Training Institute and Orphanage in Marion, North Carolina. At some unidentified point before 1916, she received her "Pentecostal baptism of the Holy Spirit," along with healing and rejuvenation of her energy. She testified, "The old, tired feeling went like the dropping of an old garment. My memory was quickened and my nerves steadied instantly."[47] From 1916 and following, she ministered in Pentecostal circles as well as with the C&MA.[48] Especially in the early 1920s, Perry maintained a broad evangelistic and healing ministry with many signs and wonders following at Alliance and Pentecostal churches in many locations, and also ministered with the Bosworths.

Seymour Preaches in the Alliance. A significant event occurred in 1921 when William J. Seymour, catalyst of the 1906 Azusa Street revival, preached in a two-week series of meetings at the C&MA church in Columbus, Ohio. Although I have not been able to document other visits by Seymour to C&MA ministries, he did have contact with Alliance-affiliated people from time to time. He had become a friend of Bosworth early in the Pentecostal renewal and undoubtedly continued contacts with him through the years. Vice President John Salmon and Superintendent George Eldridge visited Seymour in Los Angeles about 1910.

Like Bosworth, Seymour had abandoned the evidential tongues doctrine and held a position compatible with the Alliance.[49] In 1915 he had written, "Wherever the doctrine of the baptism in the Holy Spirit will only be known as the evidence of speaking in tongues, that work will be an open door for witches and spiritualists and free lovism. That work will suffer, because all kinds of spirits can come in."[50] This was very similar to the cautions that Alliance leaders had about dangers of demonic counterfeits when seeking evidential tongues.

Even though Myland had left the Alliance church in Columbus for the Pentecostal movement nearly a decade earlier, the church apparently remained charismatic in orientation and welcomed Seymour. Mrs. Georgiana Aycock, who attended the meetings, commented of Seymour, "The glow would be on that man's face. He looked like an angel from heaven. So many wanted to hear him, they had heard of him. . . . He was no man to exalt himself, he was a humble man. When you'd meet him at the door, you could just feel . . . he was a real man of God. . . . He didn't talk much. He was not a conversationalist. He'd get off about the Lord, being true to God."[51]

Cautious Cooperation with Pentecostals in Argentina. Harry Turner, who had been appointed chairman of the Argentine Alliance mission in 1916, had left for Pentecostalism in 1918. By 1920 he had restored some personal relationships in the Alliance, particularly with F. D. Sholin, the new chairman of the Alliance mission, while continuing to maintain Pentecostal connections.[52] In 1921 acting Foreign Secretary A. C. Snead reported on Harry Turner's interest in a cooperative missions endeavor between the C&MA and Pentecostals. Even though Snead was a tongue-speaker himself, he expressed concern about the proposed arrangement, affirming Turner's willingness to combine forces with C&MA services in Argentina, but in his "new relation with the Pentecostal work . . . advise great caution on the field as to his being secured for services."[53] In spite of the cautions, those overtures of openness to collaboration cultivated more positive relationships, as Turner eventually returned to the Alliance in 1926 and served as president in the 1950s.

C&MA and Assemblies of God Divide Mission Work. H. W. Cragin had served the Alliance in mission fields in South America for many years. After his 1923 furlough from the Alliance mission in Ecuador, he returned returned to Ecuador. However, he was soon asked to return to the United States to do evangelistic work for a year. Rather than leave the field, he resigned from the Alliance mission in Ecuador and joined the Assemblies of God, pioneering their work in Peru. The C&MA had made plans to enter Peru as well. Learning from the dispute several years earlier when W. W. Simpson returned to the Tibetan mission field under the banner of the Assemblies of God, this time both the C&MA and Assemblies demonstrated a magnanimous gesture of cooperation. Rather than compete with each other or wrangle over one another's territory and people, they agreed to divide the missionary work in Peru between the two organizations.[54]

Meetings with Pentecostals. In 1921 Assemblies of God minister John Waggoner held meetings in Warren, Ohio, in conjunction with the Alliance church he had formerly pastored there.[55] In 1920 Baptist pastor P. C. Nelson received Spirit baptism with tongues and became an independent Pentecostal evangelist. For a time, his beliefs seemed to be compatible with the C&MA and he was a featured speaker in many Alliance meetings.[56] The Alliance Weekly listed his ministry itinerary and reported that he held revival meetings "under the auspices of" the C&MA.[57] He contributed articles to The Alliance Weekly and held meetings in Toronto with Bosworth and Oswald J. Smith and in Kansas City with W. C. Stevens.[58] However, Nelson affiliated with the Assemblies of God about five years later.

Ramabai Associates Appointed as C&MA Missionaries. In 1922 Mr. and Mrs. Albert Norton, son and daughter-in-law of the elder Albert Norton who had been involved with Ramabai's Pentecostal revival at Mukti in India, were appointed to Palestine as C&MA missionaries.[59] The elder Albert had received the baptism in the Spirit with tongues in 1906.[60] The Nortons had been long-time friends with the Alliance mission in India, and Ramabai, who had recently passed away in 1922, had deeded her ministry over to the Alliance in her will. So it seemed natural to begin a new chapter in their ministry with the Alliance. The elder Albert died about a year later and it appears that the younger Nortons left the Palestinian field, but seeds of their brief work and anointing in Palestine bore fruit about two years after that. A Pentecostal-like revival, not unlike the revival in Mukti, broke out in the Palestinian Alliance work in 1925 with visions, dreams and power encounters leading to conversions.[61]

Montgomerys' Continued Connections. George and Carrie Judd Montgomery continued to maintain connections with the C&MA through the 1920s even though they had joined the Assemblies of God. George continued to serve as an Honorary Vice President until his death in 1930 and contributed articles to *The Alliance Weekly.*[62] Carrie showed her continued fondness for Simpson, frequently referring to him in her monthly periodical *Triumphs of Faith* and including reprints of numerous articles by Simpson.

Associations with Aimee Semple McPherson. In 1923 Kenneth MacKenzie cited Rader, Richey, Bosworth, and Aimee Semple McPherson as examples of genuine healing ministries.[63] It is significant that MacKenzie, a close associate of Simpson, would regard McPherson so highly. Oswald J. Smith claimed that McPherson did not teach tongues as the initial evidence of the baptism in the Spirit.[64] Pentecostal historian Edith Blumhofer further confirms that after 1919 McPherson did not teach evidential tongues.[65] In fact, even some in her day questioned whether she could be considered a Pentecostal and she herself avoided the term.[66]

At any rate, Alliance leaders of that period of time were comfortable with her ministry and actively participated in her meetings.[67] In 1921 and 1922 Methodist pastor Dean Arthur C. Peck, one time a Field Superintendent in the C&MA, sponsored and managed her meetings in Denver.[68] In July 1922, a "Four-Square Gospel Association" of community ministers was formed out of a McPherson campaign in Oakland, California. The Alliance Church in the city, pastored by R. H. Moon, became the meeting place for a "preacher's prayer meeting" from that group of ministers called "for the purpose of praying for the baptism of the Holy Spirit."[69] Moon testified of McPherson's meetings:

> As a pastor who sat on the platform and listened to almost every one of the messages, I am glad to say that nothing but a Scriptural, sane, old-fashioned gospel was preached. There was not even a tinge of fanaticism or wild fire present in any of the meetings. . . . Personally I was glad for the message of the necessity of the baptism with

the Holy Ghost for the believer subsequent to conversion. It is this message that has precipitated a revival in my own church and has rekindled the old passion for souls.[70]

In 1926 former C&MA President Paul Rader preached at McPherson's Angelus Temple for three months in her absence.[71] As she became more controversial over time, however, the Alliance, Rader, and even some Pentecostal leaders like Charles Price, seemed to have backed off from active support for her ministry.[72]

Price/McCrossan Meetings Plant Alliance Churches. Congregational minister Charles Price received Spirit baptism with tongues in 1921 under the ministry of Aimee Semple McPherson. As a result he launched out into an independent Pentecostal ministry, ministering both in Pentecostal and non-Pentecostal circles, and becoming a friend of Bosworth. On November 21, 1922, Presbyterian minister and Greek professor T. J. McCrossan attended Price's evangelistic and healing meeting in Albany, Oregon. There he received the baptism in the Spirit, falling under the power of the Spirit and being enraptured with a vision for more than an hour, but did not speak in unknown tongues.[73] McCrossan records his testimony of that night, using the editorial "we":

> When praying earnestly one night . . . , the blessed Holy Spirit came down upon us. We saw a light, far brighter than the noon-day sun—a perfect blaze of glory. Then hundreds of tongues of fire seemed to dart forth upon and about us. Then for an hour or more great billows of glory, indescribably beautiful from the standpoint of light and colors, began to roll through our soul like mighty breakers over a sandy beach. Did any outsider need to tell us that the Holy Spirit had entered our life in a new way? No, indeed. Then the blessed Spirit took possession of our tongue, and for an hour or more made us praise the Lord Jesus in a way we had never praised Him before. We were literally speaking with another tongue as the Spirit gave to us to utter forth, but it was all in English. [74]

Price, who had prayed over McCrossan, gives this account of that same night:

> That night Pentecost was repeated. And as the showers of blessing fell I saw that minister prostrate under the power of God. He became one of my dearest friends, Dr. T. J. McCrossan, versed as few men are in Hebrew and Greek, and a minister and educator of years standing. I knew as he lay there under the mighty power of God that Jesus was answering his prayer. That night he saw things with the eyes of the soul. The following night he stood in the armory crowded to the doors with hungry folk who were seeking God and said, "I would not take a million dollars for the hours I spent with God last night."[75]

As a result, McCrossan became a close friend and associate of Price, frequently traveling and ministering with him. Just as McCrossan had fallen under the power of the Spirit, so when he prayed for others many also fell under the same power. In one particular instance, Price asked McCrossan to join him in laying on hands praying for a Chinese pastor's wife who was dying from tuberculosis. McCrossan described what happened: "The result was that God sent a mighty power (somewhat like bolts of electricity) down our arms into her body. Personally, we could hardly endure it, but we knew well it was God answering prayer, for we saw that she had fallen into a peaceful sleep." For about half an hour she lay still on the platform, though "her dress was constantly twitching and moving just over her lungs. Suddenly she leaped to her feet perfectly well."[76] Later, he wrote of the phenomena:

> We have discovered that this power is not hypnotism. . . . this is not devil power. . . . All who are genuinely under this power praise the Lord Jesus in a marvelous manner. Many of them have visions of their Lord in Heaven. Some see Him on the cross, and, praise God, many are baptized with the Holy Ghost before the Holy Spirit is through with them. Does Satan so act?"[77]

McCrossan left the Presbyterian church he was pastoring in 1923, transferred his ordination to the C&MA, and formed Spring Hill Gospel Tabernacle in Albany, an interdenominational church affiliated with the C&MA. He also began teaching classes at Simpson Bible Institute.[78] In 1923, 1924, and 1927 Price conducted evangelistic and healing meetings in Winnipeg, Victoria, and Hamilton, Canada in cooperation with C&MA and other churches, with McCrossan assisting him. His meetings were instrumental in stirring ministers of various denominations to join the C&MA and of founding C&MA churches.[79] In March 1923 Methodist pastor John F. Dimmick attended the meetings in Victoria, British Columbia, with his daughter Ruby who had infantile paralysis for eight years. She was miraculously healed and Dimmick joined the C&MA in 1926, pastoring for fourteen years until his retirement. In 1929 he pastored the church McCrossan founded in Albany, Oregon. His daughter attended Simpson Bible Institute in Seattle and was engaged in Christian work.[80]

The Kenyon Connection. E. W. Kenyon is usually acknowledged as the father or grandfather of the modern faith movement even though he was not a Pentecostal in the classic sense. He maintained a positive relationship with the C&MA for several years. At some point in his experience he had experienced speaking in tongues, and had even applied for credentials in the Assemblies of God. However, he withdrew and maintained a viewpoint similar to the Alliance on the evidential tongues issue: "They declare that no one ever received the Holy Spirit unless he has received a physical manifestation. They do not believe that God is in the midst of people unless there is sense evidence. . . . You do not need Sense Knowledge evidence to prove that you have received the Holy Spirit. . . .

Your confidence is not in any physical manifestation or physical evidence. It is always in the Word of God."[81] Also, like the C&MA, he warned about seeking after manifestations: "When people seek experiences for a long time, demons often take advantage and become their helpers. . . . Experience-seekers are always unstable in their faith. . . . The people who are seeking this [speaking in tongues] are not spiritually minded."[82]

Kenyon had been invited on one occasion as a guest speaker by Simpson for an Easter service at his Gospel Tabernacle.[83] Under the leadership of Rader that relationship continued to grow. In February 1922, New England Scottish C&MA evangelist E. J. Evans and Paul Rader had correspondence with E. W. Kenyon about his school Bethel Bible Institute in Spencer, Massachusetts, apparently about some association or cooperation.[84] A year later *The Alliance Weekly* reported that Kenyon's school was "in friendly relationship with the Alliance." Later in April, the students of Bethel Bible Institute attended meetings with C&MA president Paul Rader.[85]

In January 1924 an Alliance missionary addressed the students of Bethel Bible Institute.[86] Kenyon relocated to California, and in February 1925, after having left the presidency of the C&MA, Rader assumed the presidency of Bethel Bible Institute, serving until September 1926.[87] Eventually, Kenyon became more independent and did not circulate as much in Pentecostal or C&MA circles, although he later maintained a friendship with F. F. Bosworth.

---

1. Paul Rader, "The Vision and the Passion," AW, May 25, 1918, 115.

2. Paul Rader, "Send Me," AW, Sept. 25, 1920, 401.

3. Paul Rader, "Annual Report of the President of The Christian and Missionary Alliance," AW, May 29, 1920, 133.

4. Editorial, AW, Oct. 30, 1920, 481.

5. Paul Rader, "At Thy Word—A Farewell Message," AW, Nov. 20, 1920, 532. For another incident, see also Paul Rader, "Devil Possession," AW, Nov. 12, 1921, 547.

6. Paul Rader, "The Fulness of the Holy Ghost," Jan. 19, 1924, 752.

7. Niklaus, et al., *All For Jesus*, 146.

8. For more on the life of Paul Rader and these issues, see Larry K. Eskridge, "Only Believe: Paul Rader and the Chicago Gospel Tabernacle, 1922-1933," Masters Thesis, University of Maryland, 1985; James L. Snyder, *Paul Rader: Portrait of an Evangelist (1879-1938)* Ocala, FL: Fellowship Ministries, 2003.

9. F. F. Bosworth, *Christ the Healer* (Grand Rapids, MI: Fleming H. Revell, 1973), 223-229; R. H. Moon, "When God Visited Lima, Ohio," AW, Sept. 25, 1920, 414; "A Revival of Healing," AW, Oct. 23, 1920, 473-474.

10. Bosworth, *Christ the Healer*, 213-221; "The Household of Faith," AW, Dec. 18, 1920, 606; E. D. Whiteside, "An Apostolic Revival," AW, Dec. 25, 1920, 616.

11. AW, Jan. 22, 1921; "Testimonies to Divine Healing from the Bosworth Meetings," AW, Feb. 5, 1921, 716; "The Outpouring of the Spirit in Revival," AW, Feb. 12, 1921, 732, 748. See also Bosworth, *Christ the Healer*, 221-223.

12. F. F. Bosworth, "They Rehearsed All That God Had Done with Them," LRE, Mar. 1921, 5.

13. J. D. Williams, "The Bosworth Revival Campaign in St. Paul," AW, Apr. 23, 1921, 90.

14. "The Bosworth Meetings," *The Pentecostal Evangel*, Apr. 2, 1921, 7.

15. Bosworth, *Christ the Healer*, 229-234.

16. Cited in Reynolds, *Footprints*, 387.

17. Reynolds, *Rebirth*, 69-70.

18. Ibid., 70.

19. Editorial, AW, June 30, 1923, 289.

20. Oscar Blomgren, Jr., "Fred F. Bosworth: Man of God, Part VI: An Old Message Brings New Hope," *Herald of Faith*, Apr. 1964, 9; Eunice M. Perkins, *Fred Francis Bosworth: Joybringer Bosworth, His Life Story*, Second Edition (Detroit, MI, 1927), 190. According to Bosworth family members, she had a strong personality and was quite active in the ministry.

21. "Tent Meeting in East Orange, New Jersey," AW, July 30, 1921, 314.

22. "Revival in Baltimore, Md.," AW, Nov. 26, 1921, 586.

23. Led by Pastor Staudt, they voted 16 to 3 to leave the Alliance, eventually joining the Assemblies of God. Minutes of Special Business Meeting of the Baltimore Branch of the C&MA, Baltimore, MD, June 4, 1923.

24. Editorials, AW, July 31, 1920, 273; W. E. Farr, "A Layman's Labors," AW, Aug. 7, 1920, 301.

25. Rev. F. H. Rossiter, "Revival in Memphis," AW, Sept. 4, 1920, 366.

26. "These Signs Shall Follow," AW, Oct. 2, 1920, 429.

27. "Editorials," AW, Jan. 1, 1921, 627, 636.

28. Blumhofer, *The Assemblies of God*, 256.

29. See Editorial, AW, Jan. 7, 1922, 673; Harry W. Lucas, "Revival at Washington, Pa.," AW, Jan. 7, 1922, 682; AW, Jan. 14, 1922, 698; "God Honors Faith in Bosworth Meetings," Apr. 15, 1922, 75; AW, June 3, 1922, 188; "Bosworth Campaign," AW, June 17, 1922, 219; Editorial, July 8, 1922, 257; "Household of Faith," AW, Aug. 5, 1922, 334; "Household of Faith," AW, Sept. 7, 1922, 390; "Bosworth Campaign in Jersey," Nov. 18, 1922, 570.

30. AW, Feb. 29, 1927, 127; see also "The Death of Warren Collins," AW, Jan. 29, 1927, 75.

31. "The Household of Faith," AW, Jan. 6, 1923, 690; AW, Feb. 21, 1925, 126. Betts eventually joined the Assemblies of God in 1942.

32. Katherine Elise Chapman, "Milestones in Detroit," AW, Dec. 17, 1921, 635.

33. "Household of Faith," AW, Mar. 25, 1922, 30; "Household of Faith," AW, Apr. 15, 1922, 78; "Household of Faith," AW, July 1, 1922, 254; "Bosworth Campaign in Jersey," AW, Nov. 18, 1922, 570; AW, Dec. 30, 1922, 658.

34. See "Household of Faith," AW, Mar. 4, 1922, 814; "Household of Faith," AW, Apr. 15, 1922, 79; AW, June 10, 1922, 206; "Household of Faith," AW, June 24, 1922, 238-239; "Household of Faith," AW, July 22,.1922, 303; "Revival Fires Continue," AW, Aug. 12, 1922, 346; "Household of Faith," AW, Sept. 9, 1922, 414; "Testings and Triumphs in Chicago, AW, Oct. 22, 1922, 474; AW, Dec. 2, 1922, 608.

35. Richey had left the Assemblies of God after a controversy over his marrying a woman who had previously been divorced due to her first husband's infidelity. Initially, he held credentials with the Alliance, but in 1921 the Alliance tightened up its policy on divorced and remarried workers, and thus was disqualified. Yet he continued to minister actively in the C&MA without credentials for about 15 years, and his father soon joined the C&MA for a decade.

36. *Out of Zion*, 188-189.

37. "Household of Faith," AW, Feb. 3, 1923, 739; "Household of Faith," AW, Mar. 24, 1923, 62; "Household of Faith," AW, Mar. 31, 80-81; "Household of Faith," AW, May 12, 1923, 182; "Household of Faith," AW, June 23, 1923, 278; Editorial, AW, July 7, 1923, 298; "Triumphs in Tulsa," AW, July 21, 1923, 338; "Household of Faith," AW, Aug. 11, 1923, 391; "Household of Faith," AW, Sept. 22, 1923, 486; "Further Reports from Tulsa, Oklahoma," AW, Oct. 20, 546.

38. "Household of Faith," AW, Aug. 11, 1923, 391. See also, Eloise May Richey, What God Hath Wrought (Houston, TX: Full Gospel Advocate, 1925), 109.

39. McCrossan, Christ's Paralyzed Church X-Rayed, 267.

40. "Household of Faith," AW, Mar. 24, 1923, 62; "Household of Faith," AW, May 12, 1923, 182; Katherine Elise Chapman, "A Rising Tide in Detroit," AW, June 2, 1923, 228; Editorial, AW, June 30, 1923, 289; "The Bosworth Campaign in Atlanta," AW, Sept. 8, 1923, 450; "Revivals in Oregon," AW, Sept. 18, 1923, 468; "Household of Faith," AW, Oct. 13, 1923, 534. See also Robert Bryant Mitchell, Heritage and Horizons (Des Moines, IA: Open Bible Publishers, 1982), 61-62.

41. Dixon, A Romance of Faith, 73-75.

42. G. N. Eldridge, "Appreciations," AW, Dec. 27, 1919, 238.

43. Editorials, AW, Jan. 31, 1920, 309.

44. "Ripe and Ready," AW, June 12, 1920, 166.

45. Editorial, AW, Mar. 22, 1924, 50.

46. Mattie E. Perry, Christ and Answered Prayer: Autobiography of Mattie E. Perry (Nashville, TN: Benson, 1939), 145.

47. Perry, 72.

48. Perry spoke at Pentecostal meetings at the Stone Church in Chicago and the Findlay Convention in Ohio. For her Pentecostal ministry, see Mattie Perry, "God's Stamp of Approval upon a Life," LRE, Feb. 1917, 2, "Stone Church Convention," LRE, Apr. 1917, 12; "Healing of Cancer," LRE, Jan. 1920, 14; Mattie E. Perry, "A Call to Prayer," LRE, Feb. 1920, 8-9. For her C&MA ministry, see "Revival Reports," AW, Aug. 21, 1921, 362; "The Household of Faith," AW, Nov. 25, 1922, 590; Perry, Christ and Answered Prayer, 230-258.

49. Douglas J. Nelson, For Such a Time as This: The Story of Bishop William J. Seymour and the Azusa Street Revival, Ph.D. dissertation, May 1981, University of Birmingham, England, 269.

50. William J. Seymour, The Doctrines and Disciplines of the Azusa Street Apostolic Faith Mission of Los Angeles, California, reprint, ed. Larry Martin (Joplin, MO: Christian Life Books, 2000), 26. See also pp. 48, 62,81-83, 87, 88.

51. Ibid.

52. Reynolds, Rebirth, 207.

53. C&MA Board of Manager Minutes, Apr. 26, 1921.

54. C&MA Board of Manager Minutes, Apr. 1, 1924, Aug. 13, 1934; conversation with Assemblies of God historian Gary McGee.

55. "The Household of Faith," AW, May 7, 1921, 125.

56. "Household of Faith," AW, June 25, 1921, 237; see also AW, July 2, 1921, 250; AW, July 9, 1921, 257.

57. W. C. Stevens, "The Nelson Meetings in Kansas City," AW, July 16, 1921, 282; see also "Household of Faith," AW, July 16, 1921, 285; "Revival Campaign," June 30, 1921, 314; AW, Feb. 18, 1922, 778; AW, Nov. 12, 1921, 554.

58. P. C. Nelson, "The Lord's Doings in Toronto," Sept. 10, 1921, 410; P.C. Nelson, "Objections to Healing," AW, Feb. 11, 1922, 762; Stevens, "The Nelson Meetings in Kansas City," 282.

59. Foreign Dept. Minutes, C&MA Board of Manager Minutes, June 16, 1922.

60. R. V. Burgess, "Ramabai, Saravati Mary (Pandita)," NIDPCM, 1018.

61. Laura G. Beecroft, "The Day of His Power—The Spirit's Working in Palestine," AW, Apr. 11, 1925, 248-249.

62. George S. Montgomery, "He Shall Sit as a Refiner," AW, July 12, 1924, 24.

63. Kenneth MacKenzie, "Are There Modern Miracles?", AW, Sept. 29, 1923, 493.

64. Nienkirchen, 39n60.

65. Blumhofer, *Aimee Semple McPherson*, 214, 221.

66. Daniel Mark Epstein, *Sister Aimee: The Life of Aimee Semple McPherson* (New York, San Diego, London: Harcourt Brace Jovanavich, 1993), 216, 265-266; Blumhofer, *Aimee Semple McPherson*, 185-186, 219-221.

67. Aimee Semple McPherson, *This Is That: Personal Experiences, Sermons and Writings of Aimee Semple McPherson, Evangelist* (Los Angeles, CA: Echo Park Evangelistic Assn., 1923), 203, 482, 485.

68. Ibid., 365, 457.

69. Ibid., 482-483, 491.

70. Ibid., 492.

71. There is debate over whether or not Rader spoke in tongues. I had heard some years ago from some long forgotten Alliance source that Rader did speak in tongues. His book *Harnessing God* shows a very positive attitude toward tongues, almost as if he is speaking from experience, but he does not come right out and say it. See Paul Rader, *Harnessing God* (New York: George H. Doran Co., 1926), 99-101. An article by D. M. Panton in 1926 expressed his displeasure that Rader had gone over to the Pentecostals, evidently because he had preached for McPherson. D. M. Panton, "Supernatural Deception," *The Dawn*, Vol. 3, No. 3 (June 15, 1926), 100. It is possible that these statements might have been the basis of my Alliance source that claimed Rader spoke in tongues. However, Oswald J. Smith wrote in response that his friend Paul Rader did not, in fact, speak in tongues. *The Dawn*, Vol. 3, No. 5 (Aug. 14, 1926), 211. Rader's biographer, Larry Eskridge does not believe that Rader spoke in tongues, although it is possible that eventually he did, but did not broadcast it because he was bridging between Pentecostals and non-Pentecostals. He was definitely against the evidential tongues doctrine. While it is possible that he may have spoken in tongues in 1926 or subsequently, at this time there is no concrete evidence to conclude that he did.

72. Blumhofer, *Aimee Semple McPherson*, 322.

73. T. J. McCrossan, *Speaking with Other Tongues: Sign or Gift—Which?* (Harrisburg, PA: Christian Publications, 1927); Charles S. Price, *The Story of My Life* (Pasadena, CA: Charles S. Price Publishing Co., 1935), 50; Charles S. Price, *See God!* (Pasadena, CA: Charles S. Price Publishing Co.), 80-81.

74. McCrossan, *Speaking with Other Tongues*, 34-35; Price, *The Story of My Life*, 50.

75. Price, *See God!*, 80-81.

76. T. J. McCrossan, *The Bible and Its Eternal Facts* (Youngstown, OH: Clement Humbard, 1947), 192-194; McCrossan, *Christ's Paralyzed Church X-Rayed*, 258-260.

77. T. J. McCrossan, *Bodily Healing and the Atonement* (Youngstown, OH: Clement Humbard, 1930), 111-112.

78. "Household of Faith," AW, July 21, 1923, 342; "Household of Faith," AW, Apr. 12, 1924, 110; "Northern Pacific Paragraphs," AW, Apr. 19, 1924, 126; Reynolds, *Rebirth*, 226-228.

79. Reynolds, *Rebirth*, 169-170, 226-228, 214, 217.

80. Ibid., 226-228.

81. E. W. Kenyon, *The Two Kinds of Faith*, (Seattle, WA: Kenyon's Gospel Publishing Co., 1942) 15-16, 31; see also Joe McIntyre, *E. W. Kenyon: The True Story* (Lake Mary, FL: Creation House, 1997), 34-35, 132, 144, 289, 355. Ironically, Kenneth Hagin, who extensively propagated Kenyon's teachings, especially on revelation and sense knowledge, did not accept Kenyon's view on evidential tongues.

82. E. W. Kenyon, *In His Presence: The Secret of Prayer. A Revelation of What We Are in Christ*, 21st edition (Lynnwood, WA: Kenyon's Gospel Publishing Co., 1969), 124-125.

83. Dale H. Simmons, *E. W. Kenyon and the Postbellum Pursuit of Peace, Power, and Plenty* (Lanham, MD and London: Scarecrow Press, 1997), 295; Joe McIntyre, *E. W. Kenyon: The True Story*, 197, 273.

84. C&MA Board of Manager Minutes, Feb. 15, Feb. 16, 1922.

85. "Household of Faith," AW, Feb. 17, 1923, 170; "Household of Faith," AW, Apr. 21, 1923, 130.

86. "Household of Faith," AW, Jan. 26, 1924, 780.

87. Letter to Geir Lie from John Beauregard, Gordon College Archivist, Nov. 4, 1993, citing the book of minutes of Bethel Bible Institute. Courtesy of Norweigian Pentecostal Archivist Geir Lie.

MORE CHARISMATIC MANIFESTATIONS AND PRACTICE

While supernatural manifestations may not have been reported as frequently in the 1920s as the previous decade and a half, by no means did they cease in the Alliance. In April 1921, A. E. Funk reported on the Pittsburgh C&MA Convention, saying it was like the 5th and 19th chapters of Acts with extraordinary meetings and special miracles.[1] Acts 5 is uniquely significant for supernatural revelatory knowledge, signs and wonders, healings, and exorcisms. Acts 19 records speaking in tongues, prophesying, healing and exorcism through the use of cloths as a point of contact of faith. By pointing out these particular chapters of Acts, Funk seems to be indicating that phenomena unique to these chapters had occurred in these meetings. As further support for such charismatic manifestations, Simpson's article "A Plea for the Supernatural" was reprinted in the December 1921 issue of *The Alliance Weekly*.[2]

The Alliance continued to teach the baptism in the Holy Spirit as an empowering and sanctifying experience subsequent to salvation that can be accompanied with or without manifestations. In 1924, for example, nineteen-year old Richard Harvey was seeking to be filled with the Spirit and looking for some feeling and outward manifestation. He did not receive the feeling or outward manifestation, but he did experience a new power over a bad temper and power to cast out demons, and consequently had a powerful evangelistic ministry with the Alliance with signs and wonders following.[3]

ELECTRIC SENSATIONS, PROPHECY, AND TONGUES

Mention of sensations of electrical-like power occurred periodically in *The Alliance Weekly*. In 1920 a woman testified of a sensation of power like electricity vibrating through her whole being. As a result, she was filled with the Spirit and received a dramatic healing.[4] In 1921 an article recorded testimony of a woman healed of infantile paralysis and stroke while electrical shocks went through her body.[5]

Though there is not a lot of mention about gifts such as prophecy and tongues in Alliance documents during this period of time, there are a few indications that they were still viewed positively among Alliance leadership. Less than a year after Simpson's death, one of Simpson's messages from 1897 at Nyack on the future of the C&MA was cited in an editorial note in *The Alliance Weekly* and was considered a prophecy come true.[6] Apparently the editorial staff of the periodical believed that Simpson exercised a genuine gift of predictive prophecy. Two years later Robert Jaffray reported in the *Weekly* what he called "a prophetic incident."[7]

Late in 1920, Mary Mullen, who had received tongues in 1907, passed away. As a former C&MA missionary, evangelist, and founder of the "Mary B. Mullen School for Colored People," she was highly regarded. A tribute to her in *The Alliance Weekly* called her "a woman of more than ordinary spiritual gifts."[8]

The editorial staff of the *Weekly*, which included Frederick Senft, Walter Turnbull, A. C. Snead, and H. M. Shuman, encouraged active receptivity to the supernatural gifts of the Spirit. In an editorial commenting on tongues and prophesying in Acts 19, the writer asked, "Have you entered upon your Pentecostal inheritance?"[9] The obvious implication is that such gifts were part of the believer's inheritance.

In his 1923 Annual China Report, Robert Jaffray related an amazing story of Mr. Wong, a Bible school student and interpreter for missionaries in China. While imprisoned by kidnappers, he saw a vision and received a special gift of tongues. His sudden outburst in tongues frightened them and enabled him to escape.[10]

POWER ENCOUNTERS, DREAMS, VISIONS, AND RAISING THE DEAD

In August 1920 an Alliance missionary reported that a man in Congo apparently was dead for several hours, then came back to life and told of vision of an encounter with angels.[11] In another issue the same month a woman testified that she had a vision of the Cross and the blood of Christ accompanying her healing.[12] Another article in *The Alliance Weekly* featured a dream from the Lord.[13] Shortly after Simpson's death, Robert Jaffray wrote about a power encounter, recounting the story of a skeptical young man who became converted after seeing the sick healed and demons cast out.[14] In December 1921 an article reported a revival in the Alliance work in India with the blind receiving sight and demons cast out in three exorcisms.[15]

TEACHING ON CHARISMATIC THEMES

Spiritual Warfare. The C&MA continued to engage actively in spiritual warfare and exorcism.[16] In 1920 W. T. MacArthur recalled an earlier incident in which he and Simpson discerned and dealt with a demonized woman who ultimately did not want to get rid of her demon companion.[17] Three years later another article by MacArthur, entitled "Healing from Deafness and Deliverance from Demons," recounted his experience of what might be called today a word of knowledge or discernment of spirits: "The conviction seized me that there was no disease present, but simply an evil spirit," which was then cast out of an eight-year old boy.[18]

In 1923 former Presbyterian layman John MacMillan began missionary ministry with the C&MA, launching a broad ministry of spiritual warfare for more than 30 years. He utilized 1 John 4:1-3 method of testing spirits by addressing the spirits with the question, "Has Jesus Christ come in the flesh?" and wrote on "The Authority of the Believer." He would later become associate editor of *The Alliance Weekly*, a professor at Nyack and a member of the C&MA Board of Managers. In 1929 W. C. Stevens commented on Mark 16 in articles on healing, that there is a "very wide range of demon presence and power" and a "close alliance between demonism and disease." Rather than "demon possession, he used the term "demonism" akin to the contemporary terminology "demonization."[19]

Authority of the Believer. Alliance leaders further developed the concept of the authority of the believer, taught in germinal form by A. B. Simpson, A. T. Pierson, and others. In 1920 *The Alliance Weekly* featured an article referring to Isaiah 45:11 on the controversial interpretation of commanding God as authority that God has given the obedient and sanctified believer.[20] In 1924 Gregory Mantle wrote two articles on Luke 10:19, redemption rights and authority of the believer.[21] In 1928 Simpson's article entitled "The Hand upon the Throne" on the authority of the believer was reprinted.[22] In 1929 articles on the "enthronement" and victory of the believer[23] and "A Power Attorney from God"[24] appeared in *The Alliance Weekly*.

Territorial Spirits. The spiritual warfare movement of the last decade of the 20th century and early 21st century in the charismatic and Third Wave movements has emphasized doing warfare with principalities and powers, spirits that exercise power over a geographical region or territory. The C&MA became pioneers in teaching an embryonic form of the concept of territorial spirits, especially through the Alliance missions in China in the 1920s. In 1920 a revival in South China was stirred by the preaching of Presbyterian missionary Jonathan Goforth preaching in the C&MA missions. Alliance missionary Mrs. L. L. Hess reported of the meetings that principalities and powers in the air and the prince of the kingdom of China were hindering the revival, but through much prayer there was a breakthrough on the tenth day with weeping and confession with more than 700 inquiring about salvation.[25]

In 1927 Robert Jaffray wrote on territorial spirits, saying, "There is today a Prince of Tibet, of Afghanistan, of Cambodia, of Arabia, of Mohammedanism, of Bolshevism, who are prepared to defend their lands."[26] In 1929 his colleague John MacMillan appealed for intercessors at home "to roll back the powers of the air, and make it possible to bring the Truth to bear on these regions where the devil is blocking the way."[27] While Alliance leaders did not use the current terminology "territorial spirits," they understood the concept of demonic strongholds over a region. Decades later MacMillan declared that the "principalities" of Ephesians 6:12 are "satanic princes, angels whose principalities cover the countries of this world."[28] He had viewed his battle for Isabel's life in 1926 as an "infernal fiat" intended to crush them because they were dislodging the spirits that held the territories of the Philippines in darkness.

EMOTIONAL DEMONSTRATIONS ENCOURAGED —DANCING, HOLY LAUGHTER, ETC.

In the decade after Simpson's death, Alliance leaders continued to encourage emotional demonstrations, as long as they were not unbridled and fleshly. In July 1920, W. W. Newberry, who had written a book several years earlier about true and false manifestations, wrote article entitled "David Brings the Ark to Jerusalem" in *The Alliance Weekly* about dancing before the Lord as a manifestation of the joy of the Lord He considered dancing as a demonstration of the moving of the Holy Spirit: "There is a degree of joy in the Holy Spirit that manifests itself in physical demonstrations that cannot be denied or resisted without resisting the Holy Spirit." He cautioned on one hand, "There is, however, great need in that every movement of the flesh be held in the place of crucifixion in all these demonstrations."

On the other hand, he warned those who would criticize all such displays, "The dancing and holy joy that David manifested aroused antagonism in the heart of Michal. She despised him in her heart. The power of the Holy Spirit on God's people has often brought down upon them the indignation and opposition of half-hearted Christians. They condemn all religious fervor as fanaticism. Judgment came on Michal . . . and it has often happened that people who have criticized the power of the Holy Spirit on other people have suffered in their experience."[29] Two years later, an article on "Revivals of the Spirit" by Dr. George Shaw of the Nyack Missionary Training Institute cited people spontaneously singing, shouting, laughing, dancing, uplifted hands without worked-up emotion.[30]

CONTINUED CAUTIONS

All of these manifestations and cooperation with Pentecostals or former Pentecostals should not, however, be interpreted as the Alliance becoming more Pentecostal. They continued to maintain a middle of the road position, not accepting uncritically all that went on in Pentecostal circles, nor accepting all charismatic practice and phenomena as from God. During the decade after Simpson's death, there were some continued concerns about charismatic/Pentecostal excesses, though surprisingly fewer cautions, most of them occurring in the year following Simpson's death. This may have been to reaffirm that the Alliance was continuing to maintain Simpson's position affirm a change in leadership.

Just three months after Simpson's death, Jaffray, a tongue-speaker, wrote that it is possible to speak with tongues of men and of angels and have the gift of prophecies and know all mysteries and knowledge and faith, but lack love and be nothing.[31] In the next issue Alliance missionary and pastor W. W. Newberry, known for both his openness and caution toward charismatic manifestations, wrote that manifestations of the Spirit do not attract the flesh.[32] Other articles in the year after Simpson's death reaffirmed the Alliance stance of believing in the supernatural, but continued to maintain that tongues is not required as the evidence of the filling of the Spirit and that caution needs to be exercised in accepting all manifestations as from God.[33]

MORE CONFLICT AND DEFECTIONS

In addition, this continued openness to charismatic belief and practice does not mean that all was rosy in the Alliance. As C&MA leaders jockeyed for new leadership positions and influence after Simpson's death, there does appear to have been some conflicts arising between the more charismatically-oriented and those who were more cautious of such practices. One such example of this may be observed in June 1920, as some apparent friction arose between Foreign Secretary Robert Glover and the pro-charismatic A. C. Snead, as Glover opposed Snead's nomination as Recording Secretary of the C&MA.[34] Having overseen the contentious departure of W. W. Simpson from the Tibetan mission field over the issue of evidential tongues, Glover appears to have been anxious about those, like Snead, who in his eyes may have been too enthusiastic about charismatic manifestations. Glover soon left the Alliance, opposing the leadership of Rader, and Snead was eventually promoted to his position of Foreign Secretary.

On the other side, others who perceived the Alliance as not Pentecostal enough also left the C&MA. In June 1920 a report came from Kansu, West China that their woman Bible teacher left to join the Pentecostals and left the C&MA mission without trained help for city and village work.[35] Also in 1920 Victor Plymire, a C&MA missionary to the Tibetan region, received the baptism in the Spirit with tongues at Lancaster, Pennsylvania, while on furlough. He was ordained by the Assemblies of God in 1922, going back to Tibet as a missionary under their denomination.[36]

In 1920 C. A. Ingalls, newly-installed as the pastor of the Alliance church in Beaver Falls, Pennsylvania, received Spirit baptism with tongues under the ministry of former Alliance leader A. G. Ward. He embraced the Pentecostal teaching and soon left the C&MA.[37] The Alliance church in Findlay apparently suffered severe defections as Alliance pastor M. A. Dean, friend of Pentecostal leader T. K. Leonard, came in to salvage "what was left of it."[38] Dean eventually did turn the church around and it continued to be charismatically-oriented, later pastored by Etta Wurmser once again in the 1930s.

The Louis Turnbulls, who had remained with the Alliance for nearly 15 years after their Pentecostal experience, came home on furlough from India in 1921. They were invited to join the Eldridges, their kin, in their work at Bethel Temple. So at that point they left the Alliance for the Assemblies of God. It is interesting, however, that they remained in the C&MA so long. Perhaps they found the Alliance in the United States less charismatic in practice than in India, or perhaps they were just drawn to join their kin in their work, not necessarily having a problem with the C&MA.

In June 1923, the Baltimore Alliance church (which had experienced a Pentecostal revival about two years earlier), led by Pastor E. F. M. Staudt (who had spoken in tongues at Rocky Springs in 1907), voted to leave C&MA, citing "the failure of the Alliance to keep pace with the 'Latter Rain' outpouring" and "failure of the C&MA officials to cooperate with the Baltimore Branch in any aggressive way, and that the general sentiment of the Alliance is against the Latter Rain, as evidenced not only by its general attitude but also the failure to emphasize this line of teaching in its official organ 'The Alliance Weekly.'" Three of 19 voted against withdrawal, citing that they did not believe that tongues was the only evidence of the baptism in the Spirit. The new church later affiliated with the Assemblies of God.[39] The tongue-speaking Ella Bird, who had been assisting Whiteside in Pittsburgh, returned to Baltimore to salvage and rebuild the Alliance work.

Scanning the articles in *The Alliance Weekly*, it can be observed that it is true that there was not a lot of teaching along the line of the "Latter Rain," although it was not totally absent. Later issues throughout this decade would address some topics related to the Latter Rain, but not with the emphasis found in the Pentecostal movement.

---

1. Funk, "Pittsburgh Convention," AW, Apr. 9, 1921, 57.

2. A. B. Simpson, "A Plea for the Supernatural," AW, Dec. 3, 1921, 594.

3. Richard H. Harvey, *70 Years of Miracles* (Beaverlodge, Alberta, Canada: Horizon Books, 1977), 84-86.

4. Mrs. Jordan, "Standing on the Promises: God's Healing Power," AW, Mar. 13, 1920, 418.

5. "Revival Tidings," AW, Oct. 8, 1921, 474.

6. A. B. Simpson, "Spiritual Mountain Tops," AW, Sept. 25, 1920, 402.

7. Robert Jaffray, "Our Friend the Enemy," AW, Nov. 11, 1922, 552.

8. A. E. Funk, "Mrs. Mary Mullen Hench," AW, Dec. 11, 1920, 586.

9. Editorial, AW, Feb. 26, 1921, 755.

10. Robert Jaffray, 1923 China Report, AW, Dec. 1, 1923, 648.

11. H. L. Pierson, "A Congo Vision," AW, Aug. 7, 1920, 295.

12. Mrs. E. B. Hicks, "Healed for God's Glory," AW, Aug. 21, 1920, 324.

13. Paul Young, "A Dream," AW, Oct. 16, 1926, 673.

14. Robert A. Jaffray, "The Missionary Message," AW, Dec. 13, 1919, 188.

15. "Revival Meetings," AW, Dec. 10, 1921, 618.

16. M. B. Birrel, "Annual Report of the Central China Mission, 1919," AW, Nov. 13, 1920, 522.

17. MacArthur, "A Reminiscence of Rev. A. B. Simpson," AW, Aug. 21, 1920, 325-326.

18. William T. MacArthur, "Healing from Deafness and Deliverance from Demons," AW, Jan. 26, 1924, 770.

19. W. C. Stevens, "Jesus' Twofold Ministry of Teaching and Healing," AW, Aug. 10, 1929, 516ff.; W. C. Stevens, "The Recovery of the Sick," AW, Aug. 17, 1929, 529ff.

20. Raymond H. Smith, "Concerning My Sons Command Ye Me," AW, July 3, 1920, 215.

21. J. Gregory Mantle, "The Conditions of Exercising Authority," AW, Apr. 5, 1924, 83;. J. Gregory Mantle, "Authority over the Enemy, "AW, May 10, 1924, 167.

22. A. B. Simpson, "The Hand upon the Throne," AW, Mar. 3, 1928, 134-135.

23. Robert D. Kilgour, "His Enthronement and Yours," AW, Jan. 5, 1929, 1; Robert D. Kilgour, "His Victory and Yours," AW, Jan. 26, 1929, 49.

24. E. A. Coray, "A Power Attorney from God," AW, Oct. 26, 1929, 689.

25. Mrs. L. L. Hess, Preaching and Prayer or Special Services at Wuchow," AW, Apr. 24, 1920, 56.

26. R. A. Jaffray, "Our Great Unfinished Task," AW, July 9, 1927, 456.

27. John A. MacMillan, "Our Mohammedan Problem in the Philippines," AW, June 22, 1929, 404.

28. The Full Gospel Sunday School Quarterly, Aug. 9, 1953, 18; for more on MacMillan's pioneering concept of "territorial spirits" and "spiritual mapping," see "Praying Geographically," AW, Sept. 14, 1946, 579.

29. W. W. Newberry, "David Brings the Ark to Jerusalem, "AW, July 17, 1920, 252.

30. George Shaw, "Revivals of the Spirit," AW, July 1, 1922, 243.

31. Robert A. Jaffray, "The Missionary Passion," AW, Jan. 3, 1920, 254.

32. W. W. Newberry, "The Fruit of the Spirit," AW, Jan. 10, 1920

33. Edgar K. Sellow, "Baptism with the Holy Ghost," AW, June 19, 1920, 181; Frederic H. Senft, "The True and the False," AW, Dec. 18, 1920, 606.

34. C&MA Board of Manager Minutes, Apr. 26, 1921.

35. Miss E. M. Beyerle, "1920 Native Conference at Minhsien, Kansu, China," AW, June 19, 1920, 184.

36. G. W. Gohr, "Plymire, Victor Guy," NIDPCM, 991.

37. "Christ Baptizes Preacher," Word and Work, Jan. 1921, 13.

38. "The Household of Faith," AW, Mar. 27, 1920, 453.

39. Minutes of Special Business Meeting of the Baltimore Branch of the C&MA, Baltimore, MD, June 4, 1923. Staudt had spoken in tongues at the Rocky Springs Convention in 1907. Eventually, he became superintendent of the Potomac District of the Assemblies of God.

CHARISMATIC LEADERSHIP BY SENFT AND SHUMAN — THROUGH 1929

1924-1925—FREDERICK SENFT TENURE

Following Rader's departure from the presidency of the C&MA, long-time Alliance leader Frederick Senft became president, though for just a short time due to his death in November 1925. Senft was a tried-and-true Alliance man who desired to lead the Alliance back into its early principles. As early as 1902 he had written that God still works supernaturally today and that the lack of signs and wonders is due to unbelief. He believed that that the spiritual gifts in 1 Corinthians 12 are to remain in the church and signs and wonders will usher in the Second Coming.[1]

Senft had reported positively of many speaking in tongues at the C&MA church in New Castle, Pennsylvania in 1908.[2] Yet also in 1909 he had reported "some loss of members through the Pentecostal movement."[3] So he had dealt with both the positive and negative elements in the Pentecostal movement. He was both open and cautious, like Simpson, advocating discernment of true and false fire.[4] His wife had testified of experiencing holy laughter and a dramatic healing without medicine in 1894.[5] He actually was somewhat radical in his views on faith healing, commenting back in 1906 that he would not anoint a person for healing if he or she continued to take medicine.[6]

During his brief tenure, the Alliance open receptivity toward the supernatural and Pentecostal/C&MA bridge-building appears to have continued. W. C. Stevens ministered in both Alliance and Pentecostal circles, contributing an article to *The Pentecostal Evangel* and working with Pentecostal evangelists.[7] In June 1924 Robert Jaffray was elected Vice President of the C&MA.[8] This indicates great confidence in and respect for this tongue-speaking missionary statesmen. However, Jaffray later turned it down, believing that he was called to remain on the mission field and commenting that it would be a demotion for him.

T. J. McCrossan became more active in Alliance circles during Senft's presidency, also acting as a bridge-builder between Pentecostals and the Alliance.

In 1924 he began teaching courses on Workers Training Class, Homiletics, and Methods of Christian Work and Greek at Simpson Bible Institute.[9] McCrossan was a featured speaker at the C&MA General Council in June 1925[10] and contributed articles to *The Alliance Weekly*.[11]

From 1924-1926 young Kathryn Kuhlman attended Simpson Bible Institute in Seattle. McCrossan's daughter Charlotte was also a student there and she and Kathryn become lifelong friends.[12] Years later, Kuhlman reestablished her old connections with the C&MA, providing funds to help Alliance missionary needs and to establish several C&MA churches overseas.[13]

Former Pentecostals Continue to Minister in the C&MA. During Senft's time in office, former Pentecostal ministers, including Bosworth, Mitchell, Benham, and Richey continued to minister openly in the Alliance, and Pentecostal-like revivals continued to surge and bring growth. Many healings were reported as well as some demons cast out. R. A. Forrest assisted in some of the meetings.[14] John H. Bostrom, an evangelist with the Assemblies of God since 1920, joined the Alliance in November 1924, becoming pastor of the charismatically-oriented Alliance church in Boone, Iowa, through 1927, then serving the Alliance as an evangelist through 1930.[15] His brothers William and Albert (A. N.) also left the Assemblies about the same time, and A. N. joined the Alliance, but stayed with the Alliance, pastoring and planting churches throughout his long ministry.[16]

Benham continued to minister with a C&MA group from Seattle. He conducted meetings in Eugene, Oregon, using young musicians from Simpson Bible Institute. Among the many miracles and healings that took place, a crippled girl was anointed with oil and her body began to shake and she fell under the power of the Spirit. After about an hour she walked off the platform without her crutches.[17]

Evangelist Raymond T. Richey held a series of meetings in the St. Petersburg/Tampa area of Florida. Out of those meetings a group of people founded The Gospel Tabernacle, a non-denominational church affiliated with the C&MA and pastored by William T. Watson. In 1932 Watson founded Florida Bible Institute, which was then affiliated with the C&MA—now known as Trinity College.[18] A young student at the Institute by the name of Billy Graham served as youth minister at the Tampa Gospel Tabernacle in the latter 1930s. Following Richey's campaign in Houston in 1924, an official Alliance work was established. Forrest did follow-up, teaching on fundamental "Full Gospel" truths. An amazing 927 people were enrolled in his Bible class.[19]

The Alliance Weekly reported Hardy Mitchell's evangelistic campaigns at the Alliance Tabernacles in St. Paul and Duluth, Minnesota, Albany, Oregon, as well as in several C&MA churches in the Northwest District, and following Bosworth at Binghamton, New York. Pastor E. E. Johnson at St. Paul affirmed, "Brother Mitchell's ministry is safe and solid and bears permanent fruitage."[20] In 1925 Hardy Mitchell became pastor of the charismatic C&MA church in Oakland, California.[21]

During this time F. F. Bosworth also continued to have a high profile in the Alliance. His book *Christ the Healer* was published in 1924, containing sermons and testimonies of healing from Alliance meetings. Articles by Bosworth on faith and healing were published in the *Alliance Weekly*.[22] In 1925 F. F. Bosworth was a featured speaker at the C&MA General Council.[23] Oswald J. Smith's 1925 book on the baptism in the Spirit, published by the C&MA, reaffirmed the Alliance position of not seeking after manifestations.[24] Bosworth, a friend of Smith, wrote the Foreword to his book.

In April 1925, evangelist Alonzo Horn, formerly with the Assemblies of God but now with the C&MA, led a revival in Alliance church in Huntingdon, Pennsylvania, where "some laughed with exceeding joy." According to one older Alliance leader, he had heard reports that some spoke in tongues during his Pennsylvania revival meetings.[25]

Charismatic Revival in Palestine. Veteran C&MA missionary Laura G. Beecroft reported power encounters and supernatural working of the Holy Spirit in Palestine. When E. O. Jago preached, "the Spirit was poured out upon us, till it seemed almost like another Pentecost." A Moslem had a vision of Jesus, heard an audible voice, and was converted. A Jewish girl had a dream of Jesus speaking to her in Hebrew, and a Moslem girl had a vision. Beecroft reported, "Nearly every case of conversion among them [Moslems] was preceded by a vision of Christ."[26]

More Revivals. In 1925 membership doubled in one year in the Alliance church in Atlanta, where Dr. Ira David was pastor and where Bosworth had held a campaign in March.[27] In November 1925, E. N. Richey, the Pentecostal father of Raymond T. Richey spoke at the C&MA church in Albany, New York, pastored by F. L. Squires.[28] The junior Richey had conducted his largest evangelistic and healing campaign in Albany the year prior. The senior Richey had received Spirit baptism with tongues in 1906 under through the ministry of Charles Parham at Dowie's Zion City in Illinois (along with Bosworth). Though he had been an Assemblies of God leader, it is significant that he held credentials with the C&MA for ten years in the 1920s and early 1930s.

In July 1924, foreign secretary A. C. Sneed related in his Annual Report several power encounters, including an instant healing of a woman left to die, divine protection, and a vision of Jesus leading to conversion.[29] In November 1924, Pastor F. H. Rossiter, who had been involved in the 1907 revival, prayed for the sick and a totally blind man was healed. Also, a woman felt a "warming and gentle electric shock go through the affected part of her body and the pain left her immediately."[30] Other articles recounted dreams, visions, miracles, and divine protection.[31]

Virginia Berg—A "Pentecostal" Alliance Evangelist/Pastor. H. E. and Virginia Berg were evangelists credentialed with the C&MA about 1923 in San Francisco, ministering in both Alliance and Pentecostal churches. Virginia was acclaimed in Pentecostal circles as a "Pentecostal preacher of power" and "a woman of rare intellectual gifts with the passion for souls and under a mighty Baptism in the Holy Spirit."[32] In 1925, Senft and District Superintendent R. A. Forrest called the Bergs to Miami to salvage the floundering church there. Within ten months the congregation had grown from 50 to more than 500 and built a tabernacle seating more than four thousand. Virginia was installed as the pastor with her husband assisting as a Bible teacher. She also hosted evangelistic campaigns with Raymond Richey and child evangelist Uldine Utley (with whom she had ministered in California).[33]

A TONGUE-SPEAKER BECOMES C&MA PRESIDENT

In late 1925 Frederick Senft died after being in office less than two years. H. M. Shuman, a tongue-speaker, became president, serving until 1954.[34] Shuman had been involved in the early Ohio revival, and had served as Superintendent for that district, adjudicating the controversies over evidential tongues and Pentecostal excesses.[35] He had also pastored the more charismatically-oriented Alliance churches in Washington and New Castle, Pennsylvania, and Wilmington, Delaware. In the early years of his tenure it would appear that the same charismatic openness continued to be maintained in the Alliance. In his 1927 Annual Report President Shuman continued to affirm the Alliance emphases on the full gospel, sanctification, and the baptism in the Holy Spirit.[36]

Continued Ministry by Former Pentecostals and Others. Richey, Mitchell, Horn and the Bosworth brothers continued evangelistic and healing meetings through the C&MA in the late 1920s, sometimes teaming up together in joint meetings. Forrest continued to assist Richey frequently with his meetings.[37] After one of Richey's meetings in Florida William G. Weston, dying of a heart condition, received miraculous healing, later becoming a renowned Alliance evangelist.[38] In 1926 Hardy Mitchell resigned as pastor of the C&MA Gospel Tabernacle in Oakland to reenter evangelistic work, returning to the Alliance Tabernacle in St. Paul pastored by E. E. Johnson, and helping with music for the Colored Quintette.[39] By 1926 E. N. Richey, Raymond's father, had switched his credentials from the Assemblies of God to the C&MA, along with his associate, E. G. Gerhart. The church they pastored in Houston "became the largest full-gospel church in South Texas during the 1920's."[40]

Former Assemblies of God evangelist Thomas J. O'Neal, served as Assistant Superintendent of the Southern District and pastored Alliance works in Oklahoma.[41] In 1927 Alonzo Horn held evangelistic meetings in Pennsylvania, assisted by young Roland Gray, in which many salvations and "several miracles of healing" took place.[42]

Another Revival in India. A group of about fifty missionaries from various missions and denominations gathered together at Christmas time in 1925 to tarry and pray for the "promise of the Father." Those days were described as "days of heaven on earth." Two were baptized in the Spirit with tongues at that time, and they continued to seek the Lord. A missionary who received her Pentecostal baptism recounted that in March 1926, "One of the Alliance missionaries whose witness God is mightily using" held a week of revival meetings at a school, and teachers came from other locations. She testified, "The power surely came down like rain. . . . The fire is spreading by leaps and bounds into many places." Thirty-six people received a Pentecostal baptism, seventeen in one day, including six or seven teachers and at least one Alliance missionary.[43]

Glenn V. Tingley. In 1925 a young Free Methodist pastor named Glenn V. Tingley received the baptism in the Spirit with tongues after some contact with a C&MA prayer group led by Mrs. Rexroat in Burbank, California. As a budding young evangelist, he was heavily recruited by the Assembly of God church in Monrovia, California. They insisted they would not take "no" for an answer, even showing up at Tingley's home with a moving van, appealing with him to come and stay in the parsonage until he made a final decision. He turned them down, however, and instead decided to join the C&MA.

C. H. Chrisman, Superintendent of the California District, offered him a position pioneering a new Alliance church in Santa Monica in February 1926. This began a lifelong pastoral and evangelistic ministry in the C&MA. He developed a friendship with Southern District Superintendent R. A. Forrest, who discussed with him the great movings of God through Bosworth and Richey. Eventually, Forrest asked him to pastor a difficult church in Ensley, Alabama, with a view of planting a new work in Birmingham. Using the Tabernacle methodology of Paul Rader to establish the church there and pioneering as a radio revival preacher, Tingley's ministry mushroomed, the church in Birmingham eventually growing to more than a thousand. Tingley developed a strong healing ministry and also operated with a prophetic gifting, including what some today call a "word of knowledge."[44] In one dramatic incident, Tingley recounted:

> A woman who continually prayed for her cruel and drunken husband told us that he had cursed "that religious program" to which she listened daily. Finally, one day he was so enraged at her devotion that he picked up the radio and crashed it on the floor. Miraculously, the little shattered box kept right on talking!
>
> He had just raised his foot to smash it into silence when my voice challenged him:
>
> "You may not want to hear what I have to say! You may throw this radio on the floor! You may stomp it to pieces, but friend, God loves you and Christ died for your sins!"
>
> Amazed and gasping, the man turned to his wife and screamed, "He sees me! He actually sees what I'm going to do!"[45]

The man came to Tingley's Gospel Tabernacle and turned his life to Christ. Through Tingley's ministry in Birmingham in training young leaders over the years, more than thirty Alliance branches were formed.[46] Tingley eventually became a national evangelist for The Christian and Missionary Alliance.

Turner Returns to the Alliance. Harry L. Turner, who had formerly served as Field Director of the C&MA in Argentina, was pastoring a church in Winnipeg with the Pentecostal Assemblies of Canada. The church split in 1924, and the independent break-off church pastored by Turner eventually joined the C&MA in 1926 and Turner returned to the Alliance.[47] Evidently, in his eight years of ministry in Pentecostal circles, he became disillusioned with the movement. Later, as president of the Alliance in 1960, Turner had a negative assessment of the Pentecostal movement.[48]

Additional Charismatic/Pentecostal Connections. The *Alliance Weekly* continued to report that the time of miracles has not passed and the latter rain revival may still be expected.[49] In August 1926, in an unusual service at the Atlanta Gospel Tabernacle pastored by Dr. Ira David, the congregation sang and marched in a circle in the church, giving an offering for the financial debt of the building.[50] The following year, writing on "The Presence of God," David testified, "There is a Holy Ghost laugh, the laugh, from your feet to the roof of your head, contagious."[51]

In February 1926 Charles Price dedicated Lighthouse Temple in Eugene, Oregon, at that time the second largest Pentecostal church in the United States. Among those who attended were Alliance leaders T. J. McCrossan and E. O. Jago.[52] Jago, who had a friendly relationship with the Stone Church more than a decade earlier and pastored the charismatically-oriented Alliance church in Brockton, Massachusetts, had seen a charismatic renewal in the Alliance in Palestine in 1925 and worked with the charismatically-oriented Nortons. He appears to have maintained ongoing fellowship with Pentecostals.[53] By 1928 Jago was serving on the C&MA Board of Managers and as Superintendent of the New England District.[54]

ALLIANCE LEADERS ON SPEAKING IN TONGUES

During the latter part of the 1920s several Alliance leaders continued to affirm the reality and value of speaking in tongues and other gifts.

Kenneth MacKenzie—Don't Judge. In several articles Simpson's close friend and associate Kenneth MacKenzie supported speaking in tongues. He wrote that where tongues are used for edification, "the use of an unknown tongue cannot be disputed."[55] Further, MacKenzie affirmed, "If a devout believer has the assurance of having received the gift [tongues] and it tends to edification both to himself and to others, the Lord be praised. Let not others judge him."[56]

This latter statement is especially significant, because some evangelical leaders such as G. H. Lang and D. M. Panton had criticized the tongue-speaking experiences of some Alliance leaders and friends of the C&MA. Lang had years earlier written a critique of tongues in which he claimed that the experiences of Alliance missionary Kate Knight and Simpson's friends T. B. Barrett and Alexander Boddy were false. Panton, who had been strongly critical of the Pentecostal movement, insisted that *all* tongues be tested according to 1 John 4:1-3: "No spirit-movement or spirit-action must ever be accepted without submission to, and authentication by, the Divine Tests."[57] He even criticized C&MA evangelist F. F. Bosworth for not having his tongue or those of others for whom he prayed tested by this procedure.[58] MacKenzie's article would especially seem to be aimed as a response to Panton's criticism of Bosworth's tongues experience and his insistence that all tongues be tested.

There has been speculation through the years, both by some Pentecostals and also hopeful, well-meaning, charismatically-oriented Alliance people that Simpson eventually did speak in tongues. However, MacKenzie affirmed that Simpson did not speak in tongues.[59] Since MacKenzie was an intimate friend and associate of Simpson, he would certainly know if Simpson had done so.

T . J. McCrossan—Don't Seek, But Accept. McCrossan, who often assisted independent Pentecostal evangelist Charles Price in his meetings as well as speaking in C&MA conferences, taught a series of meetings in Victoria, Canada, in 1927, including many who had been touched by Price's meetings. As a result, a C&MA church was formed.[60] In the same year, McCrossan's book, *Speaking in Other Tongues: Sign or Gift Which?*, was published by the C&MA. In it, he presented the most thorough expansion and exposition of the early C&MA two-fold caution of not seeking after manifestations and not forbidding speaking in tongues. McCrossan's book demonstrates several significant observations:

- The Alliance position of not seeking and not forbidding tongues continued to be maintained.

- There was continued real concern for the counterfeit, even by those who were quite open to charismatic phenomena and maintained friendships with Pentecostals.

- Such concern did not hinder Alliance leaders from desiring that tongues and other gifts be manifested.

- Alliance people were being encouraged to express and allow the manifestation of speaking in tongues in Alliance services.[61]

Ira David—Ideal of All Gifts in a Local Church. In 1928 Dr. Ira David wrote on 1 Corinthians 12-14, saying of spiritual gifts, "An ideal New Testament church would have all of them effective among the believers."[62] This reaffirmed the position that the Alliance had taken in 1907 and 1914 that speaking in tongues should have a place in every Alliance church. However, his mention that this is an "ideal" may indicate that this was no longer true of all Alliance churches. David also appealed to the need for unity as at Pentecost in Acts 2, writing,

"Frustration and division! This is the devil's device against every Full Gospel work."[63]

Statement Drafted on Baptism in the Spirit and Gifts. In 1927 Walter Turnbull and C. H. Chrisman, both of whom had been involved in earlier Alliance charismatic revivals, authored a doctrinal and mission statement called "The Message of the Christian and Missionary Alliance." The document included statements about the "Sanctifying Baptism of the Holy Ghost." They wrote about four "points of contact" with God, one of which was "an act of appropriating faith," sounding very similar to Oral Roberts' later teaching. On spiritual gifts they reaffirmed the historic and ongoing Alliance position:

> Every disciple of Christ ought to have some special manifestation of the Holy Ghost and some gift for Christian service. . . . These gifts are conferred by the Holy Ghost Himself in His sovereign will according to individual fitness and for the completeness and profit of the whole body of Christ. He knows the gift that will best enable us to glorify Him and help other. No disciple can expect to receive all these gifts. It is unscriptural and unreasonable to say that any one gift is the criterion of having received the Holy Ghost. . . . Let us covet earnestly the best gifts, but chiefly the gifts of useful and effectual spiritual ministry.[64]

More Openness to Supernatural. Several articles in *The Alliance Weekly* in the late 1920s continued to encourage openness to charismatic phenomena and practice.[65] Simpson's article "Aggressive Christianity" was reprinted, affirming that the C&MA believes in the supernatural.[66] One article described the outpourings as like the Welsh revival occurring in China.[67] Another article featured a power encounter in Indochina (Annam or Vietnam) in which a woman blind for sixty years was healed and eyesight restored. Hundreds became Christians as a result.[68] An October 1928 article reported about an eight year-old boy ill with St. Vitus Dance who was anointed with oil. As a few drops of oil were dropped on his head, "Instantly God's power came on him till he screamed from the shock. His muscles relaxed and he was put to bed." Every symptom was gone in four weeks.[69]

Other Pentecostal Connections. Although in the 1920s the Stone Church in Chicago became identified with the Assemblies of God, some connections with the Alliance remained. *The Latter Rain Evangel* published sermons delivered by W. T. MacArthur in the Alliance Gospel Tabernacle[70] and an article by R. A. Jaffray.[71] Ella Rudy, sister-in-law of Walter Turnbull and Alliance missionary to South China who had been involved early in the Pentecostal revival in Ohio, preached at the Stone Church in 1926.[72]

In the summer of 1926, T. H. Nelson from Zion City Pentecostal movement spent three weeks teaching at the C&MA convention in Iowa.[73] *The Alliance Weekly* reported in 1927 that in French West Africa "the Pentecostal Mission is doing excellent work."[74] Apparently they were working in cooperation with the Alliance mission work in West Africa, which included the tongue-speaking missionaries Kate Driscoll and Sally Botham. Articles by Pentecostal leader A. W. Orwig appeared in *The Alliance Weekly* in three successive years from 1926 to 1928.[75]

During the 1920s, M. A. Dean, who had experienced the Pentecostal revival in the Alliance in its early days, served as pastor of the Alliance church in Findlay, Ohio. He was "an intimate friend of long standing" with Pentecostal leader T. K. Leonard. Leonard and former District Superintendent Isaac Patterson, "also a close friend of twenty-eight years," presided at Dean's funeral in 1928.[76] Etta Wurmser, who was serving as principal of the Pentecostal school in Findlay in the 1920s and had served as Alliance pastor/local superintendent in Findlay earlier, soon returned to pastor the church for the next two decades. She was listed in 1929 as vice president of the National and International Pentecostal Missionary Union.[77]

Pentecostal Child Evangelist Preaches for the Alliance. In 1924 Uldine Utley, an eleven-year old girl who was saved and baptized in the Spirit with tongues in one of McPherson's meetings, received a powerful prophetic anointing as an evangelist. She preached in many Pentecostal meetings, some with Alliance/Pentecostal evangelist Virginia Berg, becoming known as "the world's youngest evangelist."[78] An Alliance church was formed out of her evangelistic campaign in Savannah, Georgia, growing to three hundred by 1926.[79] During a Sunday evening service at the Alliance church in Savannah, Georgia, in July 1926, a father rushed forward to the platform asking for prayer for his five-year old daughter. She had collapsed in the meeting, was not breathing, and had no pulse. Many said she was dead, but others continued praying. After fifteen minutes of prayer, a pulse returned, and after about ten minutes of additional prayer, the girl was completely restored.[80]

The Alliance openly accepted young Utley's ministry, as she preached, even in Pentecostal circles, "We must not seek the tongues, but the Author of tongues, which is Jesus Christ."[81] She began to preach to thousands in Atlanta, Miami, Brooklyn, and other locations "under the auspices of" the C&MA.[82]

FURTHER CONFLICTS AND HARBINGERS OF DECLINE

The Canadian Alliance and Pentecostalism. As mentioned earlier, Harry Turner left the Pentecostal Assemblies of Canada in 1926 and returned to the Alliance. Rev. A. G. Philpotts had affiliated his church, Elim Tabernacle, with the Pentecostal Assemblies of Canada in 1926, but left in 1928, becoming "undenominational." S. M. Gerow, who had pastored the charismatically-oriented Alliance churches in Akron and Detroit (and who had mentored Tozer), conducted an Alliance convention at Elim Tabernacle in December 1928, introducing the congregation to Alliance beliefs and practices. On May 1, 1929, the church officially affiliated with the C&MA, changing its name to Alliance Tabernacle, and Philpotts became credentialed with the Alliance.[83]

Yet other congregations and members in Canada defected to Pentecostalism. Canadian Alliance historian Lindsey Reynolds reported, "During the late 1920s, the fast growing appeal of Pentecostal teaching and experience coupled with the aggressive national organization of the Pentecostal Assemblies of Canada impacted heavily on the Alliance. . . . The Alliance in eastern Canada in the 1920s experienced something similar with respect to the Pentecostal movement as the Alliance in the United States had experienced twenty years earlier."[84]

Conflict in Salem, Oregon. Not all contacts with Pentecostals were positive elsewhere as well. About 1926 an evangelist named Moore was leading meetings for several weeks in the Alliance church in Salem, Oregon, co-pastored by H. E. Caswell and his wife Alice. Evidently, Moore began teaching Pentecostal doctrine (probably evidential tongues). The Alliance board asked him to stop the meetings, so he resumed the meetings in another location. Many of those attending the meetings went with Moore and left the Alliance church.[85] The Caswells were not opposed to charismatic manifestations, as Alice had been involved in the Pentecostal revivals in the Alliance in New York years earlier, but they insisted on maintaining the Alliance position against evidential tongues.

More Traces of Waning Interest. Some indication that all Alliance leaders were not happy with the direction in which the Alliance was moving may be found in an alleged interchange between an aged Alliance leader, A. E. Funk, and former C&MA pastor, David McDowell, who had become an Assemblies of God leader. Assemblies of God historian Brumback cites McDowell, who was then the Assemblies Assistant General Superintendent, as reporting that Funk told him in a conversation in 1927, "David, the Alliance has missed God." McDowell responded, "Brother Funk, God honored the Alliance by laying the baby on its doorstep. But you refused the responsibility, and now the sad thing about your statement is that it is too late now—the baby has grown up!"[86]

While Pentecostals have seized on the alleged incident as proof of their beliefs, most Alliance leaders have ignored or dismissed the alleged incident as not factual, or out of context. Alliance historian John Sawin, who had done considerable research on the Alliance relationship to Pentecostalism, called his statement "perplexing," commenting, "The statement, taken at face value, isn't true. I doubt Funk said it, unless it occurred in a qualifying statement."[87] Funk died the same year, and I have not been able to find corroborating evidence of his supposed regret. That Funk was charismatically-oriented is probable, as characterized by his earlier reporting cited in Chapter 16, and perhaps by 1927 he felt the Alliance was beginning to drift from its earlier cautious but expectant openness.[868]

In February 1927 Walter Turnbull wrote an article on "Mother Shipton's Prophecy," exposing it as a hoax.[89] This is especially significant because in 1911 *The Alliance Weekly* had reported the testimony of Anna Shipton's vision and dream of heaven as if it were genuine.[90] Turnbull, who had been involved in the charismatic revival in the Alliance mission work in India, was nevertheless aware that not all such manifestations proved to be from God. Since this particular prophecy had been accepted in earlier Alliance circles, they may have had egg on their face. The embarrassment of supporting what turned out to be a false prophecy may have contributed to the eventual backing away from the Pentecostal movement.

It would seem that some Alliance leaders who had been involved in the early Pentecostal revival began to have more negative evaluations of the movement. In 1928 Walter Turnbull wrote, "It is not sufficient that we be saved and victorious and that signs and wonders occur. If we are satisfied there, we are satisfied with less than God's great pattern."[91] In typical Alliance fashion he was not disparaging or discouraging signs and wonders, but urging people not to focus on them.

Also as some of the more charismatically-oriented of the Alliance began to die off, such as Funk, Collins, Whiteside, etc., or be less involved due to age, it would appear that some less-charismatically inclined began to gain power in leadership capacities. Those strongly inclined toward charismatic manifestations began to be concerned about signs of over-cautiousness or waning active expectancy of the supernatural.

In the late 1920s Hardy Mitchell seems to have disappeared from the Alliance scene, resurfacing in the Assemblies of God in 1947 just months before his death. Orville Benham gradually began to affiliate with the Open Bible Standard movement about 1926-27, joining the Board of Directors of the Bible Standard Theological School and joining together his publication *The Overcomer* with the publication *Bible Standard* in 1928. *The Overcomer* thus became the official publication of the Bible Standard, Inc., organization.[92] After nearly a decade in the Alliance, R. H. Moon returned to the Assemblies of God about 1928.

F. F. Bosworth and his brother B. B. separated their ministries about 1927. F. F. remained with the Alliance for a period of time but gradually became more independent, eventually embracing the British Israelism heresy in the 1930s and losing favor with the Alliance, while B. B. remained in the C&MA throughout his life. John Bostrom left the Alliance about 1930.

In 1929 Joseph Ellison, the Home Secretary of the C&MA for Great Britain, wrote a letter, published in several periodicals, including *The Alliance Weekly*, which disavowed any "identification of interest or fellowship between" the C&MA and the "Foursquare Gospel Movement."[93] Though the letter pointed out similarities between the two movements, it is significant that he was claiming that there was no interest or fellowship between the two. Even though, as we have seen above, in the earlier part of the decade there was indeed fellowship and interest between the two movements, that cooperation had diminished, probably due to the controversies surrounding Aimee Semple McPherson.

---

1. F. H. Senft, "The Unchangeable Christ," CMAW, June 21, 1902, 359.

2. CMAW, Jan 25, 1908, 284.

3. F. H. Senft, "In the Sunny South," CMAW, Mar. 27, 1909, 437.

4. Frederic H. Senft, "The True and the False," AW, Dec. 18, 1920, 606.

5. "From Grace to Glory," CAMW, Mar. 9, 1894, 265; Mrs. Frederick H. Senft, "Jesus My Physician," CAMW, Mar. 9, 1894, 275.

6. F. H. Senft, "Divine Healing," CMAW, June 30, 1906, 394-395.

7. W. C. Stevens, "The Cross and Sickness," *The Pentecostal Evangel*, Aug. 23, 1924, 6; W. C. Stevens, "The Nelson Meetings in Kansas City," AW, July 16, 1921, 282.

8. Editorials, AW, June 7, 1924, 246. See also A. W. Tozer, *Let My People Go* (Harrisburg, PA: Christian Publications, 1947), 81-82.

9. "Northern Pacific Paragraphs," AW, Apr. 19, 1924, 126; conversation with McCrossan's daughter Mrs. Landis.

10. AW, June 13, 1925, 402.

11. T. J. McCrossan, "The Bible, Its Christ, and Modernism," AW, Nov. 7, 1925, 748.

12. Her departure from the school was evidently not on positive terms, but she was asked to leave due to sneaking out of her dorm for an apparent tryst with a male student. The male student later became a C&MA missionary, and she enrolled at Aimee Semple McPherson's L.I.F.E. Bible College. Conversation with Wayne Warner.

13. Wayne Warner, *Kathryn Kuhlman: The Woman Behind the Miracles* (Ann Arbor, MI: Servant Publications, 1993), 31-34; Ronald A. N. Kydd, *Healing through the Centuries: Models for Understanding*. Peabody, MA: Hendrickson, 1998), 194-195; conversation with Wayne Warner, conversation with Cord Cooper, son of Charlotte McCrossan Theusen.

14. "Bosworth Campaign, Indianapolis, Indiana," AW, Jan. 17, 1925, 42; AW, Feb. 21, 1925, 114; AW, Feb. 28, 1925, 143; AW, Mar. 7, 1925, 167; AW, Mar. 21, 1925, 186; "Household of Faith," AW, Apr. 4, 1925, 238; AW, June 6, 1925, 396.

15. Assemblies of God Ministerial Records, Flower Pentecostal Heritage Center; C&MA Ministerial Directories, "Personalia," AW, Oct. 11, 1930, 672. Bostrom evidently ministered independently after 1930 until 1939 when he returned to the Assemblies of God.

16. A. N.'s son Dr. Harvey R. Bostrom served as a missionary in Ecuador with the C&MA, then later taught at Wheaton College, and served as Vice President at Trinity Evangelical Divinity School and Fort Wayne Bible College. Dr. Bostrom related that his father walked by faith, never using medicine after being healed through Simpson's ministry.

17. Robert Bryant Mitchell, *Heritage and Horizons: The History of Open Bible Standard Churches* (Des Moines, IA: Open Bible Publishers, 1982), 61-63.

18. Ibid., 241-242. This church building was eventually was closed due to foreclosure for debts in depression times, but rededicated by Raymond T. Richey in 1943 and became an Open Bible Church.

19. "Household of Faith," AW, AW, Aug. 30, 1924, 150.

20. "Household of Faith," AW, June 7, 1924, 258; "Household of Faith," AW, July 19, 1924, 50; "Household of Faith," AW, Oct. 18, 1924, 260; "Household of Faith," AW, Dec. 20, 1924, 427.

21. AW, June 6, 1925, 396.

22. F. F. Bosworth, "The Critics Answered," AW, Aug. 2, 1924, 77; F. F. Bosworth, "How to Appropriate the Redemptive and Covenant Blessings of Bodily Healing," AW, Dec. 6, 1924, 397; F. F. Bosworth, "Triumphant Faith," AW, July 4, 1925, 459.

23. AW, June 13, 1925, 402.

24. Oswald J. Smith, *The Baptism with the Holy Spirit* (New York, NY: Christian Alliance Publishing Co., 1925).

25. "Revival in Huntington," AW, Apr. 25, 1925, 287; conversation with Dr. Keith Bailey.

26. Laura G. Beecroft, "The Day of His Power—The Spirit's Working in Palestine," AW, Apr. 11, 1925, 248-249.

27. "Household of Faith," Aug. 1, 1925, 534; "Household of Faith," AW, Aug. 22, 1925, 582; AW, Mar. 7, 1925, 167.

28. Editorial, AW, Nov. 14, 1925, 770.

29. A. C. Sneed, "Annual Report, Foreign Department," AW, July 5, 1924, 6.

30. F. H. Rossiter, "God's Healing Power," AW, Nov. 1, 1924, 292.

31. George T. B. Davis, "Modern Miracles in China," AW, Jan. 31, 1925, 73; M. B. Birrell, "Annual Report, Central China Missions, Christian and Missionary Alliance, for 1923: God Speaking in Dreams," AW, Mar. 5, 1924, 89.

32. "Pentecost in a Baptist Church," Word and Work, Aug. 1924, 11.

33. "Dedication of the Great Miami Tabernacle," AW, Mar. 6, 1926, 159.

34. Dr. Keith Bailey recalled that Simpson associate and evangelist E. E. Johnson told him that Shuman spoke in tongues.

35. For example, in January 1917, W. A. Cramer, Secretary of the Central District, and H. M. Shuman, Superintendent of the Central District, both tongue-speakers themselves, reported to the Board of Managers regarding the work in Akron, "The strain in the work there thro [sic] some Pentecostal wrong teaching is all healed and the work is in good condition." Report of the Secretary of the Home Dept., C&MA Board of Manager Minutes, Jan 27, 1917.

36. H. M. Shuman, "Annual Report," AW, July 9, 1927, 452.

37. See "Personalia," AW, Jan. 16, 1926, 47; "Personalia," AW, Jan. 16, 1926, 47; "Personalia," AW, Feb. 27, 1926, 143; "Personalia," AW, May 15, 1926, 327; "Personalia," AW, May 29, 1926, 334; "Personalia," AW, June 12, 1926, 391. See also "Personalia," AW, Jan. 29, 1927, 79 (Bosworth campaign in Pa.); "Personalia," AW, Feb. 5, 1927, 94 (Mitchell meetings in Houston); "Personalia," AW, Mar. 19, 1927, 191 (Mitchell at Lima, Ohio, C&MA); "Personalia," AW, Apr. 23, 1927, 271 (Horn in Pa.); "Personalia," AW, Oct. 15, 1927, 687. (Richey and B. B. Bosworth in Pa.).

38. "Rev. William G. Weston—He Loved God Fervently," Alliance Witness, Sept. 16, 1964, 8.

39. "Personalia," AW, May 8, 1926, 310.

40. Lois J. Betz, The Promise Fulfilled: The Story of Eli N. Richey and His Family," 48, unpublished paper, Assemblies of God Archives.

41. "Personalia," AW, Oct. 16, 1926, 679.

42. "Personalia," AW, Apr. 23, 1927, 271; "Personalia," AW, Apr. 23, 1927, 271. Roland Gray, Sr., was my first mentor when as a 20 year old I "sat at his feet" learning from him.

43. Outpouring in India," LRE, Apr. 1926, 15.

44. Judith Adams, Against the Gates of Hell: The Story of Glenn V. Tingley (Harrisburg, PA: Christian Publications, 1977), 41-49, 53-56.

45. Adams, 111-112. For other incidents of prophetic words or what is sometimes called word of knowledge, see pp. 83-84, 111.

46. Adams, 138.

47. Reynolds, Rebirth, 206-208.

48. Harry L. Turner, 1960 C&MA Annual Report, 21-22.

49. "Personalia," AW, May 1, 1926, 295.

50. "Personalia," AW, Aug. 28, 1926, 567.

51. Ira David, "The Presence of God," AW, July 16, 1927, 468.

52. Mitchell, 68-69.

53. Additionally, in December 1925, Jago had published an article on "Supernatural Protection" in *The Alliance Weekly*. E. O. Jago, "Supernatural Protection," AW, Dec. 26, 1925, 889.

54. AW, June 23, 1928, 403.

55. Kenneth MacKenzie, "Helps to Truth Seekers," AW, Aug. 28, 1926, 567. See also Kenneth MacKenzie, "Helps to Truth Seekers," AW, June 25, 1927, 431.

56. Kenneth MacKenzie, "Helps to Truth Seekers," AW, Oct. 15, 1927, 687.

57. D. M. Panton, "Testing the Supernatural," *The Dawn: An Evangelical Magazine*, May 15, 1925, 63.

58. D. M. Panton, "Outlook of the Hour," *The Dawn*, Feb. 15, 1926, 483; Panton, "Testing the Supernatural," 62, 67.

59. Kenneth MacKenzie, "Helps to Truth Seekers," Feb. 9, 1929, 94.

60. Reynolds, *Rebirth*, 227-228.

61. T. J. McCrossan, *Speaking in Other Tongues*, 42.

62. Ira David, "Spiritual Gifts," AW, Sept. 29, 1928, 638.

63. Ira David, "Unity and the God-Commanded Blessing," AW, Jan. 22, 1927, 53.

64. Walter Turnbull and C. H. Chrisman, "The Message of the Christian and Missionary Alliance," 1927, accessed online at http://online.cbccts.sk.ca/alliance studies/ahtreadings/ahtr_s6.html.

65. John H. Cable, "Miracles," AW, Feb. 9, 1929, 86-87, 91.

66. A. B. Simpson, "Aggressive Christianity," AW, Aug. 6, 1927, 518.

67. George T. B. Davis, "Remarkable Revivals in China," AW, Oct. 15, 1927, 680.

68. George C. Ferry, "God's Wonderful Working in Indo-China," AW, Oct. 29, 1927, 714.

69. W. J. McNaughton, "Healing of St. Vitus Dance," AW, Oct. 20, 1928, 679.

70. William T. MacArthur, "Crowned with Glory and Honor—When the Curse Is Lifted," LRE, Mar. 1925, 8; William T. MacArthur, "The Lost Crown," LRE, July 1926, 20.

71. "Our Great Unfinished Task," LRE, May 1927, 20.

72. Ella Rudy, "Perilous Days in China," LRE, Jan. 1927, 6.

73. "Personalia," AW, Aug. 21, 1926, 551.

74. Rudolph Anderson, "The Opening of Dedougou in French West Africa," AW, Nov. 19, 1927, 769.

75. A. W. Orwig, "Evil Speaking and Slander," AW, Dec. 25, 1926, 845; A. W. Orwig, "Lights or Souls—Which?," AW, July 16, 1927, 475; A. W. Orwig, "The Divine Equipment," AW, July 28, 1928, 492.

76. "Faithful Unto Death," AW, Mar. 17, 1928, 167.

77. "More About Findlay School," *Assemblies of God Heritage*, Spring 1990, 20.

78. *Word and Work*, May 1924, 16; *Word and Work*, June 1924, 15; *Word and Work*, Aug. 1924, 11.

79. "Personalia," AW, Nov. 27, 1926, 791.

80. "Personalia," AW, Aug. 14, 1926, 535.

81. Uldine Utley, "God's Love Gift to the Believer," *Word and Work*, May 1924, 3.

82. "Personalia," AW, Feb. 20, 1926, 126; "Dedication of the Great Miami Tabernacle," AW, Mar. 6, 1926, 159; Ira E. David, "Revival in Atlanta," AW, Mar. 13, 1926, 179; "Personalia," AW, Aug. 10, 1929, 525.

83. Reynolds, *Rebirth*, 168-169.

84. Ibid., 160-161.

85. Marjorie Stewart, "A Story of Pentecost in the Pacific Northwest," *Assemblies of God Heritage*, Spring 1987, 8.

86. Brumback, *Suddenly . . . from Heaven*, 95-96. Funk died later the same year in November.

87. Handwritten note by John Sawin, Nov. 23, 1988. Flower Pentecostal Heritage Center.

88. See Funk, "Pittsburgh Convention," AW, Apr. 9, 1921, 57.

89. Walter Turnbull, "Mother Shipton's Prophecy," AW, Feb. 5, 1927, 90-91.

90. CMAW, Sept. 9, 1911, 378; "A Vision from Heaven," AW, Oct. 21, 1911, 38.

91. Walter Turnbull, "The Holy Spirit and Revival," AW, Sept. 1, 1928, 565.

92. Mitchell, *Heritage and Horizons*, 81, 83-84.

93. "The Christian and Missionary Alliance," AW, July 27, 1929, 475.

1930s — Drift from Cautious Expectancy to Wary Tolerance

Dr. Arnold Cook, former president of The Christian and Missionary Alliance in Canada, has written that historical drift is inevitable as a cycle of life in churches.[1] The C&MA is no exception. Significant research has shown that the decade of the 1930s demonstrated identifiable modifications of C&MA objectives.[2] It can be discerned that this is also when the Alliance began to depart from its past decades of openness and expectancy toward charismatic practice, even though its president prayed in tongues. It is difficult to pinpoint time and place and people, but the signs are evident. As is often true with historical drift, the change is often imperceptible, like a frog in a kettle of water that does not realize the temperature is increasing to the boiling point.

Continued Evidence of Some Supernatural Beliefs and Practices

To be sure, the C&MA continued to believe in the reality of the supernatural gifts of the Spirit and continued *some* connections and cooperation with Pentecostals. In February 1930, the *Alliance Weekly* reported the death of George Eldridge. Even though he left the C&MA for the Pentecostal movement in 1916, it was warmly reported that Eldridge "for many years was one of the most honored and beloved workers in the Alliance movement."[3] Also passing away in 1930 was longtime Honorary C&MA Vice President George Montgomery in Oakland, California. It is significant that Assemblies of God pastor R. H. Moon, who had earlier served as an Alliance pastor and evangelist, officiated his funeral along with H. F. Meltzer, pastor of the charismatically-oriented Alliance Church in Oakland.[4]

In the same year William T. MacArthur wrote, "May God grant us 'full gospel' preachers."[5] Even though Pentecostals used the term to describe the baptism in the Spirit with tongues, the Alliance also continued to use the term "full gospel" until the late 1950s to indicate a gospel that included sanctification, healing and the supernatural. By then, the term had become so identified with Pentecostal beliefs that the Alliance, for the most part, abandoned the term.

MacArthur ordained one of those "full gospel" preachers later the same year, imparting supernatural spiritual gifting to him. Young pastor Richard Harvey had been praying daily for spiritual gifts, especially the gift of teaching. After several weeks he heard a voice inside him saying, "Are you not willing for me to choose the gift I want to give you?" He relented to the Lord, and soon he was ordained. At the ordination service, the speaker exhorted, "Now, when the hands of the elders are laid upon you, expect the Holy Spirit to give to you today a special gift of God for your ministry." When the elders laid hands on Harvey, MacArthur prayed, "Oh God, give the young man the gift of evangelism and whatever he needs to accompany this gift." From that day his preaching changed and people responded to his messages in droves to receive Jesus Christ as Savior and Lord.[6]

In 1931 Robert Jaffray reported several power encounters in French Indo-China. In one incident 77 people were converted through a single healing. On another occasion an opium addict was delivered and 48 boys at a reform school were saved as a result.[7] Jaffray continued to press for acts of the supernatural through C&MA ministry: "We are still living in the day and dispensation called The Acts, and it is our privilege to see the mighty working of God among the people. Ours should be a day of constant miracles, the mighty Acts of the Holy Spirit."[8]

Dr. Ira David continued to encourage the baptism in the Spirit, writing of the day of Pentecost, "They then had a collective baptism, one that loosened all tongues and set them all on fire for God at once. Each assembly of believers needs such a collective baptism of the Spirit. . . . A proper baptism of the Holy Spirit will fix our tongue so that we shall stop saying the wrong things and begin to say the right."[9]

The charismatic theme of spiritual warfare and "binding the strong man" continued to be propagated in the Alliance.[10] Significant for future Pentecostal and charismatic theology, John A. MacMillan published a series of articles in the *Alliance Weekly* in 1932, which were compiled in a book entitled *The Authority of the Believer*.[11] Embryonic teachings on the authority of the believer had developed through the Keswick, Higher Life and Wesleyan holiness movements of the late nineteenth century, teaching such concepts as "throne rights" or "throne power." However, John MacMillan was the seminal writer to expand upon and put together the most thorough presentation of the concept.[12]

In 1934 Chinese theologian and writer Watchman Nee married the daughter of a Chinese C&MA pastor.[13] His writings, which include affirmation of the supernatural, have become popular in C&MA, Keswick, and charismatic circles, and show the influence of A. B. Simpson and the Alliance. Like C&MA leaders, he also warned of fleshly and demonic counterfeits of the supernatural in books such as *The Spiritual Man*, *Spiritual Reality or Obsession*, and *The Latent Power of the Soul*.[14]

From 1934-1938, Hubert Mitchell held dual credentials with the C&MA and the Open Bible Standard Church, a Pentecostal denomination, and traveled in ministry with Paul Rader. At the invitation of Rader (whose sister was a missionary in Indonesia), Mitchell went with Rader to Indonesia and served as a missionary under the C&MA in Sumatra, partially supported by the Open Bible Church. Eventually, he worked totally with the Open Bible Standard Church.[15]

CLEAR SIGNS OF DRIFT

From "Full Gospel" to "Gospel." In spite of these indications of continued openness, however, during the 1930s there are also several signs that attitudes began to change. Ernest Wilson, who began his ministry in the C&MA in 1938, wrote a doctoral dissertation entitled *Modifications of Objectives in the Christian and Missionary Alliance.* He concluded through his research, "There has been to some degree a decline of emphasis in the CMA, upon the work of the Holy Spirit."[16] Wilson has also cited indication of "historical drift" to indicate that one time the C&MA has been closer, not so much in its beliefs, as in its practices, to the Pentecostal camp.[17] He documented the trend "away from the strong emphasis (in its infancy) on the '*Full-gospel*,' to a concept more popular (in many evangelical circles) called simply *the 'Gospel.'*"[18] Similarly, it was the conclusion of Pentecostal historian Gordon Atter that those who had spoken in tongues but stayed in the Alliance "began to minimize the value of tongues lest they be dubbed Pentecostal."[19] Alliance publications did continue to use the term "full gospel" occasionally into the 1950s, but then seem to have abandoned the terminology altogether. As one old Alliance leader put it, "The Alliance got dignity."

McCrossan's Diminishing Involvement. In 1929 while serving as an Alliance pastor and interim president of Simpson Bible Institute, T. J. McCrossan wrote his book, *Bodily Healing in the Atonement,* published in 1930. However, it was not published by the C&MA but by the Humbards, independent Pentecostals who also ministered in non-Pentecostal circles similar to the ministries of Charles Price and Carrie Judd Montgomery. Even though the C&MA believed in healing in the atonement, the C&MA publishers evidently chose not to publish the book.

McCrossan had written a section in the book on falling under the power of the Spirit, which had occurred in his own life and subsequently through his ministry.[20] According to some older Alliance leaders, some in the C&MA did not like McCrossan's involvement with the practice of falling under the power of the Spirit, and did not feel that it was "Alliance." Perhaps it was not published by the C&MA publishing house for that reason, even though the phenomenon had occurred with approval of Alliance leaders many times in the past, even Simpson.

McCrossan resigned the Gospel Tabernacle in 1935 to do itinerant traveling and teaching at Bible Conferences and seminars, traveling to England, Scotland and Ireland. He visited George Jeffreys' Pentecostal work and spoke positively of the movement. He reported that Jeffreys taught that tongues is "not the one and only sign of the baptism" as American Pentecostals teach. He also spoke encouragingly about Pastor Lewi Petrus, leader of the Pentecostal movement in Sweden.[21] His support of moderate Pentecostals that did not insist on tongues as the initial evidence of the baptism in the Spirit was virtually identical to A. B. Simpson's attitude toward earlier moderate Pentecostals such as Willis Hoover and Boddy.

However, after this, McCrossan became less active with the C&MA and did not carry Alliance credentials, returning to his original Presbyterian ordination, although his daughter and son-in-law Rev. and Mrs. Fred Landis continued in C&MA ministry throughout their career. Though his ministry took him much broader than the Alliance, why he did not keep Alliance credentials is unknown. Although his positive assessment of some Pentecostals was consistent with Simpson and earlier Alliance leaders, one wonders whether his view became in less favor with the Alliance as a whole. Regardless, it is significant that his name and writings eventually sunk into anonymity in the C&MA.

His book *Speaking in Other Tongues, Sign or Gift—Which?*, the fullest exegetical exposition on tongues in the C&MA, evidently has not been reprinted since 1938, except for a brief time in the 1960s when it was rediscovered. Nor has his book *Bodily Healing and the Atonement* been recognized. In fact, when a book review of this latter book (republished by Kenneth Hagin in 1982)[22] appeared in the *Alliance Witness* in 1984, the reviewer mentioned McCrossan as a Presbyterian, evidently knowing nothing about his thirteen years of active service in The Christian and Missionary Alliance.[23]

Former Pentecostals Leave the Alliance. By 1931, John H. Bostrom, who had ministered for six years in the C&MA went into independent evangelist ministry and eventually returned to the Assemblies of God in 1939. His brother, A. N. Bostrom, remained in the C&MA. In the mid-1930s F. F. Bosworth and Luke Rader embraced the British-Israelism heresy and did not remain in fellowship in the C&MA.[24] MacMillan wrote a series of articles against the heresy in 1934.[25] That a former Pentecostal like Bosworth had succumbed to the deception of the heresy may have been another contributing factor to the distancing of the C&MA from Pentecostalism. According to some older Alliance sources, Bosworth's book *Christ the Healer* had been required for a time for C&MA ordination studies, but was evidently replaced by S. D. Gordon's book *The Healing Christ*.

In 1936 Raymond Richey and his father E. N. Richey returned to Assemblies of God after a nearly 15-year hiatus with the Alliance.[26] These two former Pentecostals had been enthusiastically welcomed with open arms into active evangelistic and pastoral ministry in the Alliance in the 1920s, so that it is probable that both of them felt the loss of "charismatic" openness and expectancy that had characterized the C&MA in the 1920s. It was no longer the same church as when they had entered, and possibly their charismatic leanings were no longer welcomed or encouraged as before.

Significant Omissions. Further evidence of erosion of the early Alliance active expectancy of the supernatural is found in a 1930s reprint of Simpson's tract *Gifts and Graces.* As pointed out by Sandy Ayer, director of the library for the C&MA's Canadian Bible College and Canadian Theological Seminary, the reprint "tellingly omits" a section of the original tract "which warns against fearing or ignoring the spiritual gifts and provides instruction in their appropriate public use."[27] Simpson's exhortations not to fear or ignore, but expect gifts and manifestations apparently were considered by the editors and publishers in the 1930s to be too encouraging of the supernatural.

From February to April 1934, MacMillan wrote a series of articles on the Spirit-filled life, affirming the gifts, but warning that seeking manifestations can lead to fleshly or counterfeit manifestations.[28] In June MacMillan became the Associate Editor of the *Alliance Weekly.* President Shuman began doing worldwide itinerant work, so for all practical purposes, MacMillan was the acting editor for the next 18 years. In October, MacMillan, with Shuman's approval, republished in *The Alliance Weekly* Hudson Ballard's 1907 statement on tongues from the book *The Signs of the Times,* reaffirming openness to tongues and the gifts, but denying the evidence doctrine, and saying tongues is desirable, but not to be sought after.

However, an almost imperceptible, but crucial, omission from Ballard's earlier official C&MA pronouncements in 1907 and 1914 (as well as Ira David in 1928) is his avowal that every church should have some who speak in tongues.[29] This omission in 1934 shows a clear backing away from the C&MA position when Simpson was living, and the decade or so following Simpson's death.[30] It was, nonetheless, consistent with and parallel to removal of the section of Simpson's tract *Gifts and Graces.* No longer did the leadership of the C&MA expect or desire that every church would have people who pray in tongues.

Distancing from Pentecostals. Even more telling is what occurred the following month. British leader D. M. Panton wrote a letter to President Shuman expressing dismay at the favorable article on tongues in the October issue of the *Alliance Weekly.* In the 1920s Panton had written an article in his periodical *The Dawn* that advocated the testing of all tongues, and critical of Bosworth's tongue-speaking experience.[31] Since Shuman was on itinerary out of the country, acting editor MacMillan responded to his letter, saying that while the article on tongues was not written by Simpson, "it expressed his views on the subject." It is notable that MacMillan further wrote, "The Christian and Missionary Alliance has no connection in any form with Pentecostalism or the tongues Movement," a statement that does not appear to be entirely accurate in light of the examples of cooperation and openness cited above. However, it does indicate definite movement in that direction. He went on to express his own opinion that while he believed some instances of tongues "to be undoubtedly of God," yet "very little of what is known as speaking in tongues is genuine."[32]

His belief was a departure from the early Alliance position that did not cast nearly so much doubt on tongues, but similar to the conclusion to which William

Christie, his missionary colleague from West China had come. Christie had become Vice President of the C&MA, so the views of these two significant leaders seem to have influenced C&MA attitudes following this time. Further, it seems strange that he made no specific mention to Panton about the positive and genuine experiences of his tongues-speaking friends and colleagues, such as President Shuman, Ira David, Alfred Snead, Robert Jaffray, Harry Turner, his Chinese interpreter Mr. Wong, and the wives of his colleagues William T. MacArthur and William Christie.

Just three months later, in February 1935, tongue-speaking scholar Ira David warned in *The Alliance Weekly* of two extremes regarding tongues: 1) tongues as evidence, 2) tongues is from the devil.[33] With the timing of this statement, one may wonder if it was a veiled public response to Panton's letter.

In 1937 MacMillan encouraged the gift of prophecy, but like Simpson and earlier Alliance leaders cautioned that prophecy is imperfect.[34] However, in another significant departure from Simpson, he claimed that prophecy no longer consists of direct messages from God, but rather impressions.[35] In 1938 we find MacMillan criticizing some mass healing meetings.[36] He does not name names, but we might wonder if he could have been referring to Aimee Semple McPherson or Charles Price, both of whom had been in favor with Alliance leaders in the 1920s.

In May 1938, MacMillan replied to a letter from an *Alliance Weekly* reader regarding tongues, saying,

> I have been in contact closely at times with those who have spoken in tongues. In some cases, there has been a deep devotion to the Lord, and a measure of power in His service. But in other cases, there has been a lamentable lack of understanding of the Scriptures. In still other cases, I know of those who, after seeking and obtaining tongues, have found themselves greatly disappointed. . . . In yet other cases, there has been received a manifestation which has decidedly not been of God. . . . There are yet other cases where believers who have received tongues have fallen into grave sin, and have continued in the exercise of the gift while living thus.[37]

MacMillan counseled her, "instead of being troubled regarding such a gift, or allowing your mind to consider that it is something that of itself evidences special spiritual blessing, that you simply continue in an attitude of full yieldedness to God, and readiness to receive all that He desires to give you."[38] Although MacMillan gives the typical Alliance cautions, this seems to be a more positive statement regarding tongues than his reply to Panton four years earlier. His counsel of "readiness to receive all that He desires to give you" is reminiscent of Simpson's encouragements.

Some Recognition of Drift

Perhaps MacMillan, Shuman, and other members of the C&MA Board of Managers began to become aware of how far they had drifted, because numerous times in the next six years MacMillan (who was usually quiet and reserved) warned in *The Alliance Weekly* that if Alliance churches cease the shouts of "Amen!" and "Hallelujah!" in their services, God will write "Ichabod" on their doorposts for the glory of the Lord has departed that place. Though not an emotional person himself, he also wrote that occasional dancing before the Lord may be appropriate.[39] He further commended uplifted hands at General Council in 1939,[40] and continued to encourage the lifting of hands in two subsequent issues.[41] Such emotional demonstrations of worship as shouting, raising hands and, upon occasion, dancing had been a part of worship in the C&MA in earlier times, but had apparently gradually been abandoned in the 1930s. By 1940, we find MacMillan lessening the overly-cautious, negative, skeptical attitude toward the *charismata* he exhibited in 1934 and expressing a desire for pure, full exercise of gifts in the assembly.[42] Further, an article regarding the 1940 General Council wistfully acknowledged that the Alliance still uses "the phraseology of the past freely, but seldom with the fullness of its original meaning."[43]

CODIFICATION OF "SEEK NOT, FORBID NOT"

Nienkirchen concluded that Tozer coined the phrase and concept "seek not, forbid not" for the official C&MA statement in 1963.[44] However, further research indicates the motto dates from the 1930s, probably from the Board of Managers.[45] Additionally, in the late 1930s, Billy Graham attended C&MA affiliated Florida Bible Institute (and preached his first sermon at Tampa Gospel Tabernacle of the C&MA), Tampa, Florida. He recalls the "seek not, forbid not" stance on tongues being taught there.[46] By the time that Tozer and other Alliance leaders published a formal statement in 1963, the motto had been in use informally for at least 25 years. Although the motto succinctly expresses the early Alliance view, the emphasis became placed on the "seek not" to the neglect of "forbid not," resulting in a passive attitude toward expectation of supernatural spiritual gifts. Hence, the Alliance drifted from a cautious expectation to a passive, wary tolerance in the 1930s and following.

---

1. Arnold L. Cook, *Historical Drift: Must My Church Die?* (Camp Hill, PA: Christian Publications, 2000), 45-56.

2. Ernest Gerald Wilson, *The Christian and Missionary Alliance: Development and Modification of Its Original Objectives*, Ph.D. Dissertation (New York, NY: New York University, 1984).

3. AW, Feb. 15, 1930, 99.

4. AW, Mar. 14, 1931, 171-172.

5. W. T. MacArthur, "Sparks from the Anvil," AW, Feb. 15, 1930, 112.

6. Harvey, *70 Years of Miracles*, 86-87.

7. Robert Jaffray, "Miracles of Salvation and Healing in French Indo-China," AW, May 23, 1931, 332-334.

8. *The Pioneer*, V, No. 19 (1934), 24.

9. I. E. David, "The Gift of the Spirit," AW, June 20, 1931, 406; see also I. E. David, "The Gospel for All Men," AW, Aug. 23, 1931, 522.

10. O. R. Palmer, "Binding the Strong Man," AW, Jan. 25, 1930, 54.

11. John A. MacMillan, "The Authority of the Believer," AW, Jan. 9, 16, 23, 30; Feb. 6, 13, 20, 27, 1932.

12. See Paul L. King, *A Believer with Authority: The Life and Message of John A. MacMillan* (Camp Hill, PA: Christian Publications, 2001).

13. Angus Kinnear, *Against the Tide: The Story of Watchman Nee* (Wheaton, IL: Tyndale House, 1973, 1978), 14, 80, 165-166.

14. Watchman Nee, *Latent Power of the Soul* (New York, NY: Christian Fellowship Publishers, Inc., 1972); Watchman Nee, *Spiritual Reality or Obsession* (New York: Christian Fellowship Publishers, 1970); Watchman Nee, *The Spiritual Man* (New York: Christian Fellowship Publishers, Inc., 1968).

15. Mitchell, *Heritage and Horizons*, 159, 161, 189-191; conversation with Wayne Warner, Dir. of Flower Pentecostal Heritage Center, 2001.

16. Wilson, *The Christian and Missionary Alliance*, 157.

17. Ibid., 157, 168.

18. Ibid., 225.

19. Atter, 149.

20. McCrossan, *Bodily Healing and the Atonement*, 111-112.

21. McCrossan, *Christ's Paralyzed Church X-Rayed*, 219, 223-224, 312-313, 341.

22. Interestly enough, although Hagin believed in falling under the power of the Spirit and the phenomenon occurred frequently in his meetings, Hagin's edited version of McCrossan's book omitted the section dealing with the manifestation. This was probably because McCrossan did not believe that all such manifestations were from God.

23. "Book Reviews," *The Alliance Witness*, Sept. 12, 1984, 22.

24. As confirmed by older Alliance leaders.

25. J. A. MacMillan, "British Israelism—A Latter-Time Heresy," Part I, AW, Sept. 1, 1934, 548ff.; J. A. MacMillan, "British Israelism—A Latter-Time Heresy," Part II, AW, Sept. 8, 1934, 564ff.; J. A. MacMillan, "British Israelism—A Latter-Time Heresy," Part III, AW, Sept. 15, 1934, 580ff; J. A. MacMillan, "British Israelism—A Latter-Time Heresy," Part IV, AW, Sept. 22, 1934, 596ff.; J. A. MacMillan, "British Israelism—A Latter-Time Heresy," Part V, AW, Sept. 29, 1934, 612ff.

26. Richey continued to minister in some Alliance circles after departing the C&MA. See "Work and Workers," AW, July 30, 1938, 493. See also a poem by his wife Eloise May Richey two decades later, indicating a continuing influence: Edith M Beyerle, comp., "Meditations in the Word," AW, Dec. 25, 1957, 13.

27. H. D. (Sandy) Ayer, *The Christian and Missionary Alliance: An Annotated Bibliography of Textual Sources* (Lanham, MD, and London: The Scarecrow Press, Inc., 2001), 251. It should be noted that a more recent reprint of the tract by Toccoa Falls College includes the previously omitted section.

28. John A. MacMillan, "The Spirit-Filled Christian," I-VII, AW, Feb. 10, 17, Mar. 3, 10, 17, Apr. 7, 14, 1934.

29. "The Gift of Tongues," AW, Oct. 27, 1934, 677-678; Nov. 3, 1934, 694-695; Nov. 10, 1934, 710-711.

30. J. Hudson Ballard, "The Spiritual Clinic," AW, Nov. 21, 1914, 126; Ira David, "Spiritual Gifts," AW, Sept.29, 1928, 638. In January 1907, A. B. Simpson originally published Ballard's pronouncement, then republished his article in full (with the statement intact) in June of the same year as a part of the book *Signs of the Times*, the official public C&MA response to Azusa Street. In 1914 Ballard had reasserted that Alliance leaders are agreed that tongues should have a place in every church. In 1928, Ira David reaffirmed this belief. Whether this editorial excise was the work of Shuman or MacMillan is unknown, but

in the light of MacMillan's letter to Panton (see following note), it was probably MacMillan. Whether Shuman was aware of the omission is unknown, but it is a significant departure from earlier Alliance policy.

31. D. M. Panton, "The Outlook of the Hour, *The Dawn*, Feb. 15, 1926, 483; D. M. Panton, "Testing the Supernatural," *The Dawn*, May 15, 1925, 62, 67.

32. Letter from D. M. Panton to H. M. Shuman, Nov. 12, 1934; letter in reply from J. A. MacMillan to D. M. Panton, Nov. 22, 1934. See also letter in reply from D. M. Panton to J. A. MacMillan, Dec. 17, 1934. C&MA Archives.

33. Ira E. David, "Sunday School Lesson: Peter Preaches to Gentiles," AW, Feb. 23, 1935, 126.

34. John A. MacMillan, "Spiritual Balance," AW, Apr. 24, 1937, 258. See also John A. MacMillan, *The Full Gospel Sunday School Quarterly*, Nov. 30, 1941, 28.

35. John A. MacMillan, "Contacting God," AW, Nov. 9, 1940, 706.

36. John A. MacMillan, "Divine Healing," AW, July 9, 1938, 435.

37. Letter from John MacMillan to Mrs. R. V. Fagely, May 16, 1938. C&MA Archives.

38. Ibid.

39. John A. MacMillan, "With Heart and Voice, AW, May 13, 1939, 290 "The Fourfold Gospel, AW, June 10,1939, 354; John A. MacMillan, *The Full Gospel Sunday School Quarterly*, May 21, 1944, 25; "Modern Hymns," Feb. 24, 1940, 115; "Religious Enthusiasm," AW, May 14, 1938, 307.

40. John A. MacMillan, "The Fourfold Gospel," AW, June 10, 1939, 354.

41. John A. MacMillan, "The Day of Prayer," Aug. 26, 1939, 531; John A. MacMillan, "Commanding God," AW, Oct. 7, 1939, 626.

42. John A. MacMillan, "Love's Divine Overflow," AW, May 18, 1940, 306.

43. "The 1940 Council," AW, Apr. 13, 1940, 226.

44. Nienkirchen, 131-140.

45. According to Keith Bailey, the phrase was in common usage when he came into the Alliance in 1944.

46. Billy Graham, *The Holy Spirit* (Waco, TX: Word, 1978); 264-265; Mitchell, *Heritage and Horizons*, 241

TWENTY

MODIFIED STANCE OF THE 1940s AND 50s

In the 1940s and 50s we see some evidence of recovered openness toward the charismatic dimension, yet maintaining some distance from Pentecostals as well. This represents a continued modification from the early Alliance stance of cautious expectancy, though not a complete repudiation of earlier teaching and practice.

MORE CHARISMATIC MANIFESTATIONS AND EMOTION

In the fall of 1940, a revival took at the Missionary Training Institute at Nyack. One pastor who was baptized in the Spirit in the 1906 Nyack revival commented, "This is the greatest outpouring of the Holy Spirit at Nyack since 1906."[1] In October 1942, another revival broke out at Nyack with A. W. Tozer speaking. A holy hush, groaning, weeping, and holy laughter were all a part of the manifestations during this moving of the Holy Spirit.[2] Annual Council the next year featured the singing Humbard Family, who had connections both with McCrossan and Pentecostalism. Attendees at Councils in the 1940s raised their hands, reaching for the Lord with hearty shouts, Amens and Hallelujahs.[3]

In April 1948 MacMillan showed renewed openness as he quoted Paul Rader regarding earlier move of Spirit in China accompanied by a roar of prayer, weeping, thrills like electricity going through believers' bodies, and groaning. He also cited phenomena in Wesley's day like falling to ground and revelations of power of God, saying they are needed in church today.[4] In the same year *The Alliance Weekly* reprinted a statement of A. B. Simpson that spoke positively regarding emotion and powerful manifestations in the C&MA.[5] According to older Alliance leaders, another outpouring of the Spirit in revival took place at Nyack College in 1950 with manifestation of supernatural gifts and some falling under power of Spirit.[6]

Several more manifestations of holy laughter took place in the Alliance during these two decades. Late Oral Roberts University professor Dr. Charles Farah, Jr., related that in the 1940s an Alliance missionary shared about his experience of holy laughter with his father, who was a C&MA pastor in New England.[7] In

July 1944, *The Alliance Weekly* recorded an account of healing with holy laughter and weeping, affirming that the gifts of the Spirit are for today, and that prophecy is needed today to give special messages, yet also cautioning that the devil can produce miracles as well.[8] Tozer likewise wrote of seeing a man experiencing holy laughter during Communion.[9] In 1953, C&MA President Shuman recounted in the *Alliance Weekly* Louis Zwiemer's experience in 1914 of receiving the baptism in the Spirit with shouting, feeling of holy fire, and holy laughter.[10]

MODERATE OPENNESS MAINTAINED

It was in the early 1940s that Keith Bailey, later a Vice President in the C&MA, received tongues while he was in the Brethren denomination. He came into the Alliance in 1944 and commented that the "Seek Not, Forbid Not" motto was commonly cited in the C&MA by that time. Also that same summer F. F. Bosworth, who had recanted British Israelism, was welcomed back into the C&MA, speaking at the C&MA Beulah Beach conference. Bosworth and his wife Florence then held credentials with the Alliance from 1947-1951 as evangelists.[11] From 1948 to 1950 Bosworth teamed up with healing evangelist William Branham. Branham became quite controversial in some of his beliefs and practices, especially later, but apparently the Alliance leaders who continued to approve Bosworth's credentials did not have significant problems with his association with Branham at that time.[12] The Bosworth brothers both suffered from diabetes in their later years and died less than a month apart in 1958. According to family members, while dying B. B. heard a heavenly choir and F. F. saw a vision of heaven.

Alliance pastor Fred Page wrote in 1944 that the supernatural signs are needed today to fulfill the Great Commission.[13] Samuel Zwemer declared in 1948 that God is still "confirming the word with signs following (Mark 16:20)."[14] In 1949 Alliance evangelist Armin Gesswein affirmed that "charismatic operations of the Spirit" are to continue in the church, exhorting, "let us hold fast the gifts and graces of the Spirit, for they are permanent in the Church." He cited a line from Luther's great hymn: "The Spirit and the gifts are ours. . . ."[15]

In 1950 veteran missionary Earl R. Carner, who had been a part of the 1906-1909 charismatic revival in the Alliance work in India, asserted, "If all of these gifts were used under the control of the Spirit, and not abused through the working of the flesh, how much more mightily the Church would work in the world today."[16] In 1956 the Alliance affirmed, "The gift of tongues may be abused, but there is still an injunction against forbidding to speak in tongues."[17] In the same issue, an article by A. B. Simpson was reprinted in which he avowed that supernatural gifts are the privilege and heritage of the church.[18] In the same year, Edgar Truax, who began mission work with the Alliance in Thailand in 1925, asserted the need for signs and wonders to confirm the gospel.[19]

Those who have supposed that Tozer was opposed to tongues would be surprised to discover that Baptist missionary Paris Reidhead was expelled by African Inland Mission for speaking in tongues and was welcomed into the C&MA in 1952, where, according to Keith Bailey, Tozer took him under his wing. Just a few years later, Reidhead became pastor of Simpson's flagship Gospel

Tabernacle. Reidhead also had connections with Bethany Fellowship, a deeper life non-denominational group that was moderately charismatic. Tozer himself also affirmed the reality of the gifts of the Spirit, saying that missing gifts are a "tragedy in the church."[20]

Articles in the 1950s exhibit the early Alliance emphasis of affirming the reality of supernatural gifts and manifestations, but not seeking them more than God.[21] In a rare moment of recovering the earlier Alliance expectancy, Helen Sigrist wrote, "We should not seek the gifts of the Spirit for their own sake, but we should expect that it would be God's will to give them."[22] Such Alliance articles typically acknowledged the reality of the supernatural gifts, but emphasized the need for love, wisdom, balance, purity, the fruit of the Spirit and other spiritual evidences of the filling of the Spirit.[23]

WARY TOLERANCE CONTINUES

With continued openness also came repeated cautions, even from those who were quite open to charismatic manifestations. In 1940 W. T. MacArthur repeated the comment of a Pentecostal leader who admitted that there is much egotism among tongue-speakers.[24] F. H. Rossiter, who had been involved in the 1907 revival and had even invited Pentecostal evangelist Frank Bartleman to his church, cautioned against counterfeit healings and miracles, quoting Jessie Penn-Lewis.[25] Along with MacMillan's interest in Penn-Lewis' writings,[26] the Alliance at this time seemed to lean more toward her more distrustful position on spiritual gifts and manifestations than did Simpson and earlier Alliance leaders.

In 1946 another significant departure from the early Alliance viewpoint can be observed. An article in *The Alliance Weekly* by Panton (who, as mentioned earlier, in the 1920s had spoken against Bosworth's tongues experience) compared the tongues experience of British Pentecostal A. A. Boddy to mechanical inspiration of a demonic nature.[27] Boddy was a good friend of A. B. Simpson, and Simpson would never have permitted such an evaluation of his compatriot's experience to be printed in an Alliance paper. Simpson's friendship with Boddy evidently had been unknown or forgotten some three decades later. Some Alliance leaders during this period were clearly much more suspicious of unusual supernatural manifestations than Simpson and the early Alliance.

DEVELOPMENT OF SPIRITUAL WARFARE THEOLOGY
AND PRACTICE

The C&MA had been involved in spiritual warfare and deliverance ministry almost from its inception, but further developed their concepts and practices during this period of time through a number of pastors and missionaries, and especially through John MacMillan.[28] In 1942 MacMillan began publicly to advocate the 1 John 4:1-3 method of testing spirits by addressing the spirits with the question, "Has Jesus Christ come in the flesh?"[29] In 1948 MacMillan wrote a series of articles in *The Alliance Weekly* on demon possession and oppression.[30]

They were compiled together as a book originally entitled *Modern Demon Possession* (later retitled *Encounter with Darkness*).

In 1951 an extensive three-month exorcism took place at Nyack College, led by MacMillan, and assisted by professors and students who were upper classmen.[31] It served as a training ground in the art of spiritual warfare for many future pastors and missionaries. In 1952 MacMillan encountered a Nyack student who manifested a demonic tongue that had entered as a result of seeking after the gift.[32] This was evidently MacMillan's only experience of casting out a demonically-inspired tongue. However, this incident, compounded with later experiences of friends of the C&MA such as Prairie Bible Institute instructor A. E. Ruark and China Inland Mission missionary George Birch, had a negative effect upon many Alliance people, arousing fear of demonic tongues and shunning any manifestation of tongues.[33] Later ministries of K. Neill Foster (who speaks in tongues) and Gerald McGraw (a student of MacMillan's) encountered a high number of demonic tongues.[34]

Also of interest is MacMillan's embryonic concept of territorial spirits, presaging the Strategic Level Spiritual Warfare movement by decades. As early as 1946, MacMillan wrote several times on an early form of combating territorial ("geographical") spirits, calling the practice "praying geographically."[35] While he was a pioneer of the idea, there is no indication that he would go as far as the current movement in his teaching.

In the early 1950s after the extensive deliverance ministry, Nyack College established a course on spiritual warfare, taught by John MacMillan who had been a pioneer in the field. Nyack was perhaps one of the first post-secondary Christian schools to offer such a course. During the 1940s and 50s MacMillan's pamphlets on *The Authority of the Believer* were frequently published in both evangelical and Pentecostal circles. After MacMillan's death in the 1950s, the influence of MacMillan's teaching on the authority of the believer seems to have diminished somewhat in the C&MA until Keith Bailey (who had been mentored by MacMillan in deliverance ministry) republished his book in 1980 while serving as the publisher of Christian Publications.

THE IMPACT OF THE LATTER RAIN MOVEMENT

Another factor contributing to the distancing of the C&MA from Pentecostals was the "Latter Rain Movement" of 1948 and following. The movement originated in Sasketchewan in February 1948, emphasizing "spiritual gifts, which were to be received by the laying on of hands, in contrast to the old Pentecostal practice of 'tarrying' for the Holy Spirit."[36] This movement was independent of the Pentecostal denominations and especially stressed prophetic revelation, recovery of the offices of apostle and prophet, and the laying on of hands. Among some of its more extreme participants, the exalting of prophetic revelation, end times speculation, and "Manifest Sons of God" teaching developed.[37] Most of the Pentecostal denominations did not accept the movement. The movement had an impact on C&MA churches in northern US and Canada, with the result that many of the churches split.[38]

The Alliance responded by endorsing the reality of the gifts of the Spirit, but also warning of manifestations inspired by the flesh or demonic forces. In September 1948, missionary R. S. Roseberry wrote in *The Alliance Weekly* on "The Need of Spiritual Gifts," which include tongues and prophecy, but also exhorted readers to "covet earnestly the best gifts."[39] Another article by A. E. Adams in December 1948 reaffirmed need for the gifts, but again cautioned that tongues, interpretation, and prophecy may be mixed with the natural.[40] In spite of the negative fallout from the Latter Rain Movement, *The Alliance Weekly* affirmed in 1950 that God "will pour out His Spirit in a tremendous, end-time revival of His Church. . . . we are in the time when the latter rain is due."[41]

LEADERSHIP BY FORMER PENTECOSTAL—BUT ANOTHER MODIFICATION OF BELIEF

Dr. Harry Turner, former Pentecostal missionary and pastor who served in Argentina with Noel Perkin of the Assemblies of God, rose to prominence in the C&MA, becoming an instructor at the C&MA's St. Paul Bible Institute. However, by 1949 he was teaching at the institute that the *baptism with* the Spirit is received at conversion, while maintaining that there is a subsequent *filling* of the Spirit. [42] He then became president of the C&MA in 1954, serving until 1960.

Ironically, with the second consecutive tongues-speaking president, this began a shifting of terminology in the C&MA away from Simpson's language of the "baptism of the Holy Spirit" to a more Reformed/Baptistic view of the terminology. Simpson and the early Alliance had taught that 1 Corinthians 12:13 was baptism *by* the Holy Spirit *into* the Body of Christ, not the same as the baptism *in* or *with* the Spirit by Jesus in Matthew 3:11, which was a definite subsequent experience.[43] Although the terms "baptism of the Spirit" and "filling of the Spirit" continued to be used synonymously in *The Alliance Weekly* during Tozer's editorship in the 1950s, the term "baptism in the Spirit" often came into disuse.

The drift was further evident during the time when the official C&MA doctrinal statement was proposed and debated in the early 1960s. A vocal group within the Alliance wanted to do away with the idea of the filling of the Spirit as a crisis or subsequent experience, but eventually the language of crisis and subsequence was maintained. I remember as a teenager in the C&MA in the 1960s the questions of baptism and filling and subsequence being discussed rather hazily. One of my first mentors, Rev. Roland Gray, Sr., a retired evangelist who started his ministry in the Alliance in the 1920s (working with former Pentecostal Alonzo Horn), told me in 1971 that the Alliance did not teach the baptism in the Spirit like it once did.[44]

A decade later, Mabel Memmott, an Alliance pastor's widow in the Alliance church where I was pastor, told me the exact same thing!—"the Alliance doesn't teach the baptism in the Spirit like it used to." She and another older woman in the church, whose daughter and son-in-law were career missionaries with the C&MA, told me that (even with my more charismatic leanings) I was "the most

Alliance pastor the church had had in years" because I was teaching the baptism in the Spirit and other old Alliance doctrines.

A few years later I left the C&MA for a time and served in pastoral ministry in charismatic churches and as a Christian school administrator. Desiring to come back into the Alliance, I met with the District Licensing and Ordaining Committee where I was living at the time. While they were satisfied with my answers regarding speaking in tongues, some of the committee members questioned my use of the term "baptism in the Spirit." When I gave my scriptural rationale based on what I had learned years earlier in the C&MA, they responded, "We have not heard this interpretation before." Many more recent C&MA leaders seem to be more influenced by Anglican John Stott's interpretation in his book *The Baptism and Fullness of the Holy Spirit*[45] than by historic Alliance teachings and theology. In more recent years, Dr. Keith Bailey has tried to correct this drift by emphasizing the baptism in the Spirit when speaking at District Conferences of the C&MA.

C&MA CONNECTIONS WITH PENTECOSTAL LEADERS

In spite of the modifications and distancing from Pentecostalism as a whole, yet some Alliance people and leaders did maintain friendly relationships with moderate Pentecostals and some charismatic influences.

Humbard Connection. In the 1940s Clement Humbard (brother of Rex Humbard) became credentialed as an evangelist with the C&MA. Alliance evangelist Alonzo Horn had ministered with their father, A. E. Humbard,[46] and the Humbards had published several of McCrossan's books. The Humbard family was well received and ministered frequently in Alliance circles in the 1940s and 50s. In 1948, Earl Sexauer, a tongues-speaking Alliance pastor, invited Rex Humbard to preach a series of revival meetings for the opening services of his new church advertised as "Oakland's Neighborhood Church, the Cathedral of Tomorrow" in Oakland, California. It was one of the Humbards' greatest revival meetings with as many as two hundred people coming to the altar in one night.

A close friendship developed between Sexauer and Humbard. [47] Humbard would later call the church he planted in Akron, Ohio, "The Cathedral of Tomorrow," following Sexauer's lead. Humbard was invited back in 1950 to hold more revival services at Sexauer's church.[48] Just a few months later, Humbard held revival services in Birmingham, Alabama, in conjunction with the C&MA Church, pastored by Glenn Tingley. Humbard considered it one of the greatest meetings they ever had.[49]

Oral Roberts Connection. In the early 1950s, John MacMillan, respected highly among Alliance leaders for his spirit of discernment and his cautiousness openness toward the supernatural, was asked to investigate the young up-and-coming Pentecostal Holiness evangelist Oral Roberts when he conducted an evangelistic and healing crusade in New York City. Even though MacMillan had spoken negatively of some mass healing evangelists in the 1930s, he nonetheless gave his stamp of approval on Oral Roberts' ministry. According to his son Buchanan, a music professor at Nyack College, "He gave him [Oral Roberts] a clean bill of health," reporting, "There is nothing wrong with what he is teaching."[50] While MacMillan would have disagreed with the Pentecostal Holiness view of tongues as the evidence of the baptism in the Spirit, Roberts did not teach it in his crusades (similar to Aimee Semple McPherson, Charles Price and Rex Humbard).[51] MacMillan's assessment seems to have been accepted in the C&MA at that time. C&MA members attended Oral Roberts' evangelistic/healing meetings in North Carolina, Oklahoma, and Texas, and on many other occasions as well.[52]

Kathryn Kuhlman Connection. Kathryn Kuhlman, who had attended Simpson Bible Institute in the 1920s, had ongoing informal connections with the C&MA, for in the summer of 1946 she began evangelistic and healing ministry through the Gospel Tabernacle in Franklin, Pennsylvania. The church had been founded as an interdenominational church by Louis P. Lehman, Sr., a friend of the Alliance and speaker in C&MA meetings. The church later affiliated officially with C&MA.[53] I remember people from the Alliance church in which I grew up in Western Pennsylvania attending her meetings in the 1960s in Youngstown, Ohio, and Pittsburgh. I later attended some of those meetings as well. It is also significant that in 1970 Kathryn Kuhlman supported Alliance missions and church planting in Vietnam.[54]

Jack Hayford Connection. Another notable charismatic connection is the link between Jack Hayford and the C&MA. As a teenager in the late 1940s/early 1950s Hayford attended the Alliance church in Oakland where he heard his pastor, Earl Sexauer, pray in tongues. Hayford speaks warmly of his experience there, which, ironically and providentially, first introduced him to speaking in tongues.[55] Hayford eventually joined the Foursquare Church, and in 2005 was elected at its president. Hayford was the featured speaker at the annual General Council of the C&MA in Anaheim, California in 1993 and shared his experience with Pastor Sexauer.[56]

---

1. "Revival at Nyack," AW, Oct. 12, 1940, 643.

2. Thomas Moseley, "Revival at Nyack," AW, Oct. 10, 1942, 643.

3. "The General Council," AW, June 19, 1943, 286.AW, June 17, 1944, 275.

4. "Spiritual Fervor," AW, Apr. 17, 1948, 242; "Revival in Our Day," AW, Apr. 17, 1948, 242.

5. A. B. Simpson, "The Divine Vision," July 17, 1948, 462.

6. See also "Everywhere Preaching," AW, Feb. 25, 1950, 125.

7. Personal recollections of Dr. Charles Farah, Jr., concerning his father.

8. E. Fred Page, "Gifts of Healing," AW, July 29, 1944, 324-325, 336.

9. A. W. Tozer, *Worship: The Missing Jewel* (Camp Hill, PA: Christian Publications, 1992), 20.

10. H. M. Shuman, "Louis Henry Zweimer," AW, Nov. 4, 1953, 10-11.

11. Bosworth moved to South Africa in 1952 where he ministered until returning to the United States shortly before his death.

12. Branham had been associated with non-Trinitarian oneness Pentecostalism and operated with supernatural knowledge about people, which some regarded as telepathic or mediumistic. Years later he claimed he was a forerunner of the coming of Christ and was shunned by Pentecostals such as Gordon Lindsay.

13. E. Fred Page, "Divine Healing and the Great Commission," AW, Jan. 12, 1944, 52ff.

14. Samuel W. Zwemer, "Mark's Gospel and Paul's Adder," AW, Oct. 18, 1948, 660.

15. Armin R. Gesswein, "This God Is Our God," AW, Oct. 29, 1949, 694.

16. E. R. Carner, "Church Organization and Leadership," AW, Feb. 25, 1950, 128.

17. L. Jay Mapstone, "Searching the Scriptures," AW, Oct. 31, 1956, 6.

18. A. B. Simpson, "Special Spiritual Privileges," AW, Oct. 31, 1956, 6.

19. Edgar A. Truax, "Faith Works by Love," AW, Nov. 14, 1956, 3.

20. A. W. Tozer, *Tragedy in the Church: The Missing Gifts* (Camp Hill, PA: Christian Publications, 1990), 13, 25.

21. L. H. Ziemer, "Evidences of Life in the Spirit," AW, Dec. 16, 1950, 787; L. H. Zeimer, "The Gifts of the Spirit," AW, Feb. 6, 1952, 83-84; L. H. Zeimer, "Spiritual Gifts," AW, Feb. 13, 1952, 101-102, 107.

22. Helen Sigrist, "For Whom Are We Waiting?", AW, Sept. 15, 1954, 6.

23. Vance Havner, "Walking as Christ Walked," AW, Jan. 11, 1947, 24; J. A. MacMillan, "Ambassadors for Christ," AW, Feb. 14, 1948, 98; William J. McNaughton, "The Wisdom of Pentecost," AW, Mar. 31, 1951, 197; "What the Alliance Believes: Some Plain Questions Get Some Plain Answers," AW, Dec. 26, 1951, 805 806; Peter Wiseman, "Pentecostal Poise," AW, Mar. 11, 1953, 5; "The Way of Christian Love," AW, May 20, 1953, 18; William F. Nicholson, "The Unfinished Work of the Spirit: Scriptural Evidences," AW, Apr. 28, 1954, 5; A.W. Tozer, "Let's Face the Facts," AW, Nov. 16, 1955, 2; Don J. Kenyon, "The Way of Christian Love," AW, Dec. 5, 1956, 14; R. M. Kinchloe, "Three Evidences of the Baptism of the Holy Spirit," AW, Mar. 27, 1957, 3.

24. William T. MacArthur, "Gifts and Graces," AW, Feb. 10, 1940, 87.

25. F. H. Rossiter, "Can Satan Perform Miracles?," AW, Dec. 18, 1943, 809-811.

26. King, *A Case Study of a Believer with Authority*, 33-34, 117, 299-302,363-364, 373-374.

27. D. M. Panton, "Is Verbal Inspiration Mechanical?", AW, June 29, 1946, 404.

28. Rev. Fred E. Page, "Authority over Demons," AW, Apr. 17, 1943, 246-247, 250.

29. John A. MacMillan, *The Full Gospel Sunday School Quarterly*, Mar. 29, 1942, 40.

30. John A. MacMillan, "Modern Demon Possession," AW, July 24, 31; Sept 4, 11, 18, 1948.

31. See King, *A Believer with Authority*, 182-190.

32. John A. MacMillan, *Encounter with Darkness* (Harrisburg, PA: Christian Publications, 1980).

33. George A. Birch, *The Deliverance Ministry* (Camp Hill, PA: Horizon House, 1988), 141, 145-170; Dorothy Brotherton, *Quiet Warrior* (Beaverlodge, Alberta: Spectrum Publisher, 1997), 93-107, 153-161.

34. K. Neill Foster, "Glossolalia and the Ruark Procedure: Distinguishing Between True and False Utterances, "*Alliance Academic Review 1997* (Camp Hill, PA: Christian Publications, 1997), 155-168.

35. "Troubled World Waters," AW, Apr. 6, 1946, 211; "God Arms His People," AW, Nov. 9, 1946, 706. Again in April 1948 MacMillan wrote on the concept of territorial spirits. "The Need of the Nations," AW, Apr. 3, 1948, 210.

MODIFIED BELIEF AND PRACTICE—1940s AND 50s

36. R. M. Riss, "Latter Rain Movement," DPCM, 532ff.

37. The "Manifest Sons of God" teaching claimed that in the end times before the Second Coming of Christ an elite group of mature or perfected Christians would emerge.

38. Keith Bailey recalled that it split nearly every Alliance church in Minnesota.

39. R. S. Roseberry, "The Need of Spiritual Gifts," AW, Sept. 18, 1948, 595-596.

40. A. E. Adams, "Diversities of Gifts," AW, Dec. 4, 1948, 771-772, 780.

41. Arthur C. Austin, "The Coming Revival," AW, Apr. 15, 1950, 231-232.

42. Harry L. Turner, *Voice of the Spirit* (St. Paul, MN: St. Paul Bible College, 1949), 37, 38, 66. Another tongue-speaking Alliance missionary, L. Bowring Quick, in 1937 had advanced a similar viewpoint from a more Reformed/Baptistic viewpoint, similar to Third Wave teaching today. See L. Bowring Quick, *The Sevenfold Work of the Holy Spirit* (Christian Publications, 1937).

43. J. Hudson Ballard, "The Spiritual Clinic," AW, Jan 16, 1915, 254; Oswald J. Smith, *The Baptism with the Holy Spirit* (New York, NY: Christian Alliance Publishing Co., 1925), 19.

44. Rev. Gray was my first mentor and like a grandfather to me. He also cautioned about "spurious tongues" and other manifestations. In the 1920s he ministered with former Assemblies of God evangelist Alonzo Horn.

45. John R. W. Stott, *The Baptism and Fullness of the Holy Spirit* (Downers Grove, IL: InterVarsity, 1964).

46. Bob Burke, *Like a Prairie Fire: A History of the Assemblies of God in Oklahoma* (Oklahoma City, OK: Oklahoma District Council of the Assemblies of God, 1994), 24, 58.

47. Rex Humbard, *Miracles in My Life* (Old Tappan, NJ: Fleming H. Revell, 1971), 64-65.

48. Rex Humbard, *To Tell the World* (Englewood Cliffs, NJ: Prentice-Hall, Inc., 1975), 90; see also Humbard, *Miracles in My Life*, 64-65.

49. Ibid., 70-71.

50. Personal conversation with his grandson, Alan MacMillan; see also King, *A Case Study of a Believer with Authority*, 252. Roberts' teaching on the use of doctors and medicine was, in fact, more moderate than that of Simpson. MacMillan's endorsement at that time does not mean that he would necessarily have approved of all Roberts' later teachings and practices.

51. Roberts later left the Pentecostal Holiness denomination and modified his view on tongues somewhat.

52. David Edwin Harrell, *All Things Are Possible: The Healing and Charismatic Revivals in Modern America* (Bloomington, IN: Indiana University Press, 1975), 47. I have talked with other older Alliance members who attended Roberts' meetings in the 1940s and 50s. Alliance members and leaders cooperated with other Pentecostals as well. In 1954 the C&MA in Argentina participated with Pentecostal evangelist Tommy Hicks revival meetings in Buenos Aires. D. D. Bundy, "Argentina," NIDPCM, 24.

53. Warner, 113-122. Warner mentioned to me that he had visited the church during his research and found it had become affiliated with the C&MA.

54. Warner, *Kathryn Kuhlman*, 196-198.

55. Jack Hayford, *The Beauty of Spiritual Language* (Dallas, TX: Word Publishing, 1992), 29, 35.

56. Jack Hayford, "Invading the Impossible," audiotape, 1993 C&MA General Council, June 2, 1993, Anaheim, CA.

TWENTY - ONE

1960s to Present — Mixed Signals and Sparks of Recovery

The Paradox of Both Warmth and Antagonism

Possibly because of Turner's former Pentecostal connections, there seemed in the 1960s to be a warmer relationship between some Alliance leaders and Pentecostals. In his history of the Assemblies of God published in 1961, Brumback wrote concerning current relationships between the Assemblies of God and the C&MA:

> We rejoice that much of the old feeling of antagonism has disappeared. We have reason to believe that the appraisal by Dr. Wilson of the newly born Pentecostal Movement no longer stands 'as the crystalized utterance of the Society.' God . . . has begun to give us favor with our Alliance brethren who have worked closely with many of our leaders and ministers in united efforts. While still unwilling to concede the scripturalness of our "evidence" doctrine, most of them are probably able to go somewhat beyond Dr. Wilson's faint praise: "I am willing to concede that there is probably something of God in it somewhere."[1]

However, that was not uniformly true throughout the C&MA. A mixture of belief and practice could be found among Alliance churches. For instance, the Alliance Academy for missionary kids in West Africa routinely regarded tongues as demonic and burned Kathryn Kuhlman's books.[2] Interestingly enough, during the same period of time people from the C&MA church in which I grew up in Western Pennsylvania were attending Kathryn Kuhlman meetings without reproach. In 1962 a Pentecostal writer commented about the C&MA: "Once again in recent years in some of the Alliance mission fields there are Pentecostal experiences in evidence including the speaking with tongues. This is causing some consternation in the hearts of certain of their missionaries."[3] This seems to indicate that there was both openness on the part of some and alarm on the part of others.

THE "SEEK NOT, FORBID NOT" STANCE

With charismatic experiences re-emerging and various opinions being expressed both pro and con, it is not surprising that the C&MA wanted to make a measured response. Therefore, in 1963 the "seek not, forbid not" stance towards tongues became formalized in the C&MA through an official statement entitled "Where We Stand on the Revived Tongues Movement," reaffirming the gifts, but not tongues as the evidence of the filling of the Spirit or the plan of God for all.[4] While some erroneously thought the motto "seek not, forbid not" was originated by Simpson, others mistakenly concluded that it was formulated by Tozer.[5] As we have seen, the motto really was coined in the 1930s, based on earlier concepts from Simpson, but became interpreted in a passive stance, lacking the expectancy of charismatic gifts expressed by Simpson and early Alliance leaders.

One of the significant statements of the document, which has gone by virtually unnoticed in the midst of the controversy is the clause, "it [tongues] *may be present in the normal Christian assembly* as a sovereign bestowal of the Holy Spirit upon such as He wills" (italics mine). For the first time in more than three decades, Alliance leaders acknowledged that tongues could have a place in the "normal Christian assembly." While it was not a return to the early Alliance position that tongues should have a place in every church, it was a movement back in that direction.

Alliance Witness Responses
Since the *Alliance Witness* was the official publishing organ of the C&MA, its public pronouncements were considered the official Alliance word on the matter. The "Seek Not Forbid Not" statement was printed in the *Alliance Witness* in 1963. With the charismatic movement emerging on the scene, charismatic gifts could no longer be downplayed or ignored in the Alliance. Several articles sought to deal with the issue as it was arising. In 1966 *Alliance Witness* editor V. Raymond Edman wrote an article "Spiritual Discernment: Are Tongues Divine or Devilish?" Drawing upon his experience and observations as a missionary, pastor, and his 25-year tenure as president of Wheaton College, Edman concluded similar to early Alliance leaders, "The gift of tongues can be of divine or demonic origin, or of neither."[6]

A reprint of Simpson's 1897 article on the reality of the gifts and encouraging exercise of the gifts (including tongues and prophecy) appeared in the *Alliance Witness* in February 1967.[7] It was especially significant because it printed, without comment, Simpson's positive statement regarding tongues and prophecy: "Fear not to speak the message which the Holy Spirit has burned into your soul for the quickening and the rousing of your soul. It will be a word in season for some weary soul. And if you have, in some simple form, the old gift of tongues welling up in your heart, some Hallelujah which you could not put into articulate speech, some unutterable cry of love or joy, out with it!" This was the most positive statement regarding speaking in tongues that had been published by the Alliance in many years.

Another article in May 1967 entitled "Tongues in the Church" reiterated the sixty-year long stance that tongues is not the only evidence of the baptism in the Spirit and that "it is not ours to seek a particular gift but to receive the gift which He, the Holy Spirit, sees best to give us."[8] I remember as a teenager in the Alliance that all of the gifts of the Spirit were affirmed as real, but there was also a great fear of "spurious" manifestations that could be demonic. That fear seemed to keep people from wanting to experience or see the exercise of such gifts.

REVIVALS OF THE 1960S AND 1970S

The Indonesian Revival. The books *Like a Mighty Wind* and its sequel *Gentle Breeze of Jesus* by Mel Tari recount the Indonesian revival of 1965-1969 with all gifts of the Spirit and many supernatural manifestations and miracles occurring.[9] This revival also impacted the C&MA. Native Alliance pastor Franz Selan was the brother-in-law of Indonesian revival leader Mel Tari, and witnessed many of the manifestations and miracles, such as visions, healings, casting out demons (one in which a serpent actually came out of the mouth of the person being delivered), raising the dead, water turned to wine, and walking on water.[10] Selan testified, "Almost every miracle mentioned in the Bible was seen and experienced by us."[11]

In the late 1960s, the Indonesian revival had spread to Vietnam. A personal friend of mine, who was a Southern Baptist military chaplain at the time, received the baptism in the Spirit with tongues at the International Alliance Church in Saigon. However, according to my friend, the pastor was not too happy with all that was going on, especially when some began to teach tongues as the initial evidence of the baptism in the Spirit.[12]

Miraculous Evangelistic Campaigns of Richard Harvey. In the late 1960s, Alliance evangelist Richard Harvey was preaching an evangelistic campaign in his son John Harvey's C&MA church in Canberra, Australia, and held a healing service the first night. A young married woman born with one leg shorter than the other had been in constant pain all her life. When she was prayed for, the pain was gone and a scheduled surgery was cancelled. The short leg gradually grew longer.[13]

Harvey's ministry included many dramatic healings, miracles and power encounters. He remarked, "We have seen the Holy Spirit work as He did in the book of Acts." Among them, a couple had been told they could not have children. Harvey prayed for them, and soon they were able to conceive and a healthy child was born to them. Harvey also ministered in the wake of the Indonesian revival accompanying Franz Selan, with many conversions resulting, and received prophetic direction, was involved in a deliverance ministry of casting out demons, and experienced supernatural divine protection.[14]

The 1970 Asbury College Revival. In February 1970 revival burst forth upon Asbury College, with many making confession of sins, rededicating their lives to Christ and being filled with the Spirit. Asbury College and the C&MA have had a cordial relationship through the years, and many C&MA students attended Asbury College, so it is not surprising that the revival overflowed into the C&MA in subsequent months.[15]

The Asbury revival was not a charismatic revival *per se*, but many people did receive tongues and other gifts as an overflow of the revival, although this was downplayed by Asbury officials.[16] My own baptism in the Spirit and later gift of tongues was as a result of this overflow, after a ministry team of Asbury students testified of the revival at Asbury with hands raised high at the C&MA church I was attending while in college in Pennsylvania. I later ministered together at a Mahaffey camp meeting with some Asbury students who had experienced tongues and other charismatic manifestations. In 1974 Asbury Seminary president Frank B. Stanger wrote a book entitled *The Gifts of the Spirit*, published by the C&MA publishing house, in which he cautioned against the two extremes of "charisphobia" and "charismania."[17]

The 1971-1972 Vietnam Revival. The stage for revival was set in South Vietnam as charismatic leaders such as Kathryn Kuhlman, Oral Roberts, and Corrie Ten Boom all visited the Alliance mission in the late 1960s and early 1970s.[18] In 1970 Kathryn Kuhlman met with Alliance missionaries Garth Hunt and Jim Livingston. She donated $250,000 to Alliance missions, also providing educational funds for the children of C&MA missionary Ed Thompson who was martyred in Vietnam.[19]

Missionaries Garth and Betty Hunt and Jim and Jean Livingston began praying for a fresh infilling of the Spirit. By June 1971 at the annual field conference in Saigon other missionaries were also seeking God for revival and a fresh touch from the Lord. Featured speaker William E. Allen, pastor of the Alliance church in Mansfield, Ohio, shared about how his church was impacted by the 1970 Canadian revival. Dutch Alliance missionary Teo van der Welle, who had experienced tongues, felt impressed by God to fly to Saigon to provide counsel and prayer. Missionaries Charles Long and Bob McNeel experienced holy laughter as they prayed and praised God, and McNeel was healed of a peptic ulcer. In the fall, missionary Orrel Steinkamp was teaching a course on the history of revivals at the Nhatrang Theological Seminary. The students were stirred to pray for revival.[20]

About the same time, at the urging of Jonathan Goforth's daughter, young C&MA evangelist Ravi Zacharias preached 2-5 sermons a day in Vietnam. Students in the seminary responded with deep repentance, restoration of broken fellowship, renewal of desire to reach people for Christ. Several weeks later revival broke out in the Alliance Seminary on Friday, December 3.[21] Steinkamp's book, *The Holy Spirit in Vietnam*, recounts the ensuing revival, including dreams, visions, healings, tongues, miracles, exorcisms, an angelic choir, tremors, resurrection from the dead, shaking, falling under the power of the Spirit, visions of soldiers in white guarding Christian villages, and other supernatural phenomena. Steinkamp emphasized that these manifestations were not sought, but happened spontaneously.[22] Many Alliance missionaries spoke in tongues, including Garth Hunt and Jim Livingston.[23] In 1973 the revivals in Indonesia, Cambodia, and Vietnam were recounted in a special Alliance publication reporting on Alliance missions.[24] This was probably the most similar revival to the early Alliance outpourings, but was not reported as widely or fully in Alliance circles as the early revivals.

Revival Spills Over into Dalat School, Malaysia. In March 1972 Teo van der Welle spoke at the spiritual emphasis week at the Alliance's Dalat School in Penang, Malaysia. Sharing about the gifts of the Spirit, he encouraged the missionaries and students to ask God for "power tools." Several spoke in tongues and manifested other gifts such as words of wisdom and knowledge, prophecy, and interpretation of tongues. Missionary nurse Joy Boese recounted of her experience of tongues, "There welled up deep within me a fresh spring of spiritual water—bubbling and bubbling. . . . Everything seemed to have come into a deeper dimension." One student who was an MK (Missionary Kid) from Vietnam spoke in perfect Thai, though she had never learned the language.[25]

The 1973 West African Revival. In surprising contrast to the vitriolic anti-Pentecostal sentiment on the West Africa C&MA mission field in the 1960s, in August 1973, Assemblies of God French missionary Jacques Giraud teamed up with the C&MA in Ivory Coast for an evangelistic and healing campaign. Many power encounters of healings and exorcisms resulted in conversions. Among the miraculous occurrences, a blind man received his sight and a demonized hunchback was delivered and healed.[26]

RESPONSES TO THE CHARISMATIC MOVEMENT
IN THE 1970S AND 1980S

Openness and Tension. The "Seek Not, Forbid Not" statement of 1963 was a recognition of the emerging charismatic movement, or what the statement called "the revived tongues movement," and many of the articles in the *Alliance Witness* on the gifts of the Spirit were in response to this pervasive movement. In the 1970s, the charismatic movement was embraced by some C&MA churches with varied responses. Some people and churches left the C&MA when they found restrictions too confining or faced too much opposition. Some churches and pastors went beyond the Alliance guidelines and either left or were forced out of the Alliance. Others functioned within Alliance guidelines and were able to remain. Still others maintained a position similar to the early C&MA, but encountered opposition because of the drift that had occurred in the Alliance. As a result, some pastors, people, and churches who would have been accepted by early Alliance leaders had to leave the Alliance. I was one of those who wanted to stay in the Alliance but in the early 1980s found it difficult to minister within the C&MA for a time.

C&MA African-American pastor Frederick K. C. Price received baptism in the Spirit with tongues in 1970 and began teaching the Word of Faith message, influenced by Kenneth Hagin.[27] In 1972 he spoke at the Pittsburgh Charismatic Conference and also at the Alliance Church where I was serving as Youth and Assistant Pastor. In 1973 Price, who had become popular as a Word of Faith teacher, left the C&MA and founded Crenshaw Christian Center in Los Angeles.

In 1972 an editorial in *Alliance Witness* spoke of openness to the gifts of the Spirit, including tongues and interpretation, saying, "If the church of Jesus Christ recovers the apostolic emphasis on the gifts of the Spirit, we believe the result will be an era of church growth unparalleled since the first century."[28] This seemed to signal openness to the burgeoning charismatic movement.

Advocating the Testing of Tongues. It appeared that the Alliance was endeavoring to maintain that historic balance of openness and caution, avoiding the extremes of charisphobia" and "charismania," as Stanger's book had counseled. However, in 1974 significant serious admonitions were published in the *Alliance Witness*, which unwittingly tilted the balance toward "charisphobia" in the Alliance. Dr. Gerald McGraw, professor at the C&MA-affiliated Toccoa College, wrote an article in the *Alliance Witness*, declaring that although there could be genuine manifestations of tongues, tongues need to be tested because 80-90% of those he had tested have been false. Having been a student of MacMillan, he advocated the 1 John 4:1-3 method of testing by addressing the spirits with the question, "Has Jesus Christ come in the flesh?"[29] This procedure became used more broadly, and in many places in the Alliance became the litmus test for determining the authenticity of tongues.

This was followed in 1975 by C&MA evangelist K. Neill Foster's book *Help! I Believe in Tongues: The Third View of Tongues* (later retitled *The Third View of Tongues*), in which he tells of his own personal experience of speaking in tongues. At the same time, he warned that he had also cast out dozens of demonic tongues of those seeking a manifestation or an evidence, using the 1 John 4:1-3 methodology of testing spirits.[30] While still warning of the dangers of spurious tongues, his approach was more positive and moderate than McGraw's, advocating a "gentle maybe" attitude toward tongues. The use of the 1 John 4 testing procedure has become commonplace among deliverance ministry in the C&MA. Many ministers in the Alliance who speak in tongues and are also involved in deliverance ministry have encountered demonic tongues.

However, there is disagreement within the C&MA on the validity and extent of use of the 1 John 4 testing procedure. C&MA minister Albert Runge disavows the testing procedure, determining that it is unreliable because one cannot trust information gleaned from conversing with demons.[31] Keith Bailey, who himself speaks in tongues, has encountered more than a dozen demonic tongues and uses the procedure generally but not exclusively. He disagrees with some of McGraw's conclusions and extensiveness of use of the procedure and does not believe that all experiences of tongues need to be tested, although he is concerned about the possibility of a large number of spurious tongues in the Pentecostal and charismatic movements. Another C&MA missionary and professor with an extensive deliverance ministry makes use of the procedure, but believes McGraw's application of the procedure to be prone to manipulation and skewed conclusions.

SIGNIFICANT STUDIES ON *CHARISMATA* IN THE ALLIANCE

Evearitt's 1976 Survey. In 1976 Daniel Evearitt, for his Masters thesis at Nyack College, conducted a representative survey of ministers in the C&MA regarding beliefs and practices of spiritual gifts in Alliance churches. He found that 53% of C&MA churches surveyed had someone who speaks in tongues and 8% had someone who has gift of interpretation.[32] Because more than half of Alliance churches had someone who speaks in tongues, yet few had the gift of interpretation, he concluded (typical of a passive "seek not" view), "Someone is seeking rather than waiting on the Holy Spirit for their gift or else the Spirit is giving this gift more liberally in these days."[33] From his perspective, this appeared to be an unusually high percentage of tongues experiences for Alliance churches. His conclusion demonstrates how far the C&MA attitude had departed from the early Alliance position in which it was expected that every church should have some who speak in tongues. Simpson and early Alliance leaders would bemoan the fact that nearly half of Alliance churches have no people who speak in tongues

C&MA VP's Paper on the Charismatic Movement. In 1977 Dr. Keith Bailey, Vice President of North American Ministries of the C&MA, who came into the Alliance as a tongue-speaker in 1944, presented a paper at a C&MA District Superintendents' Conference, entitled "Dealing with the Charismatic in Today's Church." In it, he maintained some distance from the charismatic movement, but also affirmed the Alliance belief in the gifts. He advocated allowing speaking in tongues and interpretation to take place in Alliance meetings, which to his knowledge he had not seen in his more than thirty years in the Alliance. He estimated that about 20% of C&MA pastors and missionaries speak in tongues.[34] Bailey questioned the practice of singing in tongues without interpretation and the terminology of "prayer language." He did not seem to be familiar with the fact that singing in tongues without interpretation had at least occurred occasionally in Alliance history. His counsel to allow tongues and interpretation in Alliance meetings has seemed to gone unheeded in most C&MA circles since then, though the tide may slowly be turning.

Other Studies and Presentations. In May 1979 missiologist and church growth expert Donald McGavran spoke at the C&MA General Council, Lincoln, Nebraska on power encounters, entitled "Signs and Wonders: A Way to Salvation." John Wimber, founder of Vineyard Ministries, remarked that a transcript of this message "propelled me a few years ago to begin to research the arena of Signs and Wonders."[35]

Alliance pastor John Packo's book *Find and Use Your Spiritual Gifts* was published in 1980. While acknowledging the reality of all supernatural gifts of the Spirit, Packo maintained the more wary tolerance stance toward tongues, citing the studies of Foster and others about the high percentage of demonic tongues tested in their ministries.[36]

As cited earlier, in 1984 a Ph.D. Dissertation by Ernest Wilson, an Alliance minister who had served in the C&MA since 1938, addressed the observation and problem of modification and historical drift in Alliance teaching and practice, including teaching and practices regarding healing, sanctification and the gifts of the Spirit, and modification from "full gospel" to "the gospel"[37]

C&MA historian John Sawin brought to light Simpson's diary and some of the early Alliance charismatic history through his paper "The Response and Attitude of Dr. A.B. Simpson and the Christian and Missionary Alliance to the Tongues Movement of 1906-1920" presented at the Society for Pentecostal Studies (SPS) conference in 1986.[38]

Nienkirchen's Controversial Book. In 1992, Charles Nienkirchen, a professor at the C&MA's Canadian Theological Seminary, published his book *A.B. Simpson and the Pentecostal Movement.* Expanding upon Sawin's research, this was a landmark book in several ways:

- Apart from Sawin's SPS presentation, this book was the first published study to document C&MA charismatic history (aside from some briefer Pentecostal accounts of some of the early C&MA).

- It was controversial because Nienkirchen claimed Simpson was a seeker of tongues and Tozer was a revisionist advocating a new policy of "seek not, forbid not."

- Whereas Sawin's paper was basically neutral, laying down historical facts, Nienkirchen reinforced and advanced Pentecostal/charismatic claims regarding the early C&MA.

- As a result, the book received mixed reviews in C&MA circles, but, in particular, had a negative effect among C&MA leaders who considered it revisionist.

Nienkirchen's study pioneered rediscovering the C&MA's charismatic history, although, as I have shown in this research, he was mistaken about some of his conclusions about Simpson as a seeker of tongues and Tozer as a revisionist.[39]

RE-EMERGENCE OF SPIRITUAL WARFARE AND POWER ENCOUNTERS

Since at least the 1970s spiritual warfare and power encounters have been a part of teaching at Alliance colleges, and experienced frequently on mission fields. In the 1990s, German Pentecostal evangelist Reinhard Bonnke teamed up with

C&MA missions in Africa for crusades involving power encounters with healing and deliverances.

In 1998 K. Neill Foster and myself co-authored the book *Binding and Loosing: Exercising Authority over the Dark Powers* published by Christian Publications, the Alliance publishing house, in which we presented an in-depth, balanced approach to the practice. In 2001 the book *Sorting Out the Supernatural* by K. Neill Foster was published, affirming the supernatural manifestations of the Spirit, but cautioning the need for discernment of counterfeit manifestations, and differing from the historic C&MA position on the fallibility of prophecy. Also in 2001 the biography of John A. MacMillan and his teachings and practices of spiritual warfare was authored by myself. The prayer movement in the C&MA, led by Jon Graf, Fred Hartley, and others has paralleled the prayer and spiritual warfare movement in charismatic and Third Wave circles, though endeavoring to avoid the excesses of those movements.

SPARKS OF RECOVERY IN THE 1990S AND NEW MILLENNIUM

In the 1990s, some of the newer C&MA churches have adopted more contemporary, charismatic-like worship styles in their church services. Numerous pastors have been licensed and ordained in the C&MA from charismatic and Pentecostal backgrounds—Assemblies of God, Oral Roberts University, Vineyard Ministries, Rhema Bible Training Center, and other independent charismatic/Pentecostal churches. Reportedly, in the early 1990s at a Pacific Northwest District C&MA retreat, some people fell under power of the Spirit.[40]

Renewed openness to Pentecostal/charismatic leaders has been seen with charismatic leaders featured at C&MA Annual General Councils. Jack Hayford spoke at C&MA General Council in Anaheim, California and shared about his experience in the C&MA and his pastor who spoke in tongues. His book on tongues entitled *The Beauty of Spiritual Language* was openly sold at the conference. In 1996 Rev. John Guest, a charismatic Episcopalian evangelist spoke at C&MA General Council in Indianapolis, Indiana. In the 2002 General Council in Nashville, Pentecostal leader Jim Cymbala of the Brooklyn Tabernacle was a featured speaker.

In 1999, Dr. Ron Walborn, a C&MA Preacher's Kid from Western Pennsylvania with connections to the Vineyard and Third Wave movement, became Chairman of Pastoral Ministries Dept. at Nyack College. In 2001, an African-American Pentecostal minister (Church of God, Cleveland, Tennessee) served as campus pastor at Nyack College. Some professors at Nyack College and Alliance Theological Seminary consider A.B. Simpson a "Third-Waver," are open to the Toronto Blessing movement, and believe the C&MA has succumbed to rationalistic contextualism of American religious culture, especially regarding the supernatural and power encounter. C&MA leadership, located in Colorado Springs, has dialogued with Ted Haggard, pastor of the charismatic megachurch New Life Church. Haggard gained respectability from the evangelical community, serving as President of the National Association of Evangelicals and listed among the top 25 most influential evangelical leaders.

The year of 2005 was a pivotal year toward turning the C&MA back toward its roots of greater openness and expectancy of the supernatural. The Board of Directors drafted a new more positive statement on spiritual gifts to replace the "Seek Not, Forbid Not" statement of 1963, entitled "Spiritual Gifts: Expectation without Agenda."[41] This new statement is more in line with the early C&MA expectancy of the supernatural with discernment.

The renewal movement "Rekindle the Flame Gathering" coordinated by Alliance pastor Brad Bush and Jon Graf, Director of C&MA Prayer Mobilization, scheduled for May 23-25, 2006 in West Lafayette, Indiana is a step toward recovery of the early Alliance roots. New C&MA President Gary Benedict reaffirmed that the Alliance is the only non-Pentecostal denomination that publicly affirms the reality of the gifts of the Spirit. He has noted that people who are looking for the balance between *charismania* and *charisphobia* have remarked, "This is what we have been looking for! Where have you been all my life?" Although there remain pockets of resistance, the C&MA seems poised in the 21st century to return more fully to its early charismatic roots and reestablish balanced, moderate charismatic theology and practice.

---

1. Brumback, *Suddenly . . . from Heaven*, 95.

2. As recounted to me by an Oral Roberts University faculty member. She was the daughter of Open Bible Standard missionaries and was enrolled at the Alliance Academy during the same time of the child abuse at the Academy. Although she was not personally physically or sexually abused, she endured emotional abuse for her Pentecostal background and was aware of some of the other problems. It is especially ironic to note that in the 1930s the C&MA and the Open Bible Standard Churches worked cooperatively in missions.

3. Atter, 149-150.

4. "Where We Stand on the Revived Tongues Movement," *The Alliance Witness*, May 1, 1963, 5ff.; "Seek Not, Forbid Not" brochure, New York, NY: The Christian and Missionary Alliance, 1963.

5. Nienkirchen, 131-140.

6. V. Raymond Edman, "Spiritual Discernment: Are Tongues Divine or Devilish?," *The Alliance Witness*, Mar.2, 1966, 5-7, 19.

7. A. B. Simpson, "The Worship and Fellowship of the Church," *The Alliance Witness*, Feb. 1, 1967, 3-4, 16; reprinted from Simpson, "Worship and Fellowship of the Church," CMAW, Feb. 9, 1898, 125.

8. Foster C. Trout, "Tongues in the Church," *The Alliance Witness*, May 24, 1967, 5-6.

9. Mel Tari with Cliff Dudley, *Like a Mighty Wind* (Carol Stream, IL: Creation House, 1971); Mel and Nona Tari, *The Gentle Breeze of Jesus* (Harrison, AR: New Leaf Press, 1971).

10. Franz Selan, "God of Miracles," in Smalley, comp., *Alliance Missions in Indonesia*, 3:2223-2224; William W. Kerr, "Indonesian Postscript," *The Alliance Witness*, May 23, 1973, 19; Tari, *Like a Mighty Wind*. See also Harvey, *70 Years of Miracles*, 169-172; Mrs. R. K. Smith, "Miracles in Indonesia," *The Alliance Witness*, July 3, 1968, 15-17. For an extensive evaluation of the pros and cons of the impact of the Indonesian revival, see Peter R. Nanfelt, "Indonesian Awakening: Revival or Ruse?," in Smalley, *Alliance Missions in Indonesia*,3:2219-2222.

11. Selan, 2224.

12. Testimony of a personal friend, Rev. Calvin McCarter.

13. Harvey, 166-167.

14. Ibid., 156, 167, 169-183.

15. See "Asbury Aftermath," *The Alliance Witness*, Apr. 29, 1970, 5.

16. I personally knew Asbury students who had spoken in tongues, some of them from the C&MA. Asbury leaders were not pleased with the more Pentecostal beliefs that also began to spread, such as tongues as the evidence of the baptism in the Spirit. Reportedly, at that time Asbury officials forbade speaking in tongues or propagation of Pentecostal beliefs on campus.

17. F. B. Stanger, *The Gifts of the Spirit* (Harrisburg, PA: Christian Publications, 1974), 21.

18. Jean Livingston, *Tears for the Smaller Dragon* (Camp Hill, PA: Christian Publications, 1997), 127.

19. Warner, *Kathryn Kuhlman*, 196-198.

20. Livingston, 127-131; Charles E. Long, *To Vietnam with Love* (Camp Hill, PA: Christian Publications, 1995),152-159.

21. John D. Woodbridge, ed., *Ambassadors for Christ* (Chicago, IL: Moody Press, 1994), 328; Long, 157-159.

22. Orrel Steinkamp, *The Holy Spirit in Vietnam* (Carol Stream, IL: Creation House, 1973); see also "Seedtime and Harvest," *For the Lord of the Harvest: Bringing It All Together* (Harrisburg, PA: Christian Publications, [1973]), 5-6; Long, 162-171, 178-179. See also, Orrel Steinkamp, "Revival at Nhatrang Bible Institute, "*Vietnam Today*, Summer 1972, 8; Helen Evans, "Revival Spreads in the Highlands," *Vietnam Today*, Winter 1972, 8.

23. Jim Livingston was on my original Licensing and Ordaining Committee for the Southwestern District of the C&MA in 1979, and shared with the committee that my beliefs and experiences regarding tongues were just the same as his.

24. "Seedtime and Harvest," 4-7.

25. Joy Boese, *Adventures in Learning to Trust God* (West Conshohocken, PA: Infinity Publishing, 2005, 49-55.

26. John Wimber, "Studies in the Miraculous: Case Histories," *Signs, Wonders and Church Growth* (Placentia, CA: Vineyard Ministries, Intl., 1984), 5-6; see also M. Fred Poling, "It Is Happening in the Ivory Coast," *The Alliance Witness*, Sept. 26, 1973, 14-15.

27. G. W. Gohr, "Price, Frederick K. C.", DPCM, 727.

28. Robert Cowles, "What Happened to Spiritual Gifts?," *The Alliance Witness*, Aug. 30, 1972, 23.

29. Gerald E. McGraw, "Tongues Should Be Tested," *The Alliance Witness*, June 5, 1974.

30. K. Neill Foster, *The Third View of Tongues* [originally published as *Help! I Believe in Tongues: The Third View of Tongues* (Minneapolis, MN: Bethany House Publishers, 1975)].

31. Albert Runge, "Exorcism: A Satanic Ploy?", *His Dominion* 8, no. 4 (Spring 1987), 13-14.

32. Daniel J. Evearitt, "The Gifts of the Holy Spirit and Their Nature and Presence in Churches of the Christian and Missionary Alliance in the United States," Masters of Professional Studies Thesis, Nyack College, Nyack, NY, 1976. See also Daniel Evearitt, "The Social Aspects of the Ministry and Writings of Albert B. Simpson," M. A. Thesis, Drew University, 1976.

33. Ibid., 142.

34. Keith M. Bailey, "Dealing with the Charismatic in Today's Church." A paper presented at the District Superintendent's Conference of The Christian and Missionary Alliance, Feb. 28-Mar. 2, 1977, Nyack, New York.

35. John Wimber, "Introduction," *Signs, Wonders and Church Growth*.

36. John E. Packo, *Find and Use Your Spiritual Gifts* (Camp Hill, PA: Christian Publications, 1980), 59-63. In a further deviation from early Alliance teaching, Packo claimed tongues is not a sign of the baptism

of the Holy Spirit (p. 59). To the contrary as we have seen in this study, Simpson and other early Alliance leaders acknowledged that tongues could be *a* sign of the baptism in the Spirit, just not *the* sign.

37. Ernest Wilson, *The Christian and Missionary Alliance: Development and Modifications of Its Original Objectives*. Ph.D. Dissertation, New York University, 1984.

38. John W. Sawin, "The Response and Attitude of Dr. A. B. Simpson and the Christian and Missionary Alliance to the Tongues Movement of 1906-1920." Paper delivered at the Society for Pentecostal Studies, Costa Mesa, CA, Nov. 15, 1986.

39. See Paul L. King, "A Critique of Charles Nienkirchen's Book *A. B. Simpson and the Pentecostal Movement*," *Alliance Academic Review* (Camp Hill, PA: Christian Publications, 2000), 101ff.; Paul L. King, "'Seek Not, Forbid Not': The Christian and Missionary Alliance Position on Glossolalia," *Wesleyan Theological Journal*, Fall 2005.

40. Testimony of two C&MA ministers.

41. C&MA Board of Directors, "Spiritual Gifts: Expectation without Agenda," 2005. See on C&MA website www.cmalliance.org.

Part Five

ANALYSIS OF EARLY C&MA
CHARISMATIC BELIEF
AND PRACTICE

TWENTY-TWO

EARLY C&MA CHARISMATIC THEOLOGY

As we have seen, in the late 1800s A. B. Simpson and the fledging Christian and Missionary Alliance began to develop a charismatic theology of the Holy Spirit. That theology continued to develop and provided a distinctive charismatic theology in the midst of contrary winds of Pentecostal theology. An entire book could be devoted to describing and analyzing the distinctive charismatic theology of the C&MA, but space permits only a cursory summary here. The distinctions between Pentecostal and C&MA charismatic theology were based on the foundation of biblical hermeneutics (principles of biblical interpretation).

C&MA INTERPRETATION OF CHARISMATIC SCRIPTURES

Both the C&MA and evidential tongues people claimed their view was scriptural and the other view was unscriptural. The issue really was a matter of hermeneutics. Assemblies of God scholar Michael Girolimon claims that Simpson "overlooked references to tongues in Acts passages dealing with the Spirit baptism, and chose instead to address the issue more in the context of all the gifts in 1 Corinthians."[1]

However, Simpson and other Alliance leaders were not overlooking the tongues passages in connection with Spirit baptism in Acts, but rather were looking at the broad picture of Spirit-filling throughout Acts. They recognized that in some cases tongues did accompany the filling of the Spirit, but not in all cases. Whereas Pentecostals took a few citations as the absolute repeatable pattern, the Alliance hermeneutic took a broader view of all passages on Spirit-filling (some of which did not mention tongues), and thus could not impose an absolute pattern on the text. They would have viewed the classical Pentecostal position as *eisegesis*, reading into the text more than the text says. Ironically, they would have concurred with Pentecostal scholar Gordon Fee's interpretative counsel not to "confuse normalcy with normativeness," saying that "the precedent does not establish a norm for specific action."[2]

The Alliance hermeneutic also viewed 1 Corinthians 12:11 ("distributing just as He wills") as a controlling principle, understanding that gifts are given by the sovereignty of God; therefore, while tongues may be desirable, it is not necessarily or clearly God's plan for all to speak in tongues.[3] This is similar to Third Wave and Catholic charismatic beliefs, and many other evangelical leaders who emphasize the sovereignty of the gifts. As Simpson wrote, gifts "are not determined by our wishes but His will."[4] Tongues were to be expected as *normal* in every Alliance congregation, but not necessarily *normative* for every believer. In many congregations and missions, the majority of Alliance people in a particular location did speak in tongues in the early days, but it was not expected that all would or should.

The Alliance also had difficulties with the hermeneutics of Pentecostals who believed in "spontaneous theology," in which "some knowledge is directly imparted" by the inspiration of God.[5] Such spontaneous theology "was to take precedence over systematic theology because it represented God directing spiritual understanding to 'proceed spontaneously without labor or study from the hidden fullness of His divine nature.'"[6] Others were always looking for a "deeper sense" in Scripture, claiming, "There are many scriptures that are not only double-barreled but triple-barreled."[7] While Alliance leaders recognized that some Scriptures could have a deeper sense, they were cautious about new interpretations that went beyond Scripture.

LATTER RAIN TEACHING

The C&MA did accept a hermeneutic based on Peter's quotation and application of Joel's prophecy to the outpouring of the Holy Spirit on Pentecost (Joel 2:28-32; Acts 2:16-21). The Alliance, as did many evangelical leaders of that day, extended the application to the former and latter rains mentioned in the preceding verses in Joel 2:23-27, as a further fulfillment of the New Testament church age. As we have seen, Simpson, W. C. Stevens, G. P. Pardington, D. W. Myland, May Mabette Anderson, and a host of other Alliance leaders taught a form of "Latter Rain" theology, that God was pouring out a greater latter rain before the Second Coming of Christ. Simpson wrote in 1907: "We may . . . conclude that we are to expect a great outpouring of the Holy Spirit in connection with the second coming of Christ and one as much greater than the Pentecostal effusion of the Spirit as the rains of autumn were greater than the showers of spring. . . . We are in the time . . . when we may expect this latter rain."[8] The C&MA affirmed that the Latter Rain was falling, but did not accept all Latter Rain teaching, which they believed sometimes went beyond the clear teaching of Scripture.

C&MA VIEW OF THE BAPTISM IN THE SPIRIT

The baptism in (or, "of") the Spirit was viewed by the C&MA as a sanctifying experience, not in the Wesleyan perfectionistic sense of eradication of the old man, nor in the Keswickean sense of suppression of the old man, but rather cleansing and transformation by the indwelling presence of Christ. It was recognized as both a crisis experience at a point in time, but also a progressive experience, intensifying the Holy Spirit's work of purifying and imparting holiness.[9]

The early C&MA believed in a trinity of baptisms: (1) baptism by the Holy Spirit into the body of Christ (1 Cor. 12:13), joined with Christ at new birth, (2) baptism in water (Acts 2:38), and (3) baptism by Jesus in or with the Holy Spirit (Matt. 3:11).[10] The baptism in the Spirit was viewed as subsequent to conversion, although it could, upon occasion, occur at virtually the same time. Some later Alliance leaders would teach a more Reformed/Baptistic view (also the view of many Third Wavers today), identifying the "baptism" in the Spirit with conversion and allowing for a subsequent "filling" of the Spirit. Still, distinguishing a subsequent baptism in the Spirit was the prevailing view of Alliance leaders until the 1950s.

Simpson taught that there could be "Pentecosts and second Pentecosts."[11] Hence, he believed that he had received a genuine baptism in the Spirit many years earlier, yet he also believed God wanted to give him a "deeper and fuller baptism" that would include "complete Pentecostal fullness embracing all the gifts and graces."[12] This was terminology that he and Pentecostally-oriented Alliance leaders would use periodically. Simpson encouraged believers to claim a "mightier baptism of the Holy Ghost," a "deeper sanctification," and a "fuller baptism of the Spirit."[13] He acknowledged that "the sealing and baptism of the Spirit does not exhaust the fullness of His gracious manifestation and working."[14]

Some Alliance leaders expressed their experiences of speaking in tongues as the "residue" of the Spirit, or the "rest of the oil."[15] Alliance leaders viewed the baptism in the Spirit with the "gifts and graces" as a "fuller" baptism,[16] while Pentecostals viewed the baptism in the Spirit with tongues as the "full" baptism. Rather than viewing tongues as *the* evidence of *the* baptism in the Spirit, the Alliance allowed that tongues or other gifts could be *an* evidence of *a* baptism in the Spirit, even a *fuller* baptism; but a "full" baptism did not necessarily include tongues.

PUBLIC EXERCISE OF GIFTS

The early C&MA encouraged the public exercise of gifts and manifestations of the Spirit with balance, discernment, and decorum. As mentioned earlier, long before the Pentecostal movement arose, Simpson encouraged people to speak a word of prophetic utterance or tongues.[17]

When the Pentecostal movement appeared, Alliance leaders affirmed the validity of the gifts. Again and again, however, they appealed to the guidelines of 1 Corinthians 14 in the exercise of gifts. MacArthur, whose wife spoke in tongues, maintained, "We insisted upon holding everything strictly to the Pauline regulations. . . . We have not deviated from our first position, viz. that anything that was not Pauline was not of God, there we expect to remain."[18] Alliance leaders were especially concerned about public exercise of tongues without interpretation. At the same time, they allowed for occasional exceptions when an interpretation not vocalized, but was implicit.[19]

In time, Alliance leaders felt that the gift of tongues was intended more for personal, individual worship and prayer and had limited value publicly, so they discouraged public use of the gift unless there was clear direction from God and the 1 Corinthians 14 guidelines were adhered to strictly. Yet as late as 1927, an Alliance publication was encouraging exercise of the gifts of tongues and interpretation in public worship services.[20]

Space does not permit a survey of the early Alliance definition of various spiritual gifts. Only a cursory discussion of the more notable gifts is possible here. See Simpson's "Gifts and Grace" and other sources cited in the endnotes for more on individual gifts.[21]

PROPHECY, WORDS OF WISDOM AND KNOWLEDGE

Simpson defines prophecy as "specially denoting the ministry which gives to men the direct messages of God. It is not always the power to foretell future events. A prophet is rather a divine messenger, the man who catches the mind of his Master, and gives it out to his fellowmen at the divine direction. . . . a messenger of the very thing that God would say at the time to the generation to which he speaks or the community to whom he bears witness. . . . in the immediate power and unction of the Holy Spirit, the messages of God to men."[22] This is very similar to Third Wave theologian Wayne Grudem's definition of prophecy as "telling something that God has spontaneously brought to mind.[23] Again, similar to Grudem, Alliance leaders believed such supernatural utterances as prophecy, tongues and interpretation can be a mixture of flesh and Spirit, partially true and partially mistaken, and are not to be regarded as infallible.[24]

Such divine messages often were spoken in the first person with the person prophesying for God.[25] Anointed preaching under the immediate inspiration of the Spirit could also be considered as prophecy.[26] Although prophecy was not considered primarily foretelling, the idea was not excluded from the Alliance understanding of the prophetic gift.[27] Sometimes prophecy could be directive, such as instructing an individual to go some place.[28] More often prophecy was regarded as confirming guidance. Simpson warns about danger of too much dependency and direction on prophecies. Further, there is a danger of prophets and prophetesses claiming they are authorized by the Holy Spirit to reveal secret sins and direct the decisions of others.[29]

In the C&MA view, tongues had taken on too great an emphasis in Pentecostal circles. Thompson assured, "Tongues are desirable, yet prophecy is preferrable."[30] Bosworth cautioned against making tongues more prominent than prophecy: "The teaching on tongues as the evidence makes them more ambitious to speak in tongues than to prophesy. Prophecy, which Joel said would be the most prominent result of the Baptism in the Spirit (Joel 2:28), and which Paul taught was the most valuable 'manifestation of the Spirit,' is not sought in many Pentecostal meetings nor even recognized as an evidence of the Baptism where it is already manifested."[31] Alliance leaders cautioned not to depend on impressions, but check them out with the Word;[32] to interpret prophecy, but not to speculate,[33] and not to strain for a supernatural word.[34] Simpson was especially concerned about psychic phenomena appearing in the guise of Christian prophecy, warning against regarding prophecy like fortune telling.[35]

Simpson did not define word of wisdom and knowledge in the common way it is used in the charismatic movement, but rather similar to Grudem: "What many people today call 'word of wisdom' and 'word of knowledge' in charismatic circles, it would seem better simply to refer to as 'prophecy.'"[36] In Grudem's view, as well as the early C&MA, supernatural knowledge as revelation would be subsumed under the gift of prophecy. In the early C&MA there seemed to be a concern that such phenomena sometimes appeared to be akin to psychic phenomena and easily counterfeited, so it was not commonly practiced in the C&MA.[37] However, manifestations that are today commonly called "word of knowledge" today did occur periodically in the early C&MA, as have been cited earlier.[38]

DISCERNMENT OF SPIRITS

This was the one gift that Simpson did encourage people to seek. Of discernment, Simpson observed, "It is quite remarkable that this gift immediately precedes the last two, namely, tongues and interpretation of tongues. It would seem as if at this point there were peculiar need for the power to distinguish the false and the true. The gift of tongues above all others opened the way for scenes of much excitement and the possibility of Satanic counterfeits."[39] Likewise, Jaffray counseled, "Let us not allow the enemy so to drive us away from, and cheat us out of, the real blessings of the Spirit because he has counterfeited in some cases the gift of tongues. We have no business to be afraid of evil spirits, for His has given us 'power over all the power of the enemy,' and He can give supernatural discernment of spirits."[40] Simpson and MacArthur both appear to have exercised this gift.[41] W. T. Norton from Ramabai's Mukti Mission recalled of Simpson, "Simpson once said that he could feel the demon powers attack when on ship board, and nearing a heathen land."[42]

VARIOUS KINDS OF TONGUES

Even though Simpson never spoke in tongues, he seems to have a clear perception of the experience of tongues, probably from his close friends who received the gift. He and early Alliance leaders recognized that as Paul wrote, there are "various kinds of tongues," meaning that there are a variety of purposes and uses of speaking in tongues. Tongues could be expressed as groanings or inarticulate prayers (sometimes today referred to as proto-glossolalia).[43] Referring to "inexpressible longings" in Romans 8:26, Simpson wrote that God sometimes has to give a new tongue to adequately express the burden of the Holy Spirit's prayer.[44] Hence, praying in tongues could be especially beneficial in intercessory prayer.

Tongues could be "the express of divine emotion"[45] or "an overflowing spirit of praise."[46] As MacArthur described it, "Those who speak in tongues seem to live in another world."[47] Simpson explained it as a divine ecstasy which lifts the soul above the ordinary modes and expressions of reason and utterance. . . . The spirit is the higher element and in the gift of tongues appears to overlap the mind altogether, and find its expression in speech quite unintelligible to the person himself and yet truly expressing the higher though and feeling of the exalted spiritual state of the subject. . . . the distinct mark of divine power and presence, and a very glorious and blessed channel or direct fellowship with the heavenly world, and in some sense a real opening of the doors between the earthly and the heavenly. . . . a channel of direct worship and adoration. [48]

Value of Tongues. While it was emphasized in the C&MA that tongues is listed last in Scripture, therefore indicative of being a lesser gift, Alliance leaders nonetheless held that it was a gift of value and desirable (though not to be desired above prophecy or sought after in and of itself). Simpson affirmed the value of tongues for many as "a marked deepening of the spiritual life of our members and an encouraging increase in their missionary zeal and liberality. It would therefore, be a serious matter for any candid Christian to pass a wholesale criticism or condemnation upon such movements or presume to 'limit the Holy One of Israel.'"[49]

Jaffray listed many benefits from his experience of speaking in tongues: a deeper love for and understanding of Scripture, a sense of his weakness and the power of the power of the Name and the Blood of Jesus in prayer, greater anointing in witnessing and preaching, greater control of his tongue, and a clearer understanding of the working of the Spirit and detection of evil spirits.[50] Jaffray further explained that God often grants tongues first "to test us and see whether or not we may be trusted with greater gifts of the Spirit which may be indeed of more value in the Christian ministry."[51]

MacArthur referred to the "blessedness of this experience," calling tongues "the heavenly intoxication of the supernatural song, or the blissful agony of supernatural intercession." He asserted that "Paul had the double equipment, which he so much desired that the others also should enjoy, and declared he would pray and sing with both his spirit and his understanding."[52] His wife related of her experience of tongues, "This was like the 'residue of the oil' (Leviticus 14:18, 25) that flowed down upon the hem of Aaron's robe."[53]

Tongues of Men and Angels. Pentecostal leaders like Charles Parham and holiness churches like the Church of the Nazarene believed that only tongues identified as human languages (xenoglossa or xenolalia) could be genuine. Contrary to this belief, Simpson affirmed, "It may be a human tongue, or it may be a heavenly tongue. For the apostle distinctly speaks of both the tongues of men and of angels."[54] The early Alliance believed that upon occasion "missionary tongues" might be bestowed as a power encounter witness or for preaching in another language, but eventually came to the viewpoint that most speaking in tongues was for the purpose of intercession or worship. There were in the Alliance, however, numerous instances of tongues identified as known languages, as mentioned throughout this book, including German, Hebrew, and Arabic, as well as Indian, African, and Chinese dialects.[55]

Singing in the Spirit. Singing in the Spirit, both in tongues and in one's native tongue, occurred periodically in C&MA revivals, as have been cited earlier.[56] Singing in tongues appears to have occurred during worship services as an expression of worship, sometimes without interpretation. The heavenly melody itself seemed to be its own interpretation, not needing identifiable words.[57] An example of this occurred in early October 1907 at the C&MA convention in Simpson's Gospel Tabernacle: "A young girl came under the power and her spirit was caught up to the throne. She sang a melody, without words, that seemed to come from within the veil, it was so heavenly. It seemed to come from another world."[58]

APOSTLES AND PROPHETS

Simpson was sometimes called an apostle by others, but never encouraged the term. Rader was called a "real prophet of God."[59] However, Alliance leaders rarely called people apostles or prophets. Rather, early Alliance leaders referred to "Apostolic Christianity" or being "an apostolic church of the power of the Holy Spirit."[60] Simpson cautions that no man, whether he claims to be an apostle, prophet, or saint has any right to proclaim a message whether in known or unknown tongues with a claim that it possesses authority over their consciences. There is no new revelation, only illumination of Scripture.[61] Alliance leaders cautioned against "self-appointed prophets" who "boast of being special custodians of some phase of the full Gospel."[62] Simpson maintained that real apostles and prophets are modest, not announcing themselves.[63] Early Alliance leaders would be wary of many today who claim to be prophets and apostles.

OTHER CHARISMATIC BELIEFS AND PRACTICES

Anointing and praying over cloths was occasionally practiced in the early C&MA as a point of contact, such as in the ministry of Myland and the 1921 Pittsburgh Convention revival.[64] Alliance leaders recognized that there is some "semblance of truth" to "the charging of clothing with the power of the Holy Ghost" for healing, but there are some who have gone into the "handkerchief business" are "charlatans and pretenders." Such conduct cannot be reconciled with the "unostentatious behavior of the apostles," but is an "unwholesome love for the spectacular."[65] So the practice was used sparcely in the C&MA under limited and guarded conditions.

Dancing does not appear to have been commonplace in C&MA worship, but it did occur periodically, especially in times of revival, and was even encouraged at times.[66] Simpson spoke favorably of a "sacred dance."[67] Newberry considered dancing as a manifestation of the joy of the Lord and a demonstration of the moving of the Holy Spirit, warning that "people who have criticized the power of the Holy Spirit on other people have suffered in their experience."[68]

The phenomenon of falling under the power of the Spirit, as we have seen, occurred often in C&MA revival services, both before and after Azusa Street, sometimes on whole groups of people, and was accepted but not sought. They would not regard all such falling as from the Lord, but were not reticent or fearful of the manifestation.

---

1. Michael Thomas Girolimon, "A Real Crisis of Blessing, Part II," *Paraclete*, Spring 1993, 4.

2. Gordon D. Fee and Douglas Stuart, *How to Read the Bible for All Its Worth: A Guide to Understanding the Bible* (Grand Rapids, MI: Zondervan, 1982), 100, 101.

3. Ballard, "The Spiritual Clinic," AW, July 20, 1912, 254; Ballard, "The Spiritual Clinic," AW, July 27, 1912, 270.

4. Simpson, Editorial, AW, Feb. 14, 1914, 305. See also Simpson, "All the Blessings of the Spirit," CMAW, Sept. 29, 1906, 198; Ballard, "Spiritual Gifts with Special Reference to the Gift of Tongues," *Living Truths*, Jan.1907, 23-31; Simpson, Editorial, CMAW, Jan. 26, 1907, 1; Editorial, *The India Alliance*, Aug. 1907, 19; Pierson, "Speaking with Tongues," *The India Alliance*, Aug. 1907, 19-21; May Mabette Anderson, "The 'Latter Rain,' and Its Counterfeit," *Signs of the Times*, 136; Ramsey, "Speaking in Tongues: An Exegetical Study," CMAW, Apr. 4, 1908, 7, 17; Simpson, Editorial, CMAW, Apr. 30, 1910, 78; Ballard, "The Spiritual Clinic, "AW, Mar. 2, 1912, 343; Bosworth, *Do All Speak with Tongues?*, 13-14.

5. Espoused by former C&MA pastor D. W. Kerr. See Lewis Wilson, "The Kerr-Pierce Role in A/G Education, "*Assemblies of God Heritage*, Spring 1990, 6.

6. Blumhofer, *The Assemblies of God*, 167.

7. Taught by former Alliance pastor D. W. Myland, as cited in Blumhofer, *The Assemblies of God*, 50.

8. Simpson, "What Is Meant by the Latter Rain?," CMAW, Oct. 19, 1907, 38.

9. For more on the C&MA view of the sanctifying baptism in the Spirit, see Gilbertson, *The Baptism of the Holy Spirit*; Pardington, *The Crisis of the Deeper Life*; Samuel J. Stoesz, *Sanctification: An Alliance Distinctive* (Camp Hill, PA: Christian Publications, 1992); Gerald E. McGraw, *Launch Out! A Theology of Dynamic Sanctification* (Camp Hill, PA: Christian Publications, 2000).

10. J. Hudson Ballard, "The Spiritual Clinic," AW, Jan. 16, 1915, 254; Smith, *The Baptism with the Holy Spirit*, 19; McCrossan, *Christ's Paralyzed Church X-Rayed*, 22-23, 107-114, 154-156.

11. Simpson, *A Larger Christian Life* (1988), 42.

12. Simpson, Editorial, AW, April 11, 1914, 18.

13. Simpson, 1909 C&MA Annual Report, 36; Simpson, Editorial, AW, Apr. 11, 1914, 18.

14. Simpson, Editorial, AW, Feb. 14, 1914, 305.

15. Montgomery, "The Promise of the Father," *Triumphs of Faith*, July 1908, 1; Carrie Judd Montgomery, "The Residue of the Oil," *Confidence*, Nov. 1912, 252ff.; Carrie Judd Montgomery, "Sanctification and the Anointing of the Holy Spirit," *Confidence*, Oct. 1912, 228.

16. Myland, "A Personal Word," LRE, Oct. 1911, 11.

17. Simpson, "Worship and Fellowship of the Church," CMAW, Feb. 9, 1898, 125.

18. MacArthur, "Excerpts from Annual Reports," May 25, 1909. See also MacArthur, "Excerpts from Annual Reports," May 28, 1908.

19. For example, as cited earlier, at the Alliance Tabernacle in New Castle a woman spoke in tongues for thirty minutes, accompanied, not by verbal interpretation, but interpretation through sign language

as the crucifixion of Christ. Marsh, "The Gift of Tongues," *Living Truths*, May 1907, 259-264; see also McCrossan, *Speaking with Other Tongues*, 4.

20. McCrossan, *Speaking with Other Tongues*, 42.

21. Simpson, "Gifts and Grace," CMAW, June 29, 1907, 302; Simpson, CITB, 5:216-217.

22. Ibid.

23. Wayne Grudem, *Systematic Theology: An Introduction to Biblical Doctrine* (Leicester, England: Inter-Varsity Press; Grand Rapids, MI: Zondervan, 1994), 1049.

24. Anderson, "The Prayer of Faith," CMAW, Feb. 17, 1906, 98; Anderson, "The Prayer of Faith: Part II," CMAW, Feb. 24, 1906, 106-107; MacArthur, "The Phenomenon of Supernatural Utterance," 72-73; J. Hudson Ballard, "The Spiritual Clinic," AW, July 27, 1912, 270.

25. For examples, see "The Ninety-first Psalm," CMAW, Aug. 17, 1907, 78; Andrew Murray, "Jesus, Himself," CAMW, Mar. 16, 1894, 305-308.

26. Ballard, "The Spiritual Clinic," AW, Mar. 20, 1915, 398; Ballard, "Studies in I Corinthians," AW, June 20, 1914, 198-199; June 27, 1914, 214-215.

27. For example, in 1913 the writer of an article in *The Alliance Weekly*, reported that he prophesied that a new Navy convert would become the chaplain of a warship in less than a month. It came true as within a few weeks the man was conducting five services each Sunday. Pope, "Putting Things Right," AW, Aug. 2, 1913, 283. In the same year, British C&MA leader F. E. Marsh reported that in Silverton, Devonshire, in western England, Mrs. Thomas of Liverpool prophesied that Mrs. Jordan, an invalid who had been bedridden for five years, would be healed. Shortly, Mrs. Jordan was indeed healed and herself received a "divine message." Marsh, "Here and There," AW, Oct. 11, 1913, 23.

28. See Woodberry, "John Woodbury," AW, Oct. 22, 1938, 677; Hester, "The Lord's Doings," CMAW, Feb. 9, 1901, 84.

29. Simpson, "The Anointing," CMAW, May 23, 1908, 130.

30. Thompson, "The Corinthian Epistles: Spiritual Gifts and Graces," AW, Feb. 12, 1916, 315-316; Thompson, "The Corinthian Epistles: The Use, Abuse and Value of Gifts," AW, Feb. 26, 1916, 341.

31. Bosworth, *Do All Speak with Tongues?*, 16.

32. Montgomery, *Under His Wings*, pp. 160-161.

33. "Some Dangers in Connection with Premillennial Truth," CMAW, Jan. 14, 1905, 20.

34. Simpson, Editorial, AW, Aug. 24, 1912, 321.

35. Simpson, Annual Report, 1908.

36. Grudem, *Systematic Theology*, 1080-1082. Compare with Simpson, "Gifts and Grace," 302.

37. McDonough, "The Harvest Rain," CMAW, Feb. 5, 1910, 297, 305.

38. "Healing of Mrs. Williams," CMAW, May 9, 1890, 295-296; Stella E. Bales, "My Testimony," CMAW, April 8, 1905, 212; Lewis, *Life Sketch of Rev. Mary C. Morton*, 30-32.

39. Simpson, "Gifts and Grace," 303.

40. Jaffray, "Speaking in Tongues—Some Words of Kindly Counsel," 395.

41. Simpson, Editorial, AW, Feb. 24, 1912, 322; MacArthur, "Healing from Deafness and Deliverance from Demons," AW, Jan. 26, 1924, 770.

42. *Word and Work*, Aug. 13, 1921, 5.

43. Marsh, "Revival in the Missionary Institute at South Nyack on Hudson," CMAW, Nov. 17, 1906, 316, 318; Marsh, "The Emphasis of the Holy Spirit in the Revival at Nyack and New York," CMAW, Dec. 1, 1906, 338-339; Bullen, "Among the Nyack Students," CMAW, Dec. 8, 1906, 363. See also Frodsham, *Jesus Is*

Victor, 30,36-37; Mary A. Butterfield, "Report of the Missionary Society of the Missionary Institute, 1906-07," CMAW, July 13, 1907, 20.

44. A. B. Simpson, Editorial, CMAW, Jan. 4, 1908, 233-234; A. B. Simpson, "The Holy Spirit in Romans," CMAW, Sept. 18, 1909, 422.

45. Simpson, Editorial, AW, Feb. 14, 1914, 305.

46. Thompson, "The Corinthian Epistles: Spiritual Gifts and Graces," AW, Feb. 12, 1916, 315-316; Thompson,

"The Corinthian Epistles: The Use, Abuse and Value of Gifts," AW, Feb. 26, 1916, 341.

47. MacArthur, "The Promise of the Father and Speaking in Tongues in Chicago," CMAW, July 27, 1907, 44.

48. Simpson, "Gifts and Grace," 303

49. Simpson, C&MA Annual Report, 1907-1908.

50. Jaffray, "Speaking in Tongues—Some Words of Kindly Counsel," 395.

51. Ibid.

52. MacArthur, "The Phenomenon of Supernatural Utterance," 73.

53. Brumback, *Suddenly . . . from Heaven*, 79-80.

54. Simpson, "Gifts and Grace," 303.

55. Brumback, *Suddenly . . . From Heaven*, 77-78, 89-90; Simpson, Editorial, CMAW, June 8, 1907, 205; Frodsham, *With Signs Following*, 47, 234, 240-242; McGee, "Pentecostal Awakenings at Nyack," 24-26; Frodsham, *Jesus Is Victor*, 37-40; "A Remarkable Testimony," CMAW, Nov. 9, 1907, 98; see also Montgomery, *Under His Wings*, 168-170; Woodberry, "Report of Beulah Chapel," CMAW, May 22, 1909, 134.

56. Barratt, "The Seal of My Pentecost," 735-738; Orr, *The Flaming Tongue*, 179-180; Knight, "For His Glory, "274; "Gleanings from Nyack: South America, the Neglected Continent," CMAW, April 2, 1910, 9; Myland, *The Latter Rain Covenant*, 174-177; Cramer, "Pentecost at Cleveland," CMAW, Apr. 27, 1907, 201; Herlinger, "Testimony," CMAW, Dec. 31, 1910, 215.

57. See McCrossan, *Speaking with Other Tongues*, 4.

58. Bartleman, *Azusa Street* (1982), 111-112; Cox, *Fire from Heaven*, 68; Nienkirchen, 84-85; "Notes from the New York Convention," CMAW, Oct. 19, 1907, 48.

59. Editorial, AW, Oct. 30, 1920, 481.

60. Simpson, "Apostolic Christianity," CMAW, Jan. 26, 1901, 46.

61. Simpson, "The Holy Ghost," CMAW, April 24, 1909, 48.

62. Chrisman, "Notes from the Home Field," CMAW, Dec. 24, 1910, 205.

63. A. B. Simpson, Editorial, CMAW, Jan. 11, 1902, 24.

64. Funk, "Pittsburgh Convention," AW, Apr. 9, 1921, 57.

65. MacArthur, "Fabrics Filled with Power," AW, Sept. 14, 1912, 390.

66. Franklin, "Work at Mukti," *The India Alliance*, Feb. 1906, 89, 96; Frodsham, *With Signs Following*, 105-111; Smalley, *Alliance Missions in India*, 2:898-899; Ballentyne, "Dholka Revival," *The India Alliance*, Jan. 1907,76-77; George Shaw, "Revivals of the Spirit," AW, July 1, 1922, 243; MacMillan, "With Heart and Voice, AW, May 13, 1939, 290; "The Fourfold Gospel, AW, June 10, 1939, 354; MacMillan, *The Full Gospel Sunday School Quarterly*, May 21, 1944, 25; "Modern Hymns," Feb. 24, 1940, 115; "Religious Enthusiasm," AW, May 14, 1938, 307.

67. Simpson, "Editorial Correspondence," CAMW, April 17, 1895, 248.

68. Newberry, "David Brings the Ark to Jerusalem," AW, July 17, 1920, 252.

TWENTY-THREE

DISCERNMENT—THE SIGNATURE THEME OF THE C&MA

The hallmark of the early C&MA was discernment. It is not that no Pentecostals exercised discernment, but discernment was the special provenance of the C&MA. For twenty years before Azusa the C&MA and Simpson had both encouraged the gifts and manifestations of the Spirit and cautioned discernment. Further, more than 200 times from 1906-1919 the terms *discern* and *discernment* occur in Alliance periodicals.

Prophetically foreseeing the coming controversy, Simpson wrote in May 1906, "In these days of genuine revival and intense reaching after higher things, it is especially necessary to guard against excess even in that which is good. . . . We must be prepared to expect delusions and counterfeits at such a time as this and not discredit the true because of the false." He advised "all seekers after truth to 'try the spirits' and 'discern the things that differ.'"[1] Simpson's counsel became the benchmark for Alliance charismatic theology and practice in the following years.

As Pentecostal historian Edith Blumhofer has acknowledged, "Alliance spokespersons had an almost uncanny way of discerning potential difficulties that enthusiastic Apostolic Faith adherents seemed prone to overlook. Within several years, some Pentecostals would echo Alliance appeals for prudence and balance. For the moment, however, the cautions seemed to go largely unheeded."[2]

OPENNESS AND CAUTION—WATCHFUL, BUT NOT FEARFUL

Unlike some Pentecostals and charismatics who do not acknowledge the possibility of counterfeit gifts, the C&MA cautioned that every spiritual gift and manifestation can be counterfeited. Manifestations could be caused by the action of the flesh. Some supernatural manifestations were discerned as demonic in nature.

Due to Simpson's cautions, some Pentecostals thought Simpson was anti-tongues. On the other hand, due to historical drift and over-cautiousness, there are some in the C&MA today who believe that the greater part of the early Pentecostal movement was false. Contrary to both positions, near the end of his life Simpson wrote that he "sincerely believes that in a great number of cases at the present time the particular manifestation of speaking in tongues has been wholly genuine and in perfect harmony with godly sincerity, simplicity and love."[3] He counseled, "Do not allow the counterfeit to depreciate the genuine gold. Our attitude is both openness and caution."[4] In opposition to those who advocate a passive stance toward gifts, Simpson counseled "readiness of mind to receive."[5] He desired to welcome and embrace with expectation the charismatic dimension of the Christian life with balance and discernment.

Alliance leaders believed that this movement was genuinely the Latter Rain from God, but that it was mixed with errors and excesses. Alliance conferences encouraged manifestations of gifts, discussing issues such as "How to Secure the Largest Measure of the Holy Spirit in the Most Safe and Scriptural Way."[6]

Some Pentecostals believed that Simpson and the early Alliance were quenching the Spirit with their caution. Simpson responded that "some sincere and zealous friends are unduly sensitive about even the extremely gentle and moderate words of caution that have been expressed."[7] In reality, it is probably inevitable that some Alliance leaders did at times quench the Spirit. Nevertheless, they also were aware of the danger of being overly cautious, and urged their constituency to be not fearful. Simpson expressed concern that people might miss what God has for them because of fear.[8] To those who were fearful of spurious manifestations, Simpson counseled not to be afraid of counterfeits because God is able to save us from them, assuring, "God knows how to give without a counterfeit."[9] Citing Matthew 7:9-11, he exhorted that we should not fear, for "if a son asks bread . . . God our Father will not give a stone."[10] To the overly cautious, he cautioned that they might miss what God has for them.[11] Similarly, Robert Jaffray advised:

> There is a great danger of fear of the works of the devil to such an extent that we shall lose all courage to seek earnestly for the true and full endowment of the Spirit for which our souls hunger. I have met some who are so prejudiced on account of why that have seen that they say they have no desire to ever speak in tongues, forgetting that tongues is one of the gifts of the Spirit. Let us not allow the enemy so to drive us away from, and cheat us out of, the real blessings of the Spirit because he has counterfeited in some cases the gift of tongues. We have no business to be afraid of evil spirits, for His has given us 'power over all the power of the enemy,' and He can give supernatural discernment of spirits.[12]

Simpson on Balancing the Extremes

An analysis of Simpson's statements shows that he was not categorically against all seeking, but a particular kind of seeking. What Simpson opposed was not "seeking" per se, but rather "unduly seeking" or "the seeking of any kind of power apart from or rather than God." The implication is that seeking power or gifts in conjunction with and subordinated to seeking Christ Himself would be appropriate. Simpson also cautioned against the danger of exaggerating certain gifts, such as tongues.[13] Again and again Simpson counseled balance: "guard . . . against the two extremes of danger. . . . the danger of credulity and fanaticism. . . . the extreme of refusing to recognize any added blessing which the Holy Spirit is bringing to His people in these last days."[14]

THREE DANGERS TO WATCH FOR

In his 1907-1908 Annual Report, Simpson counseled watchfulness regarding three dangers: 1) counterfeits, 2) extravagances, 3) false teachings.[15]

Counterfeits. Alliance leaders believed that every gift and manifestation of the Spirit can be counterfeited by false spirits from below. Thus, we should not believe every spirit, but try the spirits (1 John 4:1-3).[16] They cited actual occurrences of demonic manifestations as "positive proof that demons as well as the Spirit cause speaking in tongues."[17] They affirmed the value of prophetic utterances and tongues with interpretation, but also viewed them as fallible, sometimes a mixture of truth and error, or truth tinged with the flesh.[18] Simpson cautioned, "We must not accept everything that occurs even in a deeply spiritual meeting, without trying the spirits by the Word which the Holy Spirit Himself has given."[19]

Extravagances. Alliance leaders spoke out against *spiritualist-like manifestations and imitations of animal sounds* like a dog, coyote, cat, birds, roosters, etc. Some, they discerned, were from the flesh, others from the devil.[20] Simpson asserted, "There have been many instances where [seeking for] the gift of tongues led the subjects and the audiences in to the wildest excesses and were accompanied with voices and actions more closely resembling wild animals than rational beings, impressing the unprejudiced observers that it was the work of the devil."[21]

Avoiding *disorder and confusion*, Alliance leaders affirmed "our determination to hold everything strictly to Pauline order,"[22] in reference to Paul's guidelines in 1 Corinthians 14. MacArthur reported, "Quite a few left us because we entertained the subject for even a moment, believing it all to be of the devil, while a much larger number have lost interest in us because we insisted upon holding everything strictly to the Pauline regulations. . . . we have not deviated from our first position, viz. that anything that was not Pauline was not of God, there we expect to remain."[23]

Concerned about *fanaticism*, near the end of his life Simpson continued to maintain, "There is a true and holy supernaturalism which will always be recognized by its humility, self-control, holiness, love and good fruits. But there is a loud, arrogant, presumptuous and disorderly fanaticism which scoffs at all restraints and scatters its anathemas against all that oppose it and if possible would 'deceive the very elect.'"[24]

Warning about *extremes in fasting and lack of sleep*, Alliance leaders cautioned that "a weakened body often gives the adversary easy access to the spirit."[25] Simpson expressed concern about the dangers of seeing false visions or dreams from excessive prayer, fasting and asceticism: "Good people who shut themselves up in cells and closets in weeks of fasting and prayer without proper exercise, nourishment or sleep, or without any change of mental or spiritual attention, are very apt to see visions and dream dreams that do not always come from above.[26]

Simpson warned about the dangers of counterfeit gifts through *passivity*, or a "kind of 'abandonment' urged by certain spiritual leaders that would throw our whole being open to any powerful influence and hypnotic control which the enemy might wish to exercise."[27] John MacMillan cautioned:

> The most deadly enemy of the devout believer is spiritual passivity. . . . Told that all he has to do is to 'let go and let God,' he becomes quite passive, and takes all that comes to him as the working of the divine will. As a result, he may either lose his faith, or, as many in these days have done, become the victim of false impressions and Satanic delusions. . . . There must be a positive and continuous 'transfiguring ourselves by the renewing of our mind,' if we are to advance. Let the child of God neglect prayer and the assembling with the people of God for a time, and a lowering of his spiritual life has already begun, though he may not realize it."[28]

False Teachings and Practices. Simpson's standard was adherence to sound interpretation of Scripture: "The only limiting condition is conformity to the Word of God."[29] Among the teachings and practices that Alliance leaders warned about included the following: seeking for signs and wonders rather than salvation of sinners and sanctification, insisting on tongues as the evidence, spirit of separation and controversy, following novel teachings and new leaders, little known, unwise and untried, sending inexperienced and self-appointed missionaries believing they God had given them the tongue of the people, claiming of prophetic authority like clairvoyants and fortunetellers,[30] hearing voices or accepting impressions that speak "with authority on doctrinal questions,"[31] and immorality—"pandering to lusts." [32]

TESTS FOR COUNTERFEITS

Alliance leaders used several tests to discern the presence of counterfeits, excesses and false teachings:

1. *Fruit.* Does it bring a person closer to God and encourage Christ-likeness? Jesus said, "You will know them by their fruit." (Matt. 7:16-20).[33]

2. *Gift of discernment of spirits.* Simpson wrote that in the midst of spiritual cross currents and confusion in these days, the gift of discernment is much needed.[34]

3. Peace of God vs. a Check in One's Spirit (similar to discernment of spirits). Mc-Crossan testified, "You will feel at once that it is not of God, . . . your spiritual nature will revolt."[35]

4. Tests of the Word of God. What does Scripture say about this seemingly supernatural manifestation? Is this consistent with sound doctrine and the ways in which God works? The C&MA was suspicious of anything that did not clearly show a sound interpretation of Scripture. Early on in the Pentecostal movement, the Alliance dealt with this: "Never did a soul drift into fanaticism or wildfire who did not, at first, either accept a strained or a perverted interpretation of scripture, or read into certain passages a meaning made impossible by an intelligent comparison with other passages."[36]

5. Christo-centric Tests. Is Jesus continually confessed as Lord in word and deed in the person's life (1 Corinthians 12:1)? Does the spirit behind the manifestation confess the deity and humanity of Jesus Christ?—that Jesus Christ came in the flesh (1 John 4:1-3)?[37]

6. Transmission of Unclean Spirits. Has the person experienced pain, or fallen into depression, a bad habit, temptation or sin after having hands laid on him or her?[38]

7. Occult Exposure. Has the person been involved in or exposed to psychic or occult practices, cults, or Eastern religions, or is there the possibility of other demonic activity or influence existing in the person's life?[39] Carrie Judd Montgomery observed:

> I have noticed that when people who have touched occult things are in a meeting, the devil will bring forth strange manifestations from them, and the people who have no discernment come in and say, "If that is Pentecostal power, I do not want it." Beloved, it is not the power of the Holy Spirit, but it is the evil one trying to counterfeit and seeking to turn people away from the blessed baptism of the Holy Spirit. If people desire to be filled with the Spirit of God, they must first confess their sins and be cleansed by the blood of Jesus. They must confess to other Christians if they have touched any of these abominations which God has forbidden, and they must ask believing ones to set them free before they can invite the Holy Spirit to possess the temple.[40]

Other questions considered by early Alliance and some Pentecostal leaders as possible indicators of false manifestations included the following:

- Has this manifestation been manipulated or seem harsh or strained?[41]

- During or after the manifestation, does the person have a feeling of depression, confusion, or negative attitude?[42]

- Were the person's motives impure for wanting to receive a supernatural manifestation? Was the person seeking a manifestation rather than or more than God Himself?[43]

- Is the manifestation uncontrollable (1 Cor. 14:32-33) or is there any unusual display such as barking, roaring, slithering like a snake, etc.?[44]

While these were not guarantees that the miraculous manifestation is false, they were considered as possible warning signals. Alliance leaders were also careful not to go to the other extreme of labeling everything demonic. The Alliance position has been to expect and welcome the miraculous, but not automatically accept everything that appears to be miraculous as from God. Simpson's twofold attitude was:

- "At all times my spirit has been open to God for anything He might be pleased to reveal or bestow."[45]

- "find the safe and sane balance of truth between fanaticism on the one hand and fear on the other"[46]

The Alliance forefathers were neither gullible nor skeptical. They warned both against being overly zealous of signs and wonders, and also against being overly-cautious. They encouraged people not to seek after particular manifestations *rather than* or *more than* God Himself, yet actively expect God to work signs and wonders. Simpson advised not to let excesses and counterfeits "depreciate the genuine gold." He was assured, "The best remedy for the abuse of anything is its wise and proper use."[47]

---

1. Simpson, Editorial, *Living Truths*, May 1906, 257-258.

2. Blumhofer, *The Assemblies of God*, 185.

3. Simpson, Editorial, AW, Jan. 13, 1917, 225.

4. "Annual Report of the President and General Superintendent of the C&MA, 1906-1907," CMAW, June 15, 1907, 222.

5. Simpson, Editorial, *Living Truths*, Dec. 1906, 706-710. See also Simpson, "All the Blessings of the Spirit, "CMAW, Sept. 29, 1906, 198; Simpson, Editorial, CMAW, Mar. 2, 1907, 97; Simpson, Editorial, CMAW, Apr. 6, 1907, Simpson, Editorial, CMAW, May 4, 1907, 206.

6. Simpson, Editorial, AW, Feb. 24, 1912, 322-323.

7. Ibid.

8. Simpson, Editorial, CMAW, Aug. 7, 1909, 314.

9. Simpson, "A Week of Prayer," CMAW, Feb. 6, 1909, 314.

10. Simpson, "Editorial," CMAW, Jan. 23, 1909, 280.

11. Simpson, Editorial, CMAW, Aug. 7, 1909, 314.

12. Jaffray, "Speaking in Tongues—Some Words of Kindly Counsel," 395-396, 406.

13. A. B. Simpson, "Spiritual Sanity," *Living Truths*, Apr. 1907, 196.

14. Simpson, "All the Blessings of the Spirit," CMAW, Sept. 29, 1906, 198; A. B. Simpson, "Fervor and Fanaticism," CMAW, Dec. 22, 1906, 390; Simpson, Editorial, CMAW, Apr. 6, 1907, 157; Simpson, Editorial, CMAW, Mar. 2, 1907, 97; Simpson, Editorial, *Living Truths*, Dec. 1906, 706-710; Simpson, "Spiritual Sanity, "*Living Truths*, Apr. 1907, 191; Simpson, "Gifts and Grace," 302.

15. Simpson, 1907-1908 C&MA Annual Report, 10.

16. Simpson, Editorial, CMAW, Feb. 2, 1907, 99; Simpson, CITB, 6:374-375; Simpson, Editorial, CMAW, July 25, 1908, 278.

17. Simpson and Christie, "Demon Possession in Our Mincheo Native Conference, Jan. 1908," CMAW, Apr. 18, 1908, 38-39.

18. Anderson, "The Prayer of Faith," CMAW, Feb. 17, 1906, 98; Anderson, "The Prayer of Faith: Part II," CMAW, Feb. 24, 1906, 106-107; MacArthur, "The Phenomenon of Supernatural Utterance," 72-73; Ballard, "The Spiritual Clinic," AW, July 27, 1912, 270.

19. Cunningham, "A Loving Tribute," CMAW, Dec. 21, 1907, 193. Simpson, Editorial, CMAW, Dec. 21, 1907, 198.

20. Smale, "The Gift of Tongues," *Living Truths*, Jan. 1907, 32-43; MacArthur, "The Promise of the Father and Speaking with Tongues in Chicago," CMAW, Feb. 9, 1907, 64; Rader, "At Thy Word—A Farewell Message, "AW, Nov. 20, 1920, 532.

21. Simpson, Editorial, CMAW, Feb. 2, 1907, 99.

22. MacArthur, "Excerpts from Annual Reports," May 28, 1908.

23. MacArthur, "Excerpts from Annual Reports," May 25, 1909.

24. Simpson, "The Church," AW, June 21, 1919, 195; see also Simpson, 1907-1908 C&MA Annual Report, 11.

25. May Mabette Anderson, "The Latter Rain and Its Counterfeit: Part III," *Living Truths*, Aug. 1907, 477.

26. Simpson, Editorial, *Living Truths*, Dec. 1906, 708-709.

27. Simpson, Editorial, CMAW, Mar. 16, 1907, 121; see also Simpson, "Spiritual Sanity," *Living Truths*, Apr. 1907, 195.

28. John A. MacMillan, "Spiritual Energy, " AW, June 22, 1940, 386.

29. Simpson, Editorial, AW, Jan. 13, 1917, 225.

30. Anderson, "The Latter Rain and Its Counterfeit: Part IV," *Living Truths*, Sept. 1907, 534.

31. Simpson, Editorial, AW, Feb. 22, 1913, 322.

32. Marsh, "Here and There: False Prophets," CMAW, July 29, 1911, 284.

33. Simpson, 1907-1908 C&MA Annual Report, 10-11. See also Simpson, Editorial, CMAW, July 30, 1910, 288; Smale, "The Gift of Tongues," *Living Truths*, Jan. 1907, 32-43.

34. Simpson, Editorial, CMAW, Oct. 8, 1910, 24; Simpson, Editorial, AW, Jan. 13, 1917, 225; A.B. Simpson, Editorial, *Living Truths*, July 1907, 371. Years later Tozer also echoed Simpson saying that the gift that was needed the most is the gift of discernment: "Among the gifts of the Spirit scarcely any one is of greater practical usefulness than the gift of discernment. This gift should be highly valued and frankly sought as being almost indispensable in these critical times. This gift will enable us to distinguish the chaff from the wheat and to divide the manifestations of the flesh from the operations of the Spirit." A. W. Tozer, *The Root of the Righteous* (Camp Hill, PA: Christian Publications, 1955, 1986), 153.

35. McCrossan, *Speaking with Other Tongues*, 42.

36. May Mabette Anderson, "The Latter Rain and Its Counterfeit, A Message for the Hour: Part I," *Living Truth* , July 1907, 383.

37. Rader, *Harnessing God*, 99-101.

38. Pastor Schrenck, "Dangers and Warnings," WWW, July-Aug. 1885, 211-212.

39. McCrossan, *Speaking with Other Tongues*, 32; Simpson, "Spiritual Sanity," *Living Truths*, Apr. 1907, 195.

40. Carrie Judd Montgomery, "Witchcraft and Kindred Errors," AW, Oct. 15, 1938, 661.

41. McCrossan, *Speaking with Other Tongues*, 42.

42. Ibid., 42-43.

43. McCrossan, *Speaking with Other Tongues*, 32-33.

44. Smale, "The Gift of Tongues," 32-43; MacArthur, "The Promise of the Father and Speaking with Tongues in Chicago," CMAW, Feb. 9, 1907, 64; Simpson, Editorial, CMAW, Feb. 2, 1907, 99; Rader, "At Thy Word—A Farewell Message," AW, Nov. 20, 1920, 532.

45. Simpson's diary, 1912.

46. Simpson, Editorial, AW, Jan. 17, 1914, 241.

47. A. B. Simpson, CAMW, Mar. 27, 1891, 195. Similarly, Tozer rephrased it as: "Never allow the abuse of a doctrine to cancel out its use." A. W. Tozer, cited in "Minutes of General Council 1995 and Annual Report 1994," The Christian and Missionary Alliance, 142.

TWENTY-FOUR

THE EARLY C&MA ON "SEEK NOT, FORBID NOT"

This chapter gives a brief review of the C&MA motto, "Seek Not, Forbid Not," as cited earlier, in the 1963 position statement.[1] For a comprehensive investigation and history of the concept, see my article "Seek Not, Forbid Not: The Early Christian and Missionary Alliance Position on Glossolalia" in the Fall 2005 issue of the *Wesleyan Theological Journal*.[2]

While the statement does not claim that Simpson specifically coined the axiom "Seek not, forbid not," many have assumed that the motto came from Simpson. It has thus been disseminated in several studies on the relationship of the C&MA to early Pentecostalism.[3] The more recent study by Nienkirchen entitled *A. B. Simpson and the Pentecostal Movement* documented tongues and other charismatic manifestations in the early C&MA, and was correct in determining that Simpson did not coin the phrase.[4] However, he went farther by maintaining that the "Seek not, forbid not" policy was not the position of Simpson and the early Alliance, but rather was the invention of Tozer in 1963. Citing Simpson's diary and some of Simpson's alleged comments to Pentecostal leaders, Nienkirchen claimed that Simpson was, in fact, a seeker of tongues and that Tozer was a revisionist of Alliance history, coining the "Seek Not, Forbid Not" phrase.[5] His claims have since been accepted and perpetuated in more recent studies on the Alliance and the Pentecostal movement.[6]

The reaction of Alliance leader Richard Bailey was to declare that Nienkirchen is the revisionist for claiming that Simpson was a seeker of tongues.[7] Pentecostal historian Grant Wacker is more hesitant to go as far as Nienkirchen's conclusion that Simpson's diary proves him to be a seeker of tongues, saying, "Admittedly, Simpson's language is elliptical, but taken together there can be little doubt that he sought all the gifts of the Spirit, including tongues if the Lord willed it."[8]

SUMMARY OF THE EVIDENCE FOR A "SEEK NOT" POSITION

What then is the truth? Did Simpson and the early Alliance teach the "seek not, forbid not" doctrine? Or, did Simpson really seek tongues? Was Tozer a revisionist as Nienkirchen claims? An in-depth study of the documents of the early Alliance between 1906 and Simpson's death in 1919 as presented in my article in the *Wesleyan Theological Journal* overwhelmingly demonstrates that Simpson and early Alliance leaders did indeed maintain a kind of "seek not, forbid not" position, even if not precisely stated in those very words. Between 1906 and 1919, there were at least 26 cautionary statements by Simpson and his associates in C&MA periodicals, documents and correspondence not to seek after or pursue gifts or manifestations (13 by Simpson himself),[9] and at least nine instances counseling readers not to forbid, oppose or despise tongues.[10] As early as 1883, soon after launching his healing ministry, Simpson nonetheless warned against a "wonder-seeking spirit,"[11] and would continue to do so throughout his lifetime.

IS "SEEK NOT, FORBID NOT" BIBLICAL?

Some would cite 1 Corinthians 14:1, "Desire earnestly the greater gifts," arguing that to "desire earnestly" or to "covet" (Gr., *zeeloo*) is the same as to "seek." Therefore, the language of seeking or desiring is merely semantical and thus begging the question. While not specifically critiquing the C&MA position, Rich Nathan and Ken Wilson, in their book *Empowered Evangelicals*, critique a "seek not" position in general:

> But the phrase "Seek the giver, not the gifts" deserves closer examination. As stated, the advice is not biblical. St. Paul explicitly urged us to "eagerly desire spiritual gifts, especially the gift of prophecy" (1 Cor. 14:1). This echoes his earlier encouragement to "eagerly desire the greater gifts" (1 Cor. 12:31). Perhaps it would be better (though less pithy) to say, "Seek the gifts because of the giver, but never instead of the giver."
>
> The motto "Seek the giver, not the gifts" often reveals a passive, even fatalistic approach to asking for the things God has to give. . . . But the Bible encourages us to ask.[12]

THE MEANING OF "SEEK NOT" IN THE EARLY ALLIANCE

Did, then, the early Alliance cautionary statements against seeking advocate a passive stance toward gifts and manifestations and thus contradict Paul's statements in 1 Corinthians 12:31 and 14:1? Some of their writings considered in isolation could seem to indicate so, but when those statements are compared with others, passiveness is not what they had in mind. Actually, early C&MA leaders seemed to be aware of this argument, but did not see a contradiction.

First of all, early Alliance leaders maintained that Paul's exhortations do not advocate seeking a certain gift, such as tongues, but rather earnestly desiring, coveting, or seeking gifts in general, and especially the higher gifts, those that edify others the greatest. Further, the language of Simpson and other early Alliance leaders would, in fact, echo agreement with the clarifications and modifications of Nathan and Wilson above that gifts are not to be sought *instead of* or *more than* God Himself"[13] These statements are all in harmony with Nathan and Wilson's preferred rendering, "Seek the gifts because of the giver, but never instead of the giver." This is clearly what the early Alliance intended by not seeking, not a passive attitude. As Everett acknowledges, "Simpson seems to say that the individual is not entirely passive in the operation of the gifts."[14]

The real question, therefore, is: what did the early C&MA mean by not seeking tongues or other manifestations? It is true that some in the C&MA today interpret "seek not" to mean not to desire tongues or have an expectancy of tongues, but to maintain a passive mode. i.e., "I will not desire tongues, but if God wants to give it to me, okay." In fact, the attitude in some Alliance circles has been "Seek not, forbid not, and hope not." But this is was not the early C&MA position. Early Alliance leaders encouraged earnestly desiring all that God had to give, including spiritual gifts, but without seeking after a particular manifestation.

In several cases Alliance leaders use the language of "seeking" as a positive encouragement. W. C. Stevens exhorted, "It is imperative that in these momentous days of opportunity we all become acknowledged *seekers for our personal portion of the latter rain*."[15] Jaffray counseled, "*Seek earnestly for the true and full endowment of the Spirit* for which our souls hunger." [16] Alliance leaders believed in seeking all that God has for each individual believer. W. T. MacArthur counseled to seek God, not manifestations, yet "with hearts wide open in the fullest expectancy." He explains that "we are seeking the fullness of God in a way that is acceptable to Him."[17] Eventually, after seeking the fullness of God in this manner, some of his church did speak in tongues, including his wife and perhaps himself.[18]

To Alliance leaders, it was thus appropriate to seek the "fullness of God" in a way that pleases God. That "acceptable" way was understood by the C&MA as not seeking after manifestations, but "to wait expectantly upon Him without fear of fanaticism."[19] Active expectancy of gifts without seeking gifts seems to have been the Alliance norm.

SOVEREIGN BESTOWAL OF GIFTS

Simpson and other Alliance leaders from a moderate Reformed position stressed the sovereignty of God in bestowing gifts, as interpreted in 1 Corinthians 12.[20] On this basis, Alliance leaders believed that speaking in tongues is thus not necessarily for all Christians, although this point was not frequently emphasized, occurring only once by Simpson, twice by Ballard, and once by Bosworth.[21] Nevertheless, it was implied by appealing to the sovereign will of God.

According to Pentecostal historian Brumback, early on in the revival some Alliance leaders apparently believed, at least initially, that everyone could receive tongues. Mrs. W. T. MacArthur related her experience of tongues, saying that "this was like the 'residue of the oil' (Leviticus 14:18, 25) that flowed down upon the hem of Aaron's robe, and that *God was doing this thing for all who would receive*" (italics mine). E. D. Whiteside was in charge of the prayer room at this particular time and encouraged people not to be afraid of manifestations or fanaticism.[22] Later, he also invited Azusa Street leader Frank Bartleman speak in his church several times. Apparently, he was encouraging expectation of the gift of tongues, although it is not clear that he was expecting that all could receive. In time, however, the MacArthurs, Whiteside, and other Alliance leaders eventually concluded that it could not be expected that tongues would be bestowed upon all who ask and are willing to receive, as was the experience of Simpson himself.

The point that Alliance leaders were trying to make was that while it is appropriate to desire spiritual gifts, it is not necessary or spiritually healthy to seek after certain manifestations. Simpson recorded Joseph Smale reporting that some people who did not want to speak in tongues, and even opposed tongues had themselves received the gift.[23] Admonitions against seeking tongues and other manifestations did not come only from the C&MA, however, but also from numerous Pentecostals, such as Azusa Street revival leader William Seymour and other Azusa Street leaders, British Pentecostal leader A. A. Boddy, and E. W. Kenyon, often considered the father of the modern charismatic Word of Faith movement.[24] The fact that not only early Alliance leaders but even some Pentecostals have advised against seeking is noteworthy.

THE EARLY ALLIANCE "FORBID NOT" POSITION

The early C&MA was not so focused on a "Seek Not" position that they did not allow or encourage manifestation of tongues and other supernatural gifts of the Spirit. In January 1907, J. Hudson Ballard, in a statement that would be republished later the same year as the official Alliance position, wrote, "(a) The church of Christ today may receive the Gift of Tongues. (b) Every local church of Christ should have, in some of its members, the manifestation of this gift."[25] The early Alliance taught, "Every Christian should be willing to receive this gift if it please the Spirit to bestow it upon him. It is a dangerous thing to oppose or despise this, one of the immediate manifestations of the Blessed Spirit of God."[26] Repeatedly, in the next two decades, the admonition not to forbid or despise tongues was emphasized.[27] The "seek not, forbid not" concept is undeniably found in C&MA publications from 1907 to 1927, though not stated so concisely as the 1963 document.

SIMPSON A SEEKER OF TONGUES?

Nienkirchen claimed that Simpson's diary "shows him to have been a seeker of Spirit baptism with tongues between 1907 and 1912."[28] Although Simpson never uses the word "seeking," it can be recognized that he was indeed seeking more of God and all that God desired to give to him. Alliance historian John Sawin notes that Simpson's diary does imply that he was expectant of tongues or other supernatural manifestations and that he was open to receiving anything God was willing to give.[29] Simpson taught that there could be "the Pentecosts and the second Pentecosts,"[30] so he believed he had received a genuine baptism in the Spirit many years earlier. Yet he also believed God wanted to give him a "deeper and fuller baptism" that would include "complete Pentecostal fullness embracing all the gifts and graces."

However, a careful analysis of Simpson's wording clarifies the extent of his desire. It is significant that Simpson's diary in 1907 does not specify that he was praying for tongues, but "all the gifts and graces." Simpson's mention of tongues in his 1912 entry does clearly indicate that Simpson did indeed desire to receive the gift of tongues, and could suggest that perhaps at one point he had just about come to the conclusion that God wanted him to speak in tongues.[31] Yet again, he does not specify tongues by itself, but rather "tongues *or* similar gifts." It is noteworthy that he does not write "tongues *and* similar gifts." His particular language indicates that he had a special interest in tongues of all of the gifts, but his desire was not particularly or only for tongues. He indicates that he was willing to receive anything God was willing to give, be that tongues or something else.

Yet Simpson does not use the language of "seeking." Consistent with what he had stated before throughout the preceding five years both publicly and in his diary, in 1912 Simpson says he was "open" for God to bestow anything He desires. Being actively open to gifts does not necessarily mean that he was seeking them. Although it might seem like seeking to some, a careful study of Simpson's use of the word "seek" shows that it is quite unlikely that Simpson would use the word "seeking" to describe his active openness to tongues and other gifts. He was consistently following his counsel from 1906 on to "exercise at once a wise conservatism and a readiness of mind to receive whatever God is truly sending."[32] In fact, in the light of all of Simpson's statements regarding not seeking, he likely would bristle at the claim that he was seeking tongues.[33] Some Pentecostals would even argue that the reason Simpson never spoke in tongues was because he did *not* seek tongues. Further, in 1916, four years after his diary comments, Simpson continued to maintain the inappropriateness of seeking tongues: "We draw the line when teachers and evangelists insist on preaching . . . that the manifestations in *tongues or miracles must always be sought.* . . ."[34] In thirteen references in the context of eleven statements by Simpson (one in 1906, six in 1907, three in 1908 and the one in 1916), he specifically counsels not to seek tongues or other gifts.

Simpson's Non-Passive "Seek Not" Position. But neither was Simpson passive. Rather, he actively and persistently claimed all that God had to give him. To Simpson's mind "seek not" clearly did not mean passivity. Although there was in the early C&MA a strong Reformed emphasis on the sovereignty of God, Simpson also wrote on the need for desiring something in order to receive it: "Desire is a necessary element in all spiritual forces. It is one of the secrets of effectual prayer. . . . There is no factor in prayer more effectual than love. If we are intensely interested in an object or an individual, our petitions become like living forces."[35] It is important to note that for Simpson even the first level of prayer, *asking* God for gifts, is not to be taken lightly:

> Many people are looking for some extraordinary gift, or strained experience of the Holy Spirit, when He really wants to come to you in your simple everyday life and help you to be a better wife and mother, a more kind and helpful friend, a more upright and successful business man, a more efficient employee, and a more genial, loving and unselfish member of your household and social circle. . . . Beloved, perhaps it is here that the Holy Spirit wants to come to you first before you have a right to ask Him for the gifts of prophecy, miracles or tongues. He knows better than you your place in life, the needs of those around you and the sort of grace and help best fitted to make you efficient for His glory.[36]

At the same time as he wrote this (August 1907), he indicates in his diary that he did believe that the supernatural gifts and graces of the Spirit were part the inheritance of the Christian, indeed, of his own inheritance that he could claim.

Simpson had gone beyond asking and seeking to the point of knocking, persistence to receive all that he be believed God wanted to give him—including all God's gifts and graces. It must therefore be acknowledged that he did seek (and knock), but this is not an unbridled or unlimited seeking. He does not say that he was seeking after tongues itself, although it is clear he desired the gift. Rather, he sought God and claimed whatever gifts were God's inheritance for him. It is conceivable (though speculative and unverifiable) that Simpson could have become convinced that the Holy Spirit wanted to grant him the gift of tongues and thus prayed accordingly. Such an attitude would be consistent with a scriptural "earnestly desiring" and could be considered seeking in a limited sense, but would not be "unduly" seeking, or seeking the gift more than the Giver. The evidence shows that Simpson probably continued to "earnestly desire" (and perhaps pray for) tongues until his death, yet he would not call it seeking after tongues, although others may consider his posture a form of seeking.[37] I would agree with Wacker's concession that the language of Simpson's diary is "admittedly elliptical," so we need to be careful not to put words in Simpson's mouth and claim more than he himself would claim.

To clarify the misunderstandings, the original "seek not, forbid not" position of the Alliance is in harmony *with the modifications* suggested by Nathan and Wilson: "Seek not tongues *more than or instead of* God Himself. Seek the Blesser more than the blessing." A passive stance toward receptivity to tongues or mere tolerance of tongues was not the position of Simpson and the early Alliance.

In recent years there has been some movement toward clarifying and restoring the original C&MA position. Dr. Ron Walborn, Dean of Bible and Pastoral Studies at Nyack College, suggested the more positive axiom "expectation without agenda," meaning that we can expect supernatural gifts without seeking after them with impure motives. This motto was adopted by the Board of Directors. Dr. David Schroeder, former president of Nyack College and Alliance Theological Seminary suggests the phrase "Cease Not, Compel Not" (cease not permitting and encouraging tongues and other gifts, but not insisting that people speak in tongues as a required evidence of the filling of the Spirit). Both of these statements accurately and consistently convey the early Alliance position.

WAS TOZER A REVISIONIST?

Nienkirchen surmised that the phrase "seek not, forbid not" was a late accretion by Tozer, whom he claimed was a revisionist of Alliance history and theology. The above documentation demonstrates that the "seek not, forbid not" concept occurred frequently throughout early Alliance history and was not the creation of Tozer. Further, the exact phrase "seek not, forbid not" is not a 1963 invention, but was in usage in the C&MA as early as the 1930s.

Beyond that issue is Nienkirchen's claim that Tozer was a revisionist of Alliance history and theology. Nienkirchen cites a statement of Tozer in *Wingspread*, his biography of A. B. Simpson, as evidence: "The simple fact is that Mr. Simpson was miles out ahead of these people [Pentecostals] in spiritual experience. He did not need anything they had. He had found a blessed secret far above anything these perfervid seekers after wonders could ever think or conceive."[38] Bertone goes even farther in his conclusion, claiming that Tozer rejected "the experience of glossolalia entirely."[39]

If Tozer's statement is taken in isolation from his other writings, one could get the impression that he was hostile toward Pentecostals, and, maybe, for a period of time he *was* to some extent negatively biased. In fact, Tozer may have had in front of him some evidence to support his statement.[40]

Tozer's description, written in 1943, can also be considered in light of the distancing of the C&MA as a whole from Pentecostals that took place in the 1930s. When other later comments by Tozer are taken in consideration, we find that he was much more positive toward Pentecostals than Nienkirchen and Bertone surmise:

> I have known and studied these dear brethren, and have preached to them for a long, long time. I have studied them, and I know them very well, and I am very sympathetic with them. There are some churches that are very sane and beautiful and godly. . . . The movement itself has magnified one single gift above all others, and that one gift is the one Paul said was the least. An unscriptural exhibition of that gift results, and there is a tendency to place personal feeling above the Scriptures, and we must never, never do that!"[41]

Tozer, who was known not to mince words, nonetheless, here shows a warm affection for Pentecostals, and evidently even preached in Pentecostal churches, in spite of strongly disagreeing with what he considered their excessive magnification of tongues. The evidence shows that Tozer was not opposed to tongues, only against insistence that tongues is *the* necessary evidence of the filling of the Spirit. He even asserted that the gifts of the Spirit are a "necessity in the church" and that missing gifts are a "tragedy in the church."[42]

Tozer's More Positive Attitudes Toward Tongues. Tozer's attitudes toward tongues-speakers were not all negative, and he certainly did not reject "the experience of glossolalia entirely," as Bertone maintains. I had heard a report that some of Tozer's relatives were Pentecostal, but I have not been able to verify its accuracy. If this is true, they may have influenced Tozer's views, either pro or con depending on how moderate or extreme they were. It is especially significant that H. M. Shuman, Tozer's District Superintendent who accepted him into ministry and later served as C&MA president, was a tongue-speaker. Tozer himself served as Vice President under Shuman for four years, as well as editor of the *Alliance Witness* under Shuman's leadership. Additionally, Harry Turner, successor to Shuman as President of the C&MA, had been a Pentecostal missionary. Tozer had the confidence of both of these tongue-speaking leaders, and he also had confidence in them. Rather than being opposed to tongues, Tozer knew of genuine and positive speaking in tongues and negative experiences with Pentecostals as well.

Tozer also warned against shunning the supernatural work of the Spirit because of fear of wild-eyed fanatics, saying, "Well, my brother, I will not be frightened out of my rightful heritage. I will not be scared out of my birthright because some others didn't know what to do with the birthright or have found something else that has nothing to do with the birthright. I want all that God has for me!"[43] In his last message to the C&MA, Tozer decried a neglect of the person and work of the Holy Spirit in the evangelical church of the early 1960s, saying, "Now, I am not a tongues man, and I have never been, and I have no intention to join them. But I want to tell you that I believe in the gifts of the Spirit, and I believe they ought all to be in the Church."[44]

It would seem that, over time, Tozer moderated his views of Pentecostals. According to Alliance historian John Sawin, Tozer told him he wanted to withdraw *Wingspread* from circulation because it was an "interpretation, not a biography" of Simpson.[45] Referring to Tozer's use of the word "perfervid" as "unkind," Sawin commented that Tozer "sometimes traveled miles to apologize for harsh statements he made at Council meetings."[46] Sawin's implication is that Tozer would not fully subscribe to what he had written earlier.

All of this demonstrates that Tozer, though having some earlier negative bias against at least some Pentecostals, was *not* a revisionist of Alliance history and theology. Rather, he was consistent with the beliefs of Alliance leaders of his time who believed in the gifts (some of whom even spoke in tongues) but distanced themselves from Pentecostals and, generally, from early Alliance attitudes of greater openness with caution.

EARLY ALLIANCE VIEW OF PENTECOSTALS COMPARED WITH OTHER EVANGELICALS

Another way of discerning the early Alliance attitudes toward charismatic phenomena, and in particular tongues, is by comparing the early Alliance views with the viewpoints of other evangelicals of the time toward the Pentecostal movement. Many evangelical leaders were hostile toward the Pentecostal movement.[47] In his publication *The Modern Gift of Tongues: Whence Is It?*, Brethren writer G. H. Lang condemned the tongues experience of Alliance missionary Kate Knight (whom Simpson supported). Lang also spoke negatively of T. B. Barratt, Carrie Judd Montgomery, and A. A. Boddy, all friends of Simpson.[48] Some of these leaders were from the British Keswick movement, which as a whole appeared to have negative views of the Pentecostal movement.

On the other hand, although Simpson and the early Alliance had concerns and reservations about certain elements of the Pentecostal movement and discerned some elements to be counterfeit, they had no such condemning epitaphs for the movement as a whole (as some Alliance leaders do today). Simpson spoke favorably of moderate Pentecostals such as Boddy, Barratt, Jonathan Paul, and Willis Hoover, and to a great degree approved of the Pentecostal movements in England, Europe, Argentina and Chile.[49] The Alliance even cooperated with moderate Pentecostals in joint ventures and meetings.[50] The main objection of C&MA leaders was the initial evidence doctrine, and these leaders and movements took a more moderate position on the doctrine.

Even further, Alliance leaders spoke out against the opponents of tongues and the Pentecostal movement. Prominent Keswick leader A. T. Pierson, who was respected by Alliance leaders and had been a close friend of Simpson's who had spoken at many of his meetings, nevertheless had a more negative view of tongues, concluding, "In not one instance has any good been traced to these manifestations."[51] The editor of C&MA missions periodical *The India Alliance* took issue with Pierson's conclusions, saying, "We regret, however, that the writer makes such sweeping statements in regard to the modern 'tongue' movement. . . . We believe that to many has come great blessing through this movement."[52]

Jessie Penn Lewis and Evan Roberts, in their renowned book *War on the Saints*, believed the Church was not mature enough to exercise the gift of tongues properly, saying, "Until the spiritual section of the Church of Christ are more acquainted with the counterfeiting methods of the spirits of evil, and the laws which give them power of working, any testimony to such experience as true, cannot be safely relied upon."[53] Even though Penn-Lewis and Roberts were respected by Simpson and the Alliance, the Alliance took issue with their position:

> We are in hearty sympathy with our authors in warning against danger in "seeking" to speak in tongues; but we have no sympathy with them in tying God down to any theory that makes it impossible for Him to enable one to exercise the "sign" until "the spiritual section of the Church" has mastered this "Textbook" [the book *War on the Saints*] and become "more acquainted with the counterfeit methods of the spirits of evil." This method of teaching blazes a dangerous trail.[54]

Further, the fact that Simpson and the early C&MA periodicals openly and positively published many occurrences and testimonies of speaking in tongues in its periodicals (Thomas Barratt,[55] Robert Jaffray, [56] Mary Mullen, [57] John Salmon,[58] Cora Hansen,[59] Kate Knight,[60] and W. W. Simpson.[61]) demonstrates their openness to the gift of tongues. Also significant is the fact that Pandita Ramabai, whose Mukti Mission has been known as the home of the Pentecostal revival in India, designated in her will that the C&MA become the trustee of her mission after her death. This demonstrates two significant observations: 1) that the C&MA was sufficiently open to the charismatic manifestations that occurred in her mission and were welcomed by Ramabai, 2) that the C&MA of her time was more in line with her charismatic beliefs and practices than Pentecostal missions in India which emphasized evidential tongues. All of this (and much more that I have researched but not documented here) supports Alliance historian John Sawin's conclusion, "Simpson and the Alliance rejected the evidence view, but were hospitable to the tongues movement."[62] Pentecostal historian Vinson Synan astutely notes that the "Alliance position" was "a compromise unique in the early history of the movement."[63]

NORMAL, BUT NOT NORMATIVE

Assemblies of God historian William Menzies claimed, "The 'seek not, forbid not' Alliance position effectively closed the door to Pentecostal phenomena within their ranks."[64] However, this conclusion is disproved by the many continuing evidences of tongues-speakers among Alliance leadership. Evidence shows that Pentecostal phenomena did decline in the C&MA after the 1920s, but never totally closed the door.

The sampling of documentation cited here (and the dozens of other references that could be cited) demonstrate clearly that there was a much higher degree of expectancy of tongues and other charismatic phenomena by Simpson and other early Alliance leaders than today. They did not seek after tongues or other manifestations, but they did anticipate that God would pour out them out upon the Alliance, and they actively desired all that God had for them. As Ballard reiterated of the unified C&MA belief in his day, "Alliance leaders are quite agreed in believing that speaking with tongues . . . should have a place in every Spirit-controlled church."[65] In other words, tongues was expected to be *normal* in every Alliance church, but not necessarily *normative* for every believer. The 1963 "Seek Not, Forbid Not" statement does acknowledge that tongues "may be present in the normal Christian assembly,"[66] though this has not been the expectation in most Alliance churches. The new 2005 Board of Directors statement "Spiritual Gifts: Expectation with Agenda," replacing the "Seek Not, Forbid Not" statement of 1963, is a step in returning to the early C&MA emphasis.

---

1. *The Gift of Tongues—Seek Not, Forbid Not* (Nyack, NY: The Christian and Missionary Alliance, n.d.)

2. Paul L. King, "Seek Not, Forbid Not: The Early Christian and Missionary Alliance Position on Glossolalia, *"Wesleyan Theological Journal*, Vol. 40, No. 2 (Fall 2005), 184-219.

3. See Synan, *The Holiness-Pentecostal Movement in the United States*, 145.

4. Nienkirchen, *A. B. Simpson and the Pentecostal Movement*, 139-140.

5. Ibid., 131-140.

6. See Synan's revised edition, *The Holiness-Pentecostal Tradition*, 147; Blumhofer, *The Assemblies of God*, 185; John A. Bertone, "A. B. Simpson and The Experience of Glossolalia: 'To Seek or Not to Seek, To Forbid or Not to Forbid?, accessed on the Internet, Dec. 18, 2001, at http://online.cbccts.sk.ca/alliance studies/docs/SimpsonGloss.htm; David John Smith, "Albert Benjamin Simpson: An Integrated Spirituality with Christ as the Centre," (Belleville, Ontario, Dec. 15, 1997, revised Feb. 9, 1998), 17, accessed on the Internet Feb. 25, 2002 at http://online.cbccts.sk.ca/alliance studies/dsmith/djs_spirituality.html.

7. Hartzfeld and Nienkirchen, *The Birth of a Vision*, 164. The statement by Bailey is an editorial note inserted by the publisher in the second printing of the book. For a discussion of this matter, see Paul L. King, "A Critique of Charles Nienkirchen's Book *A. B. Simpson and the Pentecostal Movement*," *Alliance Academic Review* (CampHill, PA: Christian Publications, 2000), 101-114.

8. Grant Wacker, *Heaven Below: Early Pentecostals and American Culture* (Cambridge, MA; London, Eng.: Harvard University Press, 2001), 317, note 27.

9. See Simpson, "All the Blessings of the Spirit," CMAW, Sept. 29, 1906, 198; Smale, "The Gift of Tongues, *Living Truths*, Jan. 1907, 32-43; Ballard, "Spiritual Gifts with Special Reference to the Gift of Tongues," *Living Truths*, Jan. 1907, 23-31; MacArthur, "The Promise of the Father and Speaking with Tongues in Chicago, "CMAW, Feb. 16, 1907, 76; Simpson, Editorial, CMAW, Mar. 2, 1907, 97; Simpson, "Spiritual Sanity," *Living Truths*, Apr. 1907; A. B. Simpson, Editorial, CMAW, June 29, 1907, 301; Editorial, *The India Alliance*, Aug. 1907, 19; Pierson, "Speaking with Tongues," *The India Alliance*, Aug. 1907, 19-21; A.B. Simpson, "Lengthening the Cords and Strengthening the Stakes," CMAW, Aug. 10, 1907, 62; Mullen, "Some Danger Lines," CMAW, Nov. 2, 1907, 75; Uxkull, "Experiences of God's Grace in Russia," CMAW, Jan. 11, 1908,245; Moon, "The Receiving of the Holy Ghost," CMAW, Feb. 22, 1908, 344; "South China," CMAW, Aug. 1,1908, 287-289; Ramsey, "Speaking in Tongues: An Exegetical Study," CMAW, Apr. 4, 1908, 7, 17; Simpson, "Annual Report of the C&MA 1907-1908," CMAW, 155-56, 193; Simpson, "What Hath God Wrought?, "CMAW, June 13, 1908, 170; Simpson, "Side Issues and the Supreme Object of Life," CMAW, Sept. 19, 1908,416; Boyd, "Seated with Christ," CMAW, Jan. 16, 1909, 261ff.; Sellow, "I Am Not Satisfied," CMAW, Oct. 23, 1909, 60; McDonough, "The Harvest Rain," CMAW, Feb. 5, 1910, 297, 305; Harriman, "'War on the Saints': An Analytical Study, Part III," AW, Jan. 10, 1914, 231; Eldridge, "Purified and Tried," AW, Sept. 4,1915, 357; Letter from Simpson to Mrs. M. A. Weaver, Sept. 1916.

10. Ballard, "Spiritual Gifts with Special Reference to the Gift of Tongues," *Living Truths*, Jan. 1907, 23-31; reported by Simpson in Editorial, CMAW, Jan. 26, 1907, 1; Editorial, *The India Alliance*, Aug. 1907, 19; Pierson, "Speaking with Tongues," *The India Alliance*, Aug. 1907, 19-21; Simpson, "Side Issues and the Supreme Object of Life, CMAW, Sept. 19, 1908, 416; Boyd, "Seated with Christ," CMAW, Jan. 16, 1909, 261ff.; Editorial, *The India Alliance*, May 1909, 103; Ballard, "The Spiritual Clinic," AW, Mar. 2, 1912, 343; Ballard, "Studies in I Corinthians," AW, June 20, 1914, 198-199; June 27, 1914, 214-215; Thompson, "The Corinthian Epistles: Spiritual Gifts and Graces," AW, Feb. 12, 1916, 315-316; Thompson, "The Corinthian Epistles: The Use, Abuse and Value of Gifts," AW, Feb. 26, 1916, 341.

11. Thompson, *A. B. Simpson: His Life and Work*, 140.

12. Rich Nathan and Ken Wilson, *Empowered Evangelicals* (Ann Arbor, MI: Servant Publications, 1995), 120-121.

13. Simpson, Editorial, CMAW, Mar. 2, 1907, 97; Simpson, Editorial, CMAW, Mar. 16, 1907, 121; Simpson, "Spiritual Sanity," *Living Truths*, Apr. 1907; Simpson, "Gifts and Grace," Toccoa Falls, GA: Toccoa Falls College, n.d.; Oldfield, *With You Always, the Life of a South China Missionary*, 89; Simpson, May 1908 Annual Report; MacArthur, "The Promise of the Father and Speaking with Tongues in Chicago," CMAW, Feb. 16,1907, 76; S. Armson, "Ashapur, the Village of Hope," *The India Alliance*, Sept. 1908, 26; McCrossan, *Speaking with Other Tongues: Sign or Gift—Which?*, 32; Bosworth, *Do All Speak with Tongues?*, 13-14; Rader, *Harnessing God*, 96-97.

14. Everett, 69; see Simpson, *The Holy Spirit*, 2:123.

15. Stevens, "The Latter Rain," *Living Truths*, September 1907, 530.

16. Jaffray, "Speaking in Tongues—Some Words of Kindly Counsel," CMAW, Mar. 13, 1909, 395-396, 406.

17. MacArthur, "The Promise of the Father and Speaking with Tongues in Chicago," CMAW, Feb. 16, 1907, 76.

18. MacArthur, "The Promise of the Father and Speaking in Tongues in Chicago," CMAW, July 27, 1907, 44.

19. Anderson, "The 'Latter Rain,' and Its Counterfeit," *Signs of the Times*, 136; Editorial, *The India Alliance*, Aug. 1907, 19; Pierson, "Speaking with Tongues," *The India Alliance*, Aug. 1907, 19-21; Mullen, "Some Danger Lines," CMAW, Nov. 2, 1907, 75; Moon, "The Receiving of the Holy Ghost," CMAW, Feb. 22, 1908,344; Uxkull, "Experiences of God's Grace in Russia," CMAW, Jan. 11, 1908, 245; Armson, "Ashapur, the Village of Hope," *The India Alliance*, Sept. 1908, 26.

20. Simpson, "All the Blessings of the Spirit," CMAW, Sept. 29, 1906, 198; Ballard, "Spiritual Gifts with Special Reference to the Gift of Tongues," *Living Truths*, Jan. 1907, 23-31; Simpson, Editorial, CMAW, Jan. 26, 1907,1; Editorial, *The India Alliance*, Aug. 1907, 19; Pierson, "Speaking with Tongues," *The India Alliance*, Aug. 1907, 19-21; Anderson, "The 'Latter Rain,' and Its Counterfeit," *Signs of the Times*, 136; Ramsey, "Speaking in Tongues: An Exegetical Study," CMAW, Apr. 4, 1908, 7, 17.

21. Ballard, "Spiritual Gifts with Special Reference to the Gift of Tongues," *Living Truths*, Jan. 1907, 23-31; Simpson, Editorial, CMAW, Apr. 30, 1910, 78; Ballard, "The Spiritual Clinic," AW, Mar. 2, 1912, 343; Bosworth, *Do All Speak with Tongues?*, 13-14.

22. Brumback, *Suddenly . . . from Heaven*, 79-80.

23. Smale, "The Gift of Tongues," *Living Truths*, Jan. 1907, 32-43.

24. E. Sisson, "Tongues and Prophecy," LRE, Nov. 1912, 23; Larry Martin, ed., *Holy Ghost Revival on Azusa Street: The True Believers* (Joplin, MO: Christian Life Books, 1998), 72; Bartleman, *Azusa Street* (1980), 79; Larry E. Martin, ed., *The Topeka Outpouring of 1901: 100th Anniversary Edition* (Joplin, MO: Christian Life Books, 2000), 110; A. A. Boddy, "They Two Went On," LRE, Oct. 1912, 7; Guy P. Duffield and Nathaniel M. VanCleave, *Foundations for Pentecostal Theology* (Los Angeles, CA: L.I.F.E. Bible College, 1983), 1987, 322; Eldridge, "Purified and Tried," AW, Sept. 4, 1915, 357; Letter from W. W. Simpson to A. B. Simpson, Oct. 17,1916; Kenyon, *In His Presence*, 124-125; Price, *The Real Faith*, 57; Kathryn Kuhlman, *Captain LaVrier Believes in Miracles* (Old Tappan, NJ: Spire Books, 1973), 83.

25. Ballard, "Spiritual Gifts with Special Reference to the Gift of Tongues," *Living Truths*, Jan. 1907, 23-31; reported by Simpson in Editorial, CMAW, Jan. 26, 1907, 1.

26. Ibid.

27. Editorial, *The India Alliance*, Aug. 1907, 19; Pierson, "Speaking with Tongues," *The India Alliance*, Aug. 1907, 19-21; Simpson, "Side Issues and the Supreme Object of Life, CMAW, Sept. 19, 1908, 416; Boyd, "Seated with Christ," CMAW, Jan. 16, 1909, 261ff.; Ballard, "The Spiritual Clinic," AW, Mar. 2, 1912, 343; Ballard, "Studies in I Corinthians," AW, June 20, 1914, 198-199; June 27, 1914, 214-215; Thompson, "The Corinthian Epistles: Spiritual Gifts and Graces," AW, Feb. 12, 1916, 315-316; Thompson, "The Corinthian Epistles: The Use, Abuse and Value of Gifts," AW, Feb. 26, 1916, 341; Rader, *Harnessing God*, 95-96, 99; Smith, *The Baptism with the Holy Spirit*, 44-46; McCrossan, *Speaking with Other Tongues: Sign or Gift—Which?*, 32, 42.

28. Nienkirchen, 136.

29. Sawin, "The Response and Attitude of Dr. A. B. Simpson and the Christian and Missionary Alliance to the Tongues Movement of 1906-1920," 22, 28.

30. Simpson, *A Larger Christian Life* (1988), 42.

31. Alliance historian John Sawin notes this: "Simpson saw and heard about the bestowal of the gift of tongues upon his respected friends and co-workers. . . . He wanted to receive for himself the same

gift his friends had experienced, but couldn't understand why the Lord was not pleased to bestow the gift upon him. So he continued to seek [the Lord, not tongues itself]. He gave much time praying and waiting on the Lord. The wonderful presence and power of the Spirit did come to him with renewed freshness, but not the gift of tongues. . . . His quest then, for which the diary is the record, was for a deeper, richer fullness of the Spirit than he had heretofore known, and his desire included the gift of tongues." Sawin, "The Response and Attitude of Dr. A. B. Simpson and the Christian and Missionary Alliance to the Tongues Movement of 1906-1920," 22, 28. Paper presented at the Society of Pentecostal Studies Conference, Sept. 1986, Fort Myers, Florida.

32. Simpson, "All the Blessings of the Spirit," CMAW, Sept. 29, 1906, 198.

33. Some may argue that it is a matter of semantics as to whether Simpson was "desiring" or "seeking" tongues. However, nuances in meaning are often crucial, as in the heresies declared and battles fought over a single word in the Christological controversies among early church fathers. So we must be careful not to claim what Simpson did not actually say. Examining Simpson's choice of words closely and absorbing his thought and sensing his heart, I am convinced that Simpson would bristle at the thought of calling his desire "seeking." If in 13 statements between 1906 and 1916, he counsels not to seek manifestations, and in 7 of them specifically warns not to seek tongues, to claim that he sought tongues, one would need to conclude: 1) that he flip-flopped back and forth in his belief, 2) that he was dishonest, speaking out of both sides of his mouth—publicly saying "seek not" and privately seeking, or 3) that he was schizophrenic. Yes, he was seeking—seeking more of God, seeking all that God had for him, seeking all the gifts and graces God wanted to give him which could include tongues, but again, to be consistent (which he appears to be all through the years), he would never call his desire for tongues as seeking after tongues. Call it seeking, if you want, but it was not seeking after tongues.

34. Letter from Simpson to Mrs. M. A. Weaver, Sept. 1916.

35. Simpson, *Days of Heaven on Earth*, Nov. 13, Nov. 15.

36. Simpson, "The Ministry of the Spirit," Aug. 1907, 442.

37. Montgomery, *Under His Wings*, 231.

38. Tozer, *Wingspread*, 133. Cited in Nienkirchen, 136.

39. Bertone, 13, note 46.

40. Letter from W. W. Simpson to A. B. Simpson, Oct. 17, 1916. W. W. Simpson's chief complaint was that the official C&MA Board statement presented to him by Robert Glover differed from what A. B. Simpson wrote to Mrs. M. A. Weaver, a friend of W. W. Simpson. He claimed with bitterness, "Either Glover forged the statement he handed us or you have deliberately tried to deceive Mrs. Weaver." Obviously, neither was the case. A. B. Simpson was merely paraphrasing from memory what had been written and the thought behind it. The letter to Mrs. Weaver was not meant to be a verbatim reproduction, and Simpson's recollection at this point in his aging process was likely not accurate or complete. It is possible that Glover may have been more negative toward the Pentecostal movement and thus presented the Board's letter as an ultimatum, but it is not likely that he forged anything. W. W. Simpson was quibbling over terms and wording, but the clear fact is that his position of presenting tongues as the evidence of the baptism in the Spirit was not compatible with the Alliance view.

41. A. W. Tozer, *The Tozer Pulpit* (Camp Hill, PA: Christian Publications, 1994), 1:2:99.

42. Tozer, *Tragedy in the Church*, 13, 25.

43. A. W. Tozer, *The Counselor* (Camp Hill, PA: Christian Publications, 1993), 63-64. For more on Tozer's views on the Holy Spirit and the gifts of the Spirit, see Tozer, *The Tozer Pulpit*, Volume 2. Wilson also notes that Tozer's biography of Simpson "is a more subjective interpretation" than the earlier biography by Simpson's contemporary, A. E. Thompson. Wilson, *The Christian and Missionary Alliance*, 13.

44. A. W. Tozer, *A. W. Tozer's Last Message to the Alliance* (Camp Hill, PA: Christian Publications, 2000), 13-14.

45. Handwritten note by John Sawin, Nov. 23, 1988, Flower Pentecostal Heritage Center.

46. Ibid.

47. Synan, *The Holiness-Pentecostal Movement in the United States*, 143-145; Lederle, *Treasures Old and New*, 24; Meyer, *Five Musts of the Christian Life*, 73-74.

48. G. H. Lang, *The Modern Gift of Tongues: Whence Is It?* (London: Marshall Brothers, Ltd., [1913]), 17-49; G. H. Lang, *The Earlier Years of the Modern Tongues Movement* (Enfield, Middlesex, England: Metcalfe Collier, n.d.), 27-33, 43-46, 59-60.

49. Barratt, "The Seal of My Pentecost," *Living Truths*, Dec. 1906, 735-738; Simpson, Editorial, CMAW, Apr. 29, 1911, 65; Simpson, Editorial, AW, July 6, 1912, 210; Hoover, *History of the Pentecostal Revival in Chile*, 126-128; see also Frodsham, *With Signs Following*, 175-187; Simpson, "Editorial Correspondence," CMAW, Apr. 30, 1910, 71-73, 86.

50. "Convention in Haverhill, Massachusetts," CMAW, Mar. 19, 1910, 404; "Gleanings from Nyack," CMAW, Apr. 30, 1910, 82; "Who and Where," AW, Feb. 17, 1912, 318; Simpson, Editorial, AW, May 30, 1914, 130; Simpson, Editorial, AW, Dec. 19, 1914, 177; "Ordination of Mr. George P. Simmonds," AW, Jan. 30, 1915,286; "Report on the Los Angeles Convention," AW, June 1, 1915, 158; William T. MacArthur, "The Three Components of Christians," LRE, Jan. 1918, 6-8; Montgomery, *Under His Wings*, 231. On cooperation with Cecil Polhill and the British Pentecostal Missionary Union, see C&MA Board of Manager minutes, Mar. 30, 1912; Oct. 11, 1913; Oct. 16, 1915.

51. Pierson, "Speaking with Tongues," *The India Alliance*, Aug. 1907, 21.

52. Editorial, *The India Alliance*, Aug. 1907, 19.

53. Penn-Lewis and Roberts, *War on the Saints*, unabridged edition, 297-298.

54. Harriman, "*War on the Saints*: An Analytical Study—Part III: All Thoughts from God or Satan," AW, Jan.10, 1914, 231; see also Simpson, Editorial, AW, Jan. 17, 1914, 241-242.

55. Barratt, "The Seal of My Pentecost," *Living Truths*, Dec. 1906, 735-738.

56. Jaffray, "Speaking in Tongues—Some Words of Kindly Counsel," CMAW, Mar. 13, 1909, 395-396, 406.

57. Mullen, "A New Experience," CMAW, Oct. 5, 1907, 17.

58. Salmon, "My Enduement," CMAW, Oct. 26, 1907, 54-55.

59. Hansen, "Testimony," *The India Alliance*, Aug. 1908, 22-24.

60. Knight, "For His Glory," CMAW, Jan 25, 1908, 274.

61. Simpson, "Notes from Kansu," AW, Mar. 1, 1913, 345-346.

62. Sawin, "The Response and Attitude of Dr. A. B. Simpson and the Christian and Missionary Alliance to the Tongues Movement of 1906-1920," 29.

63. Synan, *The Holiness-Pentecostal Movement in the United States*, 145.

64. Menzies, *Anointed to Serve*, 72.

65. Ballard, "The Spiritual Clinic," AW, Nov. 21, 1914, 126.

66. *The Gift of Tongues—Seek Not, Forbid Not*. While this was acknowledged, it has not been common practice since 1963 for tongues to be a normal part of Alliance church assemblies. Keith Bailey stated in 1977 that in his 30 plus years of ministry in the C&MA he knew of no public expressions of tongues and interpretation in Alliance services. Bailey, "Dealing with the Charismatic in Today's Church."

TWENTY-FIVE

The Early C&MA and Modern Faith Teaching

The modern "word of faith" movement is a subset of the charismatic and Pentecostal movements that emphasizes walking by faith. Not all Pentecostals and charismatics are in the word of faith stream, but almost all word of faith proponents are Pentecostal or charismatic. Hank Hanegraaff in *Christianity in Crisis* and Dan McConnell in *A Different Gospel*, as well as others, have claimed that modern word of faith teaching originated in cultic New Thought metaphysics.[1] Their claims have had much impact, resulting in strong aversion to faith teaching. The C&MA of the latter-20th century has distanced itself from the word of faith movement, especially through the influence of such popular critiques of the movement.

Unfortunately, the claims of Hanegraaff and McConnell were, to a great degree, based on incomplete information, misinterpretation, and flawed logic. Several more recent and more thorough scholarly studies and scientific analyses have disproven much of their thesis.[2] This is not to say that all of their criticisms have been invalidated, but rather that their main thesis of the supposed cultic New Thought metaphysical origin of modern faith teaching has been shown to be false.

It may come as an embarrassment and even shock to some in the C&MA that the early Alliance really was the chief "word of faith" movement of its day. Early Alliance faith leaders would not approve of all that is taught and practiced in the movement today, but *some* current teachings and practices are quite similar to those of the early C&MA.

The Real Origins of Modern Faith Teaching

In reality, as my Doctor of Theology dissertation *A Practical-Theological Investigation of Nineteenth and Twentieth Century Faith Theologies* (as well as other studies) has demonstrated, much (though not all) of modern faith teaching has originated in earlier 19th and early 20th century classic faith teaching from the Wesleyan, Keswick, and Higher Life holiness and healing movements. Simpson and the early C&MA seem to have been the main propagators of such faith teaching in their day. Alliance publications and Carrie Judd Montgomery's *Triumphs of Faith* carried many teachings on faith that have been perpetuated through the decades.

When this is discovered, it is not so surprising that the modern faith movement actively promotes the teaching of early Alliance leaders. Bosworth's *Christ the Healer* and McCrossan's *Bodily Healing and the Atonement* are used in courses in Kenneth Hagin's Rhema Bible Training Center, even though they are no longer promoted in the C&MA. Perriman comments, "Most of the Word of Faith arguments about faith and healing can be found in Bosworth's influential book."[3] Hagin's teaching on the authority of the believer is based heavily on John MacMillan's booklet *The Authority of the Believer*. Hagin cites Simpson, as well as George Müller, Andrew Murray and others, as sources for some of his teachings. Simpson's books have been sold in the Rhema bookstore. In fact, some Rhema graduates that I have met are more familiar Simpson's writings on prayer, faith, and healing than many C&MA people. Frederick K.C. Price, who was once a C&MA pastor before becoming an independent word of faith leader, gleaned some of his teaching from Simpson.

E. W. Kenyon, usually cited as the father or grandfather of the modern faith movement, was a friend of Simpson, Rader, Bosworth, and other Alliance leaders, although he became more of a maverick in his later years, embracing some teachings that would not be fully accepted by early Alliance leaders.

It must be acknowledged that several similarities exist between the early C&MA and the modern faith movement. For example, both believe 1) healing is a provision of the atonement of Christ for the believer; 2) since Jesus Christ is the same, yesterday, today and forever (Hebrews 13:8), healing and the supernatural power and gifts of Spirit are still operative today, and 3) as believers we have an inheritance in Christ and the right to exercise spiritual authority, 4) faith as a spiritual law and a force, among many other teachings. Writers such as Hanegraaff and John MacArthur (*Charismatic Chaos*) deny some of these truths.[4] As a result of reading such critiques without having an awareness and acceptance of historic Alliance teaching and practices, many C&MA lay people and pastors have unwittingly bought into their conclusions fully.

HEALING IN THE ATONEMENT

Simpson and the early C&MA were pioneers in the teaching on healing in the atonement. Some have thought Simpson to be the first to teach healing in the atonement, but there were many others such as Andrew Murray, R. A. Torrey, German Hebrew scholar Franz Delitzsch, German Lutheran Otto Stockmayer, Baptists A. J. Gordon and Oswald Chambers, and Princeton scholars A. A. Hodge and J. A. Alexander who supported the doctrine in some form.[5]

The difference between the early Alliance and modern faith views of healing in the atonement is that some modern faith teaching tends to make it an absolute in all cases in this life, whereas the Alliance allowed for exceptions in the sovereignty of God. Simpson associate Russell Kelso Carter explained: "Mr. Simpson has always allowed that one's time may come and the faith not be given, but the point here is that practically the position [of Simpson and the C&MA] has been one of special answers in the will of God, not a broad Atonement for all at any time."[6]

It was then the belief of the Alliance that while healing is generally provided for all believers through the atonement, God in His sovereignty may not heal all. As Simpson wrote, "We are not told that He healed all the sick, but He healed many of them. It was not universal, and it was not special. He does not heal all the sick yet, but He heals without distinction or respect of persons all that are able to touch Him and take His help according to the conditions of the gospel."[7]

USE OF DOCTORS AND MEDICINE

Most word of faith people today do not stress avoidance of doctors and medicine, although they would tend to say that the more spiritual way and the greater faith is not to use medicine or doctors (similar to Simpson and early Alliance leaders). Some of the word of faith people have modified their views, primarily for two reasons—intense criticism and their own experiences of needing to use doctors and medicine.

The early Alliance went through a similar process of modification. Carter, Simpson, and the early C&MA were more like the modern word of faith movement in many respects, later modifying their views and practices. Carter, for a time, was against the use of all medicine but in 1897 wrote *Faith Healing Reviewed after 20 Years*, recanting and moderating some of his earlier more extreme teachings on healing. He also noted that Simpson and the Alliance had modified their views.[8]

Some, looking at isolated statements out of context, have claimed that Simpson was against the use of doctors and medicine,[9] but an examination of his writings makes it clear that he was not.[10] Simpson himself did not avail himself of medical care, except for eyeglasses and throat lozenges. He suffered depression and stroke in later years, and though weak in his last months, apparently did not suffer pain. In 1906 Simpson published an article by his friend A. A. Boddy, in which he counseled, "No one should give up the doctor or medicine unless fully convinced that the Lord not only can, but *has* healed. Giving up taking medicine, or dismissing the pain-staking skillful doctor, does not necessarily show perfect trust."[11]

Still, at the same time other Alliance leaders like future C&MA president Senft declared he did not have freedom to anoint people with oil for healing if they were continuing to receive treatment from a doctor or use medicine.[12] In those early days, some Alliance leaders would not have accepted the teaching and practice of Oral Roberts in merging together medicine and prayer.

Gradually, the use of doctors and medicine was more accepted. In 1937 Simpson's close associate, Kenneth MacKenzie, humorously recalled the C&MA's earlier beliefs and the practical maturing of their understanding of health and the effects of aging:

> We were a hilarious company in those days of the flush of conquest, when with whole-souled enthusiasm, we were certified we should never have to adopt glasses, lose our teeth, behold falling or grey hair, nor suffer any impairment of physical faculties. . . . The high-flown exhilaration of those early years toned down in time, though there were radicals who would not compromise. At a convention at the Tabernacle, one woman remarked to me, "If I ever see glasses on A. B. Simpson's nose, I'll never again enter this place." One critic exultingly described a meeting for testimonies of healings, when a man arose and declared, "O yes, I know the Lord is your healer, but who is your dentist?"[13]

Alliance leaders came to recognize that while dying without sickness is an ideal to which *some* may attain, the effects of aging can occur in the most godly and strongest in faith, and doctors and medicine may be needed. Some negative attitudes toward medicine and doctors by a few persisted into at least the 1940s. I have a second cousin who attended Nyack Missionary Training Institute for a semester in the 1940s. She had trained as an osteopathic physician, but wanted to study in a Bible Institute before going into medical missions. The professor she studied under in one class had a dim view of medicine and doctors—especially women doctors.

Similarities to Oral Roberts'Teaching

Catholic scholar Prudencio Damboriena observes that the conditions for healing in Oral Roberts' book *If You Need Healing, Do These Things* "do not greatly differ from those demanded at the beginning of the century by A. B. Simpson or Mrs. McPherson."[14] Additionally, Oral Roberts' concept of seed faith originated in similar teaching by Andrew Murray and Charles Spurgeon,[15] and was taught in Alliance circles as well. Simpson's associate F. E. Marsh wrote an article "We Get in Giving,"[16] remarkably reminiscent of Roberts' seed faith motto, "We give to get to give."

The concept of making an action in faith as a point of contact, though made popular by Oral Roberts, was taught by several Alliance leaders including Simpson, Pardington, Funk, Walter Turnbull and C. A. Chrisman,[17] pre-dating Roberts' teaching by half a century. Simpson, in an article in 1906 entitled "According to Your Faith," writes about faith as a point of contact for healing.[18] The concept seems to have originated in Andrew Murray's 1884 book *Divine Healing*. He taught that the laying on of hands and anointing with oil should be regarded "not as a remedy, but as a pledge of the mighty virtue of the Holy Spirit, as a means of strengthening faith, a *point of contact* and of communion between the sick one and members of the Church who are called to anoint him with oil" [italics mine].[19]

3 John 2—"As Our Soul Prospers"

Simpson and the early Alliance understood this Scripture as a prayer inspired by God, asserting, "We may expect to be 'in health' and prosper 'even as our soul prospereth.'"[20] However, they related this primarily to health, not chiefly to financial prosperity. Simpson interpreted this Scripture to mean that health is interrelated with the spiritual and emotional state of the soul.[21] While Simpson included temporal blessing in his understanding of this invocation, he made no self-centered or materialistic application of this verse as do some prosperity teachers: "It implies that we cannot expect the Lord's blessing upon our bodies and our business, if we cherish in our hearts those spiritual conditions which bring divine chastening and produce misery and pain."[22] Senft referred to 3 John 2, saying that it involves healthy food and healthy living.[23]

Whereas modern faith teachers put a high emphasis on prosperity, Simpson quotes the German mystic John Tauler, saying, "I have never been unprosperous, for I know how to live with God."[24] He taught that a faith that is focused on God through the life of the indwelling Christ is not focused on one's own welfare. Contrary to some modern faith emphasis, Simpson realized "faith [is] yielding up the world for a better inheritance." He explained that, like Lot, people with an "earthly spirit. . . contend for the best of the land." But, in contrast, "the man of faith can let the present world go because he knows he has a better, but even as he lets it go God tells him that all things are his because he is Christ's."[25]

This is not to say that Simpson was opposed to wealth. He believed that God wants His people to prosper materially: "There is no harm whatever in having money, houses, lands, friends and dearest children if you do not value these things for themselves."[26] He also spoke of the "discipline of prosperity," that working of God in the believer's heart to be able to handle prosperity with a godly attitude.[27]

FAITH AS A LAW AND A FORCE

Hanegraaff asserts that the modem concept of faith as a creative force is metaphysical.[28] Nevertheless, to the contrary, Simpson and other classic evangelical teachers refer to faith, prayer and even God Himself as a force.[29] Holiness leaders also often spoke of laws in the sense of principles, rather than fixed mechanical laws.[30] Simpson wrote of the "law of faith" in this sense.[31] Referring to Romans 3:27, Simpson commented, "Faith is the law of Christianity, the vital principle of the Gospel dispensation. Paul calls it the law of faith in distinction from the law of works."[32]

With this understanding of spiritual laws and forces, it becomes a natural progression to view faith as a force. If God Himself is a force, then as Simpson described it, faith emanates as a force from the character of God, from His omnipotence, as "one of the attributes of God Himself."[33] Simpson frequently use of the concept of faith as a force, declaring that it is "one of the attributes of God Himself": There is no doubt that while the soul is exercising, through the power of God, the faith that commands what God commands, a mighty force is operating at that moment upon the obstacle."[34] Simpson's understanding of faith as a force is probably most influenced by Spurgeon, whom he frequently quoted, and Boardman, whose book *The Higher Christian Life* had a strong impact on him. Simpson, however, disavowed that faith is an *impersonal*, mechanistic force,[35] and distanced himself from metaphysical teaching and practices.[36] Simpson distinguishes between forces that are from God, which are living and a part of the very nature of God, and "mental force," which is not from God, but from self.

THE FAITH OF GOD

The modern faith teaching interpreting Mark 11:22 from the original Greek as "the faith of God" or "the God-kind of faith" is not original to modern teaching, but was taught in the Higher Life/Keswick movements. Simpson and the early C&MA continued to propagate the teaching actively. An article by Simpson entitled "Does God Act by Faith?" was reprinted in 1924 and again in 1927.[37] Citing Romans 4:17, Alliance leaders believed, "Faith is a characteristic of God Himself."[38] McCrossan likewise taught the concept in his writings.[39]

Though often today considered controversial, several classic leaders, including Simpson, understood that if faith is imparted by God it must be a faith that God Himself possesses and manifests as part of His divine nature, and that Jesus Christ manifested that faith of God on earth.[40] Simpson asserted, "We must claim the faith of God, letting the Spirit of Jesus sustain our faith with His strong faith."[41]

Simpson explained that the faith that does not doubt in Mark 11:22-24 and James 1:6-7 is "a special work of the Holy Ghost."[42] Applying this understanding practically to the abandoning of medical treatment, Simpson cautioned, "If you have any question about your faith for this, make it a special matter of preparation and prayer. Ask God to give you special faith for this act. All our graces must come from Him, and faith among the rest. We have nothing of our own, and even our very faith is but the grace of Christ Himself within us. We can exercise it, and thus far our responsibility extends; but He must impart it, and we simply put it on and wear it as from Him."[43]

The difference between classic Alliance understanding of the faith of God and contemporary faith teaching is that modern faith teachers assert that believers should develop and exercise this "God-kind of faith," whereas classic faith leaders who taught the "faith of God" maintained that believers receive as a special gift from God the faith of God Himself. So it is not a matter of faith in God vs. faith of God, but both. They made it clear that having the faith of God does not mean having faith in one's own faith.[44]

FAITH AND THE WILL OF GOD

Alliance leaders F. F. Bosworth and T. J. McCrossan stated that saying "if it be Thy will" can be "faith-destroying words."[45] This is a phrase that Hanegraaff attacks.[46] Contrary to Hanegraaff's claim, this belief did not come from modern faith teachers, Kenyon, or metaphysics, but from classic faith leaders like Simpson, who explained:

> The prayer for healing, "If it be His will," carries with it no claim for
> which Satan will quit his hold. This is a matter about which we ought

to know His will before we ask, and then will and claim it because it is His will. Has He given us any means by which we may know His will? Most assuredly . . . the Word of God is for evermore the standard of His will, and that Word has declared immutably that it is God's greatest desire and unalterable principle of action and will to render to every man according as he will believe, and especially to save all who will receive Christ by faith, and to heal all who will receive healing by similar faith. No one thinks of asking for forgiveness "if the Lord will." Nor should we throw any stronger doubt on His promise of physical redemption.[47]

Is Healing for All?—Faith and the Sovereignty of God

Similar to modern faith teachers, Simpson believed, "His normal provision for the believer. It is something that is included in our redemption rights, something that is part of the gospel of His grace, something that is already recognized as within His will and not requiring a special revelation to justify us claiming it."[48] Again, like modern faith teachers, Simpson indicated that faith is a key element in God's will to heal, and that lack of healing could be due to unbelief or sin.[49]

Some modern faith leaders have taken these principles as absolute, claiming it is always God's will to heal, and if healing does not take place, it is not God's fault—it is due to sin or lack of faith. However, Simpson did not make absolutes out of these principles, but made room for exceptions in the sovereignty of God: "Divine healing fully recognizes the sovereignty of God and the state and spiritual attitude of the individual."[50] Citing Paul's thorn, Simpson taught: "Paul certainly prayed until he got an answer from heaven, and so we should claim deliverance at the very least until we get a refusal as clear and divine as he did."[51]

This question of whether or not it is God's will to heal also involves the question of whether sickness comes from God. Similar to modern faith leaders, Alliance leaders did not believe as a general premise that God wills or causes sickness. They would trace the causes of sickness and suffering to the Fall and Satan's part in the matter.[52] Yet contrary to some modern faith teachers, Simpson also cautioned, "We must not carry this too far by concluding that all sickness comes directly from Satanic power. Sickness may come from a physical cause, and it may come from the direct stroke of God Himself in judgment."[53]

Revelation and Sense Knowledge

The concepts of distinguishing revelation knowledge and sense knowledge are considered by faith critics as Gnostic and cultic.[54] However, similar concepts have been taught throughout church history by evangelical leaders, including Simpson and Tozer. Simpson counseled that faith can be hindered by sight, sense, and dependence on external evidences.[55] He also asserted, "Faith always seeks its message before sense confirms it."[56] Gleaning from classic faith writers and mystics, Tozer differentiated between "three degrees of religious knowledge": by senses and reason, by faith and revelation, and by direct spiritual experience, the third being the highest form of knowledge.[57] His latter two degrees would encompass the modern faith "revelation knowledge" concept, quite similar to Kenyon, though he would differ in some of Kenyon's interpretations and applications. This demonstrates that just because some have used the concepts of revelation and sense knowledge in seemingly gnostic ways does not invalidate the concept of revelation and sense knowledge altogether.

Positive Mental Attitude and Positive Confession

McConnell claims that teaching on positive confession originates with Kenyon, and is rooted in the metaphysical cults.[58] On the other hand, Bruce Barron, author of The *Health and Wealth Gospel,* asserts, "The beginnings of positive confession with regard to healing can be spotted as far back as the work of A. B. Simpson." Both writers are mistaken, for the idea is not original with Kenyon or even Simpson. In actuality, the roots of the principle of confessing one's faith are found in eighteenth-century Methodist leaders such as John Fletcher, Hester Ann Rogers and William Corvosso, and were expanded upon and popularized by holiness leader Phoebe Palmer.[59] Later holiness leaders such as Simpson, Andrew Murray, W.E. Boardman and Hannah Whitall Smith all continued to advocate positive confession of one's faith.[60]

Simpson clearly believed a positive mental attitude contributes to healing and answered prayer:

> A flash of ill temper, a cloud of despondency, an impure thought or desire can poison your blood, inflame your tissues, disturb your nerves and interrupt the whole process of God's life in your body! On the other hand, the spirit of joy, freedom from anxious care and worry, a generous and loving heart, the sedative of peace, the uplifting influence of hope and confidence—these are better than pills, stimulants and sedatives, and the very nature of things will exercise the most benign influence over your physical functions, making it true in a literal as well as a spiritual sense, that "the joy of the Lord is your strength."[61]

He also encouraged making positive confessions of our faith: "We must confess Him as our Guardian and Deliverer. . . . We must say it as well as feel it,"[62] and "Faith will die without confession."[63] Further, in 1909 Carrie Judd Montgomery wrote in The *Alliance Weekly* on "The Power of the Tongue," based on Proverbs 18:21 ("Death and life is in the power of the tongue"). She explained "the connection between a sanctified tongue and divine health in body."[64] This popular word of faith teaching finds its origin in the early C&MA.

While faith critics rightly warn against psychological or psychic use of the mind,[65] they fail to discern that there is a valid Scriptural application of positive mental attitude and positive confession, rooted in evangelical holiness teaching. While classic teaching on positive confession sounds very similar to modern faith theology, unlike faith teachers Alliance leaders did not believe that you can "name and claim" or "confess and possess" anything you desire, use confession as an automatic formula, or make people feel guilty about making the slightest "negative confession."

ADDITIONAL DIFFERENCES BETWEEN MODERN FAITH AND CLASSIC C&MA TEACHING

This is just a sampling of comparisons and contrasts between modern faith and classic C&MA faith teaching. Many more similarities and differences could be cited. Some additional of the areas in which some modern faith leaders have deviated from such classic faith teaching taught by Alliance leaders include: having faith in one's self or one's own faith, faith as the source of healing, faith as an impersonal force that can be manipulated even by unbelievers, words as a container of faith or creator of reality, demanding from God, always praying only once, as well as many others.[66] Most modern faith teachers have embraced the tongues-as-evidence doctrine, though, ironically, E. W. Kenyon, acknowledged as the father of the movement, was against the belief. For a comprehensive comparison and contrast, see my doctoral dissertation.

There has often been a tendency to emphasize one truth emphasized to the exclusion of another truth. While claiming one's rights as a child of God was taught by early Alliance leaders, they also taught the cross and self-denial. This strong emphasis on the crucified life and Christ-centered holiness by Simpson and the faith movement of a century ago is often missing or downplayed in the modern faith movement. The real walk of faith and victory can only be lived by dying to self and being infused with the resurrection life of Christ. As Simpson wrote, "How very much of the life of faith consists in simply denying ourselves."[67] It is what Martin Luther called a theology of the cross as opposed to a theology of glory.

THE C&MA AND FAITH MOVEMENT TODAY

Today the C&MA distances itself from its radical faith past as well as from the modern faith movement. Medicine and doctors are routinely used without reproach, though there may be a few Alliance people who continue to walk by faith normally without medicine, as did my first mentor Rev. Roland Gray. Seldom in latter 20th century have Simpson's faith teachings such as faith as a law or force, the faith of God, or even point of contact been taught from Alliance pulpits. In fact, the writings of modern faith critics Hanegraaff and McConnell have been promulgated in many Alliance churches and their conclusions accepted completely and uncritically. Hanegraaff, especially, considers belief in healing in the atonement, and faith of God, faith as a law and a force (all taught by Simpson and early Alliance leaders) as heretical. Ironically, in one Alliance church with which I have had contact, they regarded the teaching on faith as a law and as a force (which Simpson taught) as heretical and cultic.

It should be noted that just as the early C&MA modified some of its more radical faith teachings, so have some word of faith leaders in recent years. As Alliance people rediscover their roots and Simpson's bold writings on faith, the tide may be turning back as some Alliance leaders have indicated an openness to faith teaching and practice, while at the same time avoiding the extremes of some in the modern faith movement as well as in the C&MA's past.

CONCLUSION

This is a brief synopsis of faith teachings in light of A.B. Simpson's writings, historic Christian and Missionary Alliance teaching and classic evangelical teaching on faith. Further analysis would reveal both additional similarities as well as additional contrasts between classic and contemporary faith teaching. For further research in this area, see my doctoral dissertation and my article "A. B. Simpson and the Modern Faith Movement" in the *Alliance Academic Review*.

Writers such as Hunt, Hanegraaff, McArthur and McConnell do expose much wrong teaching and practice in the modern charismatic and faith movements. But they also oppose positions held by classic faith and holiness leaders such as Simpson, so their conclusions must not be accepted uncritically. On the other hand, while there are elements of truth in some contemporary faith leaders' teachings, there is often also serious error. Simpson and the classic faith teachers provide a healthy balanced theology and practice of faith. We must be careful not to "throw out the baby with the bath water," i.e., abandon valid principles of faith just because they have been mixed with unsound teaching. To be strong and sound in faith, Alliance people and Christians from other backgrounds can be encouraged to recover the sound faith teachings of Simpson, MacMillan, McCrossan, and other early Alliance leaders, as well as shun unsound or imbalanced teachings.

---

1.   Hank Hanegraaff, *Christianity in Crisis* (Eugene, Oregon: Harvest House Publishers, 1993); Dave Hunt and T. A. McMahon, *Seduction of Christianity* (Eugene, Oregon: Harvest House Publishers, 1985); Dave Hunt, *Beyond Seduction* (Eugene, Oregon: Harvest House Publishers, 1987); D. R. McConnell, *A Different Gospel* (Peabody, MA: Hendrickson, 1988), John F. MacArthur, *Charismatic Chaos* (Grand Rapids, MI: Zondervan, 1992); Barron, *The Health and Wealth Gospel*; Gordon Fee, *The Disease of the Health and Wealth Gospel* (Cosa Mesa, CA: Word for Today, 1979).

2.   See Simmons, *E. W. Kenyon and the Postbellum Pursuit of Peace, Power, and Plenty*; McIntyre, *E. W. Kenyon and His Message of Faith: The True Story*; Robert M. Bowman, *The Word-Faith Controversy* (Grand Rapids, MI: Baker Book House, 2001), William DeArteaga, *Quenching the Spirit* (Lake Mary, FL: Creation House, 1996); Geir Lie, "E. W. Kenyon: Cult Founder or Evangelical Minister? An Historical Analysis of Kenyon's Theology with Particular Emphasis on Roots and Influences," Masters thesis, Norwegian Lutheran School of Theology, 1994; Derek E. Vreeland, "Reconstructing Word of Faith Theology: A Defense, Analysis and Refinement of the Theology of the Word of Faith Movement." Paper presented at the 30th Annual Meeting of the Society for Pentecostal Studies, Oral Roberts University, Tulsa, Oklahoma, Mar. 2001; Eddie Hyatt, "The Nineteenth Century Roots of the Modern Faith Movement," unpublished paper, Tulsa, OK: Oral Roberts University, Apr. 25, 1991; Andrew Perriman, ed., *Faith, Health and Prosperity* (Carlisle, Cumbria, UK; Waynesboro, GA: Paternoster Press, 2003), King, *A Practical-Theological Investigation of 19th and 20th Century "Faith Theologies."*

3.   Perriman, *Faith, Health and Prosperity*, 63.

4. MacArthur, *Charismatic Chaos*, 237-269, 314; Hanegraaff, 249-251. MacArthur denies healing in the atonement, the crisis experience of the baptism or filling of the Spirit and the gifts of the Spirit for today. Hanegraaff berates belief in healing in the atonement and exercise of spiritual authority through binding and loosing.

5. Keith Bailey, *The Children's Bread* (Harrisburg, PA: Christian Publications, 1977), 43-57.

6. Russell Kelso Carter, *Faith Healing Reviewed After Twenty Years* (Boston, Chicago: The Christian Witness Co., 1897), 113.

7. Simpson, CITB, 4:197.

8. Carter, *Faith Healing Reviewed*, 113.

9. P. G. Chappell, "Healing Movements," DPCM, 363; Dayton, *Theological Roots of Pentecostalism*, 128; Bowman, *The Word-Faith Controversy*, 61, 69, 75-77, 91, 244.10. Simpson, *Gospel of Healing*, 68; Simpson, *The Four-fold Gospel*, 48; A. B. Simpson, "Editorial," CAMW, Nov. 1890, 274; A. B. Simpson, *The Old Faith and the New Gospels* (Harrisburg, PA: Christian Publications, 1966), 59.

11. Alexander Boddy, "Health in Christ," CMAW, Sept. 1, 1906, 131.

12. Senft, "Divine Healing," CMAW, June 30, 1906, 394-395

13. Kenneth MacKenzie, "My Memories of A. B. Simpson VI," AW, Aug. 7, 1937, 500.

14. Prudencio Damboriena, *Tongues as of Fire: Pentecostalism in Contemporary Christianity* (Washington and Cleveland: Corpus Books, 1969), 134.

15. Andrew Murray, *With Christ in the School of Prayer* (Springdale, PA: Whitaker, 1981), 80; Andrew Murray, *The Secret of the Faith Life* (Ft. Washington, PA: Christian Literature Crusade, 1968), 69; Charles Spurgeon, *Faith's Checkbook* (Chicago, IL: Moody Press, n.d.), 5.

16. F. E. Marsh, "We Get in Giving," AW, Sept. 14, 1912, 397.

17. See Simpson, "According to Your Faith," CMAW, Sept. 8, 1906, 146; George P. Pardington, "Sanctification," CMAW, June 2, 1906, 348ff.; Funk, "Pittsburgh Convention," AW, Apr. 9, 1921, 57; Turnbull and Chrisman, "The Message of the Christian and Missionary Alliance."

18. Simpson, "According to Your Faith," CMAW, Sept. 8, 1906, 146.

19. Murray, *Divine Healing*, 84, 133-134.

20. Simpson, *The Gospel of Healing*, 93; see also pp. 23-24, 44-45, 59; Simpson, CITB, 6:387-388.

21. Simpson, *The Gospel of Healing*, 43-44.

22. Simpson, CITB, 6:387.

23. F. H. Senft, "Divine Healing," CMAW, June 30, 1906, 394-395

24. A. B. Simpson, *Seeing the Invisible* (Camp Hill, PA: Christian Publications, 1994), 68-69.

25. Ibid, 36.

26. Simpson, *Days of Heaven on Earth*, Oct. 6.

27. Simpson, CITB, 6:206.

28. Hanegraaff, 65-71.

29. The concept of spiritual force may be traced back at least as far as the writings of Madame Guyon, who influenced a whole host of evangelical writers: Thomas Upham, Andrew Murray, Watchman Nee, Hudson Taylor, W. E. Boardman, Jessie Penn-Lewis, A. W. Tozer, S. D. Gordon, A. T. Pierson, Charles Spurgeon, Charles Price. See King, *A Practical-Theological Investigation of 19th and 20th Century "Faith Theologies"*, 124-147.

30. Simmons, *E. W. Kenyon*, 155-156.

31. Simpson, *The Gospel of Healing*, 68.

32. Simpson, *A Larger Christian Life*, 10-11.

33. Ibid., 13.

34. Ibid.

35. Simpson, *The Fourfold Gospel*, 51.

36. Ibid., 48ff.

37. Simpson, "Does God Act by Faith," AW, July 19, 1924, 40; Simpson, "Does God Act by Faith?," AW, July 23, 1927, 485.

38. "At Home and Abroad, AW, July 16, 1927, 466.

39. McCrossan, *Christ's Paralyzed Church X-Rayed*, 320-321.

40. Simpson, *A Larger Christian Life*, 54.

41. Simpson, *The Life of Prayer*, 60, 70; Simpson, CITB, 4:591. See also Simpson, *A Larger Christian Life*, 137-38; *The Gospel of Healing*, 89, 142-143; *Seeing the Invisible*, 18.

42. Simpson, *The Gentle Love of the Holy Spirit*, 135.

43. Simpson, *The Gospel of Healing*, 88-89.

44. See also Montgomery, *The Prayer of Faith*, 50; Montgomery, *Secrets of Victory*, 28.

45. Bosworth, *Christ the Healer*, 165.

46. Hanegraaff, 271; McCrossan, *Christ's Paralyzed Church X-Rayed*, 317.

47. Simpson, *The Gospel of Healing*, 76-78.

48. Simpson, CITB, 4:336.

49. Simpson, *The Gospel of Healing*, 120-121; see also pp. 60ff.

50. A. B. Simpson, *The Lord for the Body* (Camp Hill, PA: Christian Publications, 1996), 122.

51. Ibid., 120.

52. See Simpson, *The Gospel of Healing*, 28-29, 96-99, 105; Carter, *Faith Healing Reviewed*, 6, 227.

53. Simpson, CITB, 4:335.

54. Ibid.

55. Simpson, *A Larger Christian Life*, 18.

56. Simpson, *Seeing the Invisible*, 149.

57. Tozer, *Man: The Dwelling Place of God*, 49-52; 1992:120-122; Tozer, *Faith Beyond Reason*, 1989), 39-40.

58. McConnell, 137-138.

59. See Harold E. Raser, *Phoebe Palmer: Her Life and Thought* (Lewiston, NY: The Edwin Mellen Press, 1987), 249-50.

60. Boardman, *The Higher Christian Life*, 261, 263; Murray, *Divine Healing*, 36, 27-28; Andrew Murray, *The Prayer Life* (Alresford, Hants, Great Britain: Christian Literature Crusade, 1981), 53; Hannah Whitall Smith, *The Christian's Secret of a Happy Life* (Old Tappan, NJ: Fleming H. Revell, 1942), 53, 81-83.

61. Pamphlet, "Christ for the Body" (Nyack, NY: The Christian and Missionary Alliance, n.d.), 7-8.

62. A. B. Simpson, *The Lord for the Body* (Harrisburg, PA: Christian Publications, 1959), 66.

63. Simpson, *Seeing the Invisible*, 35.

64. Carrie Judd Montgomery, "The Power of the Tongue," CMAW, Sept. 4, 1909, 376.

65. Hunt, 13ff.; Hanegraaff, 80ff.; McConnell, 138ff.

66. See my dissertation for sections discussing all of these areas.

67. Simpson, *Days of Heaven on Earth*, October 19.

TWENTY - SIX

REFLECTIONS, OBSERVATIONS, AND CONCLUSIONS

While this study has concisely but comprehensively documented the cautiously charismatic story of the C&MA, there is much I have left out for the purpose of brevity. And I believe there is still much more to be uncovered, more stories of this mighty charismatic outpouring in and through the early Alliance, as well as throughout C&MA history.

If it were not for the divisive controversies over the doctrine of tongues as the initial evidence of the baptism in the Holy Spirit, I am convinced that the Alliance would have remained charismatic—cautiously so, but clearly charismatic nonetheless. "Evidential tongues" is not nearly so much of an issue today as it was back then. Pentecostal churches such as the Foursquare Church and the Open Bible Standard Church have modified their positions on evidential tongues. Respected Pentecostal and charismatic leaders such as Jack Hayford, Oral Roberts, and David Wilkerson have backed away from a strict evidential tongues position. The charismatic and Third Wave movements have by and large modified the belief in evidential tongues.

With the loss of so many charismatically-endowed and spiritually capable people, charismatic practice became more subdued by the 1930s. In some respects, the C&MA after the 1920s became less charismatic than its pre-Azusa days. Physical manifestations such as trembling, falling under the power of the Spirit, dancing, holy laughter, etc., became less accepted due to Pentecostal excesses. Later generations scorned such manifestations, never knowing of their occurrence and acceptance in earlier Alliance history.

C&MA IMPACT ON PENTECOSTALS AND CHARISMATICS

Impact on early Pentecostals. Nienkirchen and Dayton have demonstrated that A. B Simpson was a forerunner to the Pentecostal movement, especially with his emphasis on the Fourfold gospel and the baptism of the Spirit as a subsequent sanctifying and empowering experience.[1] Brumback acknowledges the indebtedness of the Assemblies of God (AG) to the C&MA in seven areas: hymnody, most AG doctrines, numerous mature leaders for the AG, books by Simpson,

Pardington, Tozer, and other C&MA leaders as basic reading for AG ministers, the name "Gospel Tabernacle," ecclesiastical organization patterned after the C&MA, and the mission vision of the Alliance.[2]

In addition, the maturity of former Alliance leaders kept the Assemblies of God from succumbing to "Jesus Only" oneness Pentecostal movement. Simpson also had influence on independent healing evangelists like Charles Price. Aimee Semple McPherson's "Foursquare" Gospel of Jesus as Savior, Baptizer, Healer, and Coming King was adapted from Simpson's Fourfold Gospel.

Influence on more recent charismatic movements. The writings of Watchman Nee, popular in many charismatic circles, were strongly influenced by the C&MA. As mentioned earlier, Jack Hayford first became interested in speaking in tongues as a teenager from his tongue-speaking C&MA pastor. Dr. Charles Farah, Jr., professor of theology at Oral Roberts University, was son of a C&MA pastor. His theology was impacted by the C&MA. At the church he co-pastored, Tulsa Christian Fellowship, he established missions conferences based on the C&MA model. Jane Hansen, leader of the charismatic Women's Aglow, was a C&MA preacher's kid. As mentioned in the previous chapter, the C&MA was perhaps the foremost proponent of faith teaching and practice in its day, and the origin of some of the modern word of faith teaching. Donald McGavran, founder of the church growth movement, declared of the C&MA, "The Christian and Missionary Alliance is without doubt the leading missionary society of the twentieth century."[3] As mentioned earlier, Wimber was impacted by the message of McGavran at the C&MA General Council at Lincoln, Nebraska in 1979 on "Signs and Wonders: A Way to Salvation."[4] These are just a sampling of the impact of the early charismatic theology and practice of the C&MA.

RESPONSES TO C&MA CHARISMATIC HISTORY

Pentecostals and C&MA people have responded in a variety of ways to the charismatic history of the Alliance. Pentecostals tend to believe that Simpson and the C&MA quenched the Spirit and portray leaders as admitting they made mistakes in not embracing Pentecostalism more fully. Yet as Pentecostal writer Girolimon perceptively notes:

> It is questionable whether Simpson would have been able to formally endorse tongues as evidence of the Baptism, given the casual voluntary relationships of the various parts of the Alliance organization. From its inception, Simpson sought not to form a new denomination, 'but simply a fraternal union of consecrated believers in connection with various evangelical churches.'. . . Even if Simpson had personally shared with Pentecostals the teaching of tongues as evidence of the Baptism, it is extremely doubtful that he could have imposed such an understanding on his organization which was filled with many non-Pentecostals.[5]

Some within the C&MA have denied, ignored or suppressed its charismatic history. Some have acknowledged its more charismatic past but say they do not want to go so far as the early Alliance leaders. Some have emphasized the C&MA's caution to a greater degree than its early leaders. Some have interpreted the early Pentecostal years of the Alliance as a time of sifting and sorting, in which they finally reached a non-Pentecostal consensus. Some, in reaction to Alliance leaders who have been overcautious or have downplayed its charismatic history, have overreached in trying to portray the early Alliance as more charismatic than it was by claiming Simpson was a seeker of tongues or that Tozer was a revisionist. Each of these positions is not what the early C&MA taught and practiced.

WOULD SIMPSON BE THIRD WAVE OR CHARISMATIC?

Similarities of phenomena and practice in the early Alliance to the Pentecostal, charismatic and Third Wave movements include soaking prayer, shaking and trembling, falling under the power of the Spirit, holy laughter, emotional expression, repetitive singing, healing manifestations such as heat, electricity, leg-lengthening. Both believe in signs and wonders and power evangelism, both believe tongues is not the initial evidence of the filling of the Spirit. Both believe in spurious and need for discernment. Both believe in inter-denominational cooperation. Both define spiritual gifts similarly. Grudem's view of word of knowledge and wisdom is similar to that of Simpson. Both emphasize spiritual warfare. Both emphasize soaking prayer. Like Wimber, Simpson (and even Pentecostal leader Charles Parham) would have not approved of some of the Toronto Blessing phenomena, such as barking, crowing, etc. The early Alliance position on prophecy is very similar to that advocated by contemporary systematic theologian Wayne Grudem, though Grudem was not familiar with the historic C&MA viewpoint. With Grudem, Christiansen, and other charismatic leaders, the C&MA would agree that not all will speak in tongues, although it should be normal in the church.[6]

Where would Simpson and the early Alliance fit today? Based on Alliance history and theology, they would maintain friendship and dialogue with moderate charismatics, Pentecostals, Third Wavers and would share platforms, just as they did then. While they would have disagreed with some of Wimber's teachings and practices, on the basis of Simpson's relationship with moderate Pentecostal leaders such as Hoover, Boddy, Jonathan Paul, and Carrie Judd Montgomery, he likely would have fellowshipped and dialogued with Wimber and other Third Wave leaders.

The C&MA position is akin to that of charismatic Lutheran leader Larry Christiansen: "Even in Pentecostal churches not everyone speaks in tongues, and there is no scriptural warrant to believe that they will."[7] Simpson would get along well with Christiansen, and no doubt would have invited him to speak in his pulpit as he did Boddy and Jonathan Paul. Simpson and Tozer would get along well with Richard Foster, a tongue-speaking Quaker, who shares with them the great interest in the saints and mystics of the church through the centuries.[8] Charismatic leader David Shibley has spoken positively of Simpson's "seek not, forbid not" posture, saying, "How much better it would be to adopt the position held by A. B. Simpson."[9] Simpson and early Alliance leaders would agree heartily with Shibley's counsel, "It is sheer disaster to accept any expression of tongues without any attempt at discernment in this vital area. . . . The evidence of being filled with the Holy Spirit is not so much speaking in another tongue as controlling the tongue you have!"[10]

While there are many similarities to the Third Wave and modern charismatic movements, there are clear differences as well. Contrary to many Third Wavers, the Alliance believes in a subsequent baptism or filling of the Spirit. Early Alliance leaders would perceive that the Toronto blessing movement was a mixture of Spirit, flesh, and demonic. While they would agree with Grudem that tongues are not necessarily for all, they would disagree with Grudem's denial of the possibility of believers receiving a counterfeit tongue or false prophecy.[11] (It should be noted that Wimber, on the other hand, did believe gifts could be counterfeited).[12] The early Alliance put more emphasis on discernment and trying the spirits and more controls on exercise of gifts and manifestations than many Third Wavers and charismatics.

Simpson would disagree with Wimber on healing in the atonement. Wimber backpedaled on the teaching, preferring instead to call it "healing through the atonement" or an "outcome of the atonement."[13] Wimber does acknowledge, "Not all of those who believe physical healing is in the atonement conclude healing is automatic and immediate."[14] Simpson, Murray, Torrey, Carter, Chambers, and Gordon would all be examples of that statement.[15]

Early Alliance leaders would agree with the strategic level spiritual warfare movement that there is warfare against territorial spirits, but would disagree with the direct confrontational approach advocated by some.

Although Simpson was considered an apostle and a prophet,[16] he would have been critical of some elements of today's prophetic movement:

> One of the most alarming tendencies of this movement has recently developed in several places in the form of a sort of prophetic authority which certain persons are claiming over the consciences of others and men and women are seeking counsel and guidance from them in the practical matters of private duty, instead of looking directly to the Anointing which they have received of Him and obeying God rather than men. It is said that in some instances Christian men and women go to these new prophets almost as the world goes to the clairvoyant and fortuneteller.17

While the early C&MA did encourage and express emotion in worship, generally, there was less emotion in the early C&MA, and more stress on the "power of stillness." There was not as much emphasis on feelings and sensations. Due to discernment of fleshly and demonic counterfeits, there were not as many manifestations or as much emphasis. In other words, people would experience holy laughter or falling under the power of the Spirit, but it would not be as frequent or as emphasized. Healings were frequent, but they were not as sensationalized and publicized as much as in the charismatic movement today.

The gifts of the Spirit did take place in C&MA services, but there were more controls than most charismatic churches.

RECOVERING EARLY ALLIANCE VIEWS AND PRACTICES TODAY

If the policies, beliefs and attitudes of Simpson and early Alliance leaders were implemented today what would the Alliance look like? In the words of the new Board of Directors motto, the Alliance would have "expectation without agenda." Alliance leaders would encourage Alliance churches to expect signs and wonders, but not seek after them. They would expect all supernatural gifts, including tongues, to be occurring normally in every Alliance church, but would not expect that everyone should speak in tongues. Speaking in tongues would often accompany reception of the baptism or filling of the Spirit, but would not be expected to occur all of the time. More people would speak in tongues privately.

Supernatural utterances such as tongues and interpretation, prophecy, singing in tongues, words of supernatural knowledge and wisdom would be welcomed and would occur periodically without dismay or fear, but under careful guidelines with discerning assessment. Falling under the power of the Spirit, holy laughter, trembling and other similar manifestations would occur from time to time in Alliance meetings and would be accepted with discernment but not sought after, emphasized, or sensationalized. Emotional expressions, such as clapping, shouting, weeping, dancing, and trembling, would be accepted but kept in check from excessive emotionalism. Such charismatic gifts and manifestations would not be forced or sensationalized, but neither would they be feared or shunned or considered aberrant. The C&MA would be fully charismatic, but at the same time cautiously so.

WHAT THE C&MA CAN LEARN FROM ITS CHARISMATIC HISTORY

For those of us in The Christian and Missionary Alliance, we can acknowledge without fear or shame that the early Christian and Missionary Alliance was indeed charismatic in theology and practice—cautiously charismatic—but charismatic nonetheless.

We in the Alliance don't need to ignore, shun, hide from, be afraid of, or be embarrassed about our charismatic past. It is part and parcel of our Alliance heritage, and something to feel good about. We can recover our heritage and encourage what early Alliance leaders desired—that all the gifts of the Spirit, including speaking in tongues, have a place in every Alliance church. We can strive for Simpson's vision to have all the gifts of the Spirit harmoniously operating, including tongues, without controversy—charismatic without chaos. We can provide a haven for safe and discerning exercise of charismatic manifestations and a model for other churches to embrace the supernatural with discernment.

What would Simpson and early Alliance leaders say about phenomena as the Toronto Blessing movements? While it would be difficult to determine precisely what their response would be, on the basis of their responses to similar phenomena in their day, they would say that there was a mixture of Spirit, flesh and demonic in the Toronto Blessing movement, as with any revival or renewal movement. They would not dismiss the phenomena of holy laughter, trembling and shaking, or falling under the power of the Spirit as all being not from God. But they would also be very concerned about the strong emphasis on feeling, emotions, experiences, as well as lack of discernment. Like Pentecostals Seymour, Parham, and Woodworth-Etter, they would view animal-like behavior and sounds as being predominately of the flesh or demonic. They would have agreed with the decision of John Wimber and the Vineyard to require accountability and discipline to the excesses.

But like the Vineyard, they would not back away from the manifestations altogether. Rather than back away from charismatic excesses, the Alliance today can provide the banks of moderation to channel the flow of the Spirit. We can, like the early Alliance, have a safe, sound exercise of charismatic manifestations. We can, like our forefathers, guide charismatically-oriented people away from unsound practices and doctrinal aberrations, while still supporting (not merely tolerating) their charismatic manifestations. As Board of Managers secretary Hudson Ballard declared in 1914, even in the midst of controversies, losses, and excesses, "Alliance leaders are agreed that tongues should have a place in every Spirit-controlled church," so would he again declare this statement, even in the midst of the controversies and excesses in the charismatic movements today.

WHAT NON-CHARISMATIC EVANGELICALS CAN LEARN FROM THE EARLY C&MA

Evangelicals can look at early Alliance history and realize that there can be and has been a valid place for the supernatural. The C&MA was an interdenominational organization that welcomed the supernatural. Baptists, Presbyterians, holiness groups, Methodists, Episcopalians, Pentecostals—all were under the umbrella of the interdenominational Alliance seeking together a higher and deeper life in Christ. Evangelicals can see a model for a moderate, balanced exercise of spiritual gifts. There can be and have been genuine gifts of the Spirit exercised by godly, humble people. There is more of the genuine supernatural from God than many evangelicals are willing to acknowledge, and more of seemingly supernatural that is not from God than many charismatics are willing to admit.

WHAT PENTECOSTALS AND CHARISMATICS CAN LEARN FROM THE EARLY C&MA

Blumhofer acknowledges, "In a warning that might well have saved Pentecostals considerable grief, [Simpson] pleaded, 'Do not . . . tear up the foundations of your peace, your holiness, your victory and your settled Christian experience because you are seeking some larger blessing at your Father's hand. . . . There is no better preparation for the higher enduements of the Holy Ghost than to be settled and established in Christ Jesus and able to rear upon the secure foundation of the indwelling Christ the superstructure of all the fullness of God.'"[18] The cautions of early Alliance leaders, as Blumhofer has remarked, went unheeded for many years.[19] Those appeals for prudence, discernment, and balance are just as relevant for the charismatic movement today.

Further, Blumhofer notes, "The conviction that Pentecostals misread the Bible—that the Bible, although affirming the presence of tongues speech in the Early Church, neither advocated any uniform initial evidence of Spirit baptism nor distinguished between evidential tongues, the gift of tongues, and the use of tongues in private worship—was central to the crystallizing of an Alliance position on Pentecostalism."[20] The Alliance position against initial evidence is echoed today through the Third Wave movement. In Simpson's day, where evidential tongues was not made an issue, ecumenical relationships flourished. Where the possibility of counterfeits was acknowledged and discretion was exercised, cooperation existed. Where the guidelines and restrictions of 1 Corinthians 14 were adhered to, exercise of charismatic gifts was permitted and encouraged. These are valuable insights for charismatics today.

SIMPSON'S VISION—A SAFE HAVEN FOR MATURE CHARISMATIC MANIFESTATIONS

Simpson did not change his mind or shrink away from his vision of fully charismatically-endowed Alliance churches. Just as he had urged in 1909, "Why may we not have all the gifts and all the graces of the Apostolic Church blended in one harmonious whole. . . . Why may we not have all the supernatural ministries of the early Church? . . . Why may we not have the ministry of teaching, the gifts of wisdom, knowledge, the faith of primitive Christianity, and even the tongues of Pentecost, without making them subjects of controversy, without judging one another harshly, because each may have all the gifts, and all in such beautiful and blended harmony. . . ."[21] Nearly a decade later in December 1917, even after many conflicts and defections to the Pentecostal movement, Simpson repeated this desire, showing his ongoing vision for the future of the C&MA after his death.[22]

His dream was for a Christian and Missionary Alliance that is "cautiously charismatic" or "charismatic without chaos," to bring revival and power to the C&MA churches and to provide a home for those experiencing the charismatic dimension of the Christian life to express their faith in a safe and balanced atmosphere of both openness to all that the Spirit wants to do and discerning avoidance of excess and counterfeits. This is the genuine gold.

---

1. Dayton, *Theological Roots of Pentecostalism*, 22; Nienkirchen, *A. B. Simpson and the Pentecostal Movement*, 52.

2. Brumback, *Suddenly . . . from Heaven*, 94-95.

3. C&MA Advertisement.

4. John Wimber, "Introduction," *Signs and Wonders and Church Growth*.

5. Michael Thomas Girolimon, "A Real Crisis of Blessing, Part II," *Paraclete*, Spring 1993, 2-3.

6. Grudem, 1076-77.

7. Larry Christiansen, *A Message to the Charismatic Movement*, (Minneapolis, MN: Dimension Books, 1972), 71.

8. See Richard J. Foster, *Prayer: Finding the Heart's True Home* (San Francisco, CA: Harper San Francisco, 1992); Richard J. Foster, *Celebration of Discipline: The Path to Spiritual Growth* (San Francisco, CA:Harper-SanFrancisco, 1978, 1988).

9. David Shibley, *A Charismatic Truce* (Nashville, TN: Thomas Nelson Publishers, 1978), 65.

10. Ibid., 74, 111.

11. Grudem, 1076-77.

12. Wimber and Springer, *Power Healing*, 232.

13. Wimber and Springer, 155-156.

14. Ibid., 156.

15. However, Wimber misinterprets Torrey's statements on healing in the atonement, asserting: "What he means is that based on what Jesus experienced on the cross we as a consequence may experience one hundred percent healing here on earth." Wimber, 154. On the contrary, Wimber is misinformed, for Torrey also declared, "Sometimes it is God's will to heal, usually it is God's will to heal, if the conditions are met; but it is not always God's will to heal. . . . It is not always possible to pray 'the prayer of faith,' only when God makes it possible by the leading of the Holy Spirit." R. A. Torrey, *The Power of Prayer and the Prayer of Power* (Grand Rapids, MI: Zondervan, 1924), 126.

16. Thompson, *A. B. Simpson: His Life and Work*, 195.

17. Simpson, Annual Report, 1908.

18. Blumhofer, *The Assemblies of God*, 152.

19. Ibid., 185.

20. Ibid., 188.

21. Simpson, "Christian Altruism," CMAW, Aug. 7, 1909, 322.

22. Simpson, "Members of One Another," AW, Dec. 8, 1917, 148.

Appendix I: Movement among the Early C&MA and Other, Predominantly Pentecostal, Bodies

TONGUE-SPEAKERS WHO LEFT THE C&MA

Leader	C&MA Role	Date Left	Pentecostal Role
Grace Agar	Missionary	1913	Missionary
A. G. Argue	Pastor	1908?	Pastor, evangelist, Pentecostal Assemblies of Canada
Mr. and Mrs. Bailly	Missionary	1914	AG missionary
Agnes N.T. Beckdahl	Nyack student	?	AG missionary
Mr. Bell	British C&MA leader	1912	British Pentecostal leader
Gottfried F. Bender	Pastor, missionary	1912-14?	Missionary
J. T. Boddy	Pastor	1912?	Pastor
John F. Bowditch	Pastor, Boston	1918	Independent ministry
Eleanor Bowie	Nyack student	?	Missionary
George Bowie	Nyack student	?	Missionary—S. Africa
Frank M. Boyd	Nyack student	1911-12?	AG Educator
Mr. Bullen	Missionary	1914	AG missionary
Frank Casley	Pastor, church planter	1916	Founded Free Gospel churches
A.S. Copley	Evangelist	1908?	Editor, pastor
Herbert Cox	Pastor, missionary	1916	Pastor
John Coxe	Pastor	1917	AG Pastor
Sarah Coxe	Missionary	1918	AG missionary
William Coxe	Pastor	1920?	AG Pastor
H. W. Cragin	Missionary	1924	AG missionary

TONGUE-SPEAKERS WHO LEFT THE C&MA (CONTINUED)

Leader	C&MA Role	Date Left	Pentecostal Role
Charles Crawford	Pastor, DS, Dir., Boone Bible School	1916	Dir., Boone Bible School
Lillian Doll	Official worker	?	AG Missionary
Minnie Draper	Board of Mgrs.	1913	Independent ministry
George Eldridge	Pastor, Dist. Supt., Honorary VP	1916	AG Pastor, District Leader
William I. Evans	Nyack graduate, Pastor	1914	Pastor, Principal, Bethel Bible School, Dean, Central Bible Institute
J. Roswell Flower Alice Reynolds Flower	C&MA members	1908	AG pastor, Dist. Supt., Gen. Sec.
Archibald Forder	Missionary	1912?	Independent missionary
Alice Rowlands Frodsham	Nyack student	?	Wife of AG Gen. Sec. Stanley Frodsham
Laura Gardner	Missionary	1915	AG Missionary
E. T. Gelatt	Evangelist	1914	Evangelist, Christian Workers Union
L. C. Hall	Pastor	1908?	Pastor, conf. speaker, joined oneness Pentecostalism
C. A. Ingalls	Pastor	1921	Independent Pentecostal ministry
Mr. & Mrs. Ivan Kaufman	Missionary	1914?	AG Missionary
D. W. Kerr	Pastor	1914	AG Pastor
Jacob E. Kistler	Missionary	1914	AG missionary
J. R. Kline	Pastor	1914	AG pastor, AG Gen. Presbytery
Kate Knight	Missionary	1913?	Shiloh Mission, Chautauqua, NY

Leader	C&MA Role	Date Left	Pentecostal Role
David McDowell	Pastor	1912	AG Pastor, AG Gen. Supt.
Claude A. McKinney	Missionary, Pastor	1908	AG pastor
Lilian Merian	C&MA teenager	1912?	Missionary, married later AG Gen. Supt. Ralph Riggs
George and Carrie Judd Montgomery	Honorary VP Worker	1917	AG pastor
R. H. Moon	Pastor	1927	AG Pastor, evangelist
Harold & Grace Hanmore Moss	Nyack students	?	Principal, Beulah Hts. Training Ctr.
Virginia E. Moss	Nyack student	1912?	Founded Beulah Hts. Bible School, N. Bergen, NJ, 1912
George & Annie Murray	Missionaries	1910?	Missionaries
David Wesley Myland	Pastor, evangelist	1912	Bible school principal
Howard & Nettie Nichols	Missionaries	?	Missionaries
Noel Perkin	Worker	?	Missionary, pastor
J. M. Pike	Pastor, Oliver Gospel Mission, Conf. speaker	1910-11?	Joined Pentecostal Holiness Church
Morton Plummer	Pastor, conference speaker	1909-10	Christian Workers Union, pastor, conf. speaker, editor Word and Work
Victor Plymire	Missionary	1921	AG missionary
Frederick Reel	Pastor	1908?	Pastor
J. E. Sawders	Pastor	1908?	Evangelist, pastor
Louis Schneiderman	Nyack student	1908?	Missionary—S. Africa

TONGUE-SPEAKERS WHO LEFT THE C&MA (CONTINUED)

Leader	C&MA Role	Date Left	Pentecostal Role
Christian and Violet Dunham Schoonmaker	Missionaries	1915	Pastor, AG missionaries
Miss Shigallis	Missionary	1914	AG missionary
Mr. & Mrs. W. W. Simpson	Missionaries	1915	AG missionaries
Elizabeth Sisson	Friend of C&MA and speaker	1917—AG ordained	Evangelist
E. F. M. Staudt	Pastor	1923	AG pastor, DS
R. E. Sternall & Ella Hostetler Sternall	Nyack students	1911	Canadian Pentecostal pastor
Alan Swift	Nyack student, pastor	?	Missionary—England
Emily Tompkins	?	?	?
Joseph Tunmore	Lay leader?	1907–08?	AG pastor
Mr. & Mrs. Louis Turnbull	Missionary	1921	AG pastor
Harry T. Waggoner	Nyack student	1913	AG missionary
John H. Waggoner	Pastor	1914	AG pastor, evangelist
A. G. Ward	Field evang., supt.	1919	AG pastor
Mr. & Mrs. Albert Weaver	Workers, delegates	1916	Christian Workers Union, Monwait, Framingham, MA
John W. Welch	Pastor, State Supt.	1911?	AG. Gen. Supt.
Benjamin Wittich	Ger. Bapt. Pastor, C&MA affiliated	1912	Pentecostal pastor
Alice Wood	Missionary	?	AG missionary
Mr. Young	Missionary	1914	missionary

TONGUE-SPEAKERS WHO STAYED IN THE C&MA

Leader	Date Received Tongues	C&MA Role	Other Charismatic Manifestations
Ella & Emma Bird	1907	Official workers	
H. L. Blake	1906	Pastor	
Sally Botham	1907	Career missionary—West Africa	
Mrs. William Christie	1912	Missionary, wife of VP, Board of Mgrs.	Visions, dreams
Thomas A. Cullen	1907	Pastor-died 1910?	
Warren Collins	?	VP, lay worker, evang.	Healing, exorcism
Warren A. Cramer	1907	Pastor	
Mr. and Mrs. Dixon	1907	Pastors, church planters	
Kate Driscoll	?	Missionary—West Africa	
Miss Edwards	1907	Missionary—China	
Mrs. David Ekvall	1912	Missionary—China	
David Evans	?	Missionary—West Africa	
Philip Hinkey	1907	Missionary, China	healing
Mr. Hamill	1907	Missionary—China	
Cora Hansen	1907	Missionary—India	
Robert Jaffray	1907	Missionary, field Dir., VP	Dreams, visions, prophecy, discernment of spirits
Ethel Landis	1907	Missionary—China	
Mrs. William T. MacArthur	1907	Wife of DS, Board of Mgr. member	
George L. Morgan	1907	Pastor, DS	

TONGUE-SPEAKERS WHO STAYED IN THE C&MA (CONTINUED)

Leader	Date Received Tongues	C&MA Role	Other Charismatic Manifestations
Mary Mullen	1907	Missionary, Dir. African/American school	
Miss Peters	1907-08?	Missionary--India	
Mr. and Mrs. Ramsay	1907-08?	Missionaries--India	
Ella Rudy	1907?	Evangelist, missionary	
Peter Robinson	1907	African/American pastor	
C. E. Rossignol	1915	Professor, Nyack	
John Salmon	1907	Pastor, VP	Prophecy, visions, fell under power of Spirit
H.M. Shuman	1907?	Pastor, DS, Pres.	
Alfred C. Snead	1907	Foreign Secretary	Fell under power of Spirit
Samuel H. Stokes	1907	Pastor	
Rev. S. H. & Clair Switzer	1907	Pastor Bapt./C&MA	
Glenn V. Tingley	1925-26	Pastor, national evang.,	Operated in prophecy/word of knowledge
Eunice Wells	1907	Missionary--India	
Mother Whittemore	1918?	Official worker, mission	
Miss Woodworth	1907-08	Missionary--India	
Erta Wurmser	?	Supt., Bible Sch. Dir., pastor	
14 missionaries in South China	1907-08		
50 of 70 missionaries in India mission	1906-08		

TONGUE-SPEAKERS WHO LEFT AND RETURNED

Leader	C&MA Role	Date Left	Role in-between	Date Returned	C&MA Role
B. B. Bosworth	Evangelist	1913?	Evangelist	1918	Evangelist
F. F. Bosworth	Pastor/ evangelist	1913?	Pastor, Pent. Evang, AG charter member, Gen. presbyter	1918	Pastor, evangelist, Asst. DS
Ira David	Pastor, DS	1912	Pent. Evangelist,	1914	Pastor, conf. speaker, Board of Mgrs.
C. D. Sawtelle	Pastor, DS	1910	Unknown	1940s	Evangelist
Harry Turner	Missionary Field Dir.	1918	Missionary, Pastor, Pentecostal Assemblies of Canada	1926	Pastor, Bib. Institute C&MA pres.1954-1960
E.J. Witte	Pastor	1914	AG Pastor	1924	Pastor
Etta H. Wurmser	Local church Supt., Bib. School Dir.	1918-1919?	Principal of Pentecostal Bible School, VP Nat. & Intl. Pentecostal Missionary Union.	1929-1932?	Pastor

THOSE WHO LEFT THE ASSEMBLIES OF GOD (AG) FOR C&MA

Leader	AG Role	Date Left	C&MA Role
Edward Armstrong	Pastor, evangelist	1918	Evangelist
E.G. Birdsall	Asst. pastor, Bosworth associate	1918	Pastor
Orville Benham	General presbyter, pastor, evangelist	1921?	Asst. pastor, evangelist (Joined Open Bible 1927)
A. N. Bostrom	Member of A. G. Stone Church	1924?	Pastor, church planter
Alonzo Horn	Evangelist, pastor	1921?	Evangelist
Thomas J. O'Neal	Pastor, evangelist	1918	Evangelist, Asst. DS, pastor
A. T. Rape	Pastor	1918	Pastor, evangelist

THOSE WHO LEFT AG FOR A TIME, THEN RETURNED

Leader	AG Role	C&MA Dates	C&MA Role	Date Returned
Raymond Ritchey	Evangelist	1921-1936	Evangelist	1936
E. N. Ritchey	Pastor	1925-1936	Pastor	1936
John Bostrom	Pastor	1924-1930	Pastor, evangelist	1939
Hardy Mitchell	Pastor, evang.	1921-1927	Pastor, evangelist	1947
R. H. Moon?	Pastor?	1918-1927	Pastor	1927

TONGUE-SPEAKERS WHO CAME INTO THE ALLIANCE

Leader	Date Entered C&MA	Prior Denomination	C&MA Role
Glenn V. Tingley	1926	Free Methodist Church	Pastor, national evangelist, operated in prophecy/ word of knowledge
Keith Bailey	1944	Brethren	Missionary, pastor, DS, VP
Virginia Brandt Berg	1923	Independent Pentecostal	Pastor, evangelist
Clement Humbard	1943	Independent Pentecostal	Evangelist
Harry W. Lucas	1918	Independent Pentecostal, Bethel Bible Training Center	Evangelist, Pastor
A. G. Philpotts	1929	Pentecostal Assemblies	Pastor
Paris Reidhead	1953	Baptist	Pastor, Simpson's Gospel Tabernacle

CHARISMATICALLY-ORIENTED C&MA LEADERS

Leader	C&MA Role	Charismatic Giftings or Involvement (some of whom may have spoken in tongues)
William Christie	Missionary; Bd. Of Mgr., VP	Exorcism, discernment of spirits, wife and son spoke in tongues (though concerned about spurious tongues)
Frank B. Collitt	Pastor	Charismatically-oriented churches, tongues?
George W. Davis	Pastor, DS	Charismatically-oriented churches, active in charismatic revival, tongues?
M. A. Dean	Pastor	Charismatically-oriented churches, active in charismatic revival, tongues?
Herbert Dyke	Pastor, DS	Charismatically-oriented churches, active in charismatic revival, tongues?
John Fee	Missionary, pastor	Charismatically-oriented churches, active in China charismatic revival, tongues?
William Franklin	Missionary, pastor, DS	Charismatically-oriented churches, active in India charismatic revival, tongues?
R. A. Forrest	DS, founder Toccoa Bible Institute	Hosted Pentecostal speakers, recruited former Pentecostals for ministry, tongues?
A. E. Funk	Pastor, Bd. of Mgr.	Wrote positively about charismatic manifestations, concern about C&MA missing God in the Pentecostal revival, tongues?
S. M. Gerow	Pastor, Tozer mentor	Enthusiastic about Latter Rain revival, tongues?
Mr. & Mrs. S. P. Hamilton	Missionaries	Active in India charismatic revival, tongues?
Miss Mary Hastie	Supt. of churches, director of Mukti Mission	Head of charismatic Mukti Mission 1923ff., speaker and writer for Pentecostals
E. O. Jago	Missionary, DS, pastor, Bd of Mgrs.	Worked actively with Pentecostals in evangelism, participated in Pentecostal meetings, tongues?
J. V. Krall	Pastor, evangelist	Charismatically-oriented churches
Lewis J. Long	Pastor, DS	Charismatically-oriented churches, Tongues?

CHARISMATICALLY-ORIENTED C&MA LEADERS (CONTINUED)

Leader	C&MA Role	Charismatic Giftings or Involvement (some of whom may have spoken in tongues)
F. E. Marsh	Simpson associate, field evangelist	Spoke positively about charismatic manifestations, called singing in tongues "the acme of the revival"
H. F. Meltzer	Pastor	Charismatically-oriented churches, friendships with Pentecostals
Wilbur F. Meminger	DS, Field Supt., evang.	Wrote enthusiastically about charismatic manifestations
Sarah Musgrove	Pastor/local superintendent	Active in charismatic revival
W. W. Newberry	Pastor, Simpson Bible Institute	Charismatically-oriented churches
Isaac E. Patterson	Pastor, Toledo, Dist. Supt.	Preached on Latter Rain themes, involved with charismatic revivals and churches
F. J. Potter	Pastor	Charismatically-oriented churches
Paul Rader	Evangelist, pastor, President	Healing, exorcism, tongues?, spoke in Pentecostal churches
F. H. Rossiter	Pastor	Active in Pennsylvania charismatic revival, hosted Pentecostal speakers, tongues?
A. B. Simpson	Founder	Prophecy/word of knowledge, discernment of spirits, fell under power of Spirit, holy laughter, healing, people for whom he prayed fell under power of Spirit, saw visions, trembled, he endorsed moderate Pentecostal leaders
R. C. Steinhoff	Pastor, Asst. DS	Charismatically-oriented churches, tongues?
W. C. Stevens	Dean, Nyack, Simpson Bible Institute	Taught and encouraged Latter Rain revival, cooperated with Pentecostals, tongues?
Glenn V. Tingley	Pastor, evangelist	Prophecy/word of knowledge, healing, tongues
Walter Turnbull & Cora Rudy Turnbull	Missionary, Nyack Dean, VP Evang.	Active in India charismatic revival, tongues? Active in Ohio charismatic revival, tongues?
E. D. Whiteside	Pastor, Bd. of Mgrs.	Hosted Pentecostal speakers, recruited former Pentecostals, fell under power of Spirit, tongues?, holy laughter, people for whom he prayed fell under power of Spirit and spoke in tongues

EARLY CHARISMATICALLY-ORIENTED C&MA CHURCHES

Note: Since the early C&MA believed all gifts should be operating in every church, virtually every Alliance church was charismatically-oriented to one degree or another. These listed have been identified by various records.

Location	Date Charismatic Renewal Began	Pastors/Leaders
Akron, OH	December 1906	C. A. McKinney, G. M. Gerow, Steinhoff, Lucas
Albany, OR	1923	McCrossan, Dimmick
Ambridge, PA	1907	Sweeney, Meltzer, Lucas
Anderson, IN	1907-08	S. M. Stokes, Poling, Gerow
Asbury Park, NJ	1907-08	Steinhoff, Gates
Atlanta, GA	1907?	Forrest, Foster, U. Lewis, Tatnall, Ira David
Attleboro, MA	1907?	Wm. Coxe, C. E. Perry
Baltimore, MD	1907	Ella and Emma Bird, E. F. M. Staudt
Beaver Falls, PA	1907	Rossiter, Marston, R. R. Brown
Binghamton, NY	1908	E. J. Richards
Boone, IA	1907?	Crawford, Blake, Bostrom
Boston, MA	1907?	Bowditch
Bowling Green, OH	1907	Hosler
Bridgeport, CN	1907	Harriman, Robertson
Brockton, MA	1907	Ira David, Packard, Jago
Butler, PA	1907	John Coxe, Boon
Chicago, IL	1907	MacArthur
Cleveland, OH	1907	Cramer, Kerr, Huxtable, Nelson, Shuman
Columbia, SC	1907	Forrest, Huxtable
Columbus, OH	1907	Myland, Rossiter, Cramer
Corning, NY	1908	L. J. Long, W.I. McGarvey
Cranford, NJ	1907	Cromwell, Francis
Cumberland, MD	1907	Gormer, Wyre
Dallas, TX	1910/1918	Bosworth, Birdsall
Dayton, OH	1907	Rudy, Kerr, Stokes
Detroit, MI	Pentecostal church joins C&MA 1911	Sorenson, Sherman, Cramer, Lucas, Gerow
Dover, NJ	1907	Scoville, V.T. Jeffrey, Collitt
Durham, NC	1907	Steinhoff, E. E. Johnson, Garrison, Combe
Everett, WA	1907-08	York, Eddy
Findlay, OH	1907	O'Brien, Kerr, Witte, Behm, Wurmser, Dean
Flushing, OH	1907-08	Kirk, Southern, Stratton
Fort Worth, TX	1910-12?	Warren Collins

Location	Date Charismatic Renewal Began	Pastors/Leaders
Franklin, PA	1907-08	Kline, Funk, Huxtable
Grove City, PA	1907	Kline, Cottrell
Harrisburg, PA	1907-08	J.D. Smith, J.S. Moore, Rossiter
Harrison, NJ	1907-08	Switzer
Homestead, PA	1907	Sawders, Jones
Hood River, OR	1907-08	C.E. Perry
Indianapolis, IN	1907	Eldridge, Harriman, J.D. Williams, Robertson, Sneed
Houston, TX	1924	E.N. Richey, Raymond T. Richey
Jersey City, NJ	1907-08	Roberts, Francis, Robertson
Lincoln Park, PA	1907	J.T. Boddy
Lima, OH	1907-08	Arnold
Los Angeles, CA	1906-07	Ballard, Eldridge
Louisville, KY	1918?	Rape, Mantle, Lucas
Lumberton, NC	1907	F. Weiss
McKeesport, PA	1907	?
Mill Spring, NC	1907?	Shuman
Newark, NJ	1907	Thompson, Potter, Jeffrey
New Castle, PA	1907	Dyke, Shuman, Coxe
Norfork, VA	1907-08	A. J. Ramsay
Norwalk, OH	1907	Wurmser
Oakland, CA	1908?	Jaderquist, Montgomery, Dyke, Moon
Oklahoma City, OK	1923	O'Neal
Pittsburgh, PA	1907	Whiteside, Dyke, Meltzer
Pittsburgh, PA (African-American Church)	1907	Robinson
Pittston, PA	1907	O.J. Stone, Moore
Plainfield, NJ	1907-08	
Portland, OR	1907	Sawtelle, Perry, Cullen, Chrisman, Arnold, Fee, Benham
Richmond, VA	1907-08	McBain, Wm. Evans
Sandusky, OH	1907	Wurmser
Scranton, PA	1907	Geo. W. Davis, Armstrong, Coray
Seattle, WA	1907-08	Eddy, McCrossan
South Fork, PA	1907	Wm. Coxe, W.I. McGarvey

Location	Date Charismatic Renewal Began	Pastors/Leaders
Spokane, WA	1907-08	J.C. Baker, F.J. Potter, Chrisman
Springfield, MA	1907	Plummer, Cullen, Kenning, Cramer, MacArthur
Tacoma, WA	1907-09	O.J. Stone
Toledo, OH	1907	Patterson
Toronto	1907	Salmon, L.J. Long, Zimmerman
Tottenville, NY	1907	Garrison, Kline, Herbert Cox, Bender
Turtle Creek, PA	1907	Casley
Tulsa, OK	1923	Cramer
Warren, OH	1907	Waggoner
Washington, PA	1907	Shuman, Staudt, Lucas
Waynesboro, PA	1908	McDowell
Wilmington, DE	1908	G.V. Brown, John Coxe, Shuman
Windsor, Ontario, Canada	1929	A. G. Philpotts
Worchester, MA	1907-08?	Pentice, Franklin
Youngstown, OH	1907	Young, Henry, Watkins, Smith

Pentecostal/C&MA Cooperation	Pentecostal Role	C&MA Connection	
Minnie Abrams	India Mukti Mission	Joint efforts	
A.A. Boddy	Leader of British Pentecostalism		Friend of Simpson, endorsed by Simpson, shared pulpits
Archibald Forder	Independent missionary		Speaker, cooperated with C&MA missions
Willis Hoover	Leader of Chilean Pentecostalism		Friend of Simpson, endorsed by Simpson, Simpson spoke at his church and some spoke in tongues
Aimee Semple McPherson	Evangelist, pastor, founder of Foursquare Church		Preached in C&MA meetings, Foursquare founded as interdenominational group in Oakland C&MA church, Rader preached in her church, MacKenzie supported her healing ministry
Hubert Mitchell	Open Bible Standard Church leader and missionary		Joint credentials with Open Bible & C&MA as missionary to Indonesia
George & Carrie Judd Montgomery	Carrie—ordained AG pastor		Speaker, George VP until death—1930
Albert Norton	India Mukti Mission	Joint efforts	
A. W. Orwig	Azusa St. leader		*Alliance Weekly* articles, friend of George Watson
Jonathan Paul	Leader of German Pentecostalism		Friend and speaker at Simpson's church
William Piper	Pastor, Pentecostal Stone Church		Sharing pulpits, speaker at C&MA conventions
Cecil Polhill	Chair, Pentecostal Missionary Union		Jointly sponsoring missionaries
Charles Price	Independent healing evangelist		Worked with McCrossan, C&MA churches founded out of meetings
Pandita Ramabai	Founder, India Mukti mission, India Pentecostal revival		Joint efforts, deeded mission to C&MA at death
William J. Seymour	Azusa St. founder		Speaker, contact with Bosworth, Salmon, Eldridge
George D. Watson	Friend of Pentecostals such as Myland, preached in Pentecostal meetings, allowed tongues in his meetings		Frequent speaker in Alliance meetings

Index

Stanger, Frank B. 253, 255
Staudt, E.F.M. 88, 206, 215, 216, 320, 327, 329
Steinhoff, R. C. 173, 326, 327
Steinkamp, Orrel 253, 254
Sternall, Reuben E. 139; 140; 148nn3, 4; 320
Stevens, William C. 31n47, 47, 49, 98, 201, 21, 217, 266, 285, 326
Stewart, Mr. 184
Stockmayer, Otto 29, 122, 129, 298
Stokes, Samuel H. 73, 129, 322, 327
Studd, C.T. 37, 38
Swift, Alan 320
Switzer, Rev. S. H. & Clair 107n19, 128, 187, 322, 328

Tari, Mel 17, 252
Tauler, John 301
Taylor, J. Hudson 28, 36, 37, 46, 307n29
Ten Boom, Corrie 253
Third Wave 15, 212, 249, 258, 266-68, 309, 311, 312, 315
Thompson, A. E. 45n49, 183, 268
Thompson, Ed 253
Tingley, Glenn V. 199, 221-22, 246, 322, 324, 326
Tompkins, Emily 320
tongues, false 68n45, 125, 163, 173, 244, 249n44, 250, 251, 255-59, 276, 278-80,
tongues, singing in 13, 62, 72, 87, 104, 114, 256, 271, 313, 326
tongues, speaking in 13-16; 22; 26; 27; 35-39; 41; 42; 46; 49; 50; 55; 56; 58-66; 67n14; 69-80; 81n9; 82nn29, 33; 84-92; 94; 95n20; 96n36; 98-106; 109-19; 120nn29, 32; 122-26; 128-34; 139; 148; 151-56; 158-60; 162n52; 164; 166; 168-76; 177nn20, 27; 179; 181-88; 197-205; 208n71; 210-11; 213-15; 216n39; 217; 219; 220-23; 225; 226; 229n34; 234; 235; 238; 239n30; 242-47; 250-58; 260nn16, 23, 36; 265-71; 272n19; 276; 277; 283-92; 294n31; 295n33; 296n66; 305; 309-315; 321-325; 326; 330
Torrey, Reuben A. 47, 298, 312, 316n15
Tozer, A.W. 16, 23, 76, 82n46, 225, 238, 241-43, 251, 257, 281n34, 282n47, 283, 289-90, 295n43, 303, 304, 307n29, 310, 311, 325
Truax, Edgar 242,
Trudel, Dorothea 33
Tunmore, Joseph 320
Turnbull, Louis 142, 320
Turnbull, Walter 67n25, 92, 104, 114, 146, 200, 211, 224, 226, 227, 326, 330
Turner, Harry 16, 175-76, 186, 201, 222, 225, 237, 245, 290, 323

Upham, Thomas 40, 307n29
Utley, Uldine 220, 225
Uxkull, Baron 113, 120n29

Van der Welle, Teo 253, 254
Villars, Lucy 79

visions 13, 22, 23, 25, 32, 35, 39-42, 48-50, 58-64, 70, 80, 84-86, 89, 90, 94, 100-2, 104, 109, 112, 114-16, 128, 132, 134, 141, 142, 146, 149n16, 153, 154, 164, 170, 179-181, 195, 196, 202-4, 211, 219, 226, 242, 252, 253, 278, 321, 322, 326

Wacker, Grant 15, 283
Waggoner, Harry T. 320
Waggoner, John 71, 81n8, 201, 320, 329
Walborn, Ron 1, 258, 288
Ward, A. G. 78, 176, 214, 320
Warner, Wayne 40; 81n18; 96n38; 119n17; 191n59; 228nn12, 13; 239n15; 249n53
Watson, George D. 27, 61, 78, 152, 160n9, 182, 183, 190n31, 330
Watson, William T. 218
Weaver, Mr. & Mrs. Albert 118; 151; 162n52; 171; 177n22; 184; 293n9; 295nn34, 40; 320
Welch, John W. 140, 153, 160n22, 161n24, 168
Wells, Eunice 59, 322
Weston, William G. 220
White, Alma 74
Whiteside, E.D. 35, 88, 90-92, 100, 101, 104, 109, 118, 119, 196, 198, 215, 227, 285, 286, 326, 328
Whittemore, Mother 322
Wiest, Maude 58, 67
Williams, E.S. 148n4
Williams, J. D. 177n20, 197, 328
Williams, Mrs. 17n1
Wilson, Ernest 234, 257, 295n43
Wilson, Henry 60, 76, 111, 250
Wilson, Ken 284, 285, 288
Wimber, John 36, 256, 310-12, 314, 316n15
Wink, Miss 75
Witte, E. J. 157, 61n41, 188, 323, 327
Wong, Mr. 211, 237
Wood, Alice 79, 320
Woodberry, John 32-33, 135n10, 243n28
Woodward-Back, Mrs. 81n15
Woodworth, Martha 142, 322
Woodworth-Etter, Maria 24, 33, 35, 40, 41, 44n45, 152, 182, 198, 314
word of knowledge 13, 164, 212, 221, 229n45, 269, 311, 322, 324, 326
World's Faith Missionary Association 71, 72
Worsnip, Mrs. Thomas 103, 141
Worsnip, Thomas 103
Wurmser, Etta 71, 112, 157, 214, 225, 322, 323, 327, 328
xenoglossa/xenolalia 37, 66n14, 270

Yoakum, Dr. F. E. 151, 185
York, A. C. 129
Young, Mr. 170, 320

Zacharias, Ravi 253
Zwemer, Samuel 242
Zwiemer, Louis Henry 180

Printed in the United States
71815LV00006B/69